The Complete Guide to Ireland's Birds
Second Edition
Revised and Additional Text

THE COMPLETE GUIDE
TO IRELAND'S BIRDS

SECOND EDITION
Revised and Additional Text

Author
ERIC DEMPSEY

Artist
MICHAEL O'CLERY

Gill & Macmillan

Gill & Macmillan Ltd
Hume Avenue
Park West
Dublin 12
with associated companies throughout the world
www.gillmacmillan.ie

ISBN-13: 978 07171 3401 4
ISBN-10: 0 7171 3401 6
Editorial consultant: Roberta Reeners
Printed in Malaysia

*The paper used in this book is made from the wood pulp of managed
forests. For every tree felled, at least one tree is planted, thereby renewing
natural resources.*

A catalogue record is available for this book from the British Library.

9 8 7 6 5

Contents

Since the publication of the first edition of *The Complete Guide to Ireland's Birds* in 1993, interest in birds in Ireland has grown considerably. Nature education is now part of the primary school curriculum and there appears to be more of an active interest in our environment and its protection.

Sadly, since 1993, several species have shown serious declines in their breeding ranges with birds such as Skylark, Lapwing and Yellowhammer recognised as being particularly vulnerable. Other species, such as Corn Bunting and Red-necked Phalarope, can no longer be considered as Irish breeding species. On a more positive note, species such as Corncrakes appear to be maintaining their numbers with slight increases noted in some areas. Roseate Terns are also doing well on the breeding islands while an introduction programme involving Polish birds is underway to attempt to re-establish Grey Partridge as a common Irish bird. By the turn of the new millennium, the native population of Grey Partridge was estimated to be as few as 10 to 20 birds.

Ireland has also seen successful breeding of species such as Little Egret and Mediterranean Gull while birds like Reed Warblers are now a more common breeding species than before. In addition to this, over 20 new species have been recorded for the first time since 1993.

In this Second Edition we have reflected the changes that have occurred in relation to the distribution and breeding status of Ireland's birds. We have also updated the rare species section with those species recently added to the Irish list as well as some which have been recently recognised as unique species. As a result, this Second Edition provides information on all the species of birds that have been recorded in Ireland up to June 2001.

Eric Dempsey and Michael O'Clery

Acknowledgments

There are many people (too numerous to mention here) who have offered us encouragement, advice and practical help. Without them, this book would not have been possible.

We are particularly grateful to Esther Murphy for her comments, advice and continued support; to the staff at the Irish Natural History Museum, especially Pat O'Sullivan, for their co-operation and access to the skin collection; and to Gerry Lyons, Gemma Dolan, Jennifer Moonan and Peg Murphy for their practical assistance. We are also very grateful to Bob Chapman who both examined and offered invaluable advice on the species distribution maps.

Special thanks also to Fergus Fitzgerald, Aidan Kelly, Kieran Grace, Jim Dowdall, Anthony McGeehan, Jim Fitzharris, Don Conroy, Paul Milne, the late Dr Tony Whilde, Avril O'Donoghue, Paul Dempsey, Rod Tuach, Rosalind Murray and Gillian Toner for their combination of advice, encouragement, knowledge and assistance.

We would also like to thank Roberta Reeners for her enthusiasm and support.

Finally, we would like to take this opportunity to thank our families for their invaluable support and encouragement over the years, especially our parents to whom we dedicate this Second Edition.

Eric Dempsey and Michael O'Clery
May 2002

How to use this book

This book consists of three sections:

- Introduction
- Main Species Accounts
- Rare Species Accounts.

Introduction

This section gives a brief history of Irish ornithology. It discusses the importance of Ireland for birds and introduces various Irish habitats.

Main Species Accounts

This section describes the 310 species most frequently recorded in Ireland. Each description is accompanied by two illustrations. One shows the bird in a typical pose in its normal habitat, while the other shows identification features. The written description includes separate sections on the voice and diet of each species, as well as its habitat and status in Ireland. The rarer species are painted on a white background with a bold black border. Caution should be used when attempting to identify these species. Should such a bird be encountered, a careful written description should be taken and then submitted to a panel of experts for verification.

Rare Species

This section provides brief descriptions of those species which are considered to be extremely rare vagrants to Ireland. Indeed some have not been recorded in Ireland in over a century.

Understanding the maps

The maps are in three colours:

- Red shows the summer distribution.
- Blue shows the winter distribution.
- Green shows resident distribution.

Summer distribution of Merlin

Winter distribution of Merlin

Resident distribution of Red Grouse

Solid colour shows where species are generally considered common within suitable habitat.

Hatched colour shows where species are considered uncommon to rare.

Bird topography

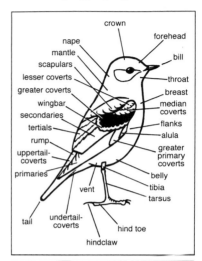

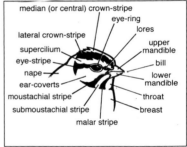

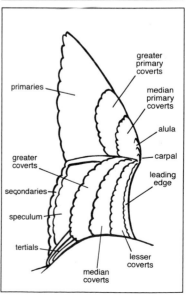

A History of Irish Birdwatching

Until relatively recently, birds were considered only for their food value, the sport which they provided, or as vermin to be eliminated. The concept of sharing our world with other species of mammals and birds came much later to Ireland than to other countries.

While little is known of the birdlife of the past, an examination of Irish literature and poetry reveals references to Bitterns, Cranes and other species which are now no longer a part of Irish avifauna. Birds such as the Wild Swans of Lir have passed into Irish folklore, while other species like the Wren hold an important part in rural customs.

On St Stephen's Day, in many parts of the country, the 'Wran Boys' can still be heard singing the ancient rhyme:

The Wran, the Wran, king of all birds,
On St Stephen's Day he got caught in the furze,
Up with the kettle and down with the pan,
A penny or tuppence to bury the Wran.

The hunting of the Wren is an ancient Irish tradition which dates back to pre-Christian times. At the winter solstice, the king decreed that, for just one day, the roles of everyone would be inverted. The king would therefore become the pauper, and the Wren, the smallest of the birds, would become the king for one day. However, on this day, the Wren had to be hunted and killed, or everyone would remain in this inverted state. Thankfully, Wrens are no longer killed during such festivities.

Further evidence of past birdlife is the fact that many species which are now rare or extinct in Ireland have old Irish names. This suggests a familiarity with the species and may indicate that these birds were quite numerous in the past.

Discoveries of ancient Irish dwellings in caves and on island crannógs have produced bones of Irish birds such as geese, ducks, crows and finches, as well as those of eagles and cranes. Even bones of the extinct Great Auk have been identified at old coastal dwellings.

The first written record of Irish bird-life can be traced back to the twelfth century when a Welsh monk, Giraldus Cambrensis, wrote a *History and Topography of Ireland*. While many observations made at the time were unreliable, he did describe species such as Ospreys, Peregrines and Dippers, and commented on the lack of Nightingales, Magpies and game-birds like Pheasant and Partridge in Ireland.

Up to the early nineteenth century, most written work referred to gamebirds. However, it was with the increased interest in the world of science which occurred in the early part of that century that the first real studies began. The first book on the birds of Ireland was written by William Thompson. It appeared as three volumes between 1849 and 1851. During the latter half of that century, and in the early years of the twentieth century, many new and young ornithologists came to prominence. Of these, R.J. Ussher was among the most influential. In 1900, he and R. Warren published the *Birds of Ireland*. The work described the distribution

and status of Irish birds. Also in 1900, another important book, *The Migration of Birds as observed at Irish Lighthouses and Lightships*, was published by R.M. Barrington. This was an extremely important account of the movements of birds off our coasts; in many ways, it was the first coastal bird observatory report.

In 1904, an important step towards bird conservation was taken with the formation of the Irish Society for the Protection of Birds. In 1921, the Ulster Society for the Protection of Birds was formed. Together, these two organisations purchased land in Mayo to protect breeding Red-necked Phalaropes. The threats to birds during the first half of this century included egg-collectors and shooting, and these societies were instrumental in the introduction of protective legislation.

Among the best known ornithologists of this period was George Humphreys who produced the *List of Irish Birds* in 1937. In 1950, the Irish Ornithologists Club was founded; in 1954, it produced the first *Irish Bird Report*. Also in 1954, three of the foremost Irish ornithologists, Major R.F. Ruttledge, Rev. P.G. Kennedy S.J., and Col. C.F. Scroope published the *Birds of Ireland*.

Another important development during this period was the establishment of bird observatories, a direct result of the interest taken in bird migration by this time. Migration was studied on the Great Saltee in Wexford; on Copeland Island, Co. Down; on Malin Head and Tory Island in Donegal; and on Cape Clear Island in Cork. Many of today's prominent ornithologists learned their trade at these observatories. The sightings from these locations formed the basis of the *Irish Bird Report* and,

Introduction

Cape Clear Bird Observatory, Co. Cork
(photo: Roberta Reeners)

in 1966, a systematic list, *Ireland's Birds*, was produced by Major Ruttledge.

A new era dawned in 1968 when the Irish Wildfowl Conservancy, the Irish Society for the Protection of Birds and the Irish Ornithologists Club amalgamated to form the Irish Wildbird Conservancy (IWC). This new society led the way in bird and habitat protection, scientific research and long-term studies carried out by amateur birdwatchers, including the Breeding and the Wintering Atlases.

The IWC still fulfils this role. It is now the largest conservation body in Ireland and has produced many publications, including the annual *Irish Birds*. This journal, while publishing scientific papers, also incorporates the *Irish Bird Report*.

Probably due to a greater awareness of the environment, the number of active amateur birdwatchers grew during the 1970s and early 1980s. Gordon D'Arcy produced *The Guide to the Birds of Ireland* during this period, while Clive Hutchinson published a book on the best birdwatching sites in Ireland. This latter book not only described the species which could be found at each site, but also provided details on the best routes to take, along with an Ordnance Survey map of each location.

With an increase in the observers, the availability of improved optical equipment and the great advances made in identification criteria, new and exciting discoveries were made. New species for Ireland were found on headlands and estuaries, while pelagic (deep water) trips off south-western Ireland found large concentrations of seabirds including the occasional Wilson's Petrel.

Reports of rare birds are now submitted to the Irish Rare Bird Committee both for acceptance and for publication in the Irish Bird Reports. In 1989, a new *Birds in Ireland* was written by Clive Hutchinson. This work detailed all bird records up to December 1986.

The interest in migration, as well as the occurrence and identification of rare and unusual species in Ireland, continued to grow. As a result of this, the Birds of Ireland News Service (BINS) was formed in 1990. BINS not only provides an information service on the sightings of unusual species found in Ireland, but also produces a new quarterly journal, *Irish Birding News*.

In recent years, new areas have been discovered as migration watchpoints. Work at Loop Head in Co. Clare and at Dunquin in Co. Kerry has proved worthwhile. Firkeel and Garinish Point in Co. Cork are also being watched on a regular basis each autumn, and this has produced many spectacular species, including Ireland's first Northern Parula. Islands such as Dursey in Cork and Tory in Donegal are again being manned in the autumn. There are undoubtedly many other areas awaiting discovery.

As concern for the environment continues to grow, the future of birds in Ireland looks good. Societies like the Irish Wildbird Conservancy continue to increase their membership. By doing so, they gain the political strength needed to ensure the protection of Irish habitats and of the birds which depend on them. Each year, more people are discovering the wealth of birdlife around them.

Youngsters who are now only learning the joy and skills of birdwatching are the prominent ornithologists of the future. It is up to us to teach them well.

Irish Breeding Birds

By comparison to Great Britain, Ireland has considerably fewer breeding species. While many of these are migratory, there are also many resident species which, while common in Britain, are rare or unusual visitors to Ireland. There are several reasons and theories why this should be.

First, Ireland has been isolated as an island for approximately 8000 years. As a result, many sedentary species including Nuthatches, Willow Tits and Tawny Owls, which do not move great distances, have not managed to cross the Irish Sea. Of other common British breeding species, Ireland has recorded Marsh Tit on only one occasion, while Green Woodpeckers are exceptionally rare visitors. Great Spotted Woodpeckers do occur more regularly, but it is believed that these birds occur during hard weather movements or irruptions from Continental Europe.

Second, migrants are at a disadvantage to resident birds. Due to mild Irish winters, its resident species generally suffer a low mortality rate. This allows them to commence breeding in the best habitats before many migrants have even arrived. With the best nesting territories and the most productive feeding areas already occupied, Ireland has fewer available niches for migratory species.

Lastly, and importantly, Ireland has fewer habitat types than Britain. Ireland contains less deciduous woodlands and Caledonian Scots pine forests, while habitats such as heaths, chalk downland and very high mountain ranges are totally absent. Such habitats attract a specialised selection of species, which explains why birds like Hobby, Woodlark,

Silage making has hastened the decline of the Corncrake (photo: Avril O'Donoghue)

Dartford Warbler, Crested Tit and Ptarmigan do not breed in Ireland.

Although Ireland has generally fewer breeding birds than other European countries, it does hold important numbers of some species which are showing a serious decline elsewhere. While seabird colonies include the largest breeding numbers of Storm Petrels in the world, Ireland also holds good breeding tern colonies. These include Arctic, Common, Sandwich and Little Terns.

More importantly, Ireland holds important numbers of the rare Roseate Tern. This species has shown a serious population decrease throughout all of Europe and North America. However, Ireland has several colonies of these terns. Due to proper management and wardening of these important colonies, along with the discovery that Roseate Terns will readily breed in special nest boxes, numbers again appear to be increasing at locations such as Lady's Island Lake in Wexford and on Rockabill Island in Dublin.

Ireland is also home to one of the largest populations of Chough to be found in Europe. While this species is relatively rare in Britain, Choughs can still be found in good numbers in northern, western and southern counties.

Of all the species which breed in Ireland, the Corncrake is the most important. Ireland now holds one of the largest concentrations of Corncrakes in western Europe. Despite exhaustive work, this species may now be sliding towards extinction. Declines in Ireland were first noted around the turn of the century. Although populations continued to decrease throughout the country, a survey carried out between 1968 and 1972 showed that Corncrakes were still present in all counties. However, work done in 1978 showed that the species was absent from many of its former breeding strongholds. It was estimated

Introduction

that approximately 1200 to 1500 pairs were present in Ireland. By 1988, the Irish breeding population was estimated to be fewer than 1000 birds. By 1992, it was considered that fewer than 400 pairs of Corncrakes were left. Studies of Corncrakes on the Shannon Callows (flood plains) involved radio-tracking individual birds. Early results from such work have shown that calling males do not necessarily mean that a pair is established in a territory. As early survey work regarded each calling male as representing a pair, it now seems that Ireland has even fewer breeding pairs than once believed.

The main reason for the decline of the Corncrake is recent changes in farming practices, in particular the cutting of silage. This requires the grass meadows to be cut earlier in the year than was formerly the practice when farmers engaged in haymaking. As a result, eggs and nests are destroyed. Very often, chicks and females, reluctant to leave the nest, are killed.

With a species such as the Corncrake on the edge of extinction, the small breeding territories which Ireland still offers are of international importance. Ireland also holds the most southern-breeding Red-necked Phalaropes in the world. This elegant species breeds occasionally at a site in Co. Mayo. At the beginning of the century, this site held up to fifty pairs. In recent years, however, only one or two birds are found annually and breeding does not always take place.

There are several other species which are declining as breeding birds in Ireland. These include Corn Bunting, Yellowhammer, Nightjar, Grey Partridge, Twite, Red Grouse, Merlin and Hen Harrier. Most of these declines are related to changes in habitat management.

A radio-tracking aerial is attached to a Corncrake as part of a continuing study of this species on the Shannon Callows (photo: Avril O'Donoghue)

There is some good news, however, and it seems that certain species are now increasing their breeding numbers in Ireland. For example, Reed Warblers, once a very rare breeding bird, are now present in good numbers in reed-beds along southern, eastern and north-eastern counties. Breeding populations of Wood Warblers and Buzzards are also increasing, while Peregrine Falcons are now back to their former numbers. Very small numbers of Garganey now also breed on a regular basis in suitable Irish wetlands.

There are also other potential breeding species. Of these, the Lesser Whitethroat, formerly a rare vagrant, is now occurring on a regular basis in spring and autumn. Several reports refer to males singing and holding territory at suitable breeding locations. In 1989, a male was heard in song at a location in the south-east. The following year, Lesser Whitethroats bred for the first time in Ireland at this site.

In 1992, Whooper Swans bred for the first time in Co. Donegal. A gull which may also possibly breed in the future is the Ring-billed Gull. First recorded in Ireland in 1979, this North American species is now frequently found in good numbers among gull flocks around Ireland.

Such colonisations are usually the result of a range expansion by a species. The best example of such expansion is the Collared Dove. This Asian species began to spread across Europe during the first half of the twentieth century. It was first recorded in Ireland in 1959 and slowly began to extend its Irish range. Now, Collared Doves breed in all counties. Such sudden range expansions can be difficult to predict. Perhaps in the next ten years, a species which is now considered rare will become a common Irish breeding bird.

Looking to the future, it seems obvious that only proper conservation actions and management policies will slow the decline of those breeding birds which are now under threat. It will be a great tragedy if, in the future, the sounds of Corncrakes and Corn Buntings are not heard in our countryside, or if the graceful Roseate Tern is no longer seen off our coasts.

Irish Races

Ireland has fewer breeding bird species than its nearest neighbours. The island has been isolated for up to 8000 years, and this has prevented many species from reaching Ireland's shores. The diversity of bird species changes from season to season. Migrants arrive each summer and winter. Even birds which are generally considered to be resident can engage in movements between countries.

However, some of our species rarely leave Ireland. In effect, these species have been isolated from their main European populations for thousands of years. They have gradually adapted to their Irish habitats and now appear significantly different from their British and European counterparts. As a result, they are considered as distinct Irish races.

Ireland has four such species. They are Coal Tit, Dipper, Jay and Red Grouse.

Coal Tit
Parus ater

Irish Coal Tits, *P.a. hibernicus,* differ from birds of the British race, *P.a. britannicus*, and the Continental race, *P.a. ater*, by showing a different plumage tone. Irish birds also show a larger bill, although this feature is impossible to discern in the field.

Irish Coal Tits are best recognised by the strong sulphur-yellow tones on the cheeks, breast and belly. Both British and Continental races show white cheeks and underparts. British birds lack the buffish tinge on the greyish-green upperparts as seen on the Irish race, while Continental birds show pure grey upperparts.

Irish Coal Tits also tend to show buff tips to the uppertail-coverts. This can give them a slight pale-rumped

Top: Typical Coal Tit of the Irish race.
Centre: Typical Coal Tit of the British race.
Bottom: Typical Coal Tit of the Continental race.

appearance. On British birds, this feature is much duller, while Continental birds do not have any suggestion of a paler rump.

While these differences appear subtle, and variations can occur, the classic Irish race of Coal Tit is very distinctive. Equally distinctive is the Continental race, and birds showing features of this race have occurred in Ireland on coastal islands in the autumn. Birds showing some or all of the characteristics of the British race are frequently recorded in Ireland, often associating with Irish birds.

Dipper
Cinclus cinclus

The Irish race, *C.c. hibernicus*, and the British race, *C.c. gularis*, of Dipper are very similar. They both show a chestnut band on the lower breast forming a border to the white gorget. This feature alone easily distinguishes them from the Continental race, *C.c. cinclus*, which shows a black lower breast and belly.

However, the Irish race does show subtle differences from the British race. The best feature is the extent and brightness of the chestnut band on the lower breast. Irish birds tend to show a narrower and duller band. Irish Dippers also show slightly darker upperparts.

Top: Typical Dipper of the Irish race.
Centre: Typical Dipper of the British race.
Bottom: Typical Dipper of the Continental race, known as the 'Black-bellied Dipper'.

Introduction

It appears that Dippers showing the features of the Irish race are also resident and breeding in parts of western Scotland.

Birds of the Black-bellied Continental race have occurred in Ireland on two occasions. One was present on the River Tolka, Dublin, during the winter of 1956, and one was found on Tory Island, Donegal, in the autumn of 1962.

Jay
Garrulus glandarius
The Irish race of Jay, *G.g. hibernicus*, appears generally darker and duller than both the British race, *G.g. rufitergum*, and the Continental race, *G.g. glandarius*.

Top: Typical Red Grouse of the Irish race.
Bottom: Typical Red Grouse of the British race.

In comparison to the British race, *hibernicus* shows darker ear-coverts, sides of the head and mantle, while the underparts of the British race are slightly paler, especially towards the vent area. The dark crown streaking on the British race tends to be thinner with broader white edges. This can give the crown a whiter appearance than seen on Irish birds. British Jays also show whiter throats and have a tendency to show a white area immediately below the eye which is rarely seen on birds of the Irish race.

The Continental race shows greyish to greyish-brown upperparts, while the underparts appear even paler than those of the British race. The dark Irish race therefore differs significantly from the Continental race.

Red Grouse
Lagopus lagopus
The Irish race of Red Grouse, *L.l. hibernicus*, shows very subtle differences compared to the British race, *L.l. scoticus*. Irish birds are generally paler than British birds.

Females especially appear paler and more yellowish, and show paler, more finely-barred underparts. The differences between males of the two races are less significant, but again, Irish birds tend to show a paler plumage and paler, finer barring.

It is believed that the paler plumage of Irish birds is an adaptation to their heather habitat which tends to have a higher content of grasses and sedges. This allows for potentially better camouflage. Equally, the darker birds of Britain are best suited to their darker heather habitat which contains a lower grass and sedge content.

As these differences are very subtle, some believe that both the Irish and British birds belong to the same race, *L. l. scoticus*.

Red Grouse itself is a race of the Willow Grouse which shows extensive white on the underparts and wings. In winter, Willow Grouse show an almost wholly white plumage. Willow Grouse occur in Scandinavia and northern Europe.

The Importance of Irish Seabird Colonies
Surrounded by food-rich waters, Ireland plays host each summer to thousands of seabirds which breed on naturally rocky islands and steep cliffs. Few European countries can surpass Ireland for the sheer numbers and variety of seabird species found along Irish coastlines.

Top: Typical Jay of the Irish race.
Centre: Typical Jay of the British race.
Bottom: Typical Jay of the Continental race.

The geographical location of these sites is extremely important, dictating the numbers and the species which are found in each. Seabirds which feed far out on open, exposed seas tend to breed on the Atlantic shoreline. Those which feed on shallower, inshore waters are usually found close to the Irish Sea.

Up to nine Irish seabird colonies contain over 10,000 pairs. Of these, six lie on the Atlantic. They are the Skellig Islands, the Blasket Islands and Puffin Island in Co. Kerry; Inishglora and Illaunmaistir in Co. Mayo; and Horn Head in Co. Donegal. The three large eastern seaboard colonies are on Rathlin Island, Co. Antrim; Lambay Island, Co. Dublin; and Great Saltee, Co. Wexford.

The largest breeding colonies of Storm Petrels in the world are found on the small, remote, rugged islands off Kerry. These islands also hold tens of thousands of Puffins and

A Puffin - Ireland's most colourful seabird (photo: Esther Murphy)

Manx Shearwaters. The rare Leach's Petrel also breeds in very small numbers on the remote islands off Co. Mayo. It is suspected that Leach's Petrels may also breed off Kerry and Donegal.

One of the most dramatic seabird colonies in Ireland is the isolated Little Skellig Island which is home to over 20,000 pairs of Gannets. Other Gannet colonies can be found on the Bull Rock, Co. Cork; Clare Island, Co. Mayo; and on the Great Saltee Island, Co. Wexford, where two separate colonies are now established. In recent years, a new and successful colony has started on the stacks off Ireland's Eye, Co. Dublin.

Fulmars, Cormorants, Shags, Kittiwakes, Greater and Lesser Black-backed Gulls and Herring Gulls breed in large numbers at suitable sites along most coastal counties. Colonies of Guillemots and Razorbills are also present in most coastal regions, but the largest numbers occur in the north and north-west. The rarer Black Guillemot is found in small numbers in most coastal regions.

Fulmars breed along most coastal counties (photo: Eric Dempsey)

Irish seabirds face many dangers. They are particularly vulnerable to pollution and oil spillages, while thousands drown in the miles of almost invisible gill nets which are laid around the coasts each year. However, the presence of such a variety and number of breeding seabirds serves as a constant reminder of the rich, clean waters which surround Ireland.

Migration

Ireland experiences vast movements of birds to and from its shores each year. In autumn, wintering waders and wildfowl arrive from their northern breeding grounds, while our summer visitors are beginning their return journey south. Other species, such as Little Stints and Curlew Sandpipers, simply use Ireland as a stopping-off point on their long flights.

In spring, this situation is reversed, with birds arriving from Africa to spend the summer here. Most people are aware of this annual spectacle and letters appear annually in the

Introduction

newspapers about sighting the first Swallow or hearing the first Cuckoo. All birdwatchers will admit to a feeling of great excitement on seeing the first migrants of the year flying in off the sea or feeding on a coastal headland.

Due to Ireland's westerly location, many species do not reach its shores. Some birds which are common in Europe are relatively rare in Ireland. In autumn and spring, rarer vagrants from Europe and Siberia do not occur here in the same numbers in which they are found in Britain.

However, Ireland's geographical location is extremely important for the occurrence of other long-distance migrants. Being on the western edge of Europe, Ireland is often the first landfall for North American species. Irish coasts also experience stunning seabird movements which make it the envy of many European neighbours.

American Vagrants

Over two thousand miles of open ocean lie between Ireland and the North American continent, a seemingly unsurmountable obstacle to the occurrence of North American species in Ireland. However, North American waders, gulls and passerines are found every autumn along western coastlines. In winter, North American ducks are also frequently found associating with commoner duck species.

Most of the waders which occur breed on the tundras of Arctic Canada. Each autumn, they begin their long southward migration to Central or South America. Many fly over the open Atlantic, performing long-distance, non-stop flights. It is during such flights that birds can get lost or

Buff-breasted Sandpiper - an annual autumn visitor to Ireland (photo: Eric Dempsey)

caught in strong weather fronts. Such fronts can sometimes cross the Atlantic rapidly, depositing weary travellers on Irish shores. It is interesting to note that most American waders which occur here are immature birds which are making the journey for the first time.

Most of these vagrants simply begin feeding and will often associate with other wader species. Among the more common American waders are Pectoral, Baird's, White-rumped and Buff-breasted Sandpipers. Long-billed Dowitchers and Wilson's Phalaropes are frequent visitors, as are American Golden Plovers. Ireland has also recorded some of Europe's rarest wader visitors, including Short-billed Dowitcher and Western Sandpiper.

Weather also plays a vital role in the arrival of North American passerines to Ireland. Most of these birds winter or migrate through the Gulf regions of Central America. Autumn is, of course, the hurricane season in these parts. Occasionally these hurricanes move north-eastwards across the Atlantic. Travelling at great speeds, they usually arrive on Irish shores as severe storms. Small and light passerines which are caught in such storms are carried helplessly with them. Many must die out at sea, but occasionally, a tiny proportion survive the ordeal and reach Irish coastal headlands and islands.

At migration watchpoints in the south-west, these birds are often found following such storms. Among the most frequently seen are Red-eyed Vireos and Rose-breasted Grosbeaks. Ireland has been graced by some of the rarest North American passerines ever to be recorded in Europe, including Philadelphia Vireo, Ovenbird, Indigo Bunting and Gray Catbird. Some birds, like Yellow-billed Cuckoos, are usually exhausted when they are found and most are discovered dead or dying. Ireland has even recorded a North American woodpecker in the shape of a Yellow-bellied Sapsucker. Belted Kingfishers have also occurred on three occasions although, regrettably, the first two birds were shot.

Ireland is also famous for the occurrence of North American gulls. Each autumn, Sabine's Gulls are seen during seawatches, while Ring-billed Gulls can occur in good numbers and at all times of the year. Other rarer gull species recorded in Ireland are Bonaparte's and Laughing Gulls. North American terns have also been found, and there are now several records of Forster's Terns, usually seen during the winter months. However, the most dramatic find was an Elegant Tern which spent almost two weeks at a tern colony in Greencastle, Co. Down, in 1982. It was also seen later that summer in Cork. This species is found on the Pacific coast of North America and this record was one of the first for the Western Palearctic.

In winter, many American ducks are found within flocks of more common species. At sea, Surf Scoters occur with the large Common Scoter flocks. On Irish estuaries, Green and Blue-winged Teals and American Wigeons are frequently found feeding alongside their European counterparts. On lakes, diving ducks such as Ring-necked Ducks can associate with Pochard and Tufted Ducks. One of the rarest species to be found in recent years is a drake Lesser Scaup which has now wintered for several years on the inland lakes of Northern Ireland.

Snow and Canada Geese can often be found among the skeins of geese which winter in Ireland each year. Some birds return to winter in the same areas year after year. Vagrants can even be found with swans, and there are now several records of Whistling Swans, the North American race of Bewick's Swan.

It is possible for any North American migrant to land in Ireland. Even the unexpected can occur, as was proved by the finding of an American Coot in Cork in 1981.

Considering the thousands of miles these birds have travelled to reach Ireland, the fact that some survive the journey at all is a testament to the strength and endurance of long-distance migrants.

Seabird Migration

While Ireland's westerly location is a disadvantage to the occurrence of European passerines, its geographical position is ideal for witnessing spectacular seabird movements in the autumn.

Many of the species, which pass in tens of thousands off south-western and western headlands and islands, are birds which breed in Ireland. These include Gannets, Fulmars, Kittiwakes, Manx Shearwaters, Storm Petrels and auks. Many of these also come from colonies in other countries. However, the most spectacular seabird movements off the Irish coasts involve not only breeding species, but also shearwaters from the South Atlantic, gulls from North America and skuas from northern breeding grounds.

Studies have indicated that such movements can almost be predicted by watching the changing weather patterns. Birds which feed out at sea or which migrate south are often blown to inshore waters by strong winds or bad weather. Strong south-westerly winds with rain, usually associated with a rapidly moving weather front, can result in a large passage of common species as well as Sooty, Mediterranean, Great and Cory's Shearwaters; Great, Pomarine and Arctic Skuas; Grey Phalaropes and

Large numbers of Great Shearwaters can occur off Ireland in some years
(photo: Anthony McGeehan)

Introduction

Sabine's Gulls. During such conditions, islands and headlands like Cape Clear and the Old Head of Kinsale, both in Cork, have proved to be the best locations.

Should such weather conditions result in strong north-westerly winds, headlands in the north and west can provide the best seawatching. Of these, the Bridges of Ross near Loop Head in Co. Clare has gained an international reputation for the birds which pass in such conditions. While thousands of commoner seabirds are seen, species such as Long-tailed Skua and Leach's Petrel pass in unprecedented numbers. Also recorded in surprisingly large numbers are Sabine's Gulls. Seawatches in the winter have resulted in the largest recorded move-ments of Little Auks off Ireland. The rare and elusive Wilson's Petrel has even been recorded off the Bridges of Ross.

In spring, while seabird passage is not spectacular, observations indicate that a good northerly movement of Pomarine Skuas takes place off southern and western coasts. Seawatching off extreme western locations has revealed that Long-tailed Skuas also move north off Irish coasts each spring.

With a greater understanding of the requirements of seabirds, pelagic trips off western and south-western coasts have been organised in recent years in an effort to locate feeding seabirds. The best feeding areas are where warm and cool waters mix, and where cool upwelling currents bring nutrients to the surface to promote the growth of plankton. This in turn supports the various fish species on which seabirds feed.

Waters over the Continental Shelf provide such ideal conditions.

Pelagic trips also attempt to attract feeding seabirds by spreading chum (an extremely strong-smelling mixture of fish oil and offal) on the surface of the sea. Such tactics have been successful on many occasions, with species such as Wilson's Petrel giving tantalising close-up views. Other species seen on the trips include Long-tailed Skuas, Sabine's Gulls, Grey Phalaropes and a variety of shearwaters.

The variety and numbers of seabirds present off Ireland each year provide birdwatchers with an opportunity to witness some of the best seabird movements in Europe. Any seabird species can conceivably pass the coastline, with extraordinary sightings including Little Shearwaters, Magnificent Frigatebirds and Black-browed Albatrosses.

New discoveries are constantly being made. In recent years, the first Soft-plumaged Petrel was recorded off Ireland. This was quickly followed by several records in successive years. An increased awareness of these and other species provides an opportunity to discover more about the exciting seabirds which can pass Irish headlands and islands. Seawatching requires skill and patience. Those who possess such qualities are usually rewarded.

The Importance of Ireland in Winter

The Irish climate, with comparatively few hard winters, allows resident birds to enjoy a relatively low winter mortality rate. Mild winters are also important for providing the rich, soft

feeding necessary for waders. The wet climate creates the suitable wetlands for wildfowl, and the relatively snow-free weather provides ideal winter feeding grounds for thousands of thrushes and finches.

Lying on the western edge of Europe, Ireland is ideally located to attract wintering wildfowl, waders and passerines from breeding grounds in Arctic Canada, Greenland, Iceland, northern Europe and Siberia.

Up to eighteen coastal and fourteen inland Irish wetland sites have now been recognised as holding internationally important populations of wildfowl and waders. Of the coastal areas, Lough Foyle, Co. Derry; Strangford Lough, Co. Down; the Shannon Estuary of Kerry, Clare and Limerick; Cork Harbour; Dundalk Bay, Co. Louth; and the North Bull Island, Co. Dublin, usually attract over 20,000 waders each winter. Irish estuaries also hold most of the Icelandic breeding population of Black-tailed Godwits; areas such as Ballymacoda in Co. Cork hold internationally important numbers of this species.

The sight of thousands of waders feeding or flying in large, dense flocks is a spectacular winter experience not to be forgotten. Equally spectacular and exciting is the sight and sound of skeins of geese arriving in Ireland each winter. Some coastal locations have attained international recognition purely based on the wintering populations of pale-bellied Brent Geese, while Lissadell in Sligo has been recognised as holding important numbers of Barnacle Geese. On the Wexford Wildfowl Reserve, up to half the world's population of Greenland White-fronted Geese can be found. The Wexford Wildfowl Reserve also attracts large numbers of Bewick's Swans, Bar-tailed Godwits and ducks annually.

Ireland's inland wetlands provide a secure and food-rich winter haven for Whooper and Bewick's Swans, Greylag Geese, many species of duck, and waders such as Curlew, Lapwing and Golden Plover.

Of the large inland lakes, Loughs Neagh and Beg of Antrim, Armagh, Derry and Tyrone hold the largest numbers of Goldeneye, Pochard and Tufted Duck to be found anywhere in Europe. Lough Neagh also attracts the largest European inland population of Scaup. Lough Corrib in Co. Galway holds an important wintering population of Pochard as well as large numbers of Coot. Other larger and deeper inland lakes do not have a significantly large wildfowl population, while smaller lakes like Lough Iron, Owel and Derravaragh are known to attract significant wildfowl numbers.

Flooded callows and marshes are important wetland areas which hold large wintering populations of waders and wildfowl. Of these, the Shannon Callows between Portumna and Athlone, the Little Brosna in Offaly and Tipperary, and the callows of the River Suck in Galway and Roscommon hold important wintering populations of Wigeon, Whooper Swans and, at some locations, Greenland White-fronted Geese. On the fringes of these wetlands, Golden Plover, Lapwing, Curlew, Black-tailed Godwit and Snipe occur in large numbers.

Off Ireland's coasts each winter, sea-duck such as Common Scoters are found in large flocks, while species such as Velvet Scoters and Long-

Exotic Waxwings occasionally grace Irish gardens in winter (photo: Anthony McGeehan)

tailed Ducks occur in smaller numbers. Other wintering species include Red-throated and Great Northern Divers, Great-crested Grebes and, in some traditional locations, Slavonian and Black-necked Grebes. Iceland and Glaucous Gulls also occur annually, usually at fishing ports, harbours or on rubbish tips.

Ireland's mild climate, with comparatively few hard winters, is a great attraction to thousands of winter thrushes. On still November nights, the thin, high-pitched calls of Redwings and Fieldfares can often be heard as the birds arrive overnight. Large, mixed flocks of these thrushes are a common winter sight in open country. They will also occasionally visit gardens in towns and cities. Colourful Bramblings can also occur with finch flocks while, along some coasts, tame and charming Snow Buntings are annual visitors.

Ireland is also an important refuge for many thousands of birds which arrive here during extremely cold weather on the Continent or in Britain. When this occurs, normal wintering numbers are

swollen considerably, but the rich winter food resources can cope adequately with such influxes. Occasionally, Ireland is graced with large numbers of Waxwings which irrupt from northern Europe. These tame berry-eaters are the most colourful and exotic species which occur in winter.

By early spring, thousands of winter visitors will have begun the long journey north to their breeding grounds. There, they will spend the brief northern summer before returning in autumn to the safe, food-rich winter haven that awaits them in Ireland.

Bird Habitats in Ireland

Ireland has a wide variety of different habitats ranging from mountains and moorland to coastal estuaries and islands. Each habitat is unique, holding specific species of birds at different times of the year. It is important to know how to birdwatch in each of these areas without causing disturbance, especially to breeding species. Equally, it is very useful to know when to visit each habitat and to know what birds to expect.

This section will examine nine different habitats in Ireland. It will suggest how and when to birdwatch in them and will indicate which species can be expected in each.

Mountains and Moorlands

Ireland is a reasonably flat country, with only 25% of the total land mass over 150m. Yet the mountains and moorlands not only provide spectacular scenery, but are also home to many species of birds. Irish mountain ranges are mostly situated around the edges of the island and as such do not suffer the harsh winter

Introduction

Many species of bird can be found on mountain and moorland (photo: Paul Dempsey)

snowfalls of similar ranges in Britain and continental Europe. However, in winter, Irish mountains and moorlands are relatively bleak, with most species moving to lower or coastal regions.

In spring, Stonechats, Wheatears, Meadow Pipits and Skylarks are found in abundance on the moorlands, while Cuckoos are reasonably common. The rocky, upland scree slopes provide an ideal habitat for Ring Ouzels, while cliff faces provide suitable breeding sites for Ravens, Kestrels and Peregrine Falcons. On moorlands, the small, agile Merlin nests in small numbers. In the north and west, a small breeding population of Golden Plovers is present. Red Grouse are also found on the mountainous moorlands, although populations appear to have declined in recent years.

Much of Ireland's moorlands are being lost to conifer plantations.

However, young plantations provide an ideal breeding habitat for Hen Harriers. Whinchats too can occur in such areas. In some of the lower stretches of moorland, the reeling of Grasshopper Warblers can often be heard. These birds are difficult to see, and are best listened for at dusk or dawn.

Birdwatching in the mountains and moorlands, although rewarding, can also be difficult. The methods employed depend on the species one wants to see and, more importantly, on one's level of fitness. Watching from a suitable vantage point can be productive and causes the least disturbance. Patient observations can result in stunning views of a variety of birds, including raptors, warblers, Ring Ouzels and Ravens. However, climbing and walking the moorlands is usually the only way of seeing Red Grouse. Along mountain tops and moorland, species including Skylarks and Meadow Pipits can be found in large numbers. In winter, Snow Buntings can occur in small flocks on higher ground.

Coniferous Forests

More and more of Ireland's mountainous regions are being covered by coniferous plantations. These mostly consist of Sitka Spruce and Lodgepole Pine, as well as some Larch, Norway Spruce, and Douglas and Noble Firs. While young plantations do offer breeding sites for Hen Harriers and Whinchats, the more mature forests, with trees closely planted side by side, provide little in the way of suitable habitat for many species. With careful searching, some specialised species can be found. The one advantage about coniferous forests is that, being mostly state-owned, access is easy. There are usually good pathways, and an effortless stroll can bring a birdwatcher into the heart of the forest. Such habitat is ideal for Siskins and Redpolls. Goldcrests and Coal Tits are common. Sparrowhawks too can be found in such areas.

The coniferous forest is home to one of the most unusual species found in Ireland, the Crossbill. These birds are found in areas where trees are heavy with cones. Their especially adapted bills, with crossed mandibles, prise open the cones and extract the seeds inside. In some years, Crossbills can occur in large flocks. They are often found perched on the tops of the trees. They are also very vocal and their distinctive, loud *chip* calls can be the first indication of their presence.

At night, Woodcocks and Long-eared Owls can be found. These are best looked for by standing still, in cover, and watching over an open space. In some coniferous forests, the rare Nightjar also occurs. The far-carrying churring song of the male is perhaps

Coniferous forest - closely-planted trees provide little in the way of suitable habitat for many species (photo: Esther Murphy)

In winter, deciduous woodlands tend to be much quieter. While resident species are still present, winter visitors can include Bramblings which are particularly partial to Beech mast. Flocks of Siskins are also frequently encountered feeding in Birches and Alders. Mixed roving tit flocks are a familiar winter sight.

Birdwatching in deciduous woodlands is best done by walking slowly and quietly. Many of the birds which are found in these woodlands are usually heard first. It is therefore advisable not just to look for birds, but to listen carefully.

Searching for nocturnal species like Long-eared Owl and Woodcock requires patience and silence. Stand in cover overlooking open tracts of woodland. Listen especially for the muffled *oo* of adult Long-eared Owls or the low, guttural song of roding Woodcocks.

one of the most dramatic songs to be heard in Ireland. Nightjars require more mature forests, usually those with large open tracts. They can also occur in forests close to open moorland and bogs.

Birdwatching in coniferous forests is best done by slowly walking the pathways, listening as well as looking. Another method is to view the forest from a height. This method is often rewarded by views of Sparrowhawks or perched Crossbills.

Deciduous Forests

Deciduous forests represent a sadly small proportion of Ireland's woodland areas. There are now few true Oak woodlands left. Many deciduous forests comprise a mixture of Oak, Ash, Hazel, Birch and smaller numbers of Yew and Elm. While not plentiful, such forests provide excellent birdwatching, particularly in summer.

Among the many species found in deciduous woodlands are resident birds like Treecreepers, Long-tailed, Great, Coal and Blue Tits, and Jays. Sparrowhawks may also find suitable nesting sites in the quieter, less disturbed parts of the woodland.

In summer, Spotted Flycatchers, Willow Warblers and Chiffchaffs are among the commoner migrants. Blackcaps can also be found, but only if there is suitable dense undergrowth. Some of the more mature woodlands are graced by the songs of the rare Wood Warbler and Redstart.

Birdwatching is at its best early in the morning when the birds are active and singing. If the weather is bad, with heavy rain, deciduous forests can seem barren and empty as birds tend to keep low and seek shelter in such conditions.

Deciduous forests represent a sadly small proportion of Ireland's woodlands (photo: Esther Murphy)

Introduction

Freshwater Rivers

Ireland's landscape contains an intricate maze of freshwater river systems. All have their beginnings in the mountain ranges. As these ranges are usually close to the sea, rivers in Ireland consist of two main types. Those that run from the seaward side of the high ground are fast-flowing and quickly make their way to the coast. These differ from the river systems that run from the landward side which tend to be slow-flowing and meandering.

On the faster uphill river stretches, species such as Dippers and Grey Wagtails can be found feeding. Dippers walk or swim under the surface of the water in search of a variety of aquatic invertebrates. Grey Wagtails are usually seen searching for insects along the banks, although they may also be found perched on small rocks in the middle of fast-flowing water. Both species can also occur on lower stretches of such rivers. Along the rocky edges of upland streams and rivers, Common Sandpipers occur in summer.

The slower rivers usually allow dense vegetation to grow along their banks. These provide ideal breeding habitats for species such as Moorhens, Reed Buntings and, in suitable areas of rushes and reeds, Sedge Warblers. Mallard also breed in the dense cover afforded by such vegetation, while Mute Swans are a common sight on these slow, wide, food-rich water systems.

Along the quieter stretches of rivers, one may be lucky to glimpse the bright turquoise shock of a Kingfisher in flight. The speed and small size of this magnificent bird often come as a surprise to many. Kingfishers prefer slow, undisturbed stretches and tend to fish from favourite perches. In discovering such a perch, patience and silence will be rewarded with stunning views. Kingfishers breed in holes which are excavated in river banks. These nesting burrows can be unobtrusive and difficult to see. Not hard to notice, however, are Sand Martins which also nest in holes on river banks. These birds are usually found in small colonies and their noisy comings and goings make them difficult to overlook.

The shallower river stretches are favourite hunting grounds for Grey Herons. These birds stand motionless, waiting patiently before stabbing at prey with their long, dagger-like bills. Heronries are often found in stands of trees along such rivers and streams.

Closer to the coast, a variety of species can be found frequenting the river systems as they reach their final destination. These include ducks, gulls and waders. In summer, terns can also feed along river systems; many inland colonies are based along such courses. On quieter coastal streams, Green Sandpipers may even be encountered. In winter, Dippers, Grey Wagtails and Kingfishers sometimes find the coastal stretches more suitable.

Birdwatching methods along rivers vary according to the type of river and its location. Slow-moving rivers are best watched by walking the banks. Many species like Mute Swans and Mallards are easy to see. Others like Kingfishers can often give just a tantalising and brief flight view. Faster, uphill river stretches are a little more difficult to watch. Check for shallow, fast-flowing water with suitable rocks on which birds may perch. Such habitat is ideal for Dippers and Grey Wagtails. These species are best found by watching from a vantage point and searching long stretches of river. At the coast, many species can be watched easily as they feed where rivers meet the sea.

Mute Swans are a common sight along slow-moving rivers (photo: Avril O'Donoghue)

Freshwater Lakes, Marshes and Reed-beds

These are among the richest bird-watching habitats in Ireland. Frequently found side by side, they provide an excellent selection of bird species at all times of the year.

Open freshwater areas vary greatly in size, from the enormous Lough Neagh to smaller, insignificant lakes.. Marshland occurs where water just covers the surface. Here, feeding on

Freshwater lakes, marshes and reed-beds are among the richest birdwatching habitats in Ireland (photo: Anthony McGeehan)

the rich nutrients, grow a selection of plants including rushes, reeds and sedges. Some of these reed-beds can become quite extensive and cover a considerable area.

Lakes are best visited in the winter when large flocks of diving ducks such as Pochard and Tufted Duck are found. Dabbling duck like Gadwall, Teal, Mallard and Wigeon also occur. In winter, ducks are shot and are usually extremely wary as a result. Care must therefore be taken not to cause further disturbance. Appearing suddenly on a lake shore or breaking the horizon usually results in absolute panic. Watching wildfowl is best done from a hide or even a car.

In summer, lakes hold a wide variety of breeding species, especially if there are some small islets. Common and Arctic Terns may occur, sometimes in large numbers if the habitat is close to the coast. Such tern colonies may even contain breeding pairs of the rare Roseate Tern. Common and Black-headed

Gulls also breed on lake islands. Common Sandpipers are another familiar species along lake shores in summer.

Swallows, Sand Martins and Swifts can be seen over lakes on balmy summer evenings. Large flocks of these agile, aerial hunters can give stunning views as they feed on the swarms of flying insects.

Birdwatching can be more difficult in marshes. These wet habitats are ideal for breeding Snipe, Redshank and Lapwing. While Redshank move to more coastal locations in winter, Snipe numbers usually increase. Occasionally the smaller Jack Snipe may occur. Such wet marshes usually contain dense vegetation where species like Mute Swans, Coots and Moorhens find suitable breeding sites. Such areas may also attract duck; the rare Garganey which now breeds in small numbers in Ireland favours the fringes of reed-beds and vegetation.

Reed-beds offer an opportunity to see and hear some specialised bird species. In the summer, a variety of migrants can be found, including

Sedge, Grasshopper and, more recently, Reed Warblers. Cuckoos are also attracted to these areas in search of suitable nests in which to lay their eggs. Other species include Reed Buntings, Coots, Moorhens and, in the evenings, Swallows and Swifts. Raptors also hunt over reed-beds and in recent years, Marsh Harriers have become annual passage migrants. It may not be too long before this powerful bird becomes a regular breeding species.

In winter, reed-beds hold a large number and variety of wildfowl, Coots and Moorhens which, in turn, attract wintering Hen Harriers and Sparrowhawks. In some extensive stretches, enormous winter roosts of Starlings can be found. Reed-beds also serve as roosts for Swallows and martins in the autumn.

Reed-beds are often extensive areas and can prove difficult to watch. Birds are often heard but not seen. This is particularly true of the Water Rail. Their high-pitched, pig-like squealing call is probably the most distinctive sound of this habitat.

At all times of the year, reed-beds are best viewed from a suitable vantage point. Patience is required but it is usually rewarded.

Farmland

Ireland is an agricultural land, with approximately 70% of the countryside consisting of farmland. Such habitat is ideal for the variety of wildlife that lives along hedgerows. Unlike many other countries, hedgerows still act as natural borders to land, and Ireland still provides some of the best examples of such habitat to be found anywhere in Europe. Among the commonest plants found in hedgerow systems are

Introduction

Hawthorn, Blackthorn, Gorse, Brambles and Dog Roses. Other climbing species can also be found, including Ivy and Woodbine.

In summer, breeding birds include Chiffchaffs, Willow Warblers, Whitethroats, Blackbirds, Song Thrushes, Greenfinches, Bullfinches and Chaffinches. The rich songs of these species are familiar features of the farmland habitat, as is the far-carrying call of the Cuckoo. Farmyards also provide suitable breeding habitat

Farmland provides an ideal habitat for a wide variety of bird species (photo: Avril O'Donoghue)

for Swallows, tits and, occasionally, Spotted Flycatchers. In cereal-growing areas, species such as Quail and Grey Partridge can occur in summer. In some regions in the midlands, west and north-west, Corncrakes can still be heard in the hay meadows. Unfortunately, this striking call, once a common sound of the Irish countryside, is now little more than a memory in many parts.

In winter, large flocks of Redwings and Fieldfares are found on open fields and along hedgerows. Skylarks and Meadow Pipits are found in abundance, while Lapwings, Golden Plovers, Curlews and Black-headed Gulls also feed in open tracts of land. Farmyards in winter can attract large mixed flocks of Greenfinches, Chaffinches and House Sparrows. Occasionally, Bramblings and Tree Sparrows can associate with these flocks.

Woodpigeons are a common sight on farmland at all times of the year, but the shyer Stock Dove can only be found in reasonably large flocks in winter.

Farmlands also provide good hunting grounds for raptors. Kestrels and Sparrowhawks are common throughout the year. Hen Harriers are occasionally found quartering over the fields in winter, taking advantage of the abundance of prey this habitat provides. Farmlands are also important for Barn Owls, providing safe nesting sites and rich food sources.

Birdwatching in farmland areas can be difficult. In summer, a walk along the hedgerows is the best method. In winter, however, it is often best to view feeding flocks of thrushes, plovers, waders and gulls from a distance. It is vital to remember that farmlands are usually privately owned, and permission should always be sought before entering any land.

Finally, it is worth noting that extraordinary species can occasionally be found on farmland. In the past, these have included Hoopoes, Cattle Egrets and even a Bald Eagle.

Estuaries

Less than 15% of the Irish coastline falls into this category. Yet coastal estuaries and mudflats are without a doubt among the most rewarding and productive habitats in Ireland. Mudflats contain countless numbers of invertebrates which provide a rich source of food for many shorebirds. An abundance of plant life can also be found on the mudflats and saltmarshes, and these attract feeding ducks and geese.

As most of the birds which feed on estuaries and mudflats are winter visitors, the best time to visit such a habitat is between late autumn and early spring when a wealth of waders including Dunlin, Knot, Bar and Black-tailed Godwit, Redshank, Curlew and Oystercatcher occur in their thousands. Golden, Grey and Ringed Plovers also occur, while ducks include Pintail, Wigeon, Teal, Shoveler, Mallard and Shelduck. Large flocks of Brent Geese also graze on these estuaries; as the winter progresses, they can become exceptionally tame.

When visiting estuaries and mudflats, the one fundamental rule which will allow for the best viewing is to arrive when the tide is either coming in, or just going out. If the tide is fully in, the birds could be roosting in an inaccessible area. Likewise, if the tide is too far out, the birds will be too far away and will not give good views. The best time is approximately one hour before high tide. Get into position and wait. As the water rises, the waders will be pushed closer and closer to the shore. They will usually be too busy feeding to notice anyone watching them. Waders, ducks and geese can be easily disturbed. Do not walk out onto the mudflat. A car is

In winter, rocky shores provide suitable feeding areas for mixed flocks of Turnstones and Purple Sandpipers. These birds are ideally suited to such habitats and seem to blend perfectly into their surroundings. Along the lower shingle shores in winter, Linnets, Twite, Meadow Pipits and, occasionally, Snow Buntings are found. In summer, these shingle areas attract a variety of breeding birds like Ringed Plovers and Oystercatchers. A small proportion of such stretches may also contain a breeding colony of Little Terns. Because these species lay their well-camouflaged eggs in shallow scrapes on the ground, they are particularly vulnerable to disturbance. Care must be taken when birdwatching in these areas, as the eggs and nests are almost invisible against the stony background.

Tidal estuaries and mudflats support many species of wader and wildfowl in winter (photo: Esther Murphy)

perhaps one of the best birdwatching hides for this habitat. Telescopes are a great advantage on estuaries and will allow excellent birdwatching from a safe distance.

In winter, coastal estuaries and mud-flats play host to a variety of raptors which prey on the large numbers of wintering birds. A close watch should always be kept for Peregrine Falcons, Merlins or even Hen Harriers. On the saltmarshes, Short-eared Owls can occasionally be found hunting during the day. Also on the marshes, Snipe and the smaller Jack Snipe can frequent the pools, while Skylarks, Meadow Pipits, finches and buntings are usually found in reasonably large numbers.

In summer, estuaries and mudflats are much quieter, less productive areas, although Shelducks, Redshanks, Curlews and some Lapwings can usually be found. Other species which

can occur in summer may include Common and Arctic Terns which can sometimes be found feeding over estuaries at high tide.

Rocky Shores and Cliffs

Shaped by the power of the sea, the rugged Irish coastline consists of mostly rocky shores and cliffs. Such habitats vary from the low, rocky, coastal shorelines of the east coast, to the high cliffs of the headlands and islands of southern and western regions. Over 85% of the coastline consists of such habitat.

Sea cliffs in summer are the most exciting and noisy places to visit. They are similar in many ways to high-rise apartment blocks. During the breeding season, thousands of

Rocky shores and cliffs represent over 85% of the Irish coastline (photo: Esther Murphy)

Introduction

Guillemots, Razorbills and Kittiwakes cram onto the narrow ledges to nest. On wider ledges, Cormorants and Shags can be found, while Fulmars tend to nest on the higher parts of the cliffs. Gulls also breed on the cliffs and on the slopes above. Care should be taken not to wander into gull colonies. Some of the larger species, like Great Black-backed Gulls, can be quite aggressive.

On some islands and headlands, Puffins can be seen on the slopes. These charming auks nest in old burrows. During the height of the breeding season, they can sometimes be seen returning from fishing trips with several sand-eels draped in their large, colourful bills.

On the more remote islands, Manx Shearwaters and Storm Petrels occur. These birds usually return to their nesting areas at night, and their strange, eerie calls add to the unforgettable experience of nights spent on such islands. Gannets also tend to breed on these islands, nesting on rocky ledges in large, extremely busy and noisy colonies. With an abundance of breeding species, such cliffs also attract Peregrine Falcons which nest on inaccessible ledges. Along the Atlantic shoreline, cliffs are also the main breeding sites for Choughs and Rock Doves.

By late summer and early autumn, most of the breeding birds have dispersed out to sea, and the cliffs are strangely silent.

Of all the habitats which birdwatchers visit, sea cliffs are the most dangerous. Extreme care must always be taken. Nesting seabird colonies are best visited from early spring to late summer. Viewing is best from a

distance, and warning signs and notices should be heeded.

Towns, Parks and Gardens

While they may not appear to be the most attractive habitats at first glance, towns, parks and gardens do hold a

Parks are like green oases in the midst of towns and cities (photo: Esther Murphy)

surprisingly large number of bird species. In busy towns, Feral Pigeons, House Sparrows and Starlings are plentiful, as are Rooks, Jackdaws and Magpies. In summer, Swifts can be seen feeding high over busy areas, while Kestrels and Peregrine Falcons can occasionally find suitable breeding sites on high-rise or derelict buildings. Grey Wagtails, normally associated with uphill rivers and

streams, are also found in Irish towns and cities in winter. In summer, this species even breeds near park ponds and streams in the heart of busy cities. Pied Wagtails also occur and can form very large winter roosts.

Parklands are like green oases in the midst of cities and towns. Breeding species include Great, Blue and Coal Tits, Dunnocks, Robins, Blackbirds, and Mistle and Song Thrushes. In more mature parks, Treecreepers or Jays may occur, while Sparrowhawks are not uncommon. In summer, Chiffchaffs may be heard singing over the noise of city traffic. In winter, parks provide ideal habitats for Redwings and Fieldfares.

Parks which have ponds usually contain resident Moorhens and Mallards, while Tufted Ducks and Coots will also take advantage of the generous food supply given by humans at these traditional, decorative ponds. Such a reliable food supply is vital for the survival of these species. Many gull species also occur on these ponds, including Herring and Black-headed Gulls. In winter, it is possible to encounter a Glaucous or Iceland Gull.

Of all the birdwatching habitats that can be visited, the favourite is undoubtedly one's own garden. In the summer, Blackbirds and Dunnocks breed in hedgerows and trees. House Sparrows and Starlings are common while, under the eaves of our roofs, House Martins build their nests. In some areas, Swifts can also be found nesting under the eaves.

Robins can breed in a variety of locations around the garden. Occasionally, Spotted Flycatchers may choose to nest in the most unlikely

Kestrels can occasionally breed on high-rise or derelict city buildings (photo: Eric Dempsey)

sites such as hanging flower baskets. In dense bushes and ivy, Wrens may be found building their complicated, rounded nests. Nest boxes are one of the best ways of attracting breeding Blue or Great Tits. Such boxes should be erected early in the year if they are to be successful.

Song Thrushes are another familiar garden breeding bird. Many gardeners welcome this species as they can keep an area clear of snails and slugs. Watch for broken shells near a stone in the garden. Song Thrushes use favourite stones as anvils to break open snail shells.

In many ways, people have become the guardians of their breeding birds. Such species as Magpies, which fulfil a vital natural role in keeping small bird populations in check, are often discouraged.

In winter, gardens become a hive of activity. Nut-feeders attract tits, Greenfinches, Siskins and, occasionally, Redpolls. In recent

years, House Sparrows and Chaffinches have learned to use these hanging feeders. Robins, Dunnocks and Blackbirds feed either on the ground or on bird tables. Berry bushes attract wintering Redwings and even Fieldfares. In some years, gardens are graced by the exotic Waxwing which feeds both on berries and, occasionally, fruit. Apples strategically placed on branches of trees provide food for Blackbirds, tits

and finches. Apples also attract Blackcaps. These shy birds are one of only two warblers which winter in Ireland. The other species, Chiffchaff, seldom visits gardens. During the winter, roving tit flocks may move through gardens and these may include Long-tailed Tits.

It is extremely important to remember that birds also need water in winter. They can often survive longer without food than without water. They need to wash and preen to keep their feathers in good shape in order to provide the warmth and insulation needed to survive cold spells. It is also vital to remember that, once you start feeding birds, they depend on that food supply for the winter. Once you start, don't stop until early April, although this will depend on weather conditions.

Birdwatching in the garden is so easy. Feeders can be gradually moved closer to windows. Before long, many birds will have become so tame that they will hardly fly away while you refill the feeders. There is nothing quite like birdwatching from the warmth and comfort of home!

Apples attract many species to gardens in winter, including Blackcaps (photo: Rod Tuach)

Divers

Great Northern Diver
Gavia immer Lóma mór

A large, thick-necked, black and white diver. Shows a long flat crown, a steep forehead, a distinctive bump where the crown meets the forehead and a long, heavy, pale grey bill. **In summer** shows a completely black head, with black and white striped patches on the sides of the neck and throat. Black upperparts show a white chequered pattern. **In winter**, the head and nape are black, contrasting strongly with the white on the throat, neck and breast. A black half collar extends from the nape onto the neck. Upperparts black. **Immatures** similar, but show pale fringes to the upperpart feathers. Deep red eye appears blackish at a distance. Flies with neck extended.

Voice and Diet
Although usually quiet, birds returning in autumn can give a far-carrying, wailing, gull-like call. Dives for fish and marine invertebrates. Can stay submerged for long periods, covering good distances under water. On occasions, this can make them difficult to relocate.

White-billed Diver (rare)
Gavia adamsii

The largest diver species, can easily be mistaken for Great Northern. **In summer**, shows a black head with striped neck and throat patches, and black upperparts showing a white chequered pattern. Shows a steep forehead, a flat crown and a bump on the upper forehead, as on Great Northern. The pale, uptilted yellowish-white bill is very striking, giving a large, Red-throated Diver-like head profile. Differs from Great Northern **in winter** by showing a diffuse brownish nape which does not contrast strongly with the paler neck. Half collar also present. Upperparts blackish-brown. **Immatures** show pale feather edges to browner upperparts. Eyes deep red.

Voice and Diet
Although rarely heard in Ireland, White-billed Diver can give a wailing, gull-like call. Dives for fish and marine invertebrates.

Black-throated Diver (rare)
Gavia arctica

An elegant species with a slender, straight bill. **In summer**, shows a matt greyish head and nape with a black chin and throat. Black and white stripes extend from the sides of the neck onto the white breast. Belly white. Black upperparts show a white chequered pattern. **In winter**, the black crown extends down to eye. The blackish-grey nape extends well onto the sides of the neck, and is strongly demarcated from the white throat. Underparts white. Shows a gently-angled forehead and a slightly rounded crown. Upperparts blackish. **Immatures** show pale fringes to upperpart feathers. Often shows a prominent white patch on the rear flanks. Eyes deep red.

Voice and Diet
Although normally quiet in Ireland, autumn birds can give a croaking-type call or a plaintive, wailing *arru-uuh*. Feeds by diving for fish and a variety of marine invertebrates. Capable of lengthy dives, moving reasonable distances when submerged.

Habitat and Status

A common winter visitor to Ireland from breeding grounds in Greenland and Iceland. Found on open seas, bays and harbours in all coastal counties. Can also occur on inland lakes and reservoirs. Arrives in Ireland in late autumn, with most birds departing by April. In early spring, some can show a full summer plumage.

Great Northern Diver

Winter

thick, heavy bill

Adult (summer)

Habitat and Status

An extremely rare winter visitor to Ireland from high Arctic regions from western Russia to Canada. Occurs on open coastal waters, bays and harbours. Can be quite approachable.

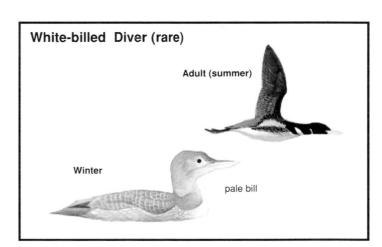

White-billed Diver (rare)

Adult (summer)

Winter

pale bill

Habitat and Status

A rare but regular winter visitor to Irish coastlines. In recent years, good numbers have been recorded annually in western, north-western and northern coastal regions. In spring, frequently reported off south-eastern counties. Usually found on open coastal waters, bays and, occasionally, harbours. Can occur on inland freshwater lakes.

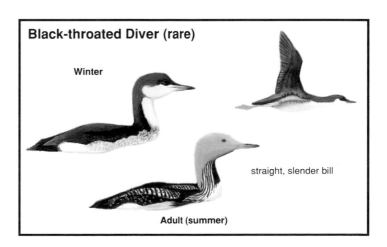

Black-throated Diver (rare)

Winter

straight, slender bill

Adult (summer)

Divers and Grebes

Red-throated Diver
Gavia stellata   Lóma rua

A small diver with a narrow, uptilted, pale greyish bill giving a distinctive head-in-the-air profile. **In summer**, shows a pale greyish head and a narrow red throat patch. Black and white stripes extend from the neck onto the sides of the breast. Upperparts brownish with small, faint, pale spots. **In winter**, appears very pale, with a grey rounded crown and nape lacking a strong contrast with the whitish throat and breast. Upperparts show pale feather edges. Can show a white flank patch but is not usually as contrasting as on Black-throated. **Immatures** appear dirtier, and show a small, dull red throat patch. Dark red eye conspicuous in a plain face.

Voice and Diet
Gives a quacking *kruuk* call and a loud, wailing *ruu-aruu*. These calls are usually heard on the breeding grounds although can often be heard in very early autumn. Dives for fish and marine invertebrates. Can move considerable distances under water.

Great Crested Grebe
Podiceps cristatus   Foitheach mór

Large, elegant, slender-necked grebe with a long, pointed, pink bill. **In summer**, shows a black crown which extends back to form a double crest. Long rufous and black feathers from the rear of crown to the throat form a frill which is used during elaborate courtship displays. Dark line extends from base of bill to eye. Diagnostic white supercilium extends from the bill over the eye and blends with the white cheeks. Throat and breast whitish. Nape and upperparts plain brown. Shaggy, pale greyish flanks can show a rufous wash. **In winter**, the head frill and long double crest are lost. Eye red. In flight, shows white patches on forewing and secondaries.

Voice and Diet
On the breeding grounds gives a variety of harsh, croaking *kar-rraar* calls and whirring notes. An active diver, feeding on fish, insects and aquatic invertebrates.

Red-necked Grebe (rare)
Podiceps griseigena   Foitheach píbrua

A smaller, stockier and thicker-necked grebe than Great Crested. In all plumages shows a black crown which extends down below eye. Cheeks dusky white. Nape and upperparts blackish-brown. Flanks pale brown but can show a striking white flash. **In summer**, lower throat, neck and upper breast chestnut-red, becoming greyish-white and diffuse in winter and lacking a strong contrast with the nape. Black bill shows a bright yellow basal patch, this being more conspicuous and extensive on **immatures**. In flight, shows white on secondaries and a white forewing patch. Eyes dark on adults, pale yellow on immatures. When diving, often leaps clear of water.

Voice and Diet
A usually silent species in Ireland. Feeds on insects, small fish and other small aquatic invertebrates. Dives below surface of water and, like other grebes, can cover good distances when submerged.

Habitat and Status

A rare Irish breeding bird found nesting on small islets on loughs or lakes. The main Irish breeding populations are based in north-western regions. A common winter visitor to all coastal counties. Found on open coastal waters, bays and harbours.

Red-throated Diver

Winter

thin, uptilted bill

Adult (summer)

Habitat and Status

A common Irish breeding bird found on inland lakes throughout the year. Builds a large floating nest among reeds and sedges, or hidden by tree branches. In winter, common in harbours and on open coastal waters in most regions. Tends to be scarce in some south-western areas. Breeding populations are highest in more northern regions of the country.

Great Crested Grebe

Winter

pink bill

Adult (summer)

Habitat and Status

A rare but regular winter visitor from the Baltic regions. Normally found on open coastal waters, bays and occasionally in harbours. Can also occur on reservoirs and inland lakes.

Red-necked Grebe (rare)

Winter

yellow base to dark bill

Adult (summer)

Grebes

Slavonian Grebe
Podiceps auritus   Foitheach cluasach

Small, solid, flat-crowned grebe with a stubby, pale-tipped black bill. **Summer adults** show a black crown separated from black cheeks and chin by golden horns extending from base of bill, through eye, and forming a crest on the rear of crown. Nape and upperparts blackish. Neck, upper breast and flanks chestnut-red. **In winter** is strikingly black and white. Crown black, extending down to the red eye and sharply demarcated from the white cheeks. Also shows a thin stripe from eye to bill, and a pale loral spot. Nape and upperparts black, contrasting with the white breast and neck. Flanks greyish. Shows white secondaries and small white wedge on forewing in flight.

Voice and Diet
A silent species in Ireland. Slavonian Grebes are active feeders, sometimes jumping clear of the water when diving. Feeds primarily on small fish, insects and other small aquatic invertebrates.

Black-necked Grebe (rare)
Podiceps nigricollis   Foitheach píbdhubh

A small grebe which can give a fluffed-up appearance. Shows a steep forehead and rounded crown. Thin black pointed bill is uptilted. **Summer adults** show a black crown which forms a stubby crest. Nape, cheeks, throat and neck black. Bright golden feathers form a fan behind the deep red eye. Flanks bright chestnut-red. **In winter**, unlike Slavonian Grebe, the black of the crown extends below the eye onto ear coverts. Cheeks, chin and throat white. Nape black, fading into the dusky-grey sides of neck. Breast white. Flanks greyish. Upperparts always blackish. In flight shows white inner primaries and secondaries, but no white on forewing.

Voice and Diet
On the breeding grounds, gives a flute-like *poe-eet* call. Silent in winter. Sometimes jumps clear of the water when diving for small aquatic invertebrates. Does not take fish as frequently as other grebes.

Little Grebe
Tachybaptus ruficollis   Spágaire tonn

Tiny, short-necked, stubby-billed grebe with a fluffed-up, short-bodied appearance. **Summer adults** show a black crown, nape and upper breast. Black on crown extends down to the eye. Cheeks, chin, throat and sides of neck deep chestnut-red. Also shows a pale yellow spot at the base of the bill. Upperparts blackish. Breast and flanks dark brownish-black, often fluffed. Sometimes shows rufous patches on rump. **In winter** shows a dark brown crown, nape and upperparts, and greyish flanks. Cheeks, throat and neck pale buff-brown with a paler breast. **Immatures** similar to winter adults, but show a dark mark below the eye. In flight shows a completely plain wing.

Voice and Diet
On the breeding grounds can give a high-pitched, rattling call. Also gives a sharp *pit-pit* or *wit-wit* call when alarmed. An active, buoyant feeder, sometimes jumping clear of the water when diving for small insects and molluscs.

Habitat and Status

An uncommon winter visitor from their breeding grounds in Iceland and Scandinavia. Found in coastal bays and harbours, often associating in small groups. Occasionally recorded on inland lakes and reservoirs, particularly in northern counties.

Slavonian Grebe

neat black crown, white cheeks

Winter

stubby dark bill with pale tip

Adult (summer)

Habitat and Status

Formerly a rare breeding species on inland lakes in western counties where small colonies may still exist. Builds a floating nest, hidden in sedges or reeds. An uncommon winter visitor from continental Europe. Found on coastal bays or freshwater areas close to the coast. Most reports refer to southern counties. Rare on inland reservoirs or lakes in winter.

Black-necked Grebe (rare)

black crown extends onto cheeks

Winter

thin, uptilted bill

Adult (summer)

Habitat and Status

A common breeding bird found on ponds, lakes, reservoirs and marshes. Builds a floating nest among reeds and sedges. In winter, common on ponds, lakes and reservoirs. Uncommon, although occasionally seen, on estuary channels and in harbours. Rarely seen on open coastal water.

Little Grebe

Adult (winter)

small, compact, stubby bill, often looks 'fluffed up'

Adult (summer)

25

Gannet, Albatross and Fulmar

Gannet

Morus bassanus   Gainéad

A large seabird with long narrow wings, a pointed tail and a spear-like bill. **Adults** are white with striking black wing tips, a creamy yellow head and black lores. Pointed bill bluish-grey with dark lines. Forward-facing eyes show a pale iris. Legs and feet greyish. **Juveniles** blackish-brown with pale speckling on upperparts and head, a paler lower breast and belly, and pale uppertail-coverts. Bill and legs dark. As birds mature, the plumage becomes gradually whiter, so that **3rd year birds** are very similar to adults but show some dark feathering on the inner wings, and can show a dark centre to the tail. Flight is graceful, with strong wing beats interspersed with long, easy glides.

Voice and Diet

Noisy on the breeding colonies with birds giving loud, barking *arrah* calls. Usually silent at sea. Feeds on a wide variety of fish which are caught by dramatic plunges into the water, sometimes from substantial heights. When a shoal of fish is located, large numbers of Gannets can be seen diving together.

Black-browed Albatross (rare)

Diomedea melanophris

An enormous seabird with extremely long, narrow wings and a chunky head and body. **Adults** show a large yellow bill with blackish basal lines, a white head with a blackish eye patch giving a frowning expression, and white underparts. Back and upperwings blackish, contrasting with the white rump and uppertail-coverts. Short tail dark greyish. Underwing shows a white central stripe with a broad black border. **Immatures** similar, but show a greyish bill, a greyish wash on the nape and hindneck, and a greyish band on the foreneck. Underwings show a very narrow, ill-defined, whitish central stripe. Glides with ease on stiff wings and can cover long distances without flapping.

Voice and Diet

A silent species, rarely heard away from the breeding grounds. Feeds on a wide variety of marine life, including fish, jellyfish and squid. Will also be attracted to offal and waste.

Fulmar

Fulmarus glacialis   Fulmaire

A rather gull-like species with a thickset neck and long, narrow, stiff wings. **Adults** and **immatures** similar, show-ing a thick, tube-nosed, yellowish bill with a green or bluish-green base. Head and neck white with conspicuous black patches in front of eyes. Back and upperwings bluish-grey with pale inner primary patches. Underwings white with dusky edges. Tail and rump pale greyish. Flight strong with long glides and rapid, stiff wing beats. Soars over breeding cliffs with skilful twists and turns. When alarmed can spurt an oily substance which is foul-smelling and repulsive. The northern phase, known as **Blue Fulmar**, shows a smoky-grey head, neck and underparts.

Voice and Diet

On the nest, gives a cackling, grunting, repeated *urg-urg-urg* call. Can also give a warning, growling call before spurting oil. Feeds on a wide range of marine fish, molluscs and crustaceans. Will also take fish offal from trawlers and can occasionally feed on carrion found at sea.

Habitat and Status

A common bird of open sea found off the Irish coastline throughout the year. Breeds at colonies on Little Skellig in Co. Kerry, on the Bull Rock in Co. Cork, at two colonies on the Saltees in Co. Wexford, and on Clare Island in Co. Mayo. In recent years a colony has become established on a sea stack off Ireland's Eye, Co. Dublin. Nests on steep, rocky cliffs.

Habitat and Status

An extremely rare vagrant from the breeding grounds in the southern hemisphere. Usually seen at sea, with records from sites in the south-west, west and south-east. While only a small number of birds have been positively identified as Black-browed, most reports of albatrosses off Ireland probably refer to this species.

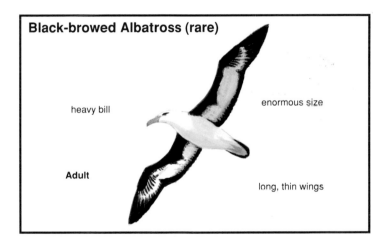

Habitat and Status

Although Fulmars first bred in Ireland as recently as 1911, they are now a widespread breeding species found nesting in most coastal counties. Found throughout the year, Fulmars are strictly pelagic, rarely venturing inland. Observations in the south-west show that Fulmar numbers reach their peak in early April and early August. Good movements also occur in December and January. Nests in small colonies on coastal cliffs. Blue Fulmars are recorded annually in small numbers.

Shearwaters

Great Shearwater
Puffinus gravis

A large shearwater which glides effortlessly on bowed wings, or flies with stiff, fast wing beats. **Adults** and **immatures** similar, showing a black bill, a dark brownish cap which contrasts strongly with a white throat, and a whitish collar which almost extends around the nape. Underparts white with diagnostic dark brownish patches on the sides of the breast, and a dark belly patch. Mantle and rump greyish-brown. Wings show greyish-brown coverts and contrasting blackish wing tips and secondaries. Whitish underwings show black edges, and black markings on the coverts and axillaries. White tips to the uppertail-coverts form a narrow horseshoe patch above the dark tail.

Voice and Diet
If close to a feeding flock of Great Shearwaters, a raucous, gull-like call can occasionally be heard. Feeds on a wide range of small fish, squid and offal from trawlers. Can be seen following trawlers out at sea.

Cory's Shearwater (rare)
Calonectris diomedea

A large shearwater which glides on bowed wings and flies in a lazy, gull-like manner. **Adults** and **immatures** show a pale bill and a rather featureless plumage. Head greyish-brown, becoming diffuse as it merges into a whitish throat. Lacks the diagnostic dark cap and pale collar of Great Shearwater. Underparts pure white with no breast or belly patches. Upperparts and wings greyish-brown, with no contrast between the wing coverts, wing tips and secondaries. Underwing clean white with dark border. Pale tips to uppertail-coverts can show as a thin, pale horseshoe patch above darker tail. Seen in silhouette or in poor conditions, Fulmars can be mistaken for Cory's Shearwater.

Voice and Diet
Cory's Shearwaters are silent away from the breeding grounds and are never heard in Irish waters. Feeds on a wide variety of small fish and crustaceans. Will readily take offal from trawlers.

Sooty Shearwater
Puffinus griseus

A distinctive, stocky bird, showing an all-dark body plumage and long, narrow wings. Head, upperparts, upperwings and tail sooty-brown. Underparts can appear slightly paler or greyish-brown. In flight, the conspicuous silvery centre to the underwing contrasts strongly with the dark plumage. Bill dark. Flies with long, angled-back wings, gliding in arcs over the water. On the water, appears wholly dark and could be mistaken for a dark-phase Arctic Skua at a distance. Could also be mistaken for Mediterranean Shearwater but the all-dark underparts, the angled-back wings, larger size and flight are diagnostic.

Voice and Diet
Silent away from the breeding grounds and at sea. Feeds on a wide range of marine life, taking small fish, squid and crustaceans.

42-50cm	**Great Shearwater**
43-49cm	**Cory's Shearwater**
38-44cm	**Sooty Shearwater**

Habitat and Status

An annual autumn visitor to Irish waters, with most records occurring between July and October. Breeds in the South Atlantic. Most are recorded from seawatching sites in the south-west or on open seas during pelagic trips. However, occasional sightings have been recorded off southern, south-eastern, eastern, north-western and western counties.

Great Shearwater

dark cap, thin white rump

brown on breast-sides and belly

Habitat and Status

A rare but annual autumn visitor to Irish waters. Breeds in Mediterranean regions and in the central Atlantic. Most Irish records refer to birds passing seawatching sites in the south-west where they have been seen from June to October. Also seen on pelagic trips where they are found in open seas, occasionally following fleets of trawlers.

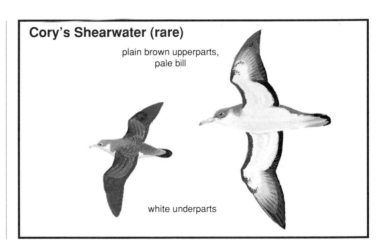

Cory's Shearwater (rare)

plain brown upperparts, pale bill

white underparts

Habitat and Status

A bird of open oceans and seas, Sooty Shearwaters are regular late summer and autumn visitors from breeding grounds in the southern hemisphere. Usually seen off seawatching points in most coastal counties, with the largest movements recorded in the south and south-west. The peak passage is normally between late August and mid-September. Also encountered on oceanic pelagic trips.

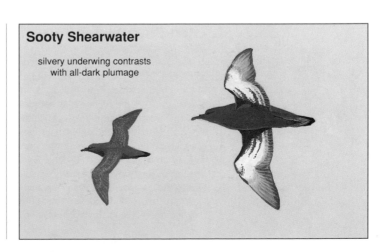

Sooty Shearwater

silvery underwing contrasts with all-dark plumage

29

Shearwaters

Mediterranean Shearwater (rare)
Puffinus mauretanicus

A brown and white shearwater, slightly bulkier and larger than Manx Shearwater, with a shortish tail and long, narrow, pointed wings. Upperparts brown, with a slightly darker brown cap fading into a paler throat. Underparts pale whitish-brown, but can show very dark underparts with a pale belly. Underwing whitish with a thick, dark border. The underwing can appear quite greyish or silvery. Bill dark. Legs pinkish. In bad light can appear all-dark, and could be confused with Sooty Shearwater. However, Mediterranean is smaller with shorter, less angled wings. Glides and shears like Manx Shearwater, but flight tends to appear more fluttery with rapid stiff wing beats.

Voice and Diet
Being silent at sea, Mediterranean Shearwaters are rarely heard in Irish waters. On breeding grounds, gives crooning and crowing calls similar to Manx Shearwaters. Feeds on a wide range of small fish and molluscs. Like other shearwaters, can also be attracted to offal from trawlers.

Manx Shearwater
Puffinus puffinus   Cánóg dhubh

A slender, black and white shearwater with long, narrow, pointed wings. Upperparts black. Crown black, extending below eye. Underparts white. Underwing white with a black border and extensive dark wing tips. Bill dark. Legs pinkish. Very distinctive in flight, with quick, stiff wing beats followed by long gliding, shearing and banking low over the waves. This flight gives contrasting flashes of the black upperparts, followed by the white underparts. In very calm weather, can fly with rapid wing beats and very little gliding, leading to confusion with Little Shearwater. However, size, long, slender wings and black crown to below eye are diagnostic.

Voice and Diet
Silent at sea. At the breeding grounds, however, Manx Shearwaters can be heard to give a range of weird, wild, crooning and crowing calls. These raucous calls are given both in flight and in the burrows. Returns to the nesting burrows at night, adding to the eeriness of the calls. Feeds on a wide range of small fish and molluscs. Will also be attracted to offal from trawlers.

Little Shearwater (rare)
Puffinus assimilis

A stocky shearwater, very similar to Manx Shearwater but noticeably smaller with shorter, blunter wings. Upperparts black. Unlike Manx, the black crown does not extend below eye, giving a whiter face with a white circle around eye. Underparts white with white undertail-coverts almost extending to tip of tail. Whitish underwing shows a blackish border, but the wing tips are not as extensively dark as on Manx. Short bill dark. Bluish legs difficult to see, but differ from the pinkish legs of Manx Shearwater. Flies with fast, auk-like, fluttering wing beats. Glides and banks less than Manx Shearwater, but the flight of Manx can vary according to weather conditions.

Voice and Diet
A silent species when found at sea. Feeds by plunging or by picking from the surface of the water while swimming. Takes a wide variety of small fish and small molluscs.

Habitat and Status

A scarce but annual late summer and early autumn visitor from breeding grounds in the western regions of the Mediterranean. Has also been recorded in winter and spring. Most sightings are from seawatching points in the south and south-west, with occasional reports from other coastal regions. Most birds are seen flying, feeding and generally associating with flocks of Manx Shearwaters at sea.

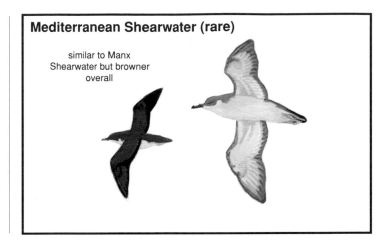

Mediterranean Shearwater (rare)

similar to Manx Shearwater but browner overall

Habitat and Status

A very common, numerous breeding seabird found off all coastal counties on passage and in summer. Winters far out into the Atlantic Ocean. Found breeding at many sites on quiet islands and headlands, with the largest concentrations in the south-west. Can pass seawatching locations in very large numbers in late summer and early autumn. Found on open sea and oceans, with occasional inland records usually referring to large inland lakes.

Manx Shearwater

strikingly black and white

white underparts

Habitat and Status

An extremely rare vagrant from breeding grounds in the Azores and Canary Islands. Most records refer to late summer and autumn with sightings primarily from the south-west and west. A bird of open sea and ocean, occasionally found moving with Manx Shearwaters.

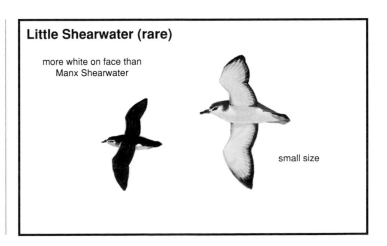

Little Shearwater (rare)

more white on face than Manx Shearwater

small size

31

Petrels

Storm Petrel
Hydrobates pelagicus   Guairdeall

A small, dark petrel with a square tail, a white rump and short, rounded wings. **Adults** and **immatures** show a sooty-black head, underparts, mantle and upperwing, contrasting strongly with a square white rump which extends onto the lower flanks. Tail dark. Upperwing plain, lacking any pale covert panel as seen on other petrel species. However, the underwing does show a striking white line on the coverts. Legs dark and short, not extending beyond tail. Bill small and dark. Flight is fluttery and bat-like, with fast wing beats interspersed with glides. When feeding, can paddle the feet in the water as it moves back and forth on raised wings.

Voice and Diet
Silent at sea. At night, around the breeding colonies, gives a variety of repeated, squeaking and growling *tur-wik* and *pee* calls. At the nest, gives a purring call which ends in a distinctive hiccup-type note. Feeds on a wide variety of marine food items, including small fish and plankton. Can also be attracted to trawlers, readily feeding on scraps and offal.

Leach's Petrel
Oceanodroma leucorhoa

A dark petrel, larger and paler than Storm Petrel, and showing long, pointed wings, a forked tail and a white rump. **Adults** and **immatures** show a dark blackish-brown head, mantle and underparts. Upperwing dark with a distinctive greyish band across the coverts. Underwing wholly dark. Narrow rump can show a dark central line, a feature only obvious at very close range. Tail dark and forked. Bill and legs dark. In flight shows long, pointed wings which are swept back at the carpals. Flight appears easy, with slow wing beats and glides. Moves back and forth across the water when feeding, pattering the feet in the water while holding the wings flat or slightly bowed.

Voice and Diet
Silent at sea. At breeding sites at night, gives a variety of chatters and screeches. At the nest, gives purring-type calls and a distinctive, wheezing *wick* call. Like Storm Petrel, feeds on a wide variety of marine food items, including small fish, plankton and occasionally trawler offal and scraps.

Wilson's Petrel (rare)
Oceanites oceanicus

A dark petrel, larger than Storm Petrel, with rounded wings, a white rump and long legs extending beyond the tail. **Adults** and **immatures** show a blackish head, mantle and body. Rounded blackish wings show a greyish upperwing panel like Leach's Petrel. Unlike Leach's, can show a pale line on the underwing. Broad white rump extends further onto flanks than on Storm Petrel. Tail square and dark. In moult, can show long outer primaries, giving the wings a pointed appearance. Bill dark. Long legs dark with yellow webbed feet. Flight direct, with fast wing beats and short glides. When feeding, dangles the long legs or patters the feet in the water. Moves slowly with wings raised high above the body.

Voice and Diet
Never heard when found at sea. Feeds on a wide range of small fish and plankton. Will also be attracted to trawlers, taking fish offal and scraps. This habit is taken advantage of by pelagic birdwatching trips which use a foul-smelling, fish-waste mixture called chum to attract seabirds.

Habitat and Status

A common bird of open sea and ocean, breeding in colonies on small, undisturbed islands. Ireland holds the world's largest breeding population of this species, with most colonies concentrated in north-western, western and south-western counties. Nests in crevices in walls, under rocks and in burrows. Following breeding, disperses to open seas, with large numbers often recorded off seawatching sites in the south-west. Birds can occasionally be found inland after storms.

Storm Petrel

tiny size

white rump

white line on underwing

Habitat and Status

An uncommon petrel, with a very small Irish breeding population based on small, remote islands off western counties. May also be breeding on islands in the north. Nests under rocks or boulders, or in burrows. Regularly reported off western and northern coasts in autumn, most notably from the Bridges of Ross, Co. Clare. Disperses to open seas and oceans at winter. Following storms, birds are occasionally wrecked by being blown close offshore.

Leach's Petrel

small size

dark underwing, pale wingbar on upperwing

long, pointed wings

Habitat and Status

A very rare, late summer or early autumn vagrant to the North Atlantic from the southern hemisphere. A bird of open seas and oceans. Recent pelagic trips off south-west Ireland have found Wilson's Petrels, indicating that this species may be numerous in offshore waters. Has also been recorded from seawatching sites in the west. Ireland's first record of this species was of one inland on Lough Erne, Co. Fermanagh, in 1891.

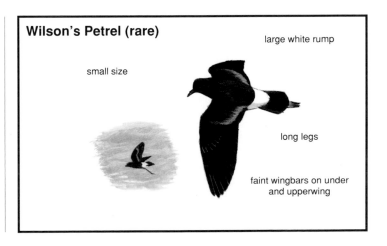

Wilson's Petrel (rare)

large white rump

small size

long legs

faint wingbars on under and upperwing

Cormorants and Ibis

Cormorant
Phalacrocorax carbo   Broigheal

A stockier, thicker-necked bird than Shag, with a heavier bill, a large area of bare skin on the lores, face and chin, and a slanted forehead. **Summer adults** show yellow around eye, a white throat and cheek patch, white head and neck feathers, a blue gloss on head and underparts, and white thigh patches. Upperparts show a bronzy gloss. **Winter adults** lack thigh patches, are less glossy, and show dark mottling on the white face patch. Eyes green. **Immatures** show a yellow or orange face, a blackish-brown plumage, mottled or whitish underparts, and brownish eyes. Legs dark. In flight appears heavy and goose-like. Swims low in the water. Often seen perched on rocks or buoys, drying open wings.

Voice and Diet
On the breeding cliffs can give low, guttural *rr-rah* calls. Rarely heard away from the breeding areas. Feeds by diving, jumping clear of the water. Takes a wide variety of fish.

Shag
Phalacrocorax aristotelis   Seaga

A smaller, thinner-necked bird than Cormorant with a steep forehead and a slim bill. **Summer adults** show a dark bill with a yellow gape line, an upcurved forehead crest, and a dark, glossy-green head, neck and underparts. Upperparts dark with a purple gloss. **In winter** shows a pale throat, a duller plumage and no crest. Eyes green. Legs dark. Brownish **immatures** show pale wing coverts, yellowish eyes and a pale brown throat and breast. Belly can also be pale. Underparts rarely as white as immature Cormorant. Legs yellow-brown. In flight appears light, with pointed wings. Tends to fly low over the water. Swims higher on the water than Cormorant. Often seen perched, drying open wings.

Voice and Diet
On the breeding cliffs can be heard to give a range of croaks, grunts and hisses. Rarely heard away from the nest. Feeds on a wide variety of small fish and some crustaceans. Jumps clear of the water when diving.

Glossy Ibis (rare)
Plegadis falcinellus

A large, all-dark, long-necked bird with a long, curved, Curlew-shaped bill. **Summer adults** appear blackish, but show a deep bronze plumage with a purple gloss on the upperparts, a green gloss on the wings and chestnut on the shoulders. Long curved bill and legs dark. In **winter**, the plumage is less glossy and appears blackish, with white streaking on the head and neck. **Immatures** appear dull brown, with very little gloss and varying amounts of mottling or streaking on the head and neck. In flight shows a slim body, long rounded wings, an extended neck and trailing legs. Flies with fast wing beats and occasional glides. Walks and feeds in a slow, methodical manner.

Voice and Diet
Although usually silent, Glossy Ibis can occasionally give a long, harsh croak. Feeds in a slow manner, picking or probing with the long bill. Takes a wide range of food items, including insects, worms, larvae and molluscs.

Habitat and Status

A common breeding species found nesting in colonies on cliffs and islands along most coastal counties. Also breeds on large inland lakes, nesting on islands and in trees. In winter, Cormorants are common and can be found on estuaries, open offshore waters, and on inland lakes, rivers and canals.

Cormorant

heavy build, striking white facial and thigh patches, yellow around eye

Adult (summer)

Habitat and Status

A common breeding species found nesting in colonies on rocky cliffs and islands off most coastal counties. Shags are more maritime than Cormorants, and are rarely found inland. In winter, occurs on open coastal waters and harbours. Found less frequently in estuaries.

Shag

forehead crest, dark around eye

Young Cormorant & Young Shag   Adult (summer)

Habitat and Status

A very rare vagrant from south-eastern Europe with only a small number of records in the last forty years. One individual, first seen at Lough Beg in Co. Cork in March 1981, was later found at Ballycotton, Co. Cork in April 1981, and remained at that locality for over two years. Found on marshes and mudflats. Will also readily perch in trees.

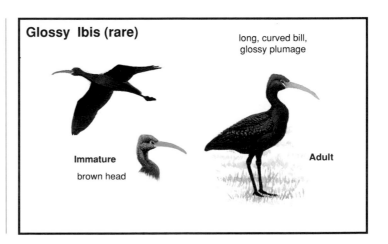

Glossy Ibis (rare)

long, curved bill, glossy plumage

Immature
brown head

Adult

Bitterns and Herons

Bittern (rare)
Botaurus stellaris   Bonnán

A stocky, short-necked, heron-like species with a pointed, dagger-like, yellowish bill, orange-yellow eyes and greenish legs. Shows a blackish crown, nape and moustachial stripe contrasting with the warm buff neck which shows brownish barring. Chin and throat whitish with brownish stripes. Pale buffish underparts show dark streaking. Upperparts warm buff and brown, with blackish-brown mottling, barring and stripes. Brownish wings show heavy, dark mottling. In flight, the large rounded wings give an owl-like impression. Legs trail behind the short, brownish, barred tail. Stretches neck upwards when alarmed, blending into and swaying with the surrounding vegetation.

Voice and Diet
Gives a loud, harsh, raucous *aarrk* when disturbed or in flight. The distinctive booming song of the male is rarely heard in Ireland. Feeds by walking in a slow, methodical, hunched manner, watching for suitable prey items. Feeds on fish, frogs, newts, small mammals and birds. Catches prey with a quick stab of the dagger-like bill.

Night Heron (rare)
Nycticorax nycticorax

A compact, short-necked heron with a thick, pointed, dark bill and deep reddish eyes. **Adults** are very distinctive, with a black loral stripe contrasting with a whitish forehead, and a black crown and nape showing long white plumes. Throat and underparts greyish-white. Mantle black, contrasting with grey wings and tail. Legs yellowish but can show red tones in spring. In flight, the black crown, nape and mantle contrast with the grey wings and tail. Flies with rapid wing beats on short, rounded wings. **Immatures** show brownish upperparts with heavy buffish-white spots and streaks, and pale, greyish-white underparts with heavy dark streaking. Active at dusk.

Voice and Diet
When leaving a roost at dusk, or when disturbed, gives a hoarse, croaking, Raven-like call. Feeds on a wide range of insects, frogs, newts, worms, molluscs and fish. Catches prey items with quick stabs of the pointed bill.

Little Bittern (rare)
Ixobrychus minutus   Bonnán beag

A tiny, skulky species with a long, dark-tipped, yellowish bill and yellow-green legs. **Males** show a black crown, a pale greyish-buff neck and pale buff underparts with orange-buff stripes. Mantle, rump and tail black, contrasting with a large pale buff patch on the black wings. Underwings show pale coverts contrasting with black flight feathers. **Females** show a dark crown, warm orange-buff tones on the nape and sides of the neck, and stronger brown stripes on the pale buff underparts. Pale-streaked, brownish upperparts contrast with an orangy carpal and a pale buff wing patch. **Immatures** brown with dark streaking. When alarmed, adopts a Bittern-like stretched-neck posture. Flight fast with shallow wing beats.

Voice and Diet
When disturbed, gives a short, abrupt, low *querk* call. Although rarely heard, the song consists of muffled, repeated, barking notes which may recall a dog barking in the distance. Feeds on fish, insects and frogs.

Habitat and Status

Bitterns bred in Munster, Connaught and Ulster up to the middle of the last century. Have since become rare visitors, with most recent records referring to winter months. During the last decade, several birds have been heard booming in suitable habitat in late spring and early summer. Found in areas of extensive reed-beds. Also found feeding among rank vegetation on the fringes of lakes and slow rivers. Can also climb reed stems. Many birds may be overlooked in dense reed-beds. Very active at dusk.

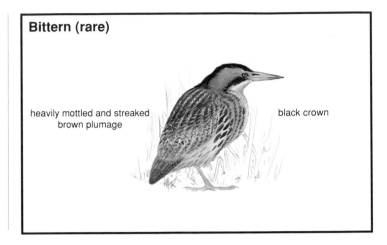

Bittern (rare)

heavily mottled and streaked brown plumage

black crown

Habitat and Status

A rare spring and autumn vagrant from southern Europe. Most records refer to southern counties. Inactive during the day, roosting in trees or bushes near marshes, rivers, swamps or lakes. Best seen at dusk when leaving the daytime roost to fly to suitable feeding areas. Feeds in shallow waters close to vegetation, hunting in a methodical manner.

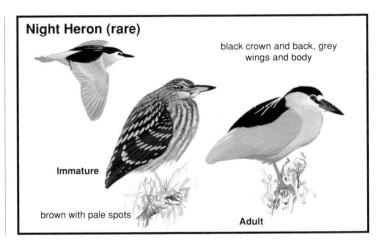

Night Heron (rare)

black crown and back, grey wings and body

Immature

brown with pale spots

Adult

Habitat and Status

A rare spring passage vagrant from continental Europe. Found in dense reed-beds or in vegetation and trees along rivers, lakes or marshes. A very skulking species which can climb up reed stems or tree branches with relative ease. Has also been recorded in open areas on coastal islands and headlands, these reports usually referring to exhausted birds or fresh arrivals. Tends to be very active towards evening.

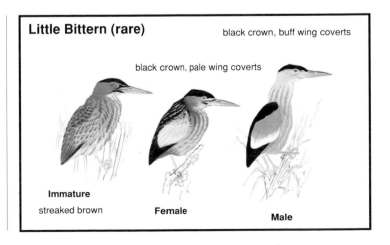

Little Bittern (rare)

black crown, buff wing coverts

black crown, pale wing coverts

Immature

streaked brown

Female

Male

Egrets, Spoonbill and Stork

Little Egret
Egretta garzetta

This elegant, thin-necked, all-white heron, with a long dagger-like bill, is unlikely to be confused with any other species. Plumage all white. **Summer adults** show two long white plumes on the head and long aigrettes (back and mantle plumes). The bare skin on the lores is yellowish in summer, being a greyish-blue out of breeding plumage. In **winter** the head plumes are lost and the aigrettes are reduced. The long, pointed, dagger-like bill is blackish. The legs are black, with contrasting yellow feet, this being difficult to observe if the bird is feeding in water. In flight, withdraws the neck and shows white, rounded wings and long, trailing legs.

Voice and Diet
Usually silent in Ireland, can give a croaking *arrk* call on occasions. Feeds actively in shallow water, catching fish, insects or frogs with quick stabs of the bill.

Spoonbill (rare)
Platalea leucorodia   Leitheadach

An unmistakable, white, heron-like bird with a long neck and legs and a distinctive long, spatulate bill. **Adults** show an all-white plumage with a yellow throat, a black, yellow-tipped bill and black legs. Shows yellowish neck plumes and a yellow ring around the base of the neck in summer. In flight, shows an outstretched neck and trailing legs. Flies with fast wing beats, interspersed with short glides. **Immature** birds are similar to adults, but show a pinkish throat and bill, as well as black tips to the wings, obvious in flight. **Immatures** also show pinkish legs. Feeds with diagnostic, side-to-side sweeps of the bill.

Voice and Diet
Although usually silent in Ireland, can occasionally give grunting-type calls. An active feeder, taking fish, molluscs and insects from shallow water by side-to-side sweeps of the sensitive bill.

White Stork (rare)
Ciconia ciconia   Storc bán

An enormous, long-necked, black and white bird with a long red bill and long red legs. Plumage all white except for black greater coverts, tertials, secondaries and primaries, which form a large glossy black wing patch. Also shows a thin black loral stripe. Eye blackish. The bright red bill is thick, long and pointed. Legs bright red. **Immatures** show a dull wing patch, a blackish tip to a reddish bill and dull red legs. Flies with long, outstretched neck and trailing legs. Wings appear long and narrow in flight and show a striking black and white underwing pattern. Flies with slow wing beats, soaring frequently. On the ground, walks slowly with outstretched neck.

Voice and Diet
A silent bird, only heard during the breeding season. Feeds on a wide variety of prey, including insects, small mammals, frogs, nestlings, fish and worms. Feeds by walking slowly, watching carefully before stabbing at prey with the long bill.

Habitat and Status

Formerly a rare vagrant from Europe, Little Egrets are now an uncommon but resident breeding species with the largest concentrations found in the southern counties. Nests in colonies in trees and bushes. Usually found in marshes, lakes and estuaries where they feed in the channels at low tide. Sometimes roosts in trees. Hard winters with prolonged snow and ice may reduce the resident population. Once hunted extensively for its plumes to service the fashion industry.

Little Egret

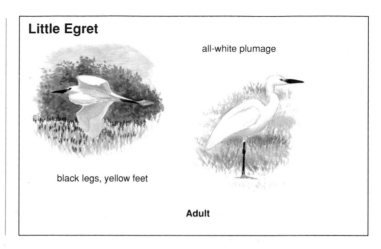

all-white plumage

black legs, yellow feet

Adult

Habitat and Status

A rare visitor from Europe, Spoonbills can occur at any time of the year, with some birds over-wintering. Feeds in shallow water and can be found on marshes or lakes. Often found on estuaries feeding in shallow channels at low tide.

Spoonbill (rare)

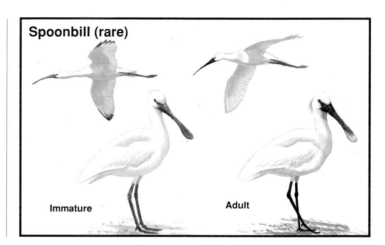

Immature

Adult

Habitat and Status

A very rare vagrant to Ireland from Europe, normally recorded in spring. Usually found on open grasslands, flooded meadows and marshes. The large size and the conspicious plumage, as well as the open habitat frequented, make this species hard to miss!

White Stork (rare)

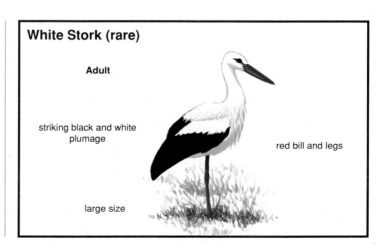

Adult

striking black and white plumage

red bill and legs

large size

Herons and Crane

Grey Heron
Ardea cinerea   Corr réisc

Large, long-necked bird with a long, stout, pointed bill. **Adults** show a white head and neck with a black crown stripe which forms a loose crest. Black stripes obvious on foreneck extending onto loose, shaggy breast. Upperparts blue-grey with a black shoulder patch and pale, elongated scapulars forming plumes. Black on sides of breast continues down as flank stripe, meeting on the ventral area. Flanks and belly white. Bill orange-yellow. Flies on bowed wings, showing contrasting grey wing coverts and blackish primaries and secondaries. Flies with neck retracted, and trailing, dull-greenish legs. **Immatures** show a dark crown, greyish sides to neck and a duller bill.

Voice and Diet
Gives a harsh, grumpy *krarnk* call, especially when disturbed. Feeds by standing patiently, watching for prey items which are caught with a fast, sudden stab of the dagger-like bill. Takes fish, insects, frogs and small mammals.

Purple Heron (rare)
Ardea purpurea

A thin-necked bird with a long, yellowish-orange bill. **Adults** show a chestnut head and neck, a pale throat and foreneck, and black crown and face stripes forming a crest. Shows a black stripe down sides of neck, with thinner black stripes on foreneck. Upperparts dark purple-grey with chestnut shoulder patch. Elongated scapulars yellow-brown. Underparts purple-chestnut with dark purple-brown flank stripe. In flight, purple-grey wing coverts do not contrast with darker flight feathers, although buff carpal patches are obvious. Underwing reddish-brown. In flight, legs trail, and the retracted neck forms a prominent bulge. **Immatures** similar, but show brownish wing coverts.

Voice and Diet
Gives a *krarnk* call similar to that of Grey Heron, although delivered in a higher-pitched tone. This call is usually given when disturbed. Feeds by stabbing fish, frogs and insects.

Crane (rare)
Grus grus

A very tall, long-necked bird with a shortish bill and long, drooping tertials. **Adults** unmistakable, with a black head showing a small red crown patch and a broad white stripe from behind eye down neck. Lower neck, breast and underparts grey. Upperparts grey with a brownish wash on mantle. Most striking feature is the long, drooping black and grey tertials which fall over the tail. In flight, shows a large wing span with darker primaries and secondaries, and a dark-tipped grey tail. Extended neck and trailing legs give an almost goose-like profile in flight. Bill dark and pointed. Legs dark. **Immatures** show a sandy-brown head and neck with an overall greyish-brown plumage.

Voice and Diet
Can give a loud *krroh* call as well as trumpeting, bugle-like calls in flight. Feeds on insects, small mammals and a wide variety of plant material and seeds.

Habitat and Status

A common resident species found throughout the country. Breeds in colonies known as heronries, building nests on tops of trees and bushes. In winter, populations may increase with the arrival of birds from Scandinavia and Britain. Found on lakes, rivers, canals, marshes and estuaries.

Grey Heron

Immature

long, white neck and long pointed bill

Adult

Habitat and Status

An extremely rare visitor from southern Europe, with most records referring to spring birds. Found in reed-beds or marshes, rarely on open estuaries or rivers. Can stand motionless for long periods within cover, making them very difficult to see on occasions.

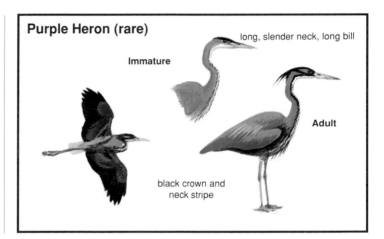

Purple Heron (rare)

Immature

long, slender neck, long bill

Adult

black crown and neck stripe

Habitat and Status

Bred in Ireland in the Middle Ages, but now only occurs as a very rare visitor from northern and central Europe. Most records refer to winter sightings. Found on marshes and open, arable lands.

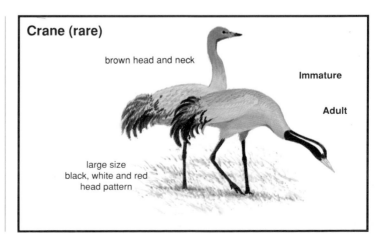

Crane (rare)

brown head and neck

Immature

Adult

large size
black, white and red
head pattern

41

Swans

Mute Swan
Cygnus olor   Eala bhalbh
Their all-white plumage, long, curved neck and their elegance in the water, often with the wings arched back, make this species easy to identify. The long, pointed tail is another useful feature, especially when birds are up-ending. **Male** (the cob) and **female** (the pen) are identical in plumage and both have orange bills with black edges and a black base which continues up to meet the dark eye. The sexes can easily be distinguished by the size of the knob on the top of the bill, which is larger and more obvious on the cob. Legs black. **Immatures** are brownish-grey in colour, with pinkish bills, and lacking the bill knob of adults.

Voice and Diet
Despite their name, Mute Swans can be surprisingly vocal. When threatened or when aggressive, they make a hissing sound. They also give a muffled 'nasal' grunt. In flight, they do not call, but the wings make a whistling, throbbing sound. Feeds on various water plants which are pulled from lake and river bottoms while up-ending. Also feeds on grasslands and cereal crops.

Bewick's Swan
Cygnus columbianus   Eala Bhewick
The smallest swan to occur in Ireland, Bewick's is more likely to be confused with Whooper than Mute. Both sexes are identical with an all-white plumage, often with pale brown staining on the head, a short, straight, thick neck and a short black and yellow bill. The combination of size and body proportions give Bewick's Swan an almost goose-like appearance. The black on the bill is more extensive than on Whooper, with the rounded, rather than wedge-shaped, yellow area being confined to the base of the bill. **Juvenile** birds have a pale greyish plumage and a pale creamy-pink bill, with the black confined to the edges and extreme tip of the bill. The **North American race**, Whistling Swan, shows a tiny yellow spot on an all-dark bill.

Voice and Diet
A quieter species than Whooper, giving a goose-like honking call. When in herds, can often give more melodic 'babbling' calls. Feeds on grass, roots and water plants, usually in large flocks, often alongside Whoopers and Mutes.

Whooper Swan
Cygnus cygnus   Eala ghlórach
The larger of the two migratory swans, Whooper is slightly smaller than Mute. Separated from Mute by the short tail and the bill colour, it is easily confused with the smaller Bewick's. Best identified by the long, slender straight neck, sloped forehead, size, and by the extent and shape of yellow on the larger bill. On Whooper, the yellow is large and triangular, with the black confined to the lower edge and tip. Like Bewick's, both sexes are identical, with an all-white plumage which sometimes shows pale brown head staining. Legs blackish. **Immatures** show a pale creamy-pink bill, with black confined to the tip, and a pale greyish plumage.

Voice and Diet
Often heard before they are seen, a loud honking-type call is delivered in flight. When displaying, a loud, excitable, trumpeting call is given. In threat displays, this trumpeting is equivalent to the aggressive hissing and arched wing display of Mute Swan. Feeds on grasses, roots and water plants, often alongside other species of swan.

Habitat and Status

A common bird found on lakes, rivers and canals throughout Ireland. A resident bird which only rarely makes long-distance movements. Gathers in large, sociable herds in winter at traditional sites. In summer, however, quite territorial and aggressive towards other pairs. Nests are enormous, round constructions found by rivers, canals and lakes, often hidden in reeds.

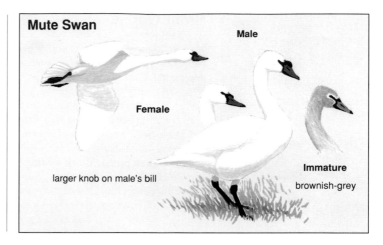

Mute Swan

Male

Female

Immature
brownish-grey

larger knob on male's bill

Habitat and Status

A common winter visitor to Ireland's lakes and marshes, they can also be found in large mixed flocks grazing on fields and sloblands. Breeding in northern Russia and Siberia, they arrive in Ireland in late autumn/early winter and leave by March or April. The North American race, known as Whistling Swan, is a rare winter visitor.

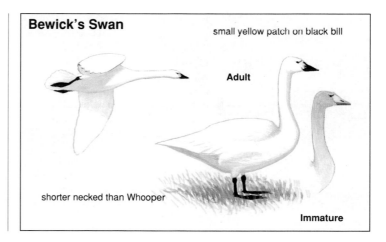

Bewick's Swan

small yellow patch on black bill

Adult

shorter necked than Whooper

Immature

Habitat and Status

A common winter visitor to lakes and marshes. Like Bewick's Swan, can also be found in large mixed flocks grazing on fields and sloblands. Breeding in Iceland and northern Europe, Whooper Swans arrive in Ireland in late autumn, and leave by mid-April, although a few may remain throughout the summer. Whooper Swans were first recorded breeding in Ireland in 1992. A pair nested and successfully reared one fledgling at an undisclosed site in the north-west.

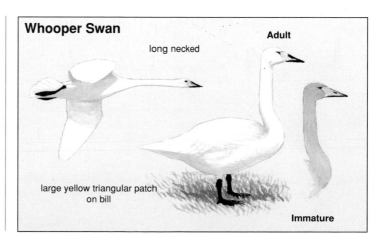

Whooper Swan

Adult

long necked

large yellow triangular patch on bill

Immature

Geese

Brent Goose
Branta bernicla   Cadhan

A small, short-necked goose with a black head, neck and breast, a small white neck collar, and dark blackish-brown upperparts. The **Pale-bellied race** shows a whitish lower breast and belly, and dark barring along whitish flanks. Undertail white. **Immatures** similar, but show a thinner neck collar and broad white edges to the wing coverts. The **Dark-bellied** eastern race is a rare visitor and shows a blackish breast, belly and flanks which do not contrast with the upper breast. **Black Brant** show a large white neck collar, dark belly and white flanks. In flight, shows a darkish upper and underwing, the pale belly contrasting with the underwings. Black tail contrasts with white uppertail-coverts. Short dark bill. Legs blackish.

Voice and Diet
A noisy species which calls both in flight and also when in feeding parties. The call is a nasal *rronk*. Grazes on coastal grasslands, on estuaries and mudflats, taking a wide variety of plant material, especially eel grass.

Barnacle Goose
Branta leucopsis   Gé ghiúrainn

A small, distinctive goose with a black crown, neck and breast and a contrasting creamy-white face which shows a black line from the dark eye to the bill. The upperparts are pale grey with broad, black, white-tipped barring. The underparts are whitish with pale grey barring on the flanks and a pure white undertail. **Immatures** similar, but show duller plumage and black speckling on the white face. In flight, the pale grey underwing with darker flight feathers distinguishes this species from Brent Goose. The upperwing is greyish with black barring. The rump and tail are black with a contrasting, broad white crescent formed by white uppertail-coverts. Legs blackish.

Voice and Diet
In flight, Barnacle Geese flocks give very distinctive, short, repeated, barking calls which may recall a pack of yelping dogs. When feeding gives a chattering *hugug, hugug* call. Feeds on grass, rushes and other plant material.

Canada Goose (rare)
Branta canadensis

A long-necked goose with a black head and neck, and a diagnostic white throat and cheek patch. The upperparts are brownish with pale fringes to the feathers. Underparts show a pale creamy breast and a brownish belly and flanks with narrow creamy barring. Undertail white. **Immatures** show a slightly duller plumage, with a brownish wash occasionally visible on throat patch. In flight, the black head and neck, the white face patch, the pale breast and dark underwing are obvious. The rump and tail are black with a contrasting, narrow white crescent formed by white uppertail-coverts. Bill and legs are blackish. There are up to ten different races, each varying in size and colour tones.

Voice and Diet
Gives a loud, trumpeting *ah-honk* call with the second note higher pitched. Feeds on grass, aquatic plants, grain and other plant matter.

Habitat and Status

A common winter visitor from the breeding grounds in Arctic Greenland and Canada. Found on coastal estuaries and mudflats, usually in noisy flocks. Can be very tame and approachable. The Dark-bellied race breed in Arctic Siberia, and is a rare winter visitor. The North American Black Brant is a very rare vagrant.

Brent Goose

Immature

Black Brant

Adult

Dark-bellied Brent

Habitat and Status

A winter visitor from breeding grounds in north-east Greenland. The main population is almost exclusively on the west coast. Also occurs along the east coast where small flocks winter on offshore islands. Found on quiet, undisturbed grazing areas, especially favouring uninhabited islands. Also found on grass and sloblands.

Barnacle Goose

dark neck,
striking whitish face

Habitat and Status

Feral populations have now established themselves in many parts of the country, having originally escaped from wildfowl collections. However, a small number of genuine birds from breeding grounds in Arctic Canada do occur. These are sometimes found grazing on open pastures and sloblands with Greenland White-fronted Geese.

Canada Goose (rare)

long, black neck,
white throat and cheek
patch

45

Geese

White-fronted Goose
Anser albifrons   Gé bhánéadanach

A thick-necked, greyish-brown goose with a striking white patch around the base of the bill. Head and neck brown, with thin black streaking on the sides of the neck. Upperparts greyish-brown with narrow, pale fringes. Underparts greyish-brown with black patches on the belly and flanks, and a thin white line along upper flanks. Undertail white. **Immatures** similar, but lack belly patches and white base to the bill. The **Greenland race** shows an orange bill and legs. The **Siberian race**, which is occasionally seen in Ireland, has a pinkish bill. In flight, shows pale coverts on a plain upperwing. Underwing dark. Rump and tail dark, with a white tail band and white uppertail-coverts.

Voice and Diet
Gives a loud, melodious, high-pitched *kow-lyok* call in flight. These calls are far-carrying, and White-fronted Geese are occasionally heard before they are seen. Feeds on grass, grain, fodder, beet and other plant material.

Pink-footed Goose
Anser brachyrhynchus   Gé ghobghearr

A small, short-necked, greyish-brown goose with a small, round-headed appearance. Head and neck dark chocolate-brown, contrasting with a pale, fawn breast. Darker rear flanks show a narrow white upperflank line. Undertail white. Upperparts pale, frosted, greyish-brown with pale greyish fringes to the feathers. Short, stubby bill is black with a pink subterminal band. Bill can sometimes show a white base. Legs deep pink. **Immatures** similar, but show a duller and browner plumage, lacking greyish tones to upperparts. In flight, shows a contrasting pale grey forewing, a darkish underwing and a white-bordered dark tail. Uppertail-coverts white.

Voice and Diet
Gives a loud, repeated *wink-wink* or *wink-wink-wink* call, which is shriller and more high-pitched than other species of grey geese. Also gives an *ang-unk* call. Feeds on grass, grain, potatoes, fodder and other plants and roots.

Bean Goose (rare)
Anser fabalis   Síolghé ghéanna

A large, long-necked, greyish-brown goose with a long-headed appearance. Head and neck dark brown with pale neck streaking. Breast pale fawn, contrasting with the darker rear flanks which show whitish edges to feathers. White upper-flank line present. Undertail white. Upperparts brownish with pale edges. Lacks the frosted appearance of Pink-footed. Long, slender black bill shows varying amounts of orange. Can also show a narrow white base to bill. Legs orange-yellow. **Immatures** similar, but show a duller, browner plumage. In flight, shows a relatively plain upperwing. Underwing dark grey. Rump, back and tail dark, with white uppertail-coverts and tail edges.

Voice and Diet
Gives a deep, often repeated *hank-hank* call. Can also give an *ang-unk* call. Both of these calls can resemble similar calls given by Pink-footed, but are lower pitched and less shrill in tone. Feeds on grass, root crops, fodder and other plant material.

Habitat and Status

Ireland holds approximately half of the world's wintering population of the Greenland race. The main population is concentrated in the south-east, with smaller numbers present in the midlands, the west and north-west. Found on open grasslands, sloblands, marshland areas and loughs. At coastal localities, can roost on estuaries or sandbanks. The Siberian race is a rare winter visitor.

White-fronted Goose

white base to bill

orange bill and legs, dark belly markings

Immature

Adult

Habitat and Status

An uncommon but regular winter visitor from breeding grounds in Iceland and Greenland. Found on open grassland, stubble fields, sloblands, lakes and wetlands. Freely associates with other goose species.

Pink-footed Goose

dark head, pink on dark bill

pink legs

Habitat and Status

A very rare winter and spring vagrant from breeding grounds in northern Europe. Found on open grasslands, sloblands and wet pastures. Occasionally found associating with other goose species.

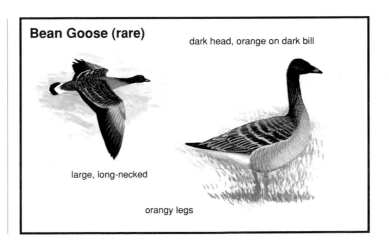

Bean Goose (rare)

dark head, orange on dark bill

large, long-necked

orangy legs

Geese and Shelduck

Greylag Goose
Anser anser   Gé ghlas

A large, thick-necked, heavy goose with a broad orange bill and pinkish legs. The head and neck are greyish-brown with dark neck streaking. Breast and belly slightly paler with variable amounts of black spotting on belly. Flanks show dark centres to the feathers with pale, greyish-brown edges. Undertail white. Upperparts pale greyish-brown with paler grey fringes to the feathers. **Immatures** similar but lack black belly spots. In flight, shows a strikingly pale grey forewing and pale grey underwing coverts. The rump is greyish. The uppertail-coverts are white and form a narrow white crescent which does not contrast strongly with the rump. Tail dark with white border.

Voice and Diet
As Greylag Geese are the original farmyard goose, the cackling, hoinking *aahng-unng-ung* call may be familiar to many. Feeds on grass, grain, roots and other plant matter.

Snow Goose (rare)
Anser caerulescens   Gé shneachta

A large goose with a broad, pale-tipped, pink bill which shows a dark cutting edge, and pinkish legs. Occurs in two forms, the white and blue phases. The unmistakable **white phase** shows an all-white plumage with black primaries and bluish-grey primary coverts. The **blue phase** shows a white head and upper neck, and dark bluish-grey lower neck, breast, mantle and underparts. The undertail can be white. The elongated scapulars show white edges. The wing coverts are pale grey. Primaries dark. In flight, the white phase shows contrasting black primaries against the all-white plumage, while the blue phase shows pale grey wing coverts and a grey rump and tail.

Voice and Diet
Gives a harsh, nasal *kaank* call as well as deep, gabbling *ung-ung* calls. Feeds on grass, fodder, grain and other plant matter.

Shelduck
Tadorna tadorna   Seil-lacha

A large duck with a bright red bill and pinkish legs. **Males** show a large bill knob, a blackish-green head and neck, and a white lower neck and upper breast. A broad, chestnut band extends from mantle onto breast. Underparts white with a black belly stripe from breast to vent. Undertail-coverts chestnut. Upperparts white with a black scapular stripe, chestnut-coloured tertials, dark green secondaries and black primaries. Bill knob reduced in winter. **Females** show no bill knob, white mottling around base of bill and duller plumage. **Immatures** blackish-grey on head and upperparts, and white below. In flight, shows a striking black and white plumage, a white rump and a white, dark-tipped tail.

Voice and Diet
Relatively noisy in the breeding season, with males giving melodious whistling calls. Females, however, give a repeated *ag-ag-ag-ag* call. Feeds on small molluscs, crustaceans and insects. Feeds by sifting in mud or by up-ending in deeper water.

Habitat and Status

A locally common winter visitor from breeding grounds in Iceland. Populations are concentrated along the northern, eastern and south-eastern counties, with smaller numbers in the south-west. In many parts of Ireland, small pockets of feral birds are present, these having escaped from wildfowl collections or even farmyards. Found on open grasslands, arable fields, marshes and lakes.

Greylag Goose

large build, heavy orange bill

grey forewing

pink legs

Habitat and Status

A rare winter visitor from Arctic Canada and north-west Greenland. Snow Geese are widely kept in captivity, but most of the records in Ireland refer to genuinely wild birds which often associate with Greenland White-fronted Geese. Most sightings occur on the North Slobs in Wexford, with other records from the midlands and west. Some birds return year after year. Found on open pastureland, sloblands and arable fields.

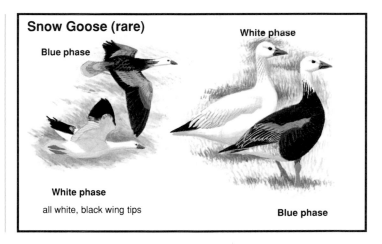

Snow Goose (rare)

Blue phase

White phase

White phase

all white, black wing tips

Blue phase

Habitat and Status

A common resident breeding species found in all coastal counties. Nests in old rabbit burrows and other holes. In July, most adults depart to moult their feathers, leaving the immatures in large crèches, usually attended by a small number of adult birds. Moulting takes place on sandbanks off north-west Germany with birds returning in early winter. Feeds on estuaries and mudflats. Nests in sand-dune systems.

Shelduck

Female

large knob on male's forehead

Immature

striking white, chestnut and dark green plumage

Male

49

Ducks

Shoveler
Anas clypeata Spadalach

A large spatulate bill gives Shoveler a striking profile. **Males** show a black bill, a glossy, dark green head and white breast. A chestnut belly contrasts with a white ventral spot and a black undertail. Upperparts white with a dark central stripe. Long black scapulars show white edges. Forewing pale blue. Shows white tips to greater coverts, a green speculum in flight, blackish primaries, a black rump and white sides to a black tail. **Female** pale brown with dark spotting, best recognised by the large bill which shows an orange cutting edge. In flight, females show a grey-blue forewing and dull green speculum. Legs and feet orange. Eye yellowish on male, duller on female.

Voice and Diet
A relatively quiet species, males can give a hollow *tunk-tunk* call, while females give quacking-type calls. Feeds by sifting the surface of the water with the large bill or by up-ending. Takes molluscs, insects, crustaceans, seeds and water plants.

Ruddy Duck
Oxyura jamaicensis

A small, dumpy, diving species with a large, broad bill and a stiff tail, which, on occasions, can be held upright. **Summer males** show a striking black crown and nape, with a pure white face and a bright blue bill. Breast, flanks and upperparts rich chestnut with white belly and undertail. Wings and tail brownish. **Winter males** show a mottled grey-brown breast and flanks, and brownish upperparts. The crown and nape are dark brown in winter with a clean whitish face and a duller bill. **Females** similar to winter males but show a dark line from base of bill onto cheeks. Females show a dull grey-blue bill. In flight, shows a plain brown upperwing and a whitish underwing panel.

Voice and Diet
Usually a quiet species, males can give low, belching calls and bill slaps and rattles. Females can also give bill slaps and rattles as well as a low hissing call. Feeds by diving for insect larvae. Also takes aquatic plant seeds.

Goldeneye
Bucephala clangula Órshúileach

A small diving duck with a peaked head, pale yellow eyes, orange-yellow legs and a blunt bill. **Males** show a dark, green-glossed head and a white spot on face at the base of the dark grey bill. Neck, breast, flanks and belly white. Upperparts black with a white, black-striped wing patch formed by white secondaries and coverts, and black scapulars. Tail greyish. Undertail-coverts black. In flight, shows a striking black and white wing pattern. Duller **females** show a reddish-brown head, a whitish neck collar, dark upperparts with grey mottling, and a greyish breast and flanks. Belly white. The dark grey bill shows an orange-yellow tip. Also shows white wing patches in flight.

Voice and Diet
Usually a silent species, males can give whistling-type calls associated with dramatic courtship displays. These displays can be seen from late winter into spring. Dives for insects, molluscs and crustaceans.

Habitat and Status

A common wintering species from Iceland, Scandinavia and northern Russia. Found on freshwater lakes and marshes, as well as estuaries and mudflats. Shoveler are a rare breeding species, nesting in grass or rushes close to water. The main breeding populations are concentrated in the midlands and north-east.

Shoveler
Male
large bill, chestnut flanks
blue forewing
Female

Habitat and Status

An uncommon species which occurs in small numbers on reservoirs and lakes. A North American species, Ruddy Ducks were introduced into Britain in the 1960s and have since become established in Ireland. Small breeding populations exist on the lakes of Northern Ireland, the midlands and south-east. Breeds in reeds and rushes.

Ruddy Duck
Male
large-headed, blue bill, white cheeks
Female
dark stripe on pale cheek

Habitat and Status

A common wintering species from northern Europe and Russia. Small numbers have been seen on occasions in summer on lakes in Northern Ireland, making Goldeneye a potential Irish breeding species. Found on coasts, bays, reservoirs and lakes.

Goldeneye
striking white spot on cheek
Male
Female
reddish-brown head

Ducks

Tufted Duck
Aythya fuligula Lacha bhadánach

A small, tufted, diving duck with yellow eyes. **Males** show a black head, breast, ventral area, tail and upperparts. Head shows a purple-blue sheen and a long crest. Belly and flanks white. **Females** are brownish on the head, upperparts, breast and tail. Flanks pale brown. Belly pale. The crest is short on females and sometimes difficult to see. **Females** can also show an area of white around the base of the bill which could lead to confusion with female Scaup. Tufted, however, lack the full-bodied, round-headed shape of Scaup and show a neater bill. **Females** can also show a whitish undertail. In flight, shows a long, broad, white wing stripe and a whitish underwing. Bill pale grey with a black tip.

Voice and Diet
Usually a silent species, males can give low whistling calls during breeding displays, females giving growling-type calls. Feeds by diving for marine invertebrates. Also feeds on aquatic plants.

Scaup
Aythya marila Lacha iascán

A large, full-bodied, round-headed diving duck with pale yellow eyes. **Males** show a black head and breast, with a green sheen to head. Belly and flanks white. Tail and undertail blackish. Mantle pale greyish with dark, narrow barring on the lower mantle. Rump black. Wing coverts blackish-grey. **Females** show a brownish head and breast, and an extensive white patch at base of bill, more extensive than that of female Tufted. In spring, can show a whitish ear covert patch. Upperparts greyish-brown. Flanks pale grey-brown, appearing broadly barred. Belly whitish. Tail and undertail brownish. In flight, shows a long, broad, white wing stripe. Broad bluish-grey bill shows a black nail.

Voice and Diet
Usually a silent species in Ireland. Females, if flushed, can give a gruff *karr* call. Dives for molluscs and crustaceans, as well as feeding on marine plants.

Ring-necked Duck (rare)
Aythya collaris

A small diving duck with a distinctive peaked rear crown and a longish tail which can be held cocked. **Males** show a black head, breast, upperparts, tail and undertail, and a faint brown neck collar. Flanks greyish, contrasting with a white crescent on the fore-flanks. Eye yellow. Bill grey with a thin white base, a broad white subterminal band, and a black tip. **Females** show a dark-greyish crown and pale lores and throat. Eye dark with a distinctive pale orbital ring which, on occasions, extends back in a line over the ear coverts. Breast and upperparts brownish with warm rufous flanks. Bill greyish with thin white subterminal band and a black tip. In flight, Ring-necked shows a greyish wing stripe.

Voice and Diet
Usually silent when found in Ireland, although females can give a growling-type call in flight. Feeds by diving for marine invertebrates. Will also feed on aquatic plants.

Habitat and Status

A common winter visitor and breeding species, found on freshwater lakes, reservoirs and small ponds. Breeds on lakes in the midlands and the north, with smaller populations in the south-east, south and west. Nests in thick cover close to water. In winter, numbers are increased with the arrival of birds from Scotland, Iceland and Europe.

Tufted Duck

black and white, tuft at rear of head

Male

Female

brown, can show some white at base of bill

Habitat and Status

A common winter visitor from breeding grounds in Iceland and Scandinavia. Found on open coastal water, bays and also on freshwater lakes close to coastal localities.

Scaup

pale grey back, stocky build

Male

Female

brownish with extensive white at base of bill

Habitat and Status

A very rare winter visitor from North America. Found on freshwater lakes, ponds and reservoirs. Can associate with flocks of Tufted Duck or Pochard. Some records refer to more than one bird. Six were seen together on a reservoir in Co. Cork in 1990.

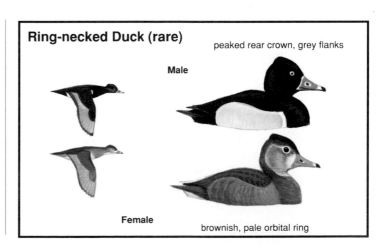

Ring-necked Duck (rare)

peaked rear crown, grey flanks

Male

Female

brownish, pale orbital ring

Ducks

Pochard
Aythya ferina   Póiseard

A diving duck with a high, domed crown and a long bill. **Males** show a rich chestnut head, a black breast, tail and undertail, and whitish-grey flanks. Upperparts pale grey. Eye reddish. Bill black with a grey central patch. **Females** show brownish crown, with paler lores and throat. Eye dark, with thin pale orbital ring which can extend back as line over ear coverts. Breast brownish with pale barring. In summer, upperparts brownish with grey scalloping. Flanks warm brown with buff scalloping. Upperparts and flanks show pale grey scalloping in winter. Tail and undertail brown. Bill dark with pale subterminal band sometimes present. In flight, Pochard shows a broad greyish wing stripe.

Voice and Diet
Usually silent, except during the breeding season when males can give a wheezing-type call. Females can give a growling call in flight. An active diving species which feeds on aquatic invertebrates and water plants.

Red-crested Pochard (rare)
Netta rufina   Póiseard cíordhearg

A large diving duck with a long neck and a rounded crown. **Males** unmistakable with a bright, slightly shaggy, golden crown, and a chestnut face. Neck and breast black, with whitish flanks becoming brownish on upper border. Belly and undertail black. Upperparts greyish-brown with a black back, rump and tail. Eye orange-red with black pupil. Bill bright red. **Females** appear capped due to a dark brownish crown and nape contrasting with a pale grey lower face and throat. Breast and flanks greyish-brown with pale barring. Ventral area pale. Upperparts and rump greyish. Eye dark. Bill dark with pinkish edges and a pink subterminal band. In flight shows a white wing stripe and pale underwings.

Voice and Diet
Rarely heard when found in Ireland. Although classed as a diving duck, Red-crested Pochard tend to feed by dabbling on the surface of the water or by up-ending. They are also known to feed on stubble and crop fields. Takes seeds, water plants and other plant material.

Ferruginous Duck (rare)
Aythya nyroca   Póiseard súilbhán

A diving duck with a sloped forehead, a peaked crown and a long, slender bill. **Males** show a dark, rich chestnut head, neck and breast, with paler chestnut flanks. Belly whitish. Undertail conspicuously white. Upperparts, rump and tail dark brown. Males show a striking white eye with a black pupil. Bill blue-grey with a paler subterminal band and a black tip. **Females** similar, but show a dark eye, a duller brown head, breast and underparts, and blackish upperparts. Sometimes an orangy loral patch can be seen. Undertail white. Females show a dark grey bill, a paler subterminal band and a black tip. In flight, shows a white wing stripe, often very extensive on males. Underwing pale.

Voice and Diet
Rarely heard when found in Ireland, although females can utter a harsh *gaaa* when disturbed. An active diving species, feeding on invertebrates, water plants and seeds.

54

Habitat and Status

A common winter visitor from Europe, with a very small breeding population concentrated in the midlands and north. In winter, the largest concentration occurs on Lough Neagh, with smaller numbers found throughout the country. Occurs on freshwater lakes, ponds and reservoirs.

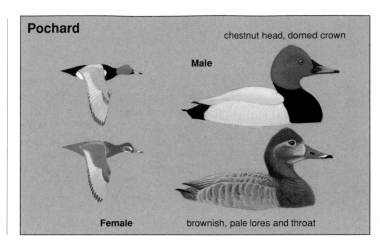

Pochard

chestnut head, domed crown

Male

Female — brownish, pale lores and throat

Habitat and Status

A very rare winter visitor from southern Europe. Red-crested Pochards are widely kept in wildfowl collections and some sightings might refer to escaped birds. Found on freshwater lakes, brackish lagoons and reservoirs. Can also be found feeding on crop and stubble fields close to water. Usually seen associating with mixed duck flocks.

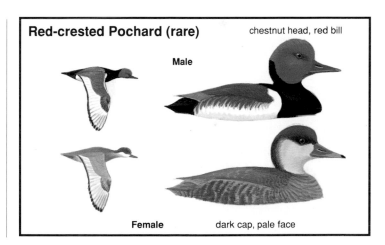

Red-crested Pochard (rare)

chestnut head, red bill

Male

Female — dark cap, pale face

Habitat and Status

A very rare winter visitor from eastern and southern Europe. Found on freshwater lakes and ponds, tending to favour those with a rich growth of vegetation. Can be found associating with flocks of Pochard. Some hybrid Pochard x Ferruginous Ducks have occurred. Ferruginous Ducks are also widely kept in wildfowl collections and some sightings might refer to escaped birds.

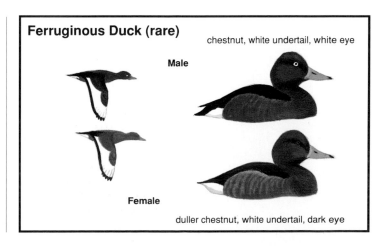

Ferruginous Duck (rare)

chestnut, white undertail, white eye

Male

Female

duller chestnut, white undertail, dark eye

Ducks

Teal
Anas crecca   Praslacha

A small duck. **Males** show a chestnut head with a buff border to green head band. Breast buff with dark spotting. Flanks grey, finely vermiculated. Yellow, black-bordered undertail patches obvious. Upperparts grey with fine vermiculations, and black and white scapular stripes. Bill dark. **Females** greyish-brown with heavy mottling, and show a dark eye-stripe on a plain face, a diagnostic white undertail-covert stripe and a pale base to bill. In flight, black and green speculum shows broad white upper border and a thin, white trailing edge. **Males** of North American race, known as **Green-winged Teal**, show a white breast stripe, a finer buff edge to head band and no white scapular stripe.

Voice and Diet
Males give a very distinctive, bell-like *prrip* call, while females give a sharp, Mallard-like *quack*. Feeds by up-ending in shallow water or by dabbling on the surface. Takes aquatic plants, seeds and aquatic invertebrates.

Garganey (rare)
Anas querquedula

A small duck which holds the rear end of the body high out of the water. **Males** show a rich brown head with a striking white stripe from above eye onto nape. A brown breast shows dark mottling. Flanks pale grey. Brown undertail shows dark spotting. Upperparts dark. Elongated scapulars show white edges. **Females** greyish-brown with broad dark mottling. Head shows a whitish supercilium contrasting with a dark crown and eye-stripe, a whitish loral patch and throat, and a dark cheek stripe. In flight, males show a grey-blue forewing, a green and black speculum, and even white upper and trailing edges. Females show duller forewing, a white trailing edge and a thin white upper edge.

Voice and Diet
Males give a distinctive, croaking, rattling call, while females give a short *quack*. Feeds on aquatic plants, seeds and invertebrates. Dabbles and immerses head in water, but rarely up-ends like Teal.

Blue-winged Teal (rare)
Anas discors   Praslacha ghormeiteach

A small duck with a broad dark bill. **Males** show a dark blue-grey head, a blackish crown and a broad white crescent between eye and bill. Breast and flanks warm buff with dark spotting. Rear flanks barred. White ventral patches contrast with black undertail. Upperparts dark with striped elongated scapulars. **Females** greyish-buff with broad, dark mottling and showing a whitish loral patch, a whitish supercilium and a broken, pale eye-ring. In flight, males show a bright blue forewing with a broad white upper edge and a dark trailing edge to a black and green speculum. Females show a duller forewing, a dark trailing edge, and an obscure whitish upper edge to a darker speculum.

Voice and Diet
A relatively silent species, males can give a soft, whistling call in flight while females give a high-pitched *quack*. Feeds by dabbling, occasionally up-ending. Takes a wide variety of aquatic plants, seeds and invertebrates.

Habitat and Status

An uncommon breeding species, found nesting on small lakes, pools and on rivers. In winter is very common, with birds from Scandinavia, Britain and Iceland wintering on lakes, marshes and on estuaries. The North American race, Green-winged Teal, is a very rare winter visitor.

Teal

striking head pattern

Male

Female

grey-brown, dark eye-stripe on plain face

Habitat and Status

An uncommon spring and autumn visitor. A very rare breeding species, with breeding records from the north and south-east. Found on freshwater lakes, pools and marshes with good reed and plant cover. Nests in dense vegetation close to water. Usually seen feeding on water along fringes of reeds and sedges.

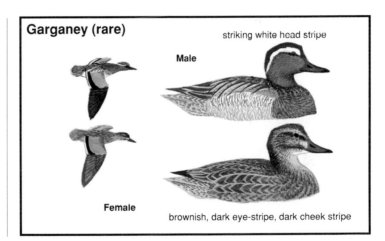

Garganey (rare)

striking white head stripe

Male

Female

brownish, dark eye-stripe, dark cheek stripe

Habitat and Status

A very rare autumn vagrant from North America, with some birds occasionally over-wintering. Found on freshwater lakes, pools and also on coastal lagoons and estuaries.

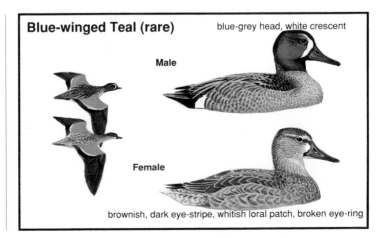

Blue-winged Teal (rare)

blue-grey head, white crescent

Male

Female

brownish, dark eye-stripe, whitish loral patch, broken eye-ring

Ducks

Mallard
Anas platyrhynchos   Mallard

A very familiar, large duck with a broad bill and orange-yellow legs. **Males** show a dark, glossy, green head, a white neck collar and purple-brown breast. Central tail feathers black and curled, contrasting with white outertail. Flanks greyish with fine vermiculations. Black undertail shows white edges. Back blackish. Upperparts greyish with fine vermiculations. Wing coverts brownish. Rump black. Bill olive-yellow with black nail. **Females** buff-brown with coarse, dark mottling. Face shows a pale supercilium and throat, and a dark eye-stripe. Bill grey with orange at base and tip. In flight, shows a black-bordered blue speculum with even, white trailing and upper edges.

Voice and Diet
The familiar, laughing *quack, quack, quack* call is given by females only. Males give soft, weak *kairp* calls, as well as grunts and whistles. Feeds by dabbling or up-ending, taking aquatic plants, seeds and invertebrates. Will also graze on crops and stubble.

Black Duck (rare)
Anas rubripes

A dark, Mallard-sized duck with bright orange-red legs. **Males** sooty-black on underparts. Pale greyish edges to tertials contrast with sooty-black upperparts. Head and throat pale buff with fine streaking. Crown and eye-stripe dark. Head contrasts with darker body. Bill olive-yellow with black nail. **Female** similar but body browner and head more coarsely streaked. Bill duller, occasionally with dark centre. Legs brownish-red. In flight, shows a black-bordered, deep blue speculum and a very thin white trailing edge. Lacks the white upper edge of speculum present on Mallard. Underwing silvery-white, contrasting strongly with dark body.

Voice and Diet
Calls similar to Mallard, with females giving *quack* calls and males giving weak *kairp* calls. Feeds by dabbling or up-ending, taking aquatic plants, seeds and invertebrates.

Gadwall
Anas strepera   Gadual

A slender duck with a steep forehead and yellowish-orange legs. **Males** greyish on head, with crown and nape streaking. Breast and flanks grey with vermiculations heaviest on breast. Stern black. Upperparts vermiculated grey with elongated buff-edged scapulars and paler grey tertials. Bill dark. **Females** show dark scalloping on brownish-grey upper and underparts. Head pale buffish-grey with dark crown and eye-stripe. Bill dark with clear-cut yellowish edges. In flight, males show a black and white speculum, a chestnut median covert panel and white trailing edge to secondaries. Females show a whitish speculum on inner secondaries and a thin white trailing edge.

Voice and Diet
Relatively silent, although males give whistling calls. Females give a high-pitched, repeated *quack* in flight and when disturbed. Feeds by up-ending or dabbling, taking aquatic plants and seeds. Occasionally feeds on stubble and crops.

Habitat and Status

An extremely common and widespread breeding species. In winter, populations increase with the arrival of birds from northern Europe. Found on lakes, ponds, marshes and estuaries. This species is widely reared and released for shooting.

Mallard

glossy green head, purple-brown breast

Male

Female

brown, orange and grey bill

Habitat and Status

An extremely rare winter visitor from North America. Found associating with Mallard on lakes, marshes and estuaries. Also found on crop and stubble fields.

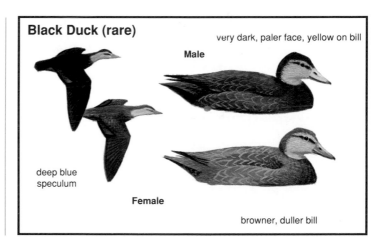

Black Duck (rare)

very dark, paler face, yellow on bill

Male

deep blue speculum

Female

browner, duller bill

Habitat and Status

A scarce breeding species, with very small populations in the south-west, west, north and south-east. Breeds on freshwater lakes with good vegetation, suitable for cover when nesting. Uncommon in winter, despite the arrival of birds from Iceland, Britain and Europe. Winters on open freshwater lakes and marshes.

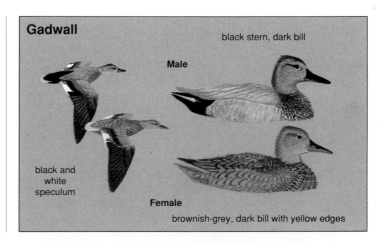

Gadwall

black stern, dark bill

Male

black and white speculum

Female

brownish-grey, dark bill with yellow edges

59

Ducks

Wigeon
Anas penelope   Lacha rua

A short-necked duck with a black-tipped, blue-grey bill. **Males** show a chestnut head, a creamy-yellow forehead and crown, a greyish-pink breast, grey, vermiculated flanks, a white ventral patch and black undertail. Belly white. Grey and white vermiculated upperparts show black- and white-edged tertials and white coverts. In flight, shows a white covert patch and a black-bordered dark green speculum. **Females** grey-brown on head with a dull, warm brown breast and flanks, a white belly and a spotted whitish undertail. Brownish upperparts show pale fringes and white-edged tertials. In flight, shows a greyish forewing. Blackish-green speculum shows a white upper edge and a pale trailing edge.

Voice and Diet
Males give a very distinctive, whistling *wheeoo* call, while females give a growling *krrr*. Feeds on a wide variety of aquatic plants and seeds. Will also graze on grasslands. Feeds on eel-grass at coastal locations in winter.

American Wigeon (rare)
Anas americana   Rualacha Mheiriceánach

Males show a steep, white forehead and crown, a flecked, pale head and neck, and a dark green eye patch. Breast and flanks pinky-brown. Belly and ventral patch white. Undertail black. Upperparts finely vermiculated pinkish-brown. Dark tertials show white edges. In flight, shows white covert patch and a dark green and black speculum. **Females** like female Wigeon, but show a greyish head with fine flecking, a darkish eye patch, an orangy breast and flanks, and a white belly and edges to brown rump. Upperparts brownish with broad, buff edges. In flight, shows white axillaries, a whitish upperwing panel, and a black and green speculum with a white trailing edge. Bill bluish-grey with black tip.

Voice and Diet
Males give a soft, repeated, whistling *whee* call, with females giving growling *krrr* calls. Feeds on a wide variety of aquatic plants and seeds. Like Wigeon, can sometimes graze on land.

Pintail
Anas acuta   Biorearrach

A long-necked, elegant duck. **Males** show a chocolate-brown head and throat, with a thin white stripe meeting white neck and breast. Belly white. Creamy ventral patch contrasts with black undertail. Fine grey vermiculations on upperparts and flanks. Tertials and elongated scapulars black with white and grey edges. White-edged black tail shows long central feathers. Bill dark grey with blue-grey edges. In flight, shows a chestnut covert panel, and a dark green and black speculum with a white trailing edge. **Females** show a plain, buff-brown head, a coarsely marked, pale grey-brown body and a longish, pointed tail. Shows a dark speculum with a white trailing edge. Bill dark greyish.

Voice and Diet
A relatively quiet species, males can give a Teal-like *krrip* call and low, whistling calls. Females give a repeated, weak, Mallard-like *quack*. Feeds by dabbling, up-ending or grazing on land. Takes a wide variety of aquatic plants, seeds and other plant material. Will also take aquatic invertebrates.

Habitat and Status

A very common winter visitor from Iceland, Scandinavia and Siberia. Very small numbers may spend the summer in Ireland, with breeding being recorded on only a few occasions in northern counties. Found on coastal estuaries, lagoons, freshwater lakes, marshes and grassland close to water.

Wigeon

creamy-yellow forehead, chestnut head

Male

Female

grey-brown head, brownish breast and flanks

Habitat and Status

A rare autumn and winter visitor from North America. Usually found associating with Wigeon. Frequents lakes, marshes, coastal lagoons and estuaries, although tends to prefer freshwater areas.

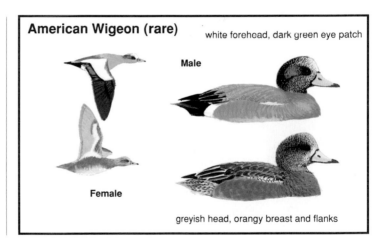

American Wigeon (rare)

white forehead, dark green eye patch

Male

Female

greyish head, orangy breast and flanks

Habitat and Status

An extremely rare breeding species, with records from the midlands and north. A scarce winter visitor from Iceland and continental Europe. Breeds on wet meadows and lakes, nesting in short vegetation. In winter is found on open freshwater lakes, coastal lagoons and estuaries.

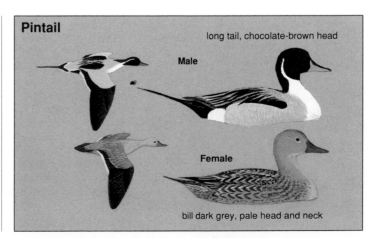

Pintail

long tail, chocolate-brown head

Male

Female

bill dark grey, pale head and neck

61

Ducks

Common Scoter
Melanitta nigra Scótar

A distinctive sea duck with a square head, a long neck and a longish tail. **Males** are totally black. Black bill shows a small knob and a yellow central patch. **Females** dark brown, with contrasting pale brown cheeks and throat. Can sometimes show pale barring on breast and flanks. Bill dark grey. **Immature males** also show a dark brown plumage with pale face patches on some birds. The longish tail can be held cocked, especially at rest. Usually dives with wings closed. In flight, appears uniformly blackish or dark brownish, with a slight contrast between the darker wing coverts and the flight feathers. When wing flapping, droops the neck and head in a distinctive S-shape.

Voice and Diet
Normally a silent species, males on the breeding grounds give high, piping, whistling calls. Females give harsh, grating calls. Feeds by diving for crustaceans, cockles, mussels, larvae and worms. Occasionally takes seeds.

Velvet Scoter
Melanitta fusca

A large, thick-necked, bulky sea duck with a wedge-shaped head. **Males** all black, with a small white crescent below the whitish eye and pure white secondaries. The large bill is orange-yellow with a black basal knob. **Females** appear dark brown, with white secondaries and pale, oval face patches on the loral area and towards the rear of the cheek. Females also show a dark eye and a greyish bill. **Immature males** lack the white eye crescent and show a duller bill. Legs orange-red. In flight, the white wing patches are striking. However, on the water, the white secondaries are not always obvious and may appear as a small white crescent towards the rear of the wing. Tends to open wings when diving.

Voice and Diet
Relatively silent when found in Ireland, although males can give a piping call in flight. Females can give a harsher *garr* call in flight. Feeds by diving for mussels, worms, crabs, shrimps and cockles.

Surf Scoter (rare)
Melanitta perspicillata

A bulky sea duck with a thick neck and a broad-based, heavy bill. **Adult males** are all black, with white forehead and nape patches, white eyes and a large, multi-coloured bill which is red and yellow towards the tip, white on the base and showing a black basal patch. **Females** are brownish with two whitish face patches on the loral area and on the cheek. Adult females may also show a small whitish nape patch. The eyes are dark and bill greyish. **Immature males** similar to females, but can show orange-yellow on the bill. **Sub-adult males** show an adult-like bill and a white nape patch, but lack the white forehead patch. In flight, the wings appear uniform. Tends to dive with open wings.

Voice and Diet
Generally a silent species, rarely heard to call in Ireland. Feeds by diving for mussels, worms, crabs, shrimps and cockles.

Habitat and Status

A rare breeding species found in small numbers on large inland lakes in the west. Common in winter, with the arrival of birds from Iceland and northern Europe. Found on open coastal water, often in very large flocks, the largest of which occur on the east, north-west and west coasts.

Common Scoter

all dark, yellow on bill

Male

Female

dark brown, pale cheeks and throat

Habitat and Status

An uncommon but regular winter visitor from northern Europe. Found on open coastal waters, usually associating with flocks of Common Scoters. Most sightings occur off the eastern coastal counties, with birds also seen off the south-west, west and north-west.

Velvet Scoter

all dark, white eye and wing patches

Male

Female

dark brown, white wing patches, pale face patches

Habitat and Status

A rare but regular winter visitor from North America. Found on open coastal water and bays, usually associating with Common Scoter flocks. Some birds are known to return to the same wintering area for several years in succession.

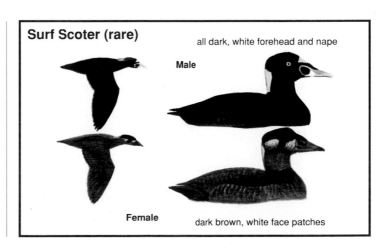

Surf Scoter (rare)

all dark, white forehead and nape

Male

Female

dark brown, white face patches

Ducks

Eider
Somateria mollissima

A stocky duck with a diagnostic wedge-shaped head. **Males** black on forehead and crown, with white stripes through pale green nape and neck patches. Face and neck white. Breast tinged pink. Belly, flanks and undertail black with white ventral patch. Upperparts black and white. Bill olive-green. In flight, black primaries and secondaries contrast with white forewing and back. **Immature males** show a dark head, mottled brown underparts and whitish upperparts. **Females** greyish-brown with heavy barring and mottling. Best told by the large, stocky size, and the wedge-shaped head profile. In flight, plain wing shows a thin white covert bar and trailing edge to secondaries.

Voice and Diet
Very vocal in late winter and early spring when males give a cooing *oo-oh-wah*, the emphasis being on the second section of the call. Females give a growling *krrr* call. Feeds by diving for mussels and other molluscs. Will also take invertebrates.

King Eider (rare)
Somateria spectabilis

Adult males show a greyish-blue crown, nape and hindneck, a greenish-white face and a black-bordered, orange-yellow shield over a bright orange-red bill. Lower neck and mantle white. Breast shows a pinkish wash. Black belly, flanks and undertail show a white ventral patch. Black upperparts show a white covert stripe with raised inner scapulars forming two prominent sails. In flight, shows white covert patch on a black wing. **Females** rufous-brown with coarse barring, a rounded rear crown, and a pale eye-ring. Short, dark bill with upcurve at gape gives a smiling expression. Bill feathering not wedge-shaped as in Eider. In flight, shows a thin pale covert bar and trailing edge to secondaries.

Voice and Diet
Although rarely heard when in Ireland, males can give a cooing *oo-ah-woo* call, similar to, but deeper in tone, than the calls given by Eider. In flight, can give a croaking call. Feeds by diving for a variety of marine molluscs, crabs and invertebrates.

Long-tailed Duck
Clangula hyemalis

A small sea duck, most likely to be seen in winter plumage when **males** show a white head, a pale pink-brown eye patch and a dark lower ear covert patch. Breast, mantle and centre of upperparts blackish. Wings blackish with white scapulars. Tail shows elongated black central feathers. Belly, flanks and undertail white. In flight shows dark wings. **Females** whitish on face and neck, with a dark crown and ear covert patch. Breast and upperparts brownish-grey. Underparts white. **Summer females** similar, but show a dark head with a pale eye patch. **Summer males** show a pale grey eye patch on a dark head, neck and breast. Bill dark grey with broad, pinkish, central band on males.

Voice and Diet
Rarely heard in Ireland. Males can occasionally give a yodelling *aw-awlee* call in spring. Females give low quacking calls. Dives for a wide variety of molluscs, crustaceans and invertebrates.

Habitat and Status

A common sea duck along the northern coastline. Scarce elsewhere, with birds occasionally wintering on the east, south-east, south-west and west coasts. Found along rocky coasts and offshore islands. Nests in down-lined hollows on short grass, bracken or heather close to water.

Eider

striking black and white plumage, green on nape

Male

Female

greyish-brown with wedge-shaped head

Habitat and Status

An extremely rare vagrant from the high Arctic regions of North America and northern Europe. Found in winter associating with Eiders. Most records refer to north, north-west and west coasts. Found along rocky coasts and offshore islands.

King Eider (rare)

grey-blue head, orange on forehead and bill

Male

Female

brown with pale eye-ring and rounded rear crown

Habitat and Status

A scarce winter visitor from northern Europe and Greenland. The largest wintering populations are based on the north and west coasts. Found on open coastal waters and bays. May be more numerous than expected, with birds wintering far offshore.

Long-tailed Duck

long tail, striking black and white plumage

Male

Female

pale head, dark crown and cheek patches

Summer Male and Female

Ducks

Red-breasted Merganser
Mergus serrator Síolta rua

A slender, thin-necked duck with a long, slightly up-curved, thin bill. **Males** show a blackish-green head with long, wispy head crests, a white lower neck and a spotted, reddish-buff breast. Vermiculated greyish flanks contrast with black and white breast sides. Mantle black. In flight, shows a white inner wing, broken by two black bars. Outer wing and leading edge black. Rump and tail greyish. Eye and bill bright red. **Females** rufous-brown on head with wispy crests, a whitish loral stripe and a whitish throat. Head colour merges into pale breast. Flanks greyish-brown. Upperparts mottled brownish-grey. In flight, shows a broken, white wing patch on the inner rear wing. Eye brownish. Bill dull red.

Voice and Diet
Usually a quiet species, males can give low, purring calls during elaborate courtship displays. Females give harsher, grating calls. Feeds by diving for fish and invertebrates.

Goosander (rare)
Mergus merganser Síolta mhór

A slender duck, very similar to Red-breasted Merganser. **Males** show a dark blackish-green head with a full, bulging rear head crest. White breast and flanks can show a pink wash. Upperparts black and white. Eye dark. Bill red. In flight, shows an unbroken, white inner wing, a black leading edge and outer wing, and a greyish rump and tail. **Females** show a dark rufous-brown head, a bulging rear head crest and a clear-cut white throat patch. Rich head colour is sharply demarcated from the pale breast. Flanks and upperparts greyish. Red bill is broader-based and shorter than on Red-breasted Merganser. In flight, females show a broken white patch on the rear inner wing.

Voice and Diet
Usually silent in Ireland. On the breeding grounds, males can give strange, twanging-type calls. Females give harsher *karr* calls. Feeds by diving for fish, also taking invertebrates.

Smew (rare)
Mergus albellus Síolta gheal

An attractive, compact diving duck with a steep forehead and a short crest. **Males** are unmistakable, with a striking black and white plumage. Head white with a large black patch around eye, a black line along rear crown, and a short crest. Breast white, with two narrow black lines on breast sides. Flanks greyish with fine vermiculations. Upperparts black and white. In flight, shows black wings with a broad white wing patch. **Females** show a reddish-brown crown and nape, with a slightly darker brown patch around the eye and a bold white cheek patch. Upperparts dark greyish with paler grey underparts. In flight, shows a whitish wing patch and a dark grey rump and tail.

Voice and Diet
Rarely heard in Ireland. An active feeder, Smew dive for small fish and invertebrates.

Habitat and Status

A common resident species breeding on inland lakes and large river systems in most regions except the south and east. A small breeding population is also present in the south-east. In autumn, large flocks of moulting birds can occasionally be seen at coastal locations. A common coastal duck in winter, found in harbours, bays and estuaries.

Red-breasted Merganser

blackish-green head, thin red bill

Male

long crest

Female

rufous-brown head merging into pale breast

Habitat and Status

A rare breeding species with small populations concentrated on remote lakes in the north-west, and mountain lakes of eastern counties. Uncommon in winter with most reports from Northern Ireland where they are annual visitors. Found on inland lakes, reservoirs and occasionally on estuaries.

Goosander (rare)

blackish-green head with distinctive shape

Male

Female

rufous-brown head, not merging into white breast

Habitat and Status

A rare winter visitor from breeding grounds in northern Europe. Found on lakes, reservoirs and occasionally on estuaries. Smew now occur annually on inland lakes and reservoirs in northern counties.

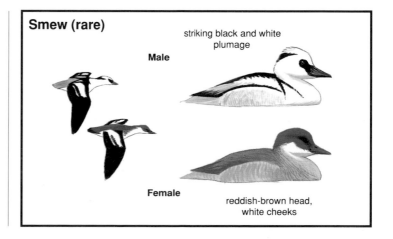

Smew (rare)

striking black and white plumage

Male

Female

reddish-brown head, white cheeks

Birds of prey

Hen Harrier
Circus cyaneus Cromán na gcearc

A slim, narrow-winged raptor. **Adult males** show whitish underparts, a white rump, a pale grey head, breast, tail and upperwing with black tips and a dark trailing edge. Underwing paler. **Females** brown above with a pale upperwing-covert panel, a large white rump and barring on a brown tail. Owl-like face streaked brown, showing a dark crescent on rear cheeks. Underparts pale with brown streaking on neck, breast and flanks. Underwing shows mottled brown coverts, barred flight feathers and a dark trailing edge. **Immatures** buffier on underparts. Legs and cere yellowish. Flies with fast wing beats and short glides. Soars on raised wings. Rounded wings show four or five fingered primaries.

Voice and Diet
Males at the breeding sites give chattering *tchuc-uc-uc* calls. Females give high-pitched *ke-ke-ke* and whistling-type calls. Feeds on a wide variety of small birds and rodents. Hunts by gliding with ease low over an area before suddenly swooping down on prey.

Montagu's Harrier (rare)
Circus pygargus Cromán liath

A light raptor, similar to Hen Harrier. **Males** grey with a white rump, a whitish belly and flank streaking. Upperwing shows black tips and a black secondary bar. Underwing shows black bars and black mottling on coverts. **Females** brown with a pale upperwing panel, a thin white rump and a barred, brown tail. Three or four fingered primaries make wings appear pointed. Face pattern diagnostic with whitish sides to head, a dark rear cheek crescent and a dark eye-stripe. Underparts pale with brown streaking. **Immatures** rufous below, and show a dark secondary bar. Legs and cere yellowish. Flight more buoyant than Hen Harrier, appearing falcon-like on occasions. Soars on raised wings.

Voice and Diet
Rarely heard on passage. Can give a soft, high-pitched *yick-yick* call when at the nest. Can also occasionally give thin *tsee* calls. Feeds on a wide range of prey items, including frogs, small birds, eggs and rodents. Will also feed on worms and large insects.

Marsh Harrier (rare)
Circus aeruginosus Cromán móna

A broad-winged, heavy raptor. **Adult males** show a dark brown mantle and wing coverts, a pale head, black wing-tips, and pale grey flight feathers. Underwing shows brown coverts, pale flight feathers and a dark trailing edge. Underparts streaked brown. Tail grey. **Adult females** are larger and show a dark brown plumage, a dark eye-stripe, and a creamy-yellow crown and throat. Underparts brown with a paler breast. Wings dark brown with creamy-yellow forewing patches on the upperwing. Tail brown. **Immatures** similar but lack forewing patches. **Immature males** show greyish inner primaries. Cere and legs yellowish. Flight heavy with deep wing beats. Glides with wings raised in a shallow V.

Voice and Diet
Usually silent on passage, with males giving shrill *key-eoo* calls only at the nesting site. Feeds on a wide range of marshland birds, mammals and frogs. Will also take eggs, nestlings and carrion.

Habitat and Status

A scarce breeding species with small numbers present in the midlands, eastern, south-western, western and northern regions. In summer, found on mountains and moorlands, nesting on the ground. Also nests in young conifer plantations. Breeding numbers appear to be declining. In winter, birds can be found in most parts of Ireland with some hunting over coastal areas. Hen Harriers can roost communally in winter. A small spring and autumn passage is noted annually in the south-west.

Habitat and Status

A rare spring and autumn passage migrant from Europe. Breeding has occurred on several occasions in eastern and south-western counties. Frequents crop fields, dune systems, reeds, moorlands and areas with young conifer plantations. On passage, found on coastal areas including headlands and islands.

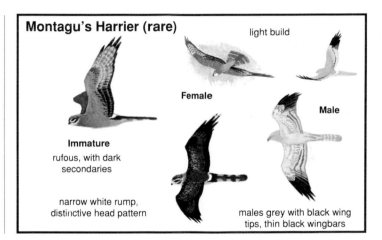

Habitat and Status

A scarce but regular spring and autumn passage migrant from Europe. Formerly a widespread breeding species, but numbers declined during the last century. In recent years, Marsh Harriers have been recorded more often and some birds have been reported summering in suitable breeding habitat. It is expected that breeding may again take place in the near future. Most reports refer to eastern, south-eastern and south-western counties. Found over large reed-beds and marshes.

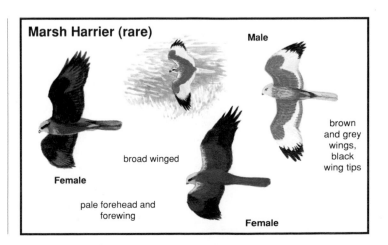

Birds of prey

Golden Eagle (rare)
Aquila chrysaetos   Iolar fíréan

A very large, powerful raptor. **Adults** show a golden-buff crown and nape, and brown upper and underparts. In flight, shows a large head and a long brownish, faintly barred tail. Long wings dark brown below, with faint barring and paler primary bases. Underparts dark brown with paler undertail-coverts. Brown upperwing shows a pale buff covert panel and greyish-brown flight feathers. Large hooked bill shows a yellow cere. Legs yellow. **Immatures** dark brown with a buff-yellow head. Dark underwing shows a striking white panel across flight feathers. White patches obvious on dark brown upperwing. Tail shows a broad white base. Soars with wings held in a shallow V.

Voice and Diet
Usually a silent species, Golden Eagle can occasionally give a whistling *wee-u* call. Hunts by flying reasonably low over the ground and swooping on prey. Feeds on a wide range of mammals and birds. Will also take carrion, which makes this species susceptible to poisoning.

White-tailed Eagle (rare)
Haliaeetus albicilla   Iolar mara

An extremely large eagle with long, broad wings and a short, wedge-shaped tail. **Adults** show a pale yellow-brown head and upper breast, brown underparts, greyish-brown upperparts and a white tail. In flight, shows a large head, dark underwings and grey-brown upperwings with yellowish coverts. Large bill pale yellow. Legs yellow. **Immatures** dark brown, with a paler breast and undertail. In flight, dark underwings show pale axillary patches and a faint covert bar. Dark brown upperwing shows a faint covert panel. Lacks white wing panels and patches of immature Golden. Short, dark tail shows white centres to feathers from below. Bill dark with a paler cere. Soars on flat wings.

Voice and Diet
Although rarely heard in Ireland, White-tailed Eagle can give a harsh, repeated *kri-ick* call. Feeds on a wide range of prey items, including fish which are snatched from, or just below, the surface of the water. Hunts low over the ground in a strong, cruising flight, taking mammals and birds. Also attracted to carrion which, like other raptors, makes them susceptible to poisoning.

Black Kite (rare)
Milvus migrans

A large, dark raptor with a shallow fork on a long tail, and long wings angled back at the carpal. Soars on flat or bowed wings. Flies with deep, elastic wing beats. **Adults** show a greyish-brown head and dark brown plumage. Breast and belly warmer brown. In flight, shows dark brown underwings with an inconspicuous pale patch on base of primaries. Upperwing dark brown with a pale covert bar. Long, slightly forked tail can appear square-ended and is often twisted in flight. Bill dark. Cere and legs yellow. **Immatures** show a brighter plumage. Appears less contrasting than Red Kite. Distant Marsh Harriers appear similar, but soar with wings held in a shallow V.

Voice and Diet
Black Kites give harsh, gull-like calls but are usually silent on passage and therefore rarely heard in Ireland. Feeds on a wide range of amphibians, birds, rodents and insects. Also attracted to carrion.

Habitat and Status

Formerly a widespread breeding species. By the first decade of the twentieth century, breeding was confined to areas in Mayo and Donegal. Now a rare visitor with most reports referring to northern and north-eastern regions. Can occur at any time of the year. As part of the 'Millennium Project', Golden Eagles are being reintroduced into Donegal in an attempt to establish a new breeding population. Frequents wild coastal islands and headlands, and inland mountainous regions.

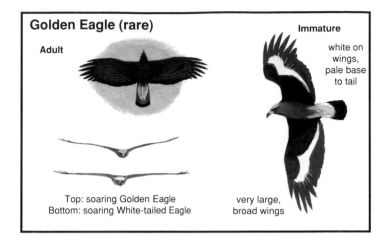

Golden Eagle (rare)

Adult

Immature

white on wings, pale base to tail

Top: soaring Golden Eagle
Bottom: soaring White-tailed Eagle

very large, broad wings

Habitat and Status

A very rare vagrant from Scotland and northern Europe. Formerly a widespread breeding species. By the turn of the twentieth century, breeding was restricted to western and south-western counties. Became extinct as a breeding species within the first decade of the twentieth century. A programme is currently taking place in Co. Kerry to reintroduce this species. Found along rocky coasts and estuaries. Perches on cliffs, trees and, occasionally, on the ground.

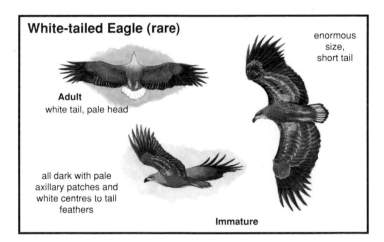

White-tailed Eagle (rare)

enormous size, short tail

Adult
white tail, pale head

all dark with pale axillary patches and white centres to tail feathers

Immature

Habitat and Status

An extremely rare vagrant from continental Europe. Most records refer to eastern, south-eastern and south-western counties, with most birds recorded in spring. Found in open areas with scattered trees or woods, and usually close to rivers and lakes. On passage can be seen anywhere along coastal counties. Can occur close to human habitation, with one record referring to a bird seen over Cork city.

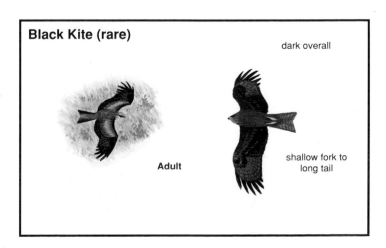

Black Kite (rare)

dark overall

Adult

shallow fork to long tail

Birds of prey

Osprey (rare)
Pandion haliaetus   Coirneach

A large raptor with a contrasting plumage. When perched, shows dark brown upperparts, a crested white crown and a striking black eye-stripe which extends down side of neck. Underparts white with a brownish breast band. Hooked bill pale with a dark tip. Legs greyish. In flight, a pale underwing shows a blackish carpal patch, a black covert bar and dark wing tips. Shortish tail is pale below, dark above, and shows narrow barring. **Immatures** show pale tips to underwing-coverts. Flies with strong, shallow wing beats on long, narrow wings. Soars on bowed wings. In the air can look gull-like. Hunts by hovering or gliding with dangled legs before plunging feet-first into the water. Shakes water from the plumage when rising.

Voice and Diet
Although seldom heard in Ireland, Osprey can give loud, repeated, whistling-type calls. Feeds exclusively on large fish which are caught from spectacular dives. Catches fish with specially-adapted talons before flying off with fish held in both feet. Always carries fish head-first.

Buzzard
Buteo buteo   Clamhán

A large, stocky, short-necked raptor with broad wings and a shortish tail. Plumage can vary greatly, but most show a dark brown head, breast and upperparts with brown mottling on underparts. Lower breast can be paler, appearing as a pale crescent. Shortish tail pale brown below, darker above, with narrow barring. Upperwing plain dark brown. Underwing shows dark brown coverts, dark carpal patches, blackish wing tips, pale base to primaries and a dark trailing edge. **Immatures** lack dark trailing edge to wings. Bill dark with a yellowish cere. Legs yellowish. Soars with wings held in a shallow V. When gliding, the wings can be held flat or just slightly raised.

Voice and Diet
Gives a distinctive, high-pitched, drawn-out, mewing *pee-oo* call. Feeds on a wide range of prey, including rats, rabbits, frogs, insects, worms and young birds. Will also be attracted to carrion. Because of this, some may die due to feeding on poison-baited carcasses.

Rough-legged Buzzard (rare)
Buteo lagopus   Clamhán lópach

A sturdy raptor, larger than Buzzard, with long wings. **Adults** show a well-defined black terminal band on a white tail with two or three narrower bands. Head and breast brown, with a paler lower breast and black belly patches. Underwing shows brown coverts, black tips to barred flight feathers, and black carpal patches. Upperwing brown with pale primary base patches. Bill dark with yellowish cere. Legs yellowish. **Immatures** similar, but show a diffuse terminal tail band, a paler, streaked head and underparts, and pale underwing coverts. Upperwings also show pale covert panels and primary patches. Flies with deep wing beats. Soars on raised wings. Hovers more than other buzzard species.

Voice and Diet
The long, mewing call is seldom given away from the breeding grounds. Feeds on a wide variety of rodents, including rabbits, rats and mice. Will also occasionally take birds.

51-60cm **Osprey**
50-57cm **Buzzard**
51-61cm **Rough-legged Buzzard**

Habitat and Status

An uncommon spring and autumn passage migrant from Europe, occurring on an almost annual basis. In recent years, birds have been reported present in suitable breeding areas in spring and late summer and it is hoped that breeding may take place in the near future. Found on large lakes and rivers, often with suitable perches such as dead trees. Also reported on passage at coastal sites. Has been seen out at sea. Can be attracted to fish farms.

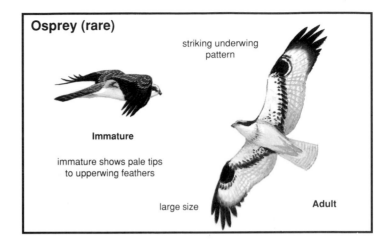

Osprey (rare)

striking underwing pattern

Immature

immature shows pale tips to upperwing feathers

large size

Adult

Habitat and Status

An uncommon breeding species with populations highest in the north-east. In recent years, Buzzards have experienced a range expansion with birds now resident and breeding in small numbers in the north-west, east and midlands. Found in a wide range of habitats including undisturbed coasts and islands, farmlands, mountains, moorlands and in wooded demesnes. Nests in trees or on cliffs.

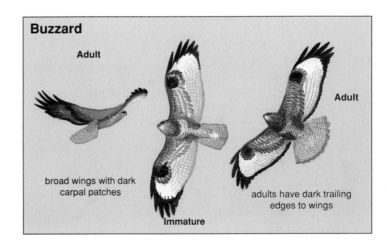

Buzzard

Adult

Adult

broad wings with dark carpal patches

adults have dark trailing edges to wings

Immature

Habitat and Status

A rare autumn and winter vagrant from Scandinavia, with most records referring to coastal counties. Frequents barren, open country and farmland. Also found on coastal dunes, marshes, headlands and islands. Most are seen on passage but some may over-winter. One bird remained on Copeland Island, Co. Down, from October 1984 to May 1985.

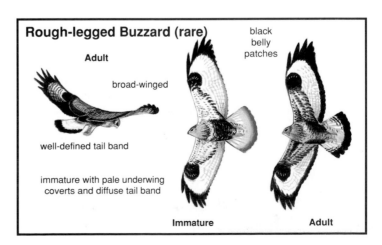

Rough-legged Buzzard (rare)

black belly patches

Adult

broad-winged

well-defined tail band

immature with pale underwing coverts and diffuse tail band

Immature

Adult

73

Birds of prey

Red Kite (rare)
Milvus milvus

A striking species with a contrasting plumage and a deeply-forked, bright orange tail. Long, narrow wings are angled back at the carpal, and are held flat or slightly bowed when soaring. Flies with deep, elastic wing beats. **Adults** show a streaked whitish head and a warm rufous-brown plumage with dark underpart streaking. In flight, shows rufous-brown underwings with conspicuous pale primary bases forming square underwing patches. Upperwing brown with a pale rufous covert panel. Long, deeply-forked, orangy tail is twisted in flight. Bill dark. Cere and legs yellow. **Immatures** as adults, but show paler underparts and a broader, paler upperwing covert panel.

Voice and Diet

Seldom heard in Ireland, Red Kites can give a shrill, mewing *weeh-oo* call which is often repeated. The call is similar to that of Buzzard, but is higher-pitched and delivered more rapidly. Feeds on a variety of small mammals, birds, amphibians and worms. Also attracted to carrion and, like other raptors, is very susceptible to poisoning.

Sparrowhawk
Accipiter nisus   Spióróg

A small raptor with yellow eyes. In flight, shows rounded wings and a long, square-ended tail. **Adult males** blue-grey on crown and upperparts, and show a white supercilium and rufous cheeks. White underparts show orange-red barring extending onto underwing coverts. Underwing flight feathers barred. Undertail shows dark bars. **Females** larger, with a grey-brown crown and upperparts, a white supercilium, and brown barring on white underparts and on underwing coverts and flight feathers. Tail shows dark bars. Bill dark. Legs and cere yellow. **Immatures** similar to females, but show pale edges to upperpart feathers and brown barring on buffish underparts.

Voice and Diet

Gives a loud, shrill, repeated *kek-kek-kek,* especially when agitated or when close to the nest. Also gives rattling calls during a slow-flapping display flight. Feeds by gliding low over the ground, along hedgerows or through trees, surprising small birds and mammals which are then swooped on. Will also chase prey into thick cover. Occasionally hunts by sitting on a hidden perch, watching over an area where birds feed regularly, and swooping down unexpectedly. Will also take large insects.

Goshawk (rare)
Accipiter gentilis

A powerful raptor, much larger than Sparrowhawk, with longer wings, a deeper chest and a rounded tail. In flight, shows a bulge to the secondaries. **Adult males** show a dark cap due to a white supercilium and nape, greyish upperparts, and dark barring on white underparts and underwing coverts. Underwing flight feathers barred. Tail shows dark bars. Larger **females** show a dark brown cap, a white supercilium and nape, brown upperparts, and barring on white underparts and underwing coverts. Undertail-coverts white. Underwing flight feathers barred. Tail shows dark bars. Eyes orange-yellow. Legs and cere yellow. **Immatures** show dark streaking on pale buff underparts.

Voice and Diet

Usually a quiet species, Goshawk can give fast, agitated *gek-gek-gek* calls if disturbed near the nest. Also engages in slow, soaring, display flights when plaintive, whistling *ee-aa* notes can be given. Feeds by flying and gliding quickly through trees, swooping on suitable prey. Will also chase prey into thick cover or out over open ground. Occasionally perches quietly, watching for prey. Takes mammals and birds up to Pheasant size.

60-66cm **Red Kite**

28-37cm **Sparrowhawk**

48-59cm **Goshawk**

Habitat and Status

A rare but regular passage migrant from breeding grounds in Wales and continental Europe. Most records refer to a period from mid-October to mid-November, and to January. Has been recorded in all provinces. In recent years, Red Kites have been recorded more frequently as a result of birds moving from Scotland where a reintroduction programme is being undertaken. Usually seen on passage over islands and headlands, or in open country close to the coast. Has also been reported inland.

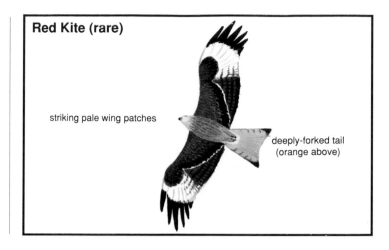

Red Kite (rare)

striking pale wing patches

deeply-forked tail
(orange above)

Habitat and Status

Probably the commonest raptor in Ireland. A resident breeding species found in all counties, frequents coniferous and mixed woodland, open farmland with scattered trees and hedgerows, parks and, especially in winter, suburban gardens. Nests high in trees, usually building close to the main trunk. In autumn, found on coastal islands and headlands, although the Irish population is usually resident. Numbers may increase in winter with the arrival of birds from Britain and Europe.

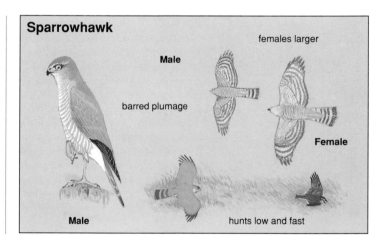

Sparrowhawk

females larger

Male

barred plumage

Female

Male

hunts low and fast

Habitat and Status

A rare passage vagrant and an extremely rare breeding species. Most suspected breeding pairs are in northern and southern regions. Frequents coniferous and mixed woodlands in both low-lying and mountainous areas. Nests in coniferous or deciduous trees. Secretive in breeding areas, but best seen in early spring when birds perform aerial displays. Occurs on passage on coastal islands and headlands, with most records referring to a period from September to mid-November.

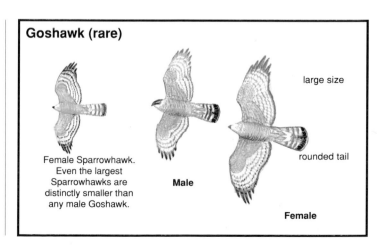

Goshawk (rare)

large size

rounded tail

Female Sparrowhawk.
Even the largest
Sparrowhawks are
distinctly smaller than
any male Goshawk.

Male

Female

Birds of prey

Kestrel

Falco tinnunculus   Pocaire gaoithe

A long-tailed falcon with pointed wings, often seen hovering in mid-air. **Adult males** show a blue-grey crown and nape, a dark moustachial stripe, black spotting on chestnut upperparts, and a black band and white tip to a grey tail. Creamy underparts show dark spotting. In flight, shows dark wing tips and dark spots on underwing coverts. **Adult females** and **immatures** show a streaked brown head, a dark moustachial stripe and heavy, dark barring on rufous upperparts. Brown tail shows dark bars and a white tip. Creamy-buff underparts and underwing coverts show heavy streaking. Shows dark tips to upperwing and barred underwing flight feathers. Legs and cere yellow.

Voice and Diet

Gives harsh, loud, repeated *kee-kee-kee* calls when agitated or close to the nest. Hunts by hovering motionless in mid-air, searching for suitable quarry below, before diving suddenly onto prey. Can snatch perched or feeding birds in a dashing swoop. Will also sit on an open perch, watching for insects. Occasionally hawks insects on the wing. Feeds on a wide range of small rodents, birds, insects and worms.

Merlin

Falco columbarius   Meirliún

A small, agile falcon with short, pointed wings. **Males** show a dark grey crown, a faint moustachial stripe, a whitish supercilium, streaked cheeks and a buff to rust-brown nape. Grey upperparts show thin streaking. Grey tail shows broad bars. Buff to rust-brown underparts show dark streaking. In flight, shows a streaked and barred underwing. **Females and immatures** show a brown crown, streaked cheeks, a diffuse moustachial stripe and a pale nape. Upperparts grey-brown. Creamy tail shows dark bars. Creamy underparts heavily streaked. In flight, shows a heavily streaked and barred underwing. Legs yellow. Cere yellow on adults, bluish on immatures.

Voice and Diet

Gives a shrill, repeated, Kestrel-like *kiik-kiik-kiik* call when agitated or disturbed at the nest. Prey consists mainly of birds, with small mammals and insects taken occasionally. Hunts by flying fast and low over the ground, sometimes snatching feeding or perched birds. Usually pursues birds with a dashing flight, following every twist and turn of the quarry until it strikes from above. Will occasionally hawk insects on the wing.

Red-footed Falcon (rare)

Falco vespertinus

Adult males show a dark grey head, upperparts and tail, silvery flight feathers, grey underparts, and red thighs, undertail and feet. Cere and eye-ring orange-red. **1st summer males** show a pale throat, orange upper breast and neck, brown flight feathers, and a barred tail. Underwing heavily barred and streaked. Thighs and bare parts yellow-orange. **Adult females** show an orange-buff crown and underparts, a white throat, and a black moustachial and eye-stripe. Upperparts and tail greyish with heavy barring. In flight, shows orange-buff underwing coverts and heavily barred flight feathers. Bare parts orange. **1st summer females** show a dark crown.

Voice and Diet

Generally silent on passage, the high-pitched *ki-ki-ki* calls only given near the nest site. Hovers with deep wing beats, but not as persistently as Kestrel. Also watches for insects on the ground from a fencepost or wires, swooping down in a shrike-like manner. Will sometimes feed on the ground, hopping, leaping and flying after prey. Hawks insects on the wing. Main prey consists of a variety of insects, but will take lizards, frogs and occasionally small mammals.

Habitat and Status

A common, widespread breeding species found in a wide range of habitats, including mountainous cliffs, moorlands and bogs, open farmland, woodlands, parks, and towns and cities. Frequently seen hovering over road verges. Nests on cliff ledges, old derelict buildings, in old nests, in hollow trees and occasionally on highrise buildings. In winter, tends to leave more mountainous areas. A small autumn and spring movement is noted annually on southern headlands and islands.

Kestrel

frequently hovers

Female

Female

Male

Habitat and Status

A scarce, resident breeding species found in all regions. In summer, found on upland moorland and bogs, on well-vegetated lake islands and in conifer plantations. Nests on the ground or in old crows' nests. In spring and autumn, a passage movement is noted on southern islands and headlands. In winter, found along coastal saltmarshes, estuaries and mudflats, and on low-lying inland bogs. Numbers probably increase in winter with the arrival of birds from Iceland and Scotland.

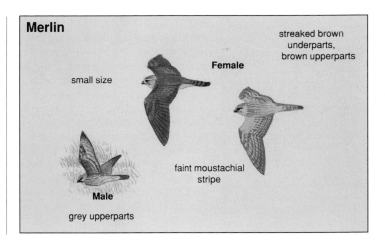

Merlin

streaked brown underparts, brown upperparts

Female

small size

faint moustachial stripe

Male

grey upperparts

Habitat and Status

An extremely rare spring and autumn vagrant from central Europe. Frequents open country with scattered scrub and trees. Many records refer to coastal islands, headlands and marshes. Also recorded inland over lakes, bogs and open parkland. On occasion, can be very tame and approachable. Can also be crepuscular in behaviour, hunting late in the evening.

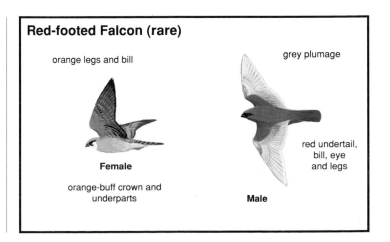

Red-footed Falcon (rare)

orange legs and bill

grey plumage

Female

orange-buff crown and underparts

red undertail, bill, eye and legs

Male

Birds of prey

Hobby (rare)
Falco subbuteo   Fabhcún coille
A slim falcon with long, Swift-like wings. **Adults** show a blackish head, a prominent black moustachial stripe and a white face. Heavily streaked, creamy underparts show bright rufous-red thighs and undertail-coverts. Upperparts slate-grey. Greyish uppertail unbarred. Shows heavily streaked and barred underwings. Pale undertail shows dark bars. Legs and cere yellow. **Immatures** show pale buff fringes to dark brown upperparts and wings. Brown uppertail unbarred, but shows a pale tip. Shows a moustachial stripe, heavily streaked, pale underparts and buffish thighs and undertail-coverts. Underwings heavily streaked and barred. Pale undertail barred. Cere bluish.

Voice and Diet
Rarely heard in Ireland, can give a clear, slow, plaintive *kew-kew-kew* call. A very agile, skilful and aerial hunter, often seen hawking insects. Will twist and turn in the air, snatching large insects in the talons and transferring them to the bill in flight. Actively pursues birds, climbing to a good height before swooping at speed. Capable of catching Swifts and hirundines in the air. Occasionally hunts by watching from a perch and swooping to the ground in a shrike-like manner.

Peregrine Falcon
Falco peregrinus   Fabhcún gorm
A powerful, stocky, heavy-chested falcon with broad, pointed wings. **Adults** show a thick, blackish moustachial stripe, a dark crown, and a white face and throat. Upperparts bluish-grey. Darker tail shows dark bars. Underparts white with fine, delicate barring. In flight, underwing shows heavy barring on flight feathers and coverts. Undertail pale with dark bars. Cere and legs yellow. **Females** larger. **Immatures** show pale-fringed, brownish upperparts, a dark moustachial stripe, and heavy streaking on creamy underparts. Dark uppertail shows pale bars. Undertail as adult. Underwing heavily barred. Cere bluish. Legs yellow. Soars on stiff, slightly bowed wings.

Voice and Diet
At the nest, gives loud, repeated, chattering, *keyak-keyak-keyak* calls. Can be very vocal during the breeding season but generally silent at other times. In winter, can occasionally give a harsh *arrk* call. Hunts by climbing to a great height and circling before diving at enormous speeds with wings held tight into the body. Snatches birds up to the size of pigeons from the air, but will also swoop through wader and duck flocks. Also takes rabbits and other smaller mammals.

Gyrfalcon (rare)
Falco rusticolus
A powerful falcon, larger and heavier than Peregrine, with broader, longer wings. **White phase** birds show a white plumage, light upperpart barring, dark wing tips and faint underpart spotting. **Dark phase** birds resemble Peregrine but show a diffuse moustachial stripe, greyish-brown upperparts, pale, streaked nape and forehead, and heavy, dark underpart spotting and barring. Heavily barred and spotted underwing coverts contrast with pale, faintly barred flight feathers. **Grey phase** birds are intermediate between light and dark phases. Cere and legs yellow. **Immatures** as adults but show clear moustachial stripes and underpart streaking. Cere and legs bluish.

Voice and Diet
Rarely heard away from the breeding grounds. Hunts low over the ground, gliding on slightly bowed wings and flying with shallow wing beats. Disturbed quarry are then chased and powerfully caught. Occasionally dives from a height with folded wings in a Peregrine Falcon-like manner. Kills a wide range of bird species. Also takes mammals, including rabbits and hares.

Habitat and Status

A rare but almost annual spring and autumn passage migrant from Europe. Most records refer to eastern, south-eastern and south-western counties, with most being recorded on headlands and islands. Also found inland over marshes, lakes and open farmland with scattered trees. In spring, most frequently sighted in May, with immature birds occurring in all autumn months. Several reports refer to birds summering in suitable breeding areas.

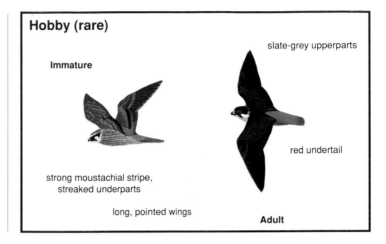

Hobby (rare)

Immature

slate-grey upperparts

red undertail

strong moustachial stripe, streaked underparts

long, pointed wings

Adult

Habitat and Status

A widespread resident breeding species found in all counties. Numbers declined dramatically in the 1950s and 1960s due to the effects of poisoning by pesticides. However, this powerful falcon can now be found in most of its former haunts. Frequents coastal and mountainous regions, nesting on cliff edges. Also found close to human habitation. In winter, most leave upland breeding areas, moving to coastal estuaries and mudflats.

Peregrine Falcon

Immature

faintly barred underparts, bluish upperparts

powerful build

Immature

Adult

Habitat and Status

A very rare vagrant from Greenland, Iceland and Scandinavia, recorded in coastal counties in all provinces. Most sightings involve white-phase-type birds. Usually found in winter and late autumn, although some reports refer to early spring. Frequents wide, open country, rocky sea cliffs and islands, mudflats, estuaries and saltmarshes. Also found over marshes and farmland close to the coast.

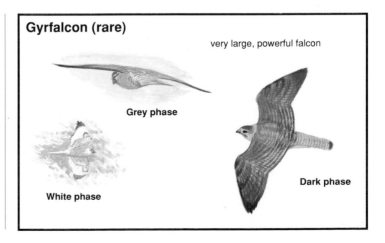

Gyrfalcon (rare)

very large, powerful falcon

Grey phase

Dark phase

White phase

Gamebirds

Red Grouse

Lagopus lagopus   Cearc fhraoigh

A dark, plump bird showing a stout, short bill and short, rounded wings. Usually only seen when flushed. **Summer males** show a deep red-brown plumage with heavy dark barring, white-feathered legs and a bright red comb above the eye. Can appear black at a distance. **Winter males** appear darker. **Females** smaller, and show a yellower plumage with coarse barring and spotting, and a less prominent red comb. **Immatures** similar to females, but lack red combs and show a duller plumage. Flushes noisily from the ground, flying with rapid, whirring wing beats and long glides on bowed wings. Red Grouse found in Ireland belong to a specific race (see Introduction).

Voice and Diet

When disturbed, gives a fast, cackling *kowk-ko-ko-ko* call. During the breeding season, Red Grouse engage in displays which involve the distinctive, crowing *go-bak, go-bak, go-bak-bak-bak-bak* call. Feeds on heather shoots, flowers and seeds. Also takes a variety of berries, buds and some insects. Will feed on cereals when available.

Grey Partridge (rare)

Perdix perdix   Patraisc

A shy, rotund species which shows short, rounded wings and a short, bright rufous tail. **Males** show an orange-red face, a grey neck and upper breast, a brown crown and nape, and pale streaking and dark spotting on brown upperparts. Pale lower breast shows a conspicuous, inverted dark chestnut horseshoe, while buff-washed flanks show chestnut barring. **Females** similar, but show a paler face, browner upperparts and a buff-grey breast. The inverted chestnut horseshoe is usually reduced to blotches on the lower breast and, on some birds, may be totally absent. Short, stout bill and legs greyish. Flies with rapid, whirring wing beats and glides on bowed wings.

Voice and Diet

When alarmed, Grey Partridge can give a slow, cackling *krikric-ric-ric-ric* call while the song consists of loud, hoarse *kirr-ic, kirr-ic* notes. Feeds on a wide variety of seeds, grain, roots, fruit and leaves. Will also take small insects such as ants. Occasionally feeds on slugs and worms.

Pheasant

Phasianus colchicus   Piasún

A large, striking species showing a very long, barred tail. **Males** show a metallic blackish-green head, bright red facial skin and small tufts on rear of crown. Some can show a white collar and eyebrow. Plumage copper-red with black crescents on underparts, and black and white fringes on upperparts. Short, rounded wings greyish-brown. In flight, shows a grey rump and a long, barred buff tail. Small bill ivory-white. **Females** show a shorter tail, a buff-brown plumage with dark barring and spotting on the breast, flanks and upperparts. **Immatures** resemble short-tailed, dull females. Flushes noisily, flying with rapid, whirring wing beats and gliding on bowed wings.

Voice and Diet

Males give distinctive, far-carrying, resonant, choking *korrk-kook* calls and a repeated *kutok, kutok* note. Females, when disturbed or alarmed, can give whistling-type notes. Feeds on a wide range of plant material, including roots, seeds, fruit, berries, leaves and stems. Will also take insects, worms, slugs and occasionally small rodents and amphibians.

Habitat and Status

A scarce but widespread resident breeding species. Found on upland blanket bog, low-lying bogs, open moorland and heather slopes. Numbers appear to be gradually declining due to habitat loss and upland management. Nests in cover of heather, rushes and tussocks on the ground. In severe winter conditions, Red Grouse can occasionally perch in bushes or trees to feed on berries. Birds of the darker British race have been introduced in the past by gun clubs.

Red Grouse

dark, plump bird

dark reddish-brown plumage with dark barring

Male **Female**

Habitat and Status

An extremely rare, resident breeding species. Formerly found in all counties, Grey Partridge now occurs only in the midlands. Found on bogs, upland moorland, marshes and pastures with hedgerow borders or overgrown verges. Also favours agricultural belts, especially wheat and corn-growing areas. A reintroduction programme involving wild birds from Poland is attempting to boost the Grey Partridge population in the midland region. Nests in dense cover on the ground.

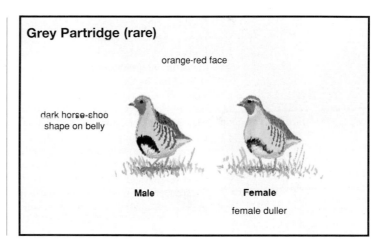

Grey Partridge (rare)

orange-red face

dark horse-shoo shape on belly

Male **Female**

female duller

Habitat and Status

An extremely common, widespread, resident breeding species found in all counties. Frequents agricultural lands, rough pastures, woodlands, upland scrub and marshes. Nests on the ground in dense cover. While large numbers are introduced into the countryside by gun clubs, the majority of Pheasants shot each year are believed to be wild birds. First introduced into Ireland from Asia in the sixteenth century.

Pheasant

Female

Male

large game bird with very long, pointed tail

81

Gamebirds and Crakes

Quail
Coturnix coturnix   Gearg

A tiny, elusive gamebird, more often heard than seen. **Adult males** show a whitish central crown-stripe, a dark crown and a whitish supercilium. Whitish throat shows a black central stripe and lower border. Underparts sandy rufous with warmer smudges on breast and black-edged, pale streaking on the flanks. Upperparts dark with buff barring and black-edged whitish streaks which are very conspicuous in flight. Tail brownish, short and appears pointed. **Females** show unmarked pale throats, brown and cream head markings, and dark spotting on breast. Bill short. Hard to flush, Quail fly short distances on bowed, sandy wings before dropping back into cover.

Voice and Diet
Adult males give a very distinctive *kwit, kwit-wit* song which is loud, repeated and far-carrying. Quail can call both by day and by night and are also ventriloquial, making their precise locations difficult to judge. Females give a low, wheezing *quep-quep* call. Feeds on a wide range of seeds and insects.

Corncrake
Crex crex   Traonach

Corncrakes are shy and hard to see, the distinctive call often being the only indication of their presence. **Adult males** show a brown, streaked crown with blue-grey cheeks and supercilium, and a chestnut eye-stripe. Breast buffish-grey with chestnut smudges on breast sides. Flanks show chestnut, white and thin black barring, fading on undertail. Upperparts show yellow-buff and greyish edges to dark-centred feathers. Wings bright chestnut, striking in flight. Short tail yellow-buff. **Females** show less grey in plumage. Short bill and legs yellow-brown. Prefers to run through thick cover, dropping quickly back into cover if flushed. Flight weak and floppy, with legs dangling.

Voice and Diet
Males give a very distinctive, loud, rasping *kerrx-kerrx* call which is repeated. Tends to call more frequently at night, but will call during the day. Feeds on seeds, plants and invertebrates.

Spotted Crake (rare)
Porzana porzana

A shy bird with a short, yellow bill showing a red base and an olive tip. Legs pale olive-green. **Adult males** show a dark, streaked crown, white spotting on rear of blue-grey supercilium and throat, and black lores. Breast brownish-grey with heavy white spotting. Flanks strongly barred brown and white with thin black edges, fading on belly. Undertail buffish. White spotting extends onto upperparts which show dark-centred feathers with greyish-brown and white edges. Tail short, and can be held cocked. **Adult females** tend to show more extensive spotting on face. **Immatures** show white spotting on a brownish-buff head and breast, a whitish throat and a dark bill with a paler base.

Voice and Diet
Gives a clear, loud, whistling *whett* call which is delivered in an explosive manner. The call is usually repeated, with birds tending to call more frequently at dusk and at night. Feeds on a wide range of plants, seeds and invertebrates.

Habitat and Status

A scarce summer visitor, with small breeding populations based at traditional sites in midland counties. Some breeding may also take place in western, northern and south-eastern regions. Seen regularly on passage on coastal headlands and islands, more frequently reported in spring than autumn. Found in crop fields and rough pastures.

Quail

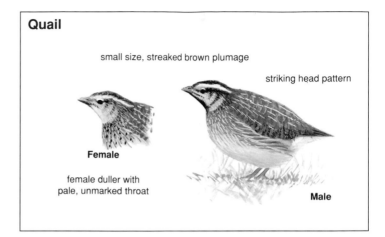

small size, streaked brown plumage

striking head pattern

Female

female duller with pale, unmarked throat

Male

Habitat and Status

Formerly an extremely common summer visitor, Corncrakes have suffered a drastic population decline during this century. Between 1968 and 1972, Corncrakes were still breeding in all counties, but now are only present in small numbers along the Shannon Callows and areas in the west and north-west, with numbers still declining. Now a rare breeding bird. Found in rough pastures, meadows, flooded meadows and crop fields.

Corncrake

greyish on neck

striking bright chestnut wings

Habitat and Status

A very uncommon visitor from Europe. Spotted Crake has been proved to breed in Ireland on just one occasion in the last century, although their shy nature may lead to birds going unnoticed. Most reports refer to autumn, with small numbers recorded in spring and summer. Several old records refer to birds being seen during winter months. Frequents areas of shallow water with dense vegetation around lakes, marshes, pools and rivers.

Spotted Crake (rare)

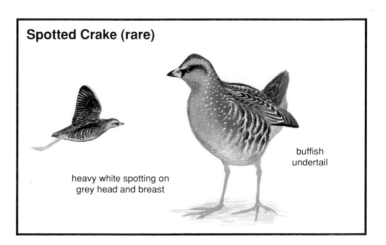

heavy white spotting on grey head and breast

buffish undertail

Rails, Moorhen and Coot

Water Rail
Rallus aquaticus   Rálóg uisce

A secretive bird with a long red bill. **Adults** show dark streaking on olive-brown crown, nape and upperparts. Wing feathers olive-brown with dark centres. Face, throat and breast blue-grey with a dark line through eye. Chin white. Flanks barred black and white. Undertail white. Eye reddish with a black pupil. Legs pinkish-brown. **Juvenile** birds show a paler bill, a whitish throat, brown mottling on buff face and underparts, and brown and buff flank barring. **Sub-adults** similar to adults, but show a large whitish chin patch, a brownish face, and dark barring on grey-brown throat and breast. Walks in a slow, deliberate manner with tail cocked. Flies on rounded wings with trailing legs.

Voice and Diet
Gives loud, explosive, pig-like squealing calls. Also gives a variety of grunting calls. Song is a rhythmic, hammering, repeated *kupp* call. Feeds on a variety of invertebrates, plants, berries and seeds.

Moorhen
Gallinula chloropus   Cearc uisce

A very distinctive bird with a brightly-coloured frontal shield and bill, and a blackish plumage. **Adults** blackish-brown on head and upperparts with short, brownish wings. Underparts greyish-black with a broad, broken, white flank stripe. Undertail white with a black central stripe. Eye reddish-brown with a black pupil. Shows a bright red frontal shield and a short, yellow-tipped red bill. Legs and feet olive-green with small red garters on tibia. **Immatures** show brownish upper and underparts, a whitish throat and belly, a buffish flank stripe, a white undertail and a greenish-brown bill. Swims buoyantly with a jerking head and cocked tail. Flies with rounded wings and trailing legs.

Voice and Diet
Gives a throaty *kurruk* alarm call and a repeated, high-pitched *krik* call. Feeds on a variety of seeds, aquatic plants, grass, worms and insects. Seldom dives for food, preferring to pick from water surface. Can also graze on pastures walking in a deliberate, hen-like manner.

Coot
Fulica atra   Cearc cheannann

A distinctive, slaty-black bird with a heavy, rotund body and short, rounded wings. **Adults** show a glossy black head with a contrasting broad, white frontal shield and a white bill. Upperparts and wings greyish-black with white tips to secondaries showing as a thin white trailing edge to the wings in flight. Underparts greyish-black. Eye reddish with a black pupil. Legs greenish-grey with red garters on the tibia and long, lobed toes. **Immatures** show brownish upperparts, a whitish face with a dark ear covert patch and a whitish neck, breast and belly. The small frontal shield and bill are greyish. Runs across the water when taking off. Flies on rounded wings with trailing legs.

Voice and Diet
Gives a high-pitched, sharp *pitt* call. Can also give a loud, piping, repeated *kock* call. Feeds by diving or by grazing on land close to water. Takes a variety of insects and other invertebrates and also aquatic plants, grasses and seeds.

Habitat and Status

A widespread, common resident species, with numbers increasing in winter due to the arrival of birds from Iceland and Europe. Found in dense reed-beds, sedges and marshes, and rivers with dense vegetation. Very difficult to see, the distinctive calls often being the only indication of a bird's presence. Nests in sedges, reeds and dense grass close to water.

Water Rail

Immature

long red bill

Adult

immature duller, with pale face and underparts

heavy black and white barring on flanks, whitish undertail

Habitat and Status

A widespread, common resident species. Found along slow streams and rivers, canals, marshes, reed-beds, lakes, flooded fields and ditches. Also found feeding on pastures and along hedgerows. Nests in reeds, grass, bushes or trees close to water.

Moorhen

Immature

red shield and bill with yellow tip

brownish, with dark bill and white on undertail

black centre to white undertail

Adult

Habitat and Status

A common, resident species with a range that is not as widespread as that of Moorhen. In winter, can gather in large flocks on lakes in the midlands, west and north. Populations may increase in winter with the arrival of birds from continental Europe. Found on areas with open water such as lakes and reservoirs, occasionally wintering in salt-water areas. Nests in reeds, grasses and other aquatic vegetation.

Coot

greyish bill

Immature

striking white shield and bill

brownish with pale underparts and dark undertail

Adult

85

Oystercatcher
Haematopus ostralegus   Roilleach

A noisy, stocky, black and white wader, best recognised by the long orange bill, which is tipped yellowish. **Summer adults** show a black head and breast, with black upperparts showing a white wingbar, obvious in flight. Underparts white. White tail shows a black subterminal band. White rump extends as a conspicuous white wedge onto back. **Winter adults** show a white band from the throat to the sides of the neck. Adults have red eyes and an orange-red eye-ring. Stout legs are flesh-pink on adults. **Immatures** show browner upperparts, a duller bill, a white neck band, yellowish eye-rings and greyish legs.

Voice and Diet
Oystercatchers are among the noisiest wading birds found in Ireland. In flight they give a loud sharp *peik,* sometimes finished with *kapeik.* In song, or when displaying over feeding territories, these notes develop into long, loud trilling calls. Probes for worms on tidal mudflats or fields. Also feeds on molluscs which are either prised or hammered open.

Black-winged Stilt (rare)
Himantopus himantopus

An elegant, black and white wader, unlikely to be confused with any other species found in Ireland. **Adults** show a white head with a black nape extending up onto the rear crown. The extent of the black on the crown varies greatly and some birds can show a completely white head. The mantle and the wings are black, with long pointed primaries giving an elegant, attenuated appearance. The underparts and the tail are white. Shows a long, thin black bill and extraordinarily long, pinkish-red legs. Usually feeds in deep water, moving with long, slow strides. In flight, shows black wings, a white wedge on the back, a white tail and long trailing legs.

Voice and Diet
The call is a short, sharp *kiyik,* repeated two or three times. This call is usually delivered in flight, when disturbed or during disputes. Feeds on insects which are picked off the surface of the water.

Avocet (rare)
Recurvirostra avosetta   Abhóiséad

A striking, black and white wader with a long, up-curved bill. The black forehead, crown and nape contrast with the white throat and neck. A strong black scapular stripe and the thick black stripe on the wing coverts form the diagnostic black oval pattern which contrasts sharply with the otherwise white upperparts. The primaries are also black. The underparts and tail are white. The long, up-curved bill is black and the legs are bluish-grey. In flight, black wing tips, and black covert and scapular stripes create a striking pattern. Feeds with distinctive side-to-side head sweeps. In deep water, head may be totally submerged.

Voice and Diet
Gives a loud, excited, fluty *klo-whitt* call when disturbed or alarmed. Also gives a shorter *klip* call. The distinctive sweeping motion when feeding allows the sensitive bill to sift water for worms, insects and crustaceans.

Habitat and Status
A very common Irish bird, primarily found on coastal estuaries and mudflats. Can form large flocks in winter. Nests in scrapes made in shingle, sand or grass, usually along coastal stretches. Rarely nests inland. In winter, can sometimes be found on playing fields or farmland where they probe for worms. A resident species, numbers increase with wintering birds from northern Europe and Iceland.

Oystercatcher
orange bill
striking black and white plumage
Adult (summer)

Habitat and Status
A very rare visitor to Ireland from southern Europe, normally seen in spring or early summer with a few autumn records. In Ireland, usually occurs singly, although small flocks have been recorded. Normally found in marshland or wetland areas with deep pools, occasionally along channels on coastal estuaries.

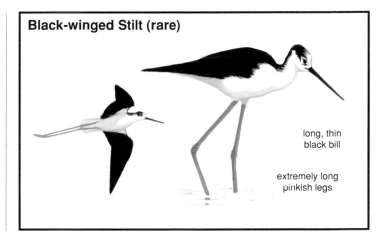

Black-winged Stilt (rare)
long, thin black bill
extremely long pinkish legs

Habitat and Status
Formerly a regular winter visitor to the east and south coasts, Avocets are now uncommon in Ireland. Breeding occurred once in the 1930s. Normally found on estuaries and mudflats as well as on shallow lagoons. Small influxes can occur, with up to twelve birds present along eastern and south-western coastal counties in November 1992.

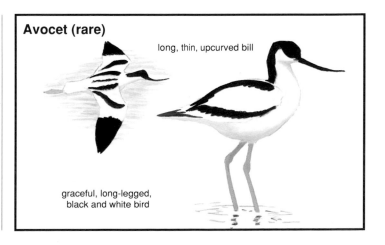

Avocet (rare)
long, thin, upcurved bill
graceful, long-legged, black and white bird

Waders

Ringed Plover
Charadrius hiaticula   Feadóg chladaigh

Small, banded plover with a striking face pattern and bright orange legs. **Breeding adults** show a white forehead patch, a black forecrown patch, and black from base of bill onto ear coverts. White supercilium above and behind dark eye. Thin, indistinct eye-ring. White throat and collar contrast with black breast band. Thick, short bill is orange with a black tip. Crown and upperparts greyish-brown. Underparts white. In **winter**, plumage and bill duller. **Immatures** show duller legs, a blackish bill, greyish-brown head and upperparts, and a white supercilium and forehead patch. Thin, brownish breast band usually incomplete. In flight, shows a white wingbar and white sides to the rump. Tail dark.

Voice and Diet
Gives a distinctive, fluty *too-ip* call which rises in pitch. On the breeding grounds, can give a trilling display song. Feeds in the typical stop-start fashion of plovers. Takes a variety of insects, molluscs and other invertebrates which are picked from the surface.

Little Ringed Plover (rare)
Charadrius dubius   Feadóigín chladaigh

A small, slim plover, with a bright yellow eye-ring and pale, flesh-pink legs. Bill short and blackish. **Breeding adults** show a black forecrown patch, a white forehead patch and black from base of bill onto ear coverts. The white supercilium extends onto crown behind black forecrown patch. White collar contrasts with black breast band. Crown and upperparts greyish-brown. Underparts white. **Winter plumage** duller. **Immatures** pale greyish-brown on head and upperparts, showing a thin yellow eye-ring but lacking a clean white supercilium and forehead patch. Thin, pale, greyish-brown breast band, usually incomplete. In flight, the upperwing appears uniform. White sides to tail and rump.

Voice and Diet
Gives a clear, whistling *pee-uu* call, which, unlike Ringed Plover, descends in pitch. This call is delivered in an abrupt fashion and is quite far-carrying. Feeds in the stop-start manner of all plovers, taking a variety of insects and molluscs which are picked from the surface of the ground.

Kentish Plover (rare)
Charadrius alexandrinus   Feadóigín chosdubh

Small, short-necked plover with a slender black bill and blackish-grey legs. **Breeding males** show a thin black line from base of bill onto ear coverts and a black forecrown patch. A white forehead patch extends back to form a broad white supercilium. Crown and upperparts sandy-brown with a rufous patch on forecrown and nape. White collar contrasts with thin, black breast patches. Underparts white. **Females** and **winter males** show sandy-brown breast patches and brown face markings, lacking any rufous tones. **Immatures** similar to females, but show pale edges to upperpart feathers. In flight, shows a white wingbar and extensive white on sides of tail. Feeds in a fast, Sanderling-like way.

Voice and Diet
Gives a sharp but soft *twit* call in flight. When alarmed can give a hard *prrip* call. Feeds in the stop-start manner of plovers, although movements appear fast and may recall Sanderling. Feeds on a wide variety of invertebrates.

Habitat and Status

A very common coastal plover found throughout the year. Breeds on shingle and sandy beaches around the coast, the nest consisting of a scrape in the ground. In autumn and winter is found in large numbers on mudflats and estuaries.

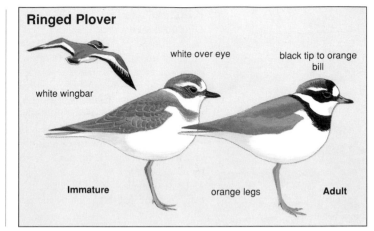

Ringed Plover

white over eye

black tip to orange bill

white wingbar

Immature

orange legs

Adult

Habitat and Status

A very rare vagrant from Europe, occurring in spring and autumn. Although breeds on inland sites such as gravel pits and shingle banks close to fresh water, they are usually seen on mudflats or coastal lakes when found in Ireland.

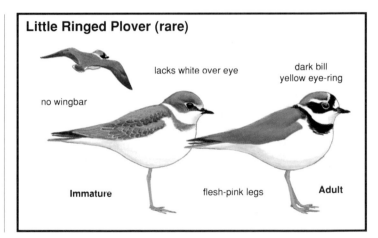

Little Ringed Plover (rare)

lacks white over eye

dark bill
yellow eye-ring

no wingbar

Immature

flesh-pink legs

Adult

Habitat and Status

A very rare vagrant from Europe with records from spring, late summer and autumn. Occurring on coastal estuaries, mudflats, wetlands and sandy areas, Kentish Plovers can be quite sociable, associating with mixed flocks of plovers and waders.

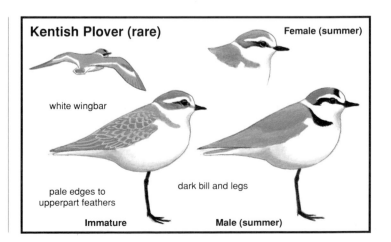

Kentish Plover (rare)

Female (summer)

white wingbar

pale edges to upperpart feathers

dark bill and legs

Immature

Male (summer)

Waders

Killdeer (rare)
Charadrius vociferus

A long-tailed plover with two blackish breast bands. **Summer males** show a black forecrown, a white forehead patch which continues under eye, black from the base of the bill onto ear coverts and an orange-red eye-ring. Whitish supercilium behind the eye. Crown and nape brown. White collar contrasts with nape and breast bands. Underparts white. Upperparts brown with long wings. **Females** duller. **Winter birds** and **immatures** lack the black on the face, immatures showing pale fringes to the upperpart feathers. In flight, shows white wingbar and a bright rust-orange rump. Tail rust-orange with white edges, a darker centre and a black subterminal band. Bill long and blackish. Legs pinkish.

Voice and Diet
The call is a most distinctive, loud, far-carrying *kill-dee*, from which the bird derives its name. Feeds in the typical stop-start fashion of plovers, taking insects, molluscs and crustaceans.

Lapwing
Vanellus vanellus   Pilibín

A distinctive plover with a broad breast band. **Summer males** show a long crest with black on the crown and face. Chin and throat black, meeting breast band. Neck white. Nape dark. Upperparts deep green with copper sheens. **Females** show white flecking on chin and throat, a shorter crest and duller upperparts. Underparts white. Undertail orange-buff. Winter adults show white chin and throat, black patches on a buff face, and buff tips to some wing feathers. **Immatures** similar but show a shorter crest and buff fringes to upperpart feathers. Flight buoyant with dark, rounded upperwings, and striking black and white underwings. Black band present on a white tail. Legs dull flesh. Bill dark.

Voice and Diet
The most distinctive call is a loud, bubbling, excited *pee-wit*, which rises in pitch on the second note. On the breeding grounds, gives a repeated *perr-u-weet-weet* call which is occasionally associated with downward plunges as part of a display flight. Feeds in the stop-start manner of plovers, taking invertebrates, insects and seeds.

Dotterel (rare)
Charadrius morinellus   Amadán móinteach

A tame plover with a large black eye and a broad supercilium which meets in a V on the nape. **Immatures** and **autumn adults** show a streaked crown and a pale buff supercilium. Breast and belly buff-brown, separated by a narrow, creamy breast band. Upper breast streaked. Upperpart feathers show pale fringes, warmer buff on immatures. In flight, appears uniform. Underwing pale. **Summer adults** show a black crown and a white supercilium and throat. A blue-grey neck and upper breast is separated from the chestnut-brown of the lower breast and upper belly by a white breast band. Belly black, undertail white. Upperpart feathers show buff fringes. Dark, short bill. Legs yellowish.

Voice and Diet
Although usually quiet when seen in Ireland, they can occasionally give a soft *peet* call which can be repeated. Dotterels can also give a trilling alarm call. Feeds in the stop-start manner of plovers, picking up a wide variety of insects, including flies, spiders and beetles.

Habitat and Status

An extremely rare autumn vagrant from North America. Found on open grasslands or ploughed fields as well as coastal marshes and fields. Some birds have over-wintered.

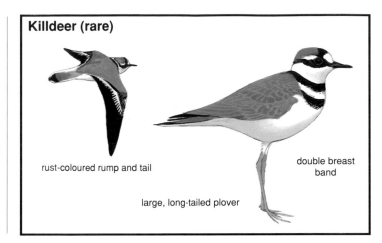

Killdeer (rare)

rust-coloured rump and tail

double breast band

large, long-tailed plover

Habitat and Status

A common bird, breeding on grasslands and grassy wetlands. In recent years breeding numbers have decreased due to habitat loss. The nest consists of a simple scrape in the ground. In winter, the population increases with the arrival of birds from northern Britain. In winter, found along the coast on mudflats and estuaries as well as far inland on open grasslands or ploughed fields.

Lapwing

long crest

rounded wings

shorter crest and buff edges to upperpart feathers

Immature

Male

Habitat and Status

A rare but regular visitor from Europe, with a single Irish breeding record from 1975 when a pair nested in Co. Mayo. Can occur in the mountainous regions of the south-west on spring migration. Most records refer to autumn, when birds are found on coastal islands or headlands. Usually seen in areas of short heather growth or on fields or grassy areas along the shore. Their excellent camouflage can make Dotterels difficult to spot.

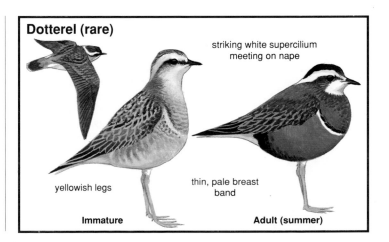

Dotterel (rare)

striking white supercilium meeting on nape

yellowish legs

thin, pale breast band

Immature

Adult (summer)

Waders

Golden Plover
Pluvialis apricaria   Feadóg bhuí

A large plover with a short dark bill, dark legs, gold-spangled upperparts and a diagnostic white underwing and axillaries. In **breeding plumage**, the face, throat, breast and belly are black, bordered by a white stripe from the supercilium, down sides of neck and breast and along flanks. Undertail white with gold and black barring. Crown, nape and upperparts are dark with gold spangling. Wing tips equal to tail length. **Immatures** and **winter-plumaged adults** show brownish upperparts with gold fringes to the feathers, a large, conspicuous black eye in a yellow-buff face and dark streaking on the breast. Belly and undertail whitish. In flight, shows a narrow white wingbar.

Voice and Diet
Gives a rather plaintive, whistling *too-lee* call, both on the ground and in flight. On the breeding grounds, gives a mournful *per-wee-oo* song, often associated with a flight display. Feeds in the typical stop-start fashion of plovers, taking insects, beetles, earthworms and other invertebrates, as well as seeds, grasses and berries.

Grey Plover
Pluvialis squatarola   Feadóg ghlas

A large, big-headed plover with a stout, dark bill, dark legs, and with black axillaries contrasting with a white underwing. **Summer adults** show a black face, breast, belly and flanks. The broad, white supercilium continues onto sides of neck and breast, but not along the flanks. Undertail always white. Crown and nape pale grey. Upperparts grey with broad black spotting. **Winter plumage** shows a large eye in a pale grey face, dark streaking on breast and light grey upperparts with dark spotting. **Immatures** similar to winter adults, but show yellowish tones to the upperparts. In flight, the upperwing shows white wing stripe. White rump obvious against the barred tail.

Voice and Diet
Gives a diagnostic, loud, whistling call, consisting of *tee-oo-ee*, the second note of which is lower in pitch. Feeds on marine molluscs, crustaceans and worms in the typical stop-start manner of plovers.

American Golden Plover (rare)
Pluvialis dominica

A medium-sized plover with a fine dark bill, long dark legs, an upright, attenuated appearance, and a diagnostic dusky-grey underwing. **Summer adults** show a black face, breast, belly, flanks and undertail. Broad white supercilium continues down, broadening and stopping abruptly on the sides of the breast. Crown and upperparts dark with pale gold spangling. Long primaries extend beyond tail, often crossing. Note tertial length is shorter than tail. **Immatures** and **winter adults** appear greyish on the upperparts, with a broad white supercilium conspicuous against a dark crown. Face and breast pale grey with faint streaking. In flight, shows a thin, pale wing stripe.

Voice and Diet
Gives a distinctive, sharp *tchoo-ee* call, which resembles that of Spotted Redshank. Can also give a *ki-ee* call. Feeds on insects, larvae, worms, molluscs, crustaceans and berries in the usual stop-start fashion of plovers.

Habitat and Status

A breeding bird found in small numbers on mountains and bogs in the west and north-west. In autumn, numbers increase dramatically with the arrival of migrant birds from Europe and Iceland, most of which over-winter. Found on arable lands and ploughed fields, both inland and along coastal areas. Also found on mudflats and estuaries in winter.

Golden Plover

gold-spangled dark upperparts

large dark eye

whitish underwing

wingtips equal to tail length

Immature   Adult (summer)

Habitat and Status

A common winter and passage visitor from the breeding grounds in western Siberia, arriving by late summer. Found on coastal estuaries, mudflats and beaches. Rarely seen on arable lands or ploughed fields. Never forms a tight feeding flock like Golden Plovers.

Grey Plover

pale face

black face and underparts
white undertail

black axillaries

yellowish tones to upperparts

Immature   Adult (summer)

Habitat and Status

A very rare vagrant from North America, found in autumn but with occasional sightings in the summer months. Frequents a variety of coastal habitats, including mudflats, marshes and areas of short cropped grass. Can sometimes be quite approachable and tame.

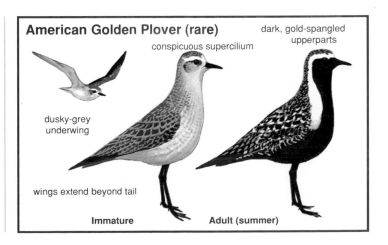

American Golden Plover (rare)

dark, gold-spangled upperparts

conspicuous supercilium

dusky-grey underwing

wings extend beyond tail

Immature   Adult (summer)

Waders

Ruff
Philomachus pugnax   Rufachán
A highly variable, small-headed, medium-sized wader with a shortish, slightly decurved bill. **Males** (Ruffs) are larger than **females** (Reeves). **Immatures** are orange-buff on the head and breast, with neat pale fringes to the dark upperpart feathers giving a strongly scalloped appearance. The belly and undertail are white. **In summer**, **adult males** show head and neck plumes which vary greatly in colour, while **females** show strong but variable markings on the head, breast and flanks. In flight, shows two white, oval rump patches, a white wing stripe and a white underwing. Bill dark with a pinkish base on adults. Leg colour varies, from greenish on immatures to orange or pink on adults.

Voice and Diet
Generally a quiet species, although a gruff *ku-uk* call can occasionally be given. Feeds in a Redshank-like manner, walking with deliberate strides, occasionally wading into deep water. Eats worms, insects, molluscs, crustaceans, as well as seeds. Probes into soft mud with the bill or picks from the surface.

Buff-breasted Sandpiper (rare)
Tryngites subruficollis
A tame, attractive wader with a short, pointed, dark bill, a large, conspicuous, black eye and mustard-yellow legs. **Immatures** show pale buff underparts, with a paler rear belly and undertail, a plain buff-coloured face, fine streaking on the crown and nape, and dark spotting on the sides of the breast. Buff-centred upperpart feathers have sharp whitish buff edges and dark submarginal crescents, giving a neat scalloped appearance. **Adults** are similar, but show dark centres to upperpart feathers with buff fringes. Buff on the underparts also extends further down. In flight, shows a plain upperwing and rump. Underwing white, with black tips to primaries, secondaries and primary coverts.

Voice and Diet
Normally a quiet species, Buff-breasted Sandpiper can give a low *pr-r-reet* call. A sharp *tic* call is also heard on occasions. Feeds in a dainty, active fashion, picking flies, insects, beetles and larvae from the ground.

Pectoral Sandpiper
Calidris melanotos
A very tame wader with a heavily-streaked breast which stops abruptly, showing a strong demarcation with the pure white belly and undertail. The slightly decurved bill is dark with a pale base. Legs yellowish. The warm crown, nape and ear coverts are streaked with a dark loral smudge, sometimes obvious before the eye. The broad supercilium is white. **Immatures** show dark-centred upperpart feathers with warm chestnut, buff and white fringes creating white braces on the mantle and scapulars. **Adults** are generally duller, especially on the upperparts. In flight, shows white sides to rump and a faint white wing stripe. Underwing white, contrasting with the streaked breast.

Voice and Diet
Pectoral Sandpipers can often be heard before they are seen, giving a distinctive, harsh, sharp *krrit* or *trrit* call which is loud and sometimes repeated. Feeds in a deliberate, steady, head-down manner, either picking from the surface or probing. Feeds on insects, larvae, worms and crustaceans.

Habitat and Status

An uncommon but regular autumn visitor from Europe, with small numbers occasionally over-wintering. Found on muddy verges of coastal, freshwater or brackish pools and lakes. Sometimes encountered on saltmarshes, although seldom seen on mudflats or estuaries.

Ruff

Males (summer) Female (reeve) Male (ruff)

Habitat and Status

A rare but regular autumn vagrant from North America. Usually found on short grass or sandy areas close to coastal marshes or lakes. Rarely found feeding in water. An extremely tame species, Buff-breasted Sandpipers are easy to overlook should they crouch down or freeze. Tends to run ahead of observers instead of flying.

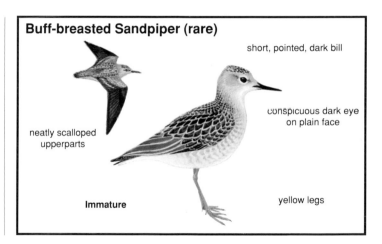

Buff-breasted Sandpiper (rare)

short, pointed, dark bill

neatly scalloped upperparts

conspicuous dark eye on plain face

Immature

yellow legs

Habitat and Status

An uncommon but regular visitor from North America, usually seen in autumn, with occasional records in summer. Found along edges of grass-fringed pools and wetlands, usually at coastal locations. Occasionally seen on open mudflats. An extremely tame bird and easy to overlook among tall grass or sedges.

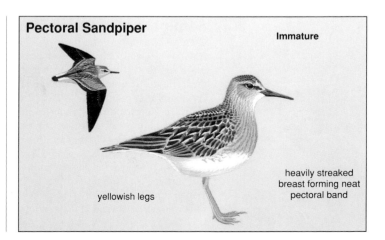

Pectoral Sandpiper

Immature

heavily streaked breast forming neat pectoral band

yellowish legs

Waders

Sanderling
Calidris alba   Luathrán

A small, hyperactive wader with a short, straight, black bill and black legs which lack a hindclaw. In **winter**, the plumage is pale grey on the upperparts, with a distinctive black patch on the bend of the wing. Underparts pure white. Occasionally seen in **summer** plumage when the head and upperparts are chestnut-brown with broad black centres to the upperpart feathers. Also shows a streaked, chestnut-brown breast band in summer. **Immatures** similar to adult winter, but show black spangled upperparts, black streaking on crown and faint streaking on the sides of the neck which can show a buff wash. In flight, shows a prominent white wingbar and white sides to rump and uppertail.

Voice and Diet
Gives a hard, quiet *kick* call, occasionally repeated. Feeds in a hyperactive fashion, almost recalling a clockwork toy. Takes a wide variety of invertebrates, including insects, worms, molluscs and small fish.

Little Stint
Calidris minuta

A tiny wader with a fine, short, black bill and black legs. **Immatures** show bright chestnut-buff edges to the upperpart feathers with white fringes to the mantle, creating the distinctive, white mantle braces. A whitish supercilium extends onto the warm brown crown, creating a diagnostic split supercilium. Ear coverts and breast sides warm buff and streaked. Underparts clean white. **Breeding adults** show streaking on a warm buff head and breast, a white throat, and chestnut-buff, dark-centred upperpart feathers with whitish fringes to the mantle. **Winter adults** show brown-grey upperparts and white underparts. Narrow white wing stripe, obvious in flight. White sides to rump.

Voice and Diet
Gives a short, sharp, high-pitched *stit* call which can be repeated. Feeds in an active fashion, taking insects, worms and molluscs, occasionally seeds. Often found among flocks of Dunlin in autumn.

Semipalmated Sandpiper (rare)
Calidris pusilla

A dull wader which shows a broad, black, 'blob-ended' bill. Black legs show partially-webbed toes, this being difficult to see. The dull **immature** plumage shows grey-brown upperparts with pale buff or whitish feather fringes. Lacks the warm tones and the striking white mantle braces of immature Little Stint. Dark streaking on the crown gives a capped effect. White supercilium does not extend onto the crown. Dark eye-stripe. Nape and breast streaked, with a pale buff wash. Underparts white. **In summer**, shows greyish-buff upperparts and a streaked breast. Crown warm brown. **Winter adults** are pale grey above and white below. Narrow white wing stripe obvious in flight. White sides to rump.

Voice and Diet
Gives a short, low-pitched, hoarse *churp* call, quite different from Little Stint. Feeds in a slower manner than Little Stint, taking a wide variety of insects, molluscs and worms.

Habitat and Status

A common winter visitor to the coastline, arriving in early autumn from breeding grounds in the Arctic. Usually found chasing the waves up and down the beach, or feeding along the tideline on debris and seaweed washed ashore. On migration, can also occur on mudflats or on coastal marshes.

Sanderling

prominent white wingbar

very pale with black carpal patch

Adult (summer)

Immature
black-spangled upperparts

Adult (winter)

Habitat and Status

A regular autumn visitor from breeding grounds in north-eastern Europe and Siberia. Occasionally recorded in winter and spring. Usually found on coastal estuaries, mudflats or lakes, often associating with large, mixed wader flocks.

Little Stint

tiny wader

white mantle braces on rufous upperparts

short, thin, black bill

plain grey upperparts

Adult winter (rare)

Immature

Habitat and Status

A very rare vagrant from North America. Usually found in the autumn on coastal mudflats, estuaries and occasionally on coastal lakes. Can often associate with mixed wader flocks.

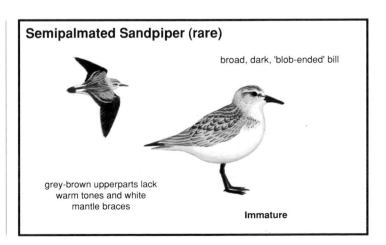

Semipalmated Sandpiper (rare)

broad, dark, 'blob-ended' bill

grey-brown upperparts lack warm tones and white mantle braces

Immature

Waders

Dunlin
Calidris alpina   Breacóg

A small wader with black legs and a blackish bill, decurved at the tip. Dunlin vary greatly in size, plumage and bill length. In **winter** shows greyish-brown upperparts. White underparts show faint streaking on the breast. **Summer adults** show a striking black belly patch and rufous edges to mantle and scapular feathers. Crown and nape warm buff, with heavy spotting on the breast. Moulting adults show a mixture of both plumages. **Immatures** show black centres and warm buff edges on mantle and scapulars. Coverts fringed buff. Breast shows a diffuse buff wash. Belly and flanks show dark spotting. In flight, shows a white wingbar, white sides to rump and uppertail, and a greyish tail.

Voice and Diet
Gives a distinctive, sharp *treep* call in flight. On the breeding grounds, the song consists of a purring trill. A fast, active feeder, probing and picking off the surface. Feeds on molluscs, worms, insects and crustaceans.

Curlew Sandpiper
Calidris ferruginea   Gobadán crotaigh

A slender wader with a long, slightly decurved bill and black legs. **Immatures** show neatly scalloped upperparts with pale fringes to the feathers. Crown and nape streaked with a well-defined supercilium. Underparts clean, creamy white, with a delicate peach wash on breast sides. **Breeding plumage** is unmistakable, with chestnut-red underparts, neck and head. Scapulars and mantle have black centres with pale and rufous fringes. Wing coverts appear greyish. **Moulting adults** can show blotchy red underparts and some dark-centred upperpart feathers. **Winter birds** are greyish-brown above and white below, with a strong supercilium. In flight shows a white rump, a dark tail and a white wingbar.

Voice and Diet
Gives a rippling, gentle *chirrup* call. Feeds by probing or picking from the surface but can wade into deep water. Takes a variety of worms, molluscs, crustaceans and insects.

Broad-billed Sandpiper (rare)
Limicola falcinellus

A small wader, with a long, black bill which shows a kink at the tip, and short dark legs. Most birds found in Ireland are **immatures**, showing neatly patterned upperparts with buff and creamy fringes to feathers, and obvious scapular and mantle stripes. Crown dark. Broad, creamy-white supercilium is split before the eye and extends onto crown to form lateral crown stripe. Dark eye-stripe. Breast shows a buff wash with light streaking. Underparts white. **Breeding adults** show heavily streaked breast and spotted flanks, a dark crown and a contrasting split supercilium. **Winter adults** grey above and white below. In flight, shows a narrow white wingbar and white sides to rump and uppertail.

Voice and Diet
Gives a distinctive, hard, trilling *chr-rr-eek* call in flight. Feeds by picking from the surface or probing in soft mud. Takes small molluscs, insects, worms and crustaceans.

Habitat and Status

An abundant autumn and winter wader, with a small breeding population based in the midlands, west and north-west. In autumn, birds arrive from Iceland and northern Europe, with large numbers wintering on estuaries, mudflats and coastal lakes. Nests in grass and tussocks on marshes, bogs and wetlands.

Dunlin

long, decurved bill
rufous upperparts

brown-grey upperparts

Adult (winter)

Adult (summer)

black belly patch

Habitat and Status

A regular autumn visitor from breeding grounds in Siberia. Occasionally seen in large numbers, with wintering birds sometimes reported. Found on coastal lakes, estuaries and mudflats. Curlew Sandpipers can associate with Dunlin flocks. Can show a tendency to feed in deeper water, making them more noticeable when in large, mixed flocks.

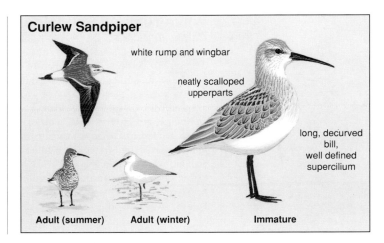

Curlew Sandpiper

white rump and wingbar

neatly scalloped upperparts

long, decurved bill, well defined supercilium

Adult (summer) **Adult (winter)** **Immature**

Habitat and Status

A very rare autumn vagrant from the breeding grounds in northern Europe. Found on coastal lake edges, estuaries, mudflats and saltmarshes, occasionally associating with Dunlin flocks.

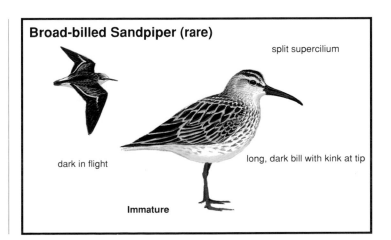

Broad-billed Sandpiper (rare)

split supercilium

dark in flight

long, dark bill with kink at tip

Immature

Waders

Knot
Calidris canutus   Cnota

A medium-sized wader with a short, straight, black bill and greenish legs. **Winter adults** are plain grey on the upperparts with pale fringed feathers. The underparts are whitish, with heavy streaking on breast, and barring on the flanks. **Immatures** similar, but show a buff wash on the breast, yellow-green legs and buffish-grey upperpart feathers appearing scalloped due to pale buff fringes and dark submarginal lines. **Summer adults** show chestnut-red face and underparts, with spotting on the sides of the breast and a barred whitish undertail. Upperparts show black-centred feathers with rufous and buff fringes. In flight, shows a narrow white wingbar, and a pale rump and uppertail.

Voice and Diet
A generally quieter wader than other species, Knot can give a soft *knut* call. Feeds in flocks, probing or picking from the surface. Eats a variety of molluscs, crustaceans, worms and insects, but can occasionally take vegetable matter.

White-rumped Sandpiper (rare)
Calidris fuscicollis

A long-winged wader with a short, straight, slightly drooped bill. In flight, shows a narrow white wingbar and a white rump similar to Curlew Sandpiper. **Immatures** show a streaked, chestnut crown, a white supercilium and streaked, rufous-washed ear coverts. The streaked nape and breast are greyish-buff, with streaking present on flanks. Underparts white. Upperparts dark with white tips to feathers, chestnut fringes to mantle and upper scapulars, and thin white mantle and scapular lines. Long primaries extend beyond tail. **Adults** show duller upperparts, with heavy streaking on breast and flanks. Bill dark with pale base to lower mandible. Legs dark.

Voice and Diet
Gives a distinctive, high-pitched *tseet* call. Feeds in a fast manner, picking from the surface or probing for small molluscs, worms and insects.

Baird's Sandpiper (rare)
Calidris bairdii

A slim, elongated wader with a short, fine, slightly drooped black bill and blackish legs. **Immatures** show a streaked, buff-brown crown and ear coverts, a whitish supercilium and a buff-washed, streaked breast which shows as a clearly defined breast band. Underparts white. Flanks unstreaked. Upperparts appear neatly scalloped with dark feathers fringed buffish-white. Long primaries extend beyond tail. In flight, shows a very narrow white wingbar and a dark rump with narrow white edges. Tail appears dark. **Adults** show buff upperparts with broad black centres to scapulars, a heavily streaked breast and clean white flanks and underparts.

Voice and Diet
Gives a short, trilling *preeep* call. Feeds in a methodical manner, preferring to pick from the surface rather than probing into soft mud. Takes a wide variety of insects, larvae, worms and small molluscs.

Habitat and Status

A reasonably common autumn and winter visitor from breeding grounds on the high Arctic regions of Greenland, Canada and Iceland. The main arrival occurs in October and by November the main wintering flocks are present. Found on coastal estuaries, mudflats and saltmarshes.

Knot

stocky build

plain grey upperparts

straight black bill, greenish legs

Adult (summer)   **Adult (winter)**

Habitat and Status

A rare but regular autumn vagrant from North America. Found on coastal estuaries, mudflats, freshwater lakes and lagoons. Often found associating with large mixed wader flocks.

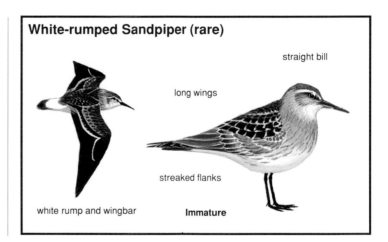

White-rumped Sandpiper (rare)

straight bill

long wings

streaked flanks

white rump and wingbar   **Immature**

Habitat and Status

A rare autumn vagrant from North America. Found on coastal estuaries, mudflats and lagoons. Has a tendency to feed higher on the shoreline than other waders, occasionally on dry ground, and seldom wading in water. Although can be found with large mixed wader flocks, tends to be less gregarious than other species and is sometimes found singly or within a small flock.

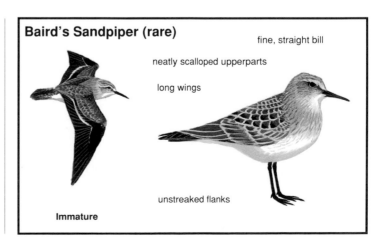

Baird's Sandpiper (rare)

fine, straight bill

neatly scalloped upperparts

long wings

unstreaked flanks

Immature

Waders

Purple Sandpiper
Calidris maritima   Gobadán cosbhuí

A tame, rather drab wader with a long, slightly decurved, yellow-based dark bill and yellowish legs. **Winter adults** show a dark grey head and upperparts, with a faint purple gloss on scapulars and mantle, and greyish fringes to the coverts. Throat and breast dark grey with streaking on breast onto flanks. Belly and undertail white. **Immatures** show rufous tones on the crown, a faint supercilium and dark upperpart feathers with whitish and buff fringes. **Summer adults** show a brown crown, a white supercilium, heavily streaked breast and flanks, and chestnut and white fringes to dark upperpart feathers. In flight, shows a striking white wingbar and white sides to the rump and the uppertail.

Voice and Diet
Gives a short, twittering *wheet* call when disturbed. Feeds on a variety of insects, molluscs and crustaceans which are found on rocky shorelines.

Temminck's Stint (rare)
Calidris temminckii

A small, dull wader with a short, fine, blackish bill and yellow-green legs. **Immatures** show a brownish crown, ear coverts and nape, a faint supercilium, a white chin and throat, and brownish upperparts with a scaly pattern due to a unique submarginal line and buff fringe to each feather. Sides of breast buff-brown, usually joining to form a breast band. Belly and undertail whitish. Tail equal to, or just longer than, wing length. **Summer adults** show black centres to mantle and scapulars with buff and grey tips, a faint supercilium and heavy streaking on the breast and head. In flight, shows a short, narrow white wingbar and diagnostic white sides to the tail and rump.

Voice and Diet
Gives a distinctive, short trilling *tirrr* call, often repeated. Feeds in a slower manner than Little Stint, occasionally with a crouched profile. Searches carefully for food items, taking a wide variety of small molluscs, insects, larvae and worms.

Least Sandpiper (rare)
Calidris minutilla

A tiny wader with a short, fine, blackish bill and yellowish legs. **Immatures** show a warm brown, streaked crown and ear coverts, a dark smudge on the lores and a white supercilium. The nape and the buffish breast are streaked. The underparts are white. Upperpart feathers show dark centres, with rufous and white edges to mantle and scapulars forming thin, white braces. Coverts show buff edges with tertials and primaries showing rufous edges. Can recall a miniature Pectoral Sandpiper. **Summer adults** show a heavily streaked breast and head, and rufous and white edges to upperpart feathers. In flight, shows a narrow white wingbar and white sides to rump and uppertail.

Voice and Diet
Gives a high-pitched *kreee* call which rises in pitch and can be repeated. Can be quite gregarious, occasionally associating with mixed flocks of waders. Feeds by picking from the surface or probing for small molluscs, insects, larvae and worms.

Habitat and Status

An uncommon winter visitor from breeding grounds in Greenland, Iceland and northern Europe. Purple Sandpipers are found along rocky shorelines, occasionally searching for prey items among seaweed. They can be extremely tame and this, as well as their coloration, can make them easy to overlook. Often found feeding with flocks of Turnstones.

Purple Sandpiper

thin white wingbar

dark wader, yellow-based dark bill

Adult (summer)   **Adult (winter)**

Habitat and Status

A very rare north European autumn vagrant. Usually seen singly, Temminck's Stints rarely associate with other waders. Frequently feeds among vegetation at wetland edges, seldom feeding on open, exposed mudflats.

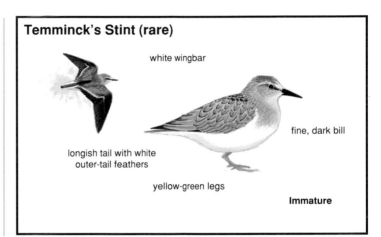

Temminck's Stint (rare)

white wingbar

fine, dark bill

longish tail with white outer-tail feathers

yellow-green legs

Immature

Habitat and Status

An extremely rare autumn vagrant from North America. Can be found on open mudflats, estuaries and beaches, sometimes with large wader flocks. Can also be found on freshwater marsh fringes and coastal lakes, feeding among vegetation. Can be quite tame.

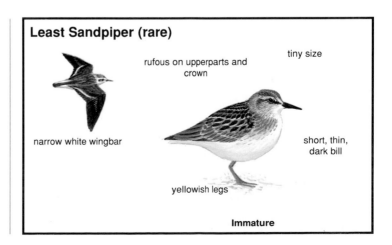

Least Sandpiper (rare)

tiny size

rufous on upperparts and crown

narrow white wingbar

short, thin, dark bill

yellowish legs

Immature

Waders

Turnstone
Arenaria interpres   Piardálai trá
A small, stocky wader with a stubby, dark bill and orange-yellow legs. **Summer males** show a white head with black crown streaking and a black line from forehead, through eye, down to broad black breast band. White neck collar contrasts with breast band. Mantle and scapulars blackish, contrasting with chestnut upperparts. Underparts white. **Females** similar, but show rufous tones to head. In **winter**, both show a duller plumage with a brownish-grey head. **Immatures** similar to winter adults, but show buff edges· to dark brownish upperpart feathers. In flight, shows blackish tail with a contrasting white uppertail, rump and back. Wing dark with a white wingbar and inner coverts. Underwing white.

Voice and Diet
When disturbed, gives a rolling *tuk-i-tuk* call, with shorter *tuk* calls given when in feeding parties. Feeds by turning over stones or tossing seaweed aside in search of food items. Will take insects, worms, crustaceans and also carrion.

Whimbrel
Numenius phaeopus   Crotach eanaigh
A short-necked wader, smaller and with a shorter, more kinked bill than Curlew. **Adults** show a distinctive head pattern of a creamy crown-stripe, a dark lateral crown-stripe, a whitish supercilium and a dark eye-stripe. Cheeks, throat and neck whitish with heavy streaking. Breast creamy with heavy streaking which extends along flanks. Belly and undertail whitish. Upperparts brownish, with pale fringes and notches on feathers. **Immatures** show a shorter bill and a warm buff wash on breast. In flight, shows a coarsely marked upperwing with a white rump and back appearing as a wedge. Tail brown with dark barring. Bill dark, occasionally with a paler base to lower mandible. Legs bluish-grey.

Voice and Diet
Gives a distinctive, whistling, rolling *ti-ti-ti-ti-ti* call which is flat-toned and delivered in a faster manner than Curlew. Feeds by probing for insects, molluscs, crabs and worms.

Curlew
Numenius arquata   Crotach
A large wader with a long, decurved bill. **Adults** pale buff on head and neck with heavy streaking. Throat pale. Breast whitish, with heavy streaks extending onto flanks. Belly and undertail whitish. Mantle and scapulars show buff edges. Coverts show dark centres with pale edges. Secondaries and greater coverts dark with pale notches. **Immatures** similar, but show a shorter bill and buff tones to breast. In flight, shows a coarsely marked plain wing with paler secondaries and greater coverts. Tail and rump white, with heavy barring and spotting. Back white and shows as a contrasting white wedge. Underwing whitish with barring. Long bill shows a pinkish base to lower mandible. Legs bluish-grey.

Voice and Diet
Gives a very distinctive, rolling, far-carrying *cour-lee* call. When alarmed, gives a repeated *kyuyu* call. Feeds by probing with the extremely long bill for molluscs, crabs, worms and insects. Will also take plant material.

Habitat and Status

A very common passage migrant and winter visitor from breeding grounds in Greenland, Iceland and northern Europe. Found feeding in parties along rocky coasts, shorelines with stones and seaweed, harbours and piers.

Turnstone

Adult (summer)

orange legs, with stubby black bill

striking black and white face, chestnut on upperparts

duller in winter

Adult (winter)

Habitat and Status

A common spring and autumn passage migrant, with small numbers present in summer. Birds occasionally winter in southern areas. Passage is recorded in early spring, as birds move north from wintering grounds in Africa to the breeding grounds of Iceland and northern Europe. Found on estuaries, mudflats, coastal wetlands and coastal pastures. Birds of the North American race, known as Hudsonian Whimbrel, are very rare vagrants, and differ by showing a brown rump and back.

Whimbrel

striking head pattern

slightly smaller and with a shorter bill than Curlew

Adult

Habitat and Status

A very common breeding species, with birds nesting on moorlands, bogs, damp meadows and farmlands. Breeding occurs in most regions, except some areas in the south-west and south-east. Winters on estuaries, mudflats and coastal grasslands. In winter, numbers increase with the arrival of birds from Scotland, northern England and Scandinavia.

Curlew

large brown wader with very long, decurved bill

Adult

Waders

Bar-tailed Godwit
Limosa lapponica   Guilbneach stríocearrach

A large wader with a long, slightly up-curved, pink-based, dark bill and dark legs. Similar to Black-tailed Godwit, but in flight shows plain wings, a barred tail and a white rump extending as a wedge up the back. In **winter**, the upperparts are brownish-grey and appear streaked. Underparts white with brownish streaking on the breast. Head brownish-grey, with a whitish supercilium most prominent behind the eye. In **summer** shows a brick-red head, a dark eye-stripe, a streaked crown and a broad supercilium. Underparts completely brick-red. Upperparts dark, with blackish, brown and chestnut notches on the feathers. **Immatures** similar to winter adults, but show a buff wash on the breast.

Voice and Diet
Calls frequently in flight, giving a low, barking *kirruk* call. Can also give a short, repeated *ik* call. Feeds by probing in soft mud, taking a variety of lugworms, flatworms and molluscs. Will also feed on insects.

Black-tailed Godwit
Limosa limosa   Guilbneach earrdhubh

A large wader with a long, straight, pink-based, dark bill and long dark legs. Similar to Bar-tailed Godwit, but shows a striking white wing stripe, a black tail and a white rump in flight. In **winter**, the grey upperparts are unstreaked. White underparts show a greyish breast. Head grey with a dark eye-stripe and a short supercilium before eye. In **summer**, shows an orangy head, a streaked crown, a dark eye-stripe and a pale supercilium fading behind the eye. Throat pale orange, with dark barring on white belly. Upperparts plain grey, with some black and chestnut feathers on mantle and scapulars. **Immatures** show a warm buff wash on the throat and breast, and orangy edges to dark upperpart feathers.

Voice and Diet
In flight, flocks give a very distinctive, repeated *wikka-wikka* call. Can also give a short *tuk* call on occasions. On the breeding grounds, Black-tailed Godwits are very noisy and give a *krru-wit-tsew* song during display flights, the emphasis being on the last phrase. The song may sound like *whatta-we-do*. Feeds by probing or picking from the surface. Takes a wide range of worms, molluscs and small crustaceans. On the breeding grounds, feeds on insects and larvae.

Long-billed Dowitcher (rare)
Limnodromus scolopaceus

A stocky wader with a very long dark bill and dull yellowish-green legs. In **summer** shows a dark crown, a broad, pale supercilium and a dark eye-stripe. Black upperpart feathers show rufous edges and whitish tips. Underparts chestnut-red, with barring on the sides of the breast onto flanks. In **winter** shows a grey crown, a whitish supercilium and a dark eye-stripe. Dark grey upperparts show pale edges to feathers. Underparts white with a grey-washed breast. **Immatures** show brownish upperparts with thin, white edges to tertials, white underparts and a buff wash on the breast. In flight, shows plain wings, and a dark, barred rump and tail contrasting with a white wedge on the back.

Voice and Diet
Gives a very distinctive *keek* call which can be repeated several times and can resemble the call given occasionally by Oystercatchers. Feeds by probing into soft mud. The feeding action has been likened to that of a sewing machine. Takes a wide variety of invertebrates.

Habitat and Status

A common winter visitor from breeding grounds in northern Europe. Birds arrive in late summer, with the peak arrival in September. Most depart in late spring, although small flocks occasionally spend the summer in Ireland. Found in all coastal counties. Feeds on sandy estuaries and mudflats. In some areas, particularly in the south-east, flocks can be found feeding on fields during high tides.

Bar-tailed Godwit

Adult (summer)

streaked brownish-grey upperparts

long, slightly up-curved bill

Adult (winter)

plain wings, barred tail and white, wedge-shaped rump

Habitat and Status

A common winter visitor from Iceland, found in all coastal counties. Also a very rare breeding species, with a small number present each summer in some midland counties. Birds begin to arrive in Ireland during the summer with the peak arrival in September and October. Found on mudflats and estuaries in all coastal counties. In spring, large numbers are found inland, feeding on the Shannon estuary and the callows of the Little Brosna and Shannon.

Black-tailed Godwit

long, straight bill

Adult (summer)

striking white wing stripe, black tail and white rump

plain, unstreaked upperparts

Adult (winter)

Habitat and Status

A rare but regular vagrant from North America. Most reports refer to autumn, with several records of birds wintering in suitable areas. Found on freshwater wetlands, feeding on the fringes of pools and lakes. Occasionally feeds along the shoreline. A shy species, easily flushed.

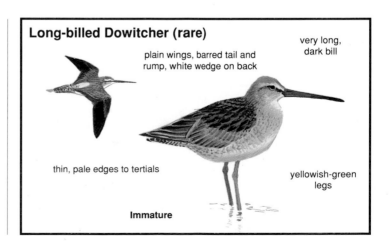

Long-billed Dowitcher (rare)

very long, dark bill

plain wings, barred tail and rump, white wedge on back

thin, pale edges to tertials

yellowish-green legs

Immature

Waders

Redshank
Tringa totanus   Cosdeargán

A medium-sized, greyish-brown wader with bright orange-red legs and a reddish base to a straight, medium-length, dark bill. In **winter**, the upperparts and head are plain greyish-brown. White eye-ring obvious against a dark eye-stripe. Underparts pale greyish-white, with dull breast and flank spotting. **Breeding birds** show heavy streaking on the head, breast and underparts. Upperparts brown, buff and cinnamon, with a variety of dark brown barring. **Immatures** show heavily streaked underparts, warm buff edges and spots to upperpart feathers, paler legs and a duller base to the bill. Easily recognised in flight by the all-white secondaries and inner primaries. Rump and back are white. Tail barred.

Voice and Diet
An extremely excitable and noisy wader which gives a loud, yelping *teeuu* call which is repeated continuously. In flight, gives a *teeu-u-u* call. During display flights on the breeding grounds, the song consists of *ty-uu* notes, delivered rapidly and loudly. Feeds by probing or picking from the surface, taking worms, insects, molluscs and crustaceans.

Spotted Redshank
Tringa erythropus

An elegant wader with long, red legs and a long, dark bill, showing a red base to the lower mandible. In **winter**, the upperparts are pale grey, underparts white. A strong white supercilium contrasts with a dark eye-stripe. In **summer**, the plumage is black, with white spots on the upperpart feathers. **Immatures** show dusky grey-brown upperparts with white spots and edges to the feathers. Told from immature Redshank by the white supercilium obvious before the eye, the longer, duller bill, and the underparts which appear more barred than streaked. In flight, shows a plain wing with a white oval on the back. This contrasts with darkish rump and tail. Legs extend well beyond the tail in flight.

Voice and Diet
Gives a very distinctive, sharp, loud *tch-uit* call in flight. They are often heard before they are seen. Feeds by picking or probing on a wide range of prey items, including molluscs, crustaceans, worms and insects.

Greenshank
Tringa nebularia   Laidhrín glas

A large, grey and white wader with a long, slightly up-curved bill and long, pale green legs. In **winter, adults** show a pale greyish-white head and grey upperparts. Faint streaking obvious on nape and sides of breast. Underparts white. **Adults in summer** show a heavily streaked head and breast, with streaking onto the flanks. The upperparts also show broad black markings. **Immatures** appear greyish-brown on the upperparts, with buff fringes on the scapulars and streaking on the head and breast sides. In flight, shows a dark, plain upperwing which contrasts with the white wedge on the back, the white rump and the pale tail which appears white at a distance. Dark bill shows a pale green base.

Voice and Diet
Gives a very loud and distinctive *tue-teu-teu* call, delivered quickly and occasionally repeated. On the breeding grounds, gives a soft, repeated *teo-oo*. Feeds in a very active manner, walking with deliberate strides, sometimes chasing prey in shallow water with lunges and sweeps. Also probes in soft mud. Takes molluscs, crustaceans, insects, worms and small fish.

Habitat and Status

A very common winter and autumn wader. Redshanks breed in very small numbers in Ireland, with breeding populations concentrated around the midlands lakes and Lough Neagh. Nests on the ground on open, wet grasslands. In autumn, numbers increase with the arrival of Icelandic birds which, together with birds from Scotland and northern England, winter in Ireland.

Redshank

all-white secondaries and inner primaries

white, wedge-shaped rump

bright orange-red legs

Adult (winter)

Habitat and Status

An uncommon visitor from breeding grounds in northern Europe. Seen in autumn and spring on passage, with small numbers wintering in Ireland. Found on coastal estuaries in winter, occasionally feeding in deep water. On passage, also recorded on brackish coastal lakes and lagoons.

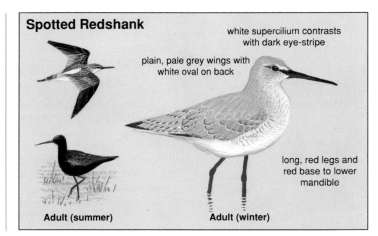

Spotted Redshank

white supercilium contrasts with dark eye-stripe

plain, pale grey wings with white oval on back

long, red legs and red base to lower mandible

Adult (summer)   **Adult (winter)**

Habitat and Status

A common autumn and winter visitor from breeding grounds in Scotland. Breeding took place in Ireland at one site in Co. Mayo in 1972 and 1974. Breeds on open moorland. Usually found on estuaries, mudflats and saltmarshes.

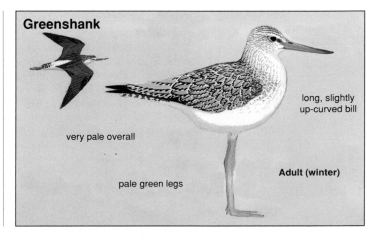

Greenshank

long, slightly up-curved bill

very pale overall

pale green legs

Adult (winter)

Waders

Wood Sandpiper
Tringa glareola   Gobadán coille

Small, slim, elegant wader, similar to Green Sandpiper, but with a long, dark-tipped bill and greenish-yellow legs. Most sightings refer to **immatures** which show a clear white supercilium beyond eye, a dark brown crown with creamy streaking, a dark eye-stripe, and coarse, pale buff spotting on brown upperparts. Underparts white with delicate breast streaking and spotting. **Summer adults** similar, but show white spotting on darker brown upperparts, and heavy streaking on foreneck and breast extending as barring onto flanks. In flight, similar to Green Sandpiper, showing a plain upperwing and a white rump, but differing by showing pale underwings and longer legs.

Voice and Diet
Wood Sandpipers give a very distinctive, rapid, high-pitched, shrill *chiff-iff-iff* call, especially when flushed. Feeds by probing in soft mud or by picking delicately from the surface of shallow pools. Feeds on a variety of insects, larvae, worms, molluscs, small crustaceans and occasionally small fish.

Lesser Yellowlegs (rare)
Tringa flavipes

A long-winged wader, larger than Wood Sandpiper, with a long, thin, dark bill, and long, bright yellow legs. **Immatures** show a white supercilium fading above eye, white streaking on a brownish-grey crown, a white eye-ring, and brownish-grey upperparts with extensive pale spotting. White underparts show dark streaking on breast and neck. **Summer adults** show heavy streaking on head and breast. Brownish upperparts show some blackish scapular and mantle feathers, and pale fringes and spots to wing feathers. **Winter adults** show white underparts and dark speckling on pale grey upperparts. In flight, shows a plain upperwing, a small, square white rump and long legs.

Voice and Diet
Gives a quiet, subdued *tu* call which is not usually repeated more than once or twice. A busy, active feeder, wading while picking or snatching food from the surface of the water or mud. Takes a variety of aquatic and land insects, larvae, worms, small fish and small crustaceans.

Greater Yellowlegs (rare)
Tringa melanoleuca

A medium-sized wader, larger than Lesser Yellowlegs and similar to Greenshank. Shows a long, dark-tipped, upturned bill and long, bright yellow legs. **Immatures** show a white supercilium, a streaked, dark grey crown, and extensive pale spotting on dark grey upperparts. Underparts white. Neck and breast streaked. **Summer adults** show a heavily streaked head and breast, and barred flanks. Dark grey upperparts show white spots and black mantle feathers and scapulars. **Winter adults** show white underparts, pale spots to grey upperparts, faint barring on flanks, and streaking on foreneck. In flight, shows a plain upperwing. Differs from Greenshank by showing a square white rump.

Voice and Diet
Gives a very loud, ringing, repeated *thew-thew-thew* call, very similar to that of Greenshank. A very busy, active feeder, often swinging the bill from side to side while wading through water. Picks or snatches from the surface of the mud or water. Rarely probes with the bill. Feeds on a variety of aquatic insects, larvae, small fish, worms, molluscs, small crustaceans and occasionally berries.

Habitat and Status

A scarce but regular autumn passage migrant from north-eastern Europe. Most records refer to August and September. Rarer in spring. Very few records refer to wintering birds. Most sightings are along eastern and southern coastal regions, although recorded in all coastal counties. Found feeding on muddy edges of coastal lakes, pools and marshes. Occasionally found along open shoreline.

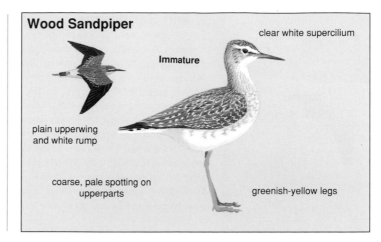

Wood Sandpiper

Immature

clear white supercilium

plain upperwing and white rump

coarse, pale spotting on upperparts

greenish-yellow legs

Habitat and Status

A rare but annual passage vagrant from North America. Most reports refer to autumn, with very small numbers recorded in spring. Birds can remain faithful to one area for lengthy periods, with some actually wintering. Most records refer to south-eastern and south-western coastal counties, but have been seen in all provinces. Frequents coastal marshes, lakes, ponds, estuaries and mudflats. Occasionally associates with other species, especially Redshanks.

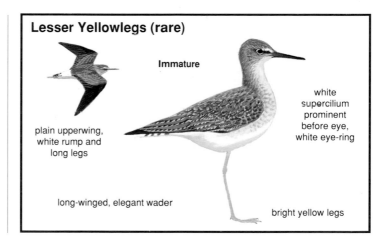

Lesser Yellowlegs (rare)

Immature

white supercilium prominent before eye, white eye-ring

plain upperwing, white rump and long legs

long-winged, elegant wader

bright yellow legs

Habitat and Status

An extremely rare vagrant from North America. All records refer to northern and south-western regions, with birds occurring in autumn, winter and, to a lesser extent, spring. Some reports refer to birds over-wintering. Usually found on coastal estuaries and mudflats. Also occurs on the fringes of lakes and marshes close to the coast. Rarely found inland, although one record refers to a bird found at Lough Beg, Co. Derry, in 1979.

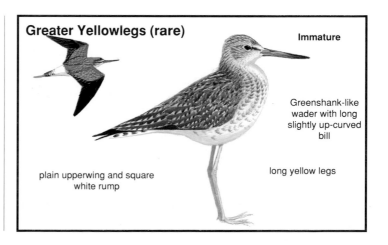

Greater Yellowlegs (rare)

Immature

Greenshank-like wader with long slightly up-curved bill

long yellow legs

plain upperwing and square white rump

Waders

Green Sandpiper
Tringa ochropus   Gobadán glas

A stocky, dark wader with yellowish-green legs. Straight bill shows a greenish base and a dark tip. **Summer adults** show dark greenish-brown upperparts with coarse pale spots, a streaked greenish-brown crown, a white supercilium before eye, and a white eye-ring. Neck and upper breast show heavy brown streaking. Underparts white. **Immatures** show buff spots on dark upperparts, a brownish-grey crown, a white eye-ring and a white supercilium before eye. Neck and upper breast brownish-grey. **Winter adults** show small buff upperpart spots and a heavily streaked neck and breast. In flight, shows a square white rump, a dark tail with strong white barring, a plain dark upperwing and a dark underwing.

Voice and Diet
When flushed, gives a loud, high-pitched *weet-tweet* call which can be repeated. Can also give a series of loud *too-leet* notes. Feeds by probing in soft mud or shallow water, taking a variety of beetles, flies, larvae and crustaceans. Can occasionally submerge head completely when feeding.

Common Sandpiper
Actitis hypoleucos   Gobadán

A small wader with a constantly bobbing long tail extending well beyond the wings. Shows dull green-yellow legs and a straight, dark-tipped brownish bill. **Summer adults** show brownish upperparts with thin streaking and barring, a brownish crown, dark lores, an indistinct, pale supercilium, and a white eye-ring. Underparts white, with brown streaking on sides of breast. **Immatures** show pale brown and dark edges to upperpart feathers, with pale tips and brown subterminal bars on coverts. Unlike Spotted, tertial edges show buff notches. In flight, shows a white wingbar and trailing edge to secondaries. Tail shows faint barring and white edges. Flies on stiff, bowed wings.

Voice and Diet
Gives a clear, distinctive *swee-wee-wee* call. On the breeding grounds, can give rapid, high *kitti-weeti* song notes which can be delivered both in flight or on the ground. Feeds in a careful, deliberate manner, picking from the surface or from vegetation. Takes a wide range of prey items, including insects, larvae, worms, molluscs, tadpoles and crustaceans. Can occasionally feed on seeds.

Spotted Sandpiper (rare)
Actitis macularia

A small wader with a constantly bobbing tail which does not extend far beyond the wings. Legs yellowish. **Summer adults** show brown spots on white underparts and streaking on sides of breast. Upperparts greyish-brown with thin barring and streaking, a white eye-ring and supercilium, and dark lores. Straight, pinkish-orange bill shows a dark tip. **Immatures** like Common Sandpiper, but show plain brownish upperparts and heavy buff, brown and black barring on the coverts. Unlike Common, shows plain edges to tertials. In flight, shows a white wingbar, a dark secondary bar, and a white trailing edge to secondaries. Dark tail barred with narrow white edges. Flies on stiff, bowed wings.

Voice and Diet
Gives a quiet, piping *peet* call which can be repeated to give a double *peet-weet* call. When flushed, this call can also be extended, giving a *peet-weet-weet-weet* call resembling that of Green Sandpiper. Like Common Sandpiper, feeds in a careful, deliberate manner, picking from the surface or from vegetation. Takes a wide range of insects, larvae, small fish, molluscs and crustaceans.

Habitat and Status

A common passage migrant from northern Europe. Most reports refer to autumn, with birds occurring from June to October. Small numbers are recorded in March and April. Birds occasionally occur in summer and winter in most regions, but uncommon in some western and north-western areas. Frequents a variety of wetland habitats, including lake fringes, pools, rivers, ditches close to marshes and lakes, and on brackish coastal lagoons.

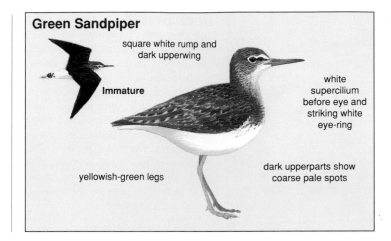

Green Sandpiper

square white rump and dark upperwing

Immature

white supercilium before eye and striking white eye-ring

yellowish-green legs

dark upperparts show coarse pale spots

Habitat and Status

A common, widespread breeding species present in most regions each summer. Small numbers winter in the south-west. Largest breeding populations are in midland and western counties. Found on edges of rocky streams and rivers, and on shingle shores of lakes. In some regions, frequents mountain lakes and rivers, while in the south-west can breed on coastal shingle areas. On passage, found on coastal estuaries and lagoons.

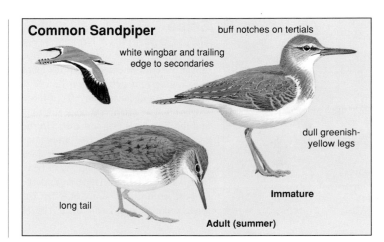

Common Sandpiper

buff notches on tertials

white wingbar and trailing edge to secondaries

dull greenish-yellow legs

Immature

long tail

Adult (summer)

Habitat and Status

An extremely rare passage vagrant from North America. All reports refer to late autumn and winter. Most sightings have been in the south and south-west, with one bird recorded in Co. Westmeath in the last century. Found on coastal estuaries, pond and lake edges, harbours and along rivers. With the exception of one bird, all Irish records refer to immature birds. It is possible that Spotted Sandpipers are frequently overlooked due to their similarity to Common Sandpiper.

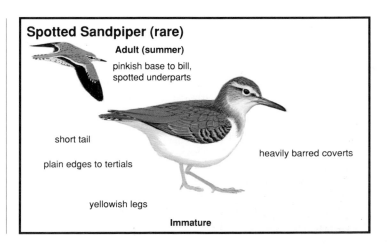

Spotted Sandpiper (rare)

Adult (summer)

pinkish base to bill, spotted underparts

short tail

plain edges to tertials

heavily barred coverts

yellowish legs

Immature

Waders

Jack Snipe

Lymnocryptes minimus   Naoscach bhídeach

Small, long-billed wader with rounded wings and prominent golden stripes on the back. When flushed, Jack Snipe fly in a straight line before quickly dropping into cover. Rarely calls when flushed. Best told from Snipe by the shorter bill, the rounded wings with a thin, pale trailing edge, prominent golden stripes on the back and by the darker tail. On the ground, shows a distinctive dark crown and a dark, isolated line within a creamy double supercilium. A dark eye-stripe continues to form a dark border to ear coverts. Underparts pale, with heavy streaking on breast and flanks. Upperparts dark, contrasting with golden upperpart stripes. Bill pale with dark tip. Legs greenish.

Voice and Diet
Usually silent when flushed, Jack Snipe can give a quiet, weak *gach* call on occasions. Feeds in a crake-like manner, picking off the surface and probing less often than Snipe. Also has a habit of bobbing the body up and down when feeding. Takes insects, worms, molluscs and seeds.

Snipe

Gallinago gallinago   Naoscach

A long-billed wader with creamy stripes on the back and crown. When flushed, usually calls loudly and flies rapidly, zig-zagging to a good height before dropping back into cover a good distance away. Told from Jack Snipe by the longer bill, less prominent back stripes, less rounded wings, and the flight pattern and call. On the ground, shows a creamy central crown-stripe and supercilium and a dark lateral crown-stripe. Dark eye-stripe does not form border to ear coverts. Underparts pale, with heavy streaking on the breast. Flanks barred. Upperparts dark with creamy back stripes. **Immatures** show buff fringes to wing coverts. Straight, dark tipped, pale brownish bill. Legs greenish.

Voice and Diet
An easily alarmed bird, flushing noisily and giving a loud, harsh *sccaap* call. On the breeding grounds, gives a short, repeated *chic* call. During display flights, dives with spread outer-tail feathers which create a rapid, muffled, 'drumming' sound. Feeds by probing deep with fast, 'sewing machine' head movements. Feeds on insects, worms and seeds.

Woodcock

Scolopax rusticola   Creabhar

A large, chunky bird with a long, heavy, straight bill and shortish legs. Unlike most waders, Woodcock are found in damp woodland areas and are usually seen at dusk and dawn. The large black eye is set high and back in the head. The steep forehead is greyish, with broad dark and pale bars on the crown and nape. Dark loral stripe present. Upperparts a complicated pattern of black, buff and cream barring with a broad, creamy mantle stripe. Underparts pale with greyish-brown barring. Sides of breast show rufous tones. In flight, shows broad, plain, rounded wings. Tail dark brown with pale tips. Bill pale pinkish with a dark tip. Short pale legs. **Immatures** similar to adults.

Voice and Diet
Usually silent when flushed, Woodcock occasionally give an almost Snipe-like *schaap* call. During the breeding season, males give a display flight (known as roding) low over treetops while giving a low, repeated, guttural song consisting of *quorr-quorr-quorr-tsietz*. Feeds on damp ground or in puddles, taking earthworms, insects and larvae.

Habitat and Status

An uncommon winter visitor from northern Europe, Jack Snipe can easily be overlooked due to their habit of remaining motionless, relying on their camouflage for safety. Found in grassy wetlands, freshwater marshes, bogs, saltmarshes and along the fringes of reed-beds. Rarely found feeding in open water or exposed mudflats.

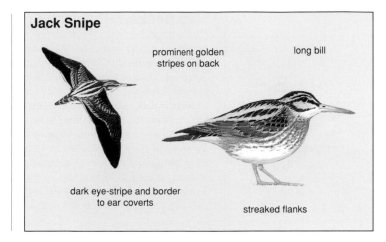

Jack Snipe

prominent golden stripes on back

long bill

dark eye-stripe and border to ear coverts

streaked flanks

Habitat and Status

A common resident breeding species, with numbers increasing in winter with the arrival of birds from the Baltic and Britain. Nests on the ground in marshes, bogs, wet fields, and river and lake shorelines. In winter found in similar habitat as well as coastal marshes. Can feed in deep, open water or on exposed mudflat areas.

Snipe

extremely long bill

creamy stripes on back

barred flanks

Habitat and Status

An uncommon but widespread breeding species, found in deciduous and coniferious woodlands with open clearings. Nests in scrapes under bracken, trees or bushes. Populations increase in winter when birds arrive from northern Britain and the Continent.

Woodcock

very long, straight bill

broad bars on crown and nape

cryptic brown, black and white plumage

Waders

Red-necked Phalarope (rare)
Phalaropus lobatus   Falaróp gobchaol

An elegant wader with a fine black bill and greyish legs. **Summer females** show a blue-grey crown and neck, darker ear coverts, a white spot above eye, a white throat, and a red foreneck extending up sides of neck to rear of ear coverts. Upperparts dark with warm buff mantle stripes and edges to wing feathers. Breast and flanks grey. Belly and undertail whitish. Tail greyish. **Summer males** drabber. In flight, shows white wing stripes and sides to uppertail coverts and rump. **Immatures** show buff upperpart stripes, a white patch on bend of wing, a whitish face with a dark crown, and a dark ear patch curving down behind eye. **Winter adults** are pale grey above and white below, with a thin black ear patch.

Voice and Diet
Gives short, low-pitched *prek* or *whit* calls. Feeds by wading or swimming buoyantly, occasionally spinning in circles or up-ending. Takes a wide range of insects and larvae, either picking them quickly from the surface of the water or from stones and vegetation.

Wilson's Phalarope (rare)
Phalaropus tricolor

An elegant wader with a long, thin bill. **Immatures** show a white head, a grey crown and a thin, greyish eye-stripe which extends onto sides of neck. Underparts white, with a greyish wash on breast. Upperparts dark with pale edges but can show grey winter feathers on mantle and scapulars. Legs yellow. Bill black. **Winter adults** pale grey above and white below. In flight, shows plain wings and a white rump. **Summer females** show a grey crown and nape, a white patch above eye, and a black eye-stripe extending down side of neck. Underparts white, with orange-buff on sides of neck onto breast. Upperparts grey, with chestnut stripes on scapulars and sides of mantle. Legs black. **Summer males** are duller.

Voice and Diet
Usually silent when found in Ireland, birds can occasionally give a nasal, grunting *chup*. By comparison with other phalarope species, Wilson's Phalarope prefers wading and walking on land to swimming, although will swim readily, spinning in circles on occasions. Takes a wide variety of insects, larvae, worms, crustaceans and seeds.

Grey Phalarope
Phalaropus fulicarius   Falaróp gobmhór

Small wader with a thick, black bill and bluish-grey legs. **Immatures** show a dark crown, a whitish face and a square, blackish ear patch which does not curve behind eye. Whitish underparts can show a peach-tinged breast. Dark upperparts show buff edges to feathers and an inconspicuous buff mantle stripe. Some grey winter feathers can show on mantle and scapulars. **Winter adults** are pale grey above and white below, with a black ear patch and a pale base to the bill. In flight, shows white wingbars and white sides to uppertail-coverts, recalling Sanderling. **Summer adults** show completely red underparts with a white face, a dark crown, lores and chin, and dark buff-fringed upperparts.

Voice and Diet
Gives a short, sharp *wit* call, higher in pitch than the similar call of Red-necked Phalarope. Feeds by swimming buoyantly, occasionally spinning, and wading. Takes a wide variety of insects, larvae, worms, molluscs and crustaceans. At sea will feed on small invertebrates picked from floating vegetation.

Habitat and Status

A rare passage migrant and former breeding species. Once bred at a site in the west where numbers dwindled since the 1920s until breeding no longer took place by the late 1990s. Has also bred at other sites in southern and western regions. Found in freshwater marshes with open pools and dense vegetation. Nests in vegetation and grass tussocks. Incubation and chick rearing performed by males only. On passage, found on coastal freshwater marshes. Winters at sea.

Red-necked Phalarope (rare)

buff stripes on upperparts

Immature

Female (summer)

fine black bill

Habitat and Status

A rare but regular autumn vagrant from North America, usually seen from August to October. Found on freshwater shallow lakes, pools, lagoons and also tidal mudflats and estuaries. Rarely seen at sea.

Wilson's Phalarope (rare)

elegant wader with long, thin bill

white rump

Female (summer)

Immature

Habitat and Status

A regular autumn passage bird, also occurring in early winter. Rarely seen on spring passage. Breeds in Arctic regions, wintering off western coasts of Africa. In autumn, especially following strong winds or gales, frequently reported from seawatching points in the west and south-west, with birds being seen in the south-east. Also found on coastal lakes, freshwater pools and marshes. Extremely tame. Will usually allow a very close approach.

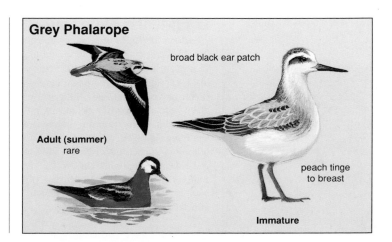

Grey Phalarope

broad black ear patch

Adult (summer) rare

peach tinge to breast

Immature

Skuas

Arctic Skua
Stercorarius parasiticus   Meirleach Artach
A light skua with narrow-based, pointed wings. **Pale-phase adults** show a dark cap, a yellowish face, whitish underparts and a diffuse breast band. Dark, plain brown upperwings show whitish shafts to outer primaries appearing as crescents on the underwing. Rump brown. Dark tail shows long, pointed, central feathers. **Dark-phase adults** show all-dark underparts and face. Bill and legs dark. **Immatures** show warm brown, buff-edged mantle, wings and rump. Crown and underparts buff with dark barring and streaking. Nape paler. In flight, shows white primary bases, barred underwing and undertail-coverts, and short, pointed central tail feathers. Bill shows a blue-grey base. Legs blue-grey.

Voice and Diet
Rarely heard when seen off Ireland. However, when in pursuit of a gull or tern, Arctic Skuas can sometimes utter hard, high-pitched *tuuk-tuuk* calls. Feeds by chasing and harassing gulls and terns, pursuing them until they drop or disgorge food. Will also feed on fish, small mammals, birds and eggs. Will readily eat carrion and offal.

Pomarine Skua
Stercorarius pomarinus   Meirleach pomairíneach
A heavy, deep-chested bird, like Arctic Skua but showing broad-based wings, and long, blunt, twisted, central tail feathers. **Pale-phase adults** show a yellowish face, a dark cap, whitish underparts and a dark breast band. Upperwing brown with whitish outer primary shafts. Underwing shows white crescents. **Dark-phase adults** show dark underparts. Heavy bill and legs dark. **Immatures** show brown, buff-edged upperparts. Head grey-brown, appearing barred. Buff underparts evenly barred. In flight, shows white primary bases, double white underwing patches, heavy barring on rump, and short, blunt, central tail feathers. Bill shows a blue-grey base. Legs greyish.

Voice and Diet
Generally silent on passage. However, the harsh, distinctive *whit-yuu* call can occasionally be given. Like Arctic Skua, Pomarines feed by chasing and harassing gulls and terns, pursuing them until they drop or disgorge food. Will also feed on fish, small mammals, birds and eggs. Also attracted to stranded fish, carrion and offal.

Long-tailed Skua (rare)
Stercorarius longicaudus   Meirleach earrfhada
A light, slender-winged skua similar to Arctic Skua. **Adults** show very long central tail feathers, a yellowish nape, a black cap, greyish upperparts and whitish underparts. In flight, greyish wings show little white on primaries and a black secondary bar. Dark underwings do not show pale crescents. In flight, **immatures** show grey-brown upperparts and wings, a black secondary bar and almost no white on primaries. Barred underwings show pale crescents. Nape and sides of head pale. Underparts greyish, breast darker. Rump, flanks and undertail heavily barred. Dark tail shows blunt central feathers, varying in length. Bill shows a bluish-grey base. Legs greyish.

Voice and Diet
On passage, Long-tailed Skuas are silent, the shrill calls only being heard on the breeding grounds. Unlike other skuas, seldom chases gulls and terns, feeding chiefly on fish caught at sea. Also attracted by carrion and offal.

Habitat and Status

A common spring and autumn passage migrant from breeding grounds in the Scottish Isles, northern Europe and Iceland. Seen on passage off islands and headlands on all coastal counties. Winters in the south Atlantic. The highest numbers are recorded in autumn, peaking in August and September. Has also been recorded on large inland lakes, with occasional reports of birds during summer months. Several reports also refer to birds seen in Irish waters in winter.

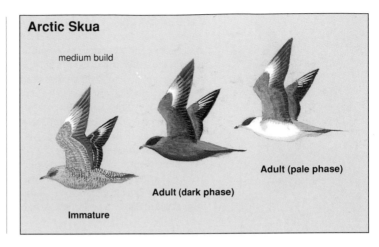

Arctic Skua

medium build

Adult (pale phase)

Adult (dark phase)

Immature

Habitat and Status

A regular but uncommon spring and autumn passage migrant. Breeds in Arctic Russia, wintering in the south Atlantic. Seen on passage off islands and headlands on all coastal counties, with most records referring to southern and western regions. The highest numbers have been recorded in spring, peaking in May. However, seawatching off western locations has revealed that large southern movements occur off Ireland in the autumn. Several reports refer to birds seen in Irish waters in winter.

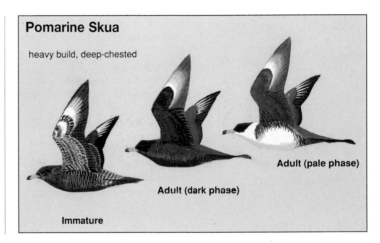

Pomarine Skua

heavy build, deep-chested

Adult (pale phase)

Adult (dark phase)

Immature

Habitat and Status

A rare but regular passage migrant from breeding grounds in Arctic Europe, with numbers fluctuating from year to year. Exceptional movements occur occasionally, with most records from western and northern coastal counties. In spring, peak movements occur in May, while late August and September provide the largest autumn counts. Has also been recorded inland. Winters in the south Atlantic.

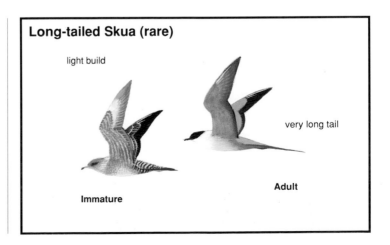

Long-tailed Skua (rare)

light build

very long tail

Adult

Immature

Skuas and Gulls

Great Skua or Bonxie
Stercorarius skua   Meirleach mór

A very large, broad-winged skua with striking white flashes across the primaries. Could be mistaken for a large immature gull, but in flight appears deeper-chested, with the bright wing flashes obvious with every deep, heavy wing beat. **Adults** show a dark brown crown, a yellowish-streaked brown neck, and streaked, brown upperparts. Dark brownish tail shows slightly elongated central feathers. Greyish-brown underparts show brown streaking on throat and along flanks. Wings brown with contrasting darker flight feathers and striking white primary flashes. **Immatures** appear darker than adults and show smaller wing flashes. Shows a large, dark, hooked bill. Legs dark.

Voice and Diet
The harsh, gruff calls are rarely heard away from the breeding grounds, but Great Skuas can occasionally give deep, guttural *tuk-tuk* calls when pursuing or attacking birds. Feeds by agilely chasing and attacking other bird species including gulls, terns and even Gannets. Usually pursues these birds relentlessly until they either drop or disgorge food. Will readily take fish, birds and eggs. Attracted by offal from trawlers.

Great Black-backed Gull
Larus marinus   Droimneach mór

A very large gull with a heavy bill and pinkish legs. **Adults** show a white head, underparts and tail. Head unstreaked in winter. Upperparts black with white scapular and tertial crescents, large white tips to black primaries, and, in flight, a white trailing edge to wing. Bill yellow with a red gonys spot. Eye yellow. **1st year birds** show a black bill, a dark eye, a whitish head and underparts, barred brownish-grey upperparts and dark primaries. In flight, tail shows an ill-defined band. **2nd years** show whiter underparts and head, a pale-based bill and some black mantle feathers. **3rd years** as adult, with some immature feathering and dark subterminal markings on bill.

Voice and Diet
Calls are louder and more powerful than Herring and Lesser Black-backed Gulls. Gives a deep, barking *aouk* call and a long, trumpeting *ee-aouk-ouk-ouk*. When disturbed on the breeding grounds, gives deep *uk-uk-uk* calls. Feeds on a wide variety of fish, molluscs, worms, crustaceans, offal and carrion. Also found at rubbish tips, feeding on scraps and waste. Will take weak or small mammals and during the breeding season kills seabirds.

Lesser Black-backed Gull
Larus fuscus   Droimneach beag

A large gull, similar in size to Herring Gull. **Adults** show a white head and underparts, and yellow legs. Head streaked and legs duller in winter. Dark grey upperparts contrast with white-tipped black primaries. Underwing dusky on inner primaries and secondaries. Bill yellow with red spot. Eye yellow with red eye-ring. **1st year birds** show a black bill, a dark eye, barred brownish upperparts, dark primaries and a whitish head and underparts. In flight, shows a broad tail band and a contrasting upperwing pattern. Legs pinkish. **2nd years** show a pale-based bill and some grey mantle feathers. **3rd years** as adult, with some immature feathering and dark subterminal markings on bill.

Voice and Diet
The calls are louder and deeper than Herring Gull. Gives a loud, deep *kyow* call and a long, shrill, trumpeting *kyee-kyee-kyee-aou-aou-aou*. When disturbed, especially on the breeding grounds, gives loud *kee-ya* calls and deep *gak-gak-gak* calls. Feeds on a wide variety of fish, molluscs, worms, crustaceans, offal and carrion. Also found at rubbish tips, feeding on scraps and waste. Will take weak, small mammals. During the breeding season, kills seabird chicks.

56-62cm **Great Skua** or **Bonxie**
69-70cm **Great Black-backed Gull**
51-56cm **Lesser Black-backed Gull**

Habitat and Status

The commonest skua species found off Ireland, they are regular autumn and spring passage migrants from breeding grounds in Iceland and the northern Scottish Isles. Seen off all coastal regions, most records refer to passage movements off seawatching points on the south-west and west coasts. Some records refer to birds present on large inland lakes in northern and midland counties. Occasionally found in Irish waters in winter.

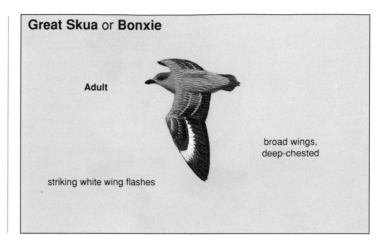

Great Skua or Bonxie

Adult

broad wings, deep-chested

striking white wing flashes

Habitat and Status

A common resident breeding species found in all coastal counties. Breeds in small colonies or singly on coastal cliffs or islands, building a large nest of feathers, plant material, seaweed and sticks. Also found breeding on lake islands at inland sites in northern and western regions. In winter, present along all coastal counties, on estuaries, mudflats or at rubbish tips. Small numbers also occur at inland sites in winter.

Great Black-backed Gull

very large size, all black back and wings

Adult (winter)

1st year

pink legs

Adult (summer)

Habitat and Status

A common breeding species found in most coastal counties. Primarily a summer visitor, arriving from southern Europe and North Africa in early spring, and departing in autumn. In recent years, large numbers winter at coastal and inland sites. Breeds in colonies on coastal headlands and islands, nesting on the ground on flat, sloping areas or on well-vegetated lake islands at inland sites. Found on estuaries, mudflats, farmlands and rubbish tips.

Lesser Black-backed Gull

dark grey upperparts, black primaries

Adult (winter)

1st year

yellow legs

Adult (summer)

121

Gulls

Herring Gull
Larus argentatus   Faoileán scadán

A familiar large gull, similar in size to Lesser Black-backed, but showing pink legs. **Adults** show a white head and underparts. Head streaked in winter. Pale grey upperparts contrast with white-tipped black primaries. Bill yellow with red spot. Eye yellow with orange-yellow ring. **1st year birds** show a pale base to black bill, a dark eye, barred brownish upperparts, dark primaries, and a pale brownish head and underparts. In flight, shows a tail band and a dark outer wing contrasting with paler inner primaries. **2nd years** show some grey mantle feathers and a blotchy tail band. **3rd years** as adult, with some immature feathering and dark subterminal markings on bill.

Voice and Diet
Gives a loud *kyow* call and a long, shrill, trumpeting *kyee-kyee-aou-aou-aou*. When disturbed, gives loud *kee-ya* calls and deep *gak-gak-gak* calls. Calls are almost identical to Lesser Black-backed, but not as deep. Feeds on a wide variety of fish, molluscs, worms, crustaceans, offal and carrion. Also found at rubbish tips, feeding on scraps and waste. Takes weak, small mammals. During the breeding season, kills seabird chicks.

Yellow-legged Gull
Larus michahellis

Adults show yellow legs, with the grey upperparts being a shade between Herring and Lesser Black-backed. Head and underparts white with little streaking in winter. Bill yellow with red gonys spot. Yellow eye shows red eye-ring. In flight, shows little white on extensive black wing tips, and dusky-grey inner primaries and secondaries on the underwing. **1st year birds** show barred, brownish upperparts, dark primaries, a whitish head and underparts, and a black bill. In flight, shows a neat tail band and contrasting wings. **2nd years** show a grey mantle and scapulars, and a well-defined tail band. **3rd years** as adult, with some immature feathering and dark subterminal markings on bill.

Voice and Diet
Gives a loud *kyo* call and a long, trumpeting *kyee-kyee-kyo-kyo-kyo*. Will also give deep *gak-gak-gak* calls. Overall, the calls are almost identical to Lesser Black-backed, being deeper in tone than those of Herring Gull. Feeds on a wide variety of fish, molluscs, worms, crustaceans, offal and carrion. Also found at rubbish tips, feeding on scraps and waste.

Laughing Gull (rare)
Larus atricilla

A medium-sized gull with a long, drooped bill. **Summer adults** show a black hood and white eye crescents. Upperparts dark grey. Long, black primaries show small white tips. Underparts white. Bill dark red with a dark subterminal bar. Legs reddish. **Winter adults** show a cleaner head with dark shading behind eye, a red-tipped, dark bill and dark legs. **1st year birds** show a dark patch behind eye onto crown, grey on nape extending onto breast and flanks, dark grey mantle, brownish coverts and long dark primaries. Bill and legs dark. Shows a dusky underwing and a broad tail band in flight. **2nd years** as adult winter, but show grey nape and underpart shading, and some brown on tail.

Voice and Diet
The laughing, crying calls from which this species derives its name are rarely heard when birds are found in Ireland. Feeds with other species of medium-sized gulls, taking a wide range of food items, including small fish, molluscs, worms and a variety of aquatic invertebrates.

Habitat and Status

An extremely common, widespread, resident breeding species found in all coastal counties. Breeds in colonies on coastal cliffs or islands. Builds a nest of feathers, seaweed and other plant material on sloping or flat ground. Also found breeding on lake islands at inland sites. In recent years has bred in towns and cities, nesting on rooftops and chimneys. In winter, present along all coastal counties, on estuaries, mudflats or at rubbish tips. Good numbers winter inland.

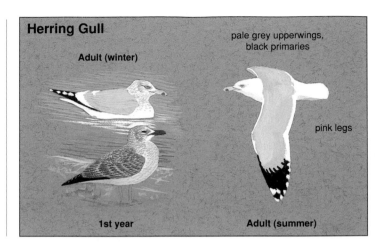

Herring Gull

Adult (winter)

pale grey upperwings, black primaries

pink legs

1st year

Adult (summer)

Habitat and Status

An uncommon vagrant from Europe, found associating with Lesser Black-backed and Herring Gulls. Can be found at any time of the year with most reports being from late autumn into winter. Most frequently seen in northern, eastern and southern counties, but has occurred in most areas. Found along coastal counties in a range of habitats including estuaries, mudflats and rubbish tips.

Yellow-legged Gull

Adult (summer)

grey upperwing

yellow legs

Top: Adult winter Lesser Black-backed Gull
Bottom: Adult winter Yellow-legged Gull.
Note unstreaked head.

Habitat and Status

A very rare vagrant from North America. Birds have been recorded in south-western, western, eastern and north-eastern regions. Records refer to summer, late autumn and winter, with the bulk of the reports involving 1st year birds. Found associating with gull flocks on coastal estuaries, mudflats, lagoons and harbours.

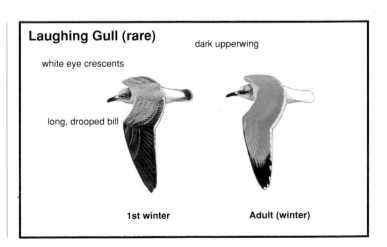

Laughing Gull (rare)

dark upperwing

white eye crescents

long, drooped bill

1st winter

Adult (winter)

123

Gulls

Glaucous Gull
Larus hyperboreus   Faoileán glas

A large, powerful gull. **Winter adults** show a streaked white head, white underparts, pale grey upperparts, and short white primaries. Eye yellow. Bill yellow with red spot. Legs pink. **1st winter birds** show delicate barring on pale buff upperparts, rump and tail, creamy underparts, and short creamy-white primaries. Heavy, pale pink bill shows a black tip. Eye dark. **2nd winters** appear whiter, show a yellow eye and a dark ring on a pink bill. **3rd winters** as adult, with buff feathers on whitish wings and tail, and black markings on yellow bill. Told from Iceland Gull by larger size, heavy bill, a flat-crowned appearance, a more aggressive expression and shorter primaries.

Voice and Diet
The most commonly heard note of this generally silent species is a deep *kyow*, similar to, but shriller than, Herring Gull. When agitated will give loud *gak-gak-gak* calls like most large gulls. Feeds on a variety of carrion, offal, fish, worms and molluscs. Also feeds on waste and scraps at rubbish tips.

Iceland Gull
Larus glaucoides

A white-winged gull, smaller than Glaucous Gull. **Winter adults** show a streaked white head, white underparts, grey upperparts, and long, attenuated white primaries. Eye yellow. Bill yellow with red gonys spot. Legs pink. **1st winter birds** show delicate mottling on pale buff upperparts and tail, creamy underparts and whitish primaries. Medium-sized dark bill shows a pinkish base. Eyes dark. **2nd winters** whiter, with a yellow eye and dark ring on pink bill. **3rd winters** as adult, with buff on whitish wings and tail, and black markings on yellow bill. Told from Glaucous by smaller size, medium-sized bill, rounded crown, gentle expression and long primary projection.

Voice and Diet
Iceland Gulls are a reasonably quiet species away from the breeding grounds. Calls are similar to Herring Gull, consisting of shriller *kyow* and agitated *gak-gak-gak* calls. Like Glaucous Gull, feeds on a variety of carrion, offal, fish, worms and molluscs. Also feeds on waste and scraps at rubbish tips.

Ivory Gull (rare)
Pagophila eburnea

A very distinctive gull, similar in size to Common Gull but with a stocky, pigeon-like build. **Adults** show a pure white plumage, a conspicuous black eye, and shortish, black legs. Bill bluish or greenish-grey with a yellow and orange tip. Could be confused with albinistic gulls of similar size, but the colour of the bill is diagnostic and should always be checked. **1st winter birds** are unmistakable, showing a white plumage with a dusky, dirty face, black-tipped primaries and tail, and varying amounts of dark spotting on the wings. Bill dark greyish with a yellowish tip. Legs blackish. Can be very tame and approachable, but very aggressive towards other gull species.

Voice and Diet
Although rarely heard, Ivory Gull can give a harsh, tern-like *kee-ar* call. Feeds on carrion, including dead fish and mammals. Will also take fish, crustaceans, molluscs and insects. Will pick food from the water in flight, often pattering its feet on the surface.

Habitat and Status

An uncommon but regular winter visitor from Iceland and Greenland. In some years, extremely large numbers have occurred. Found along most coastal counties, the highest concentrations being in northern, western and southern regions. Frequents fishing ports, harbours, docklands and rubbish tips. Occasionally found inland. Most reports refer to a period from January to early March. Smaller numbers recorded in autumn, early winter, spring, and occasionally in summer.

Glaucous Gull

large build, heavy bill

short primaries

Adult (winter)

white wing tips

1st winter

Habitat and Status

Uncommon but regular winter visitor from Greenland. Although scarcer than Glaucous Gull, large influxes can occur in some winters. Found along most coastal counties, with the highest concentrations in northern, western and southern counties. Frequents fishing ports, harbours, docklands and rubbish tips. Very rarely found inland. Most reports refer to a period from January to early April, with very small numbers seen in autumn, early winter and spring. Extremely rare in summer.

Iceland Gull

medium-sized bill

long primaries

Adult (winter)

white wing tips

1st winter

Habitat and Status

An extremely rare winter vagrant from north Greenland, Spitzbergen and other islands in the high Arctic. In winter, rarely travels farther south than the Arctic Circle. Usually found in harbours and fishing ports, feeding aggressively alongside other gulls. Perches frequently. Usually very tame. While most records refer to winter months, Ivory Gull has been recorded in late summer and late autumn. Can stay for several days in one area.

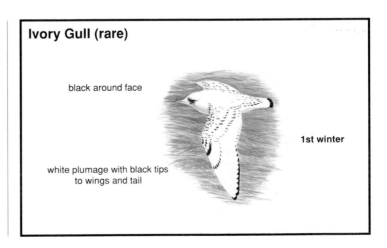

Ivory Gull (rare)

black around face

white plumage with black tips to wings and tail

1st winter

Gulls

Common Gull
Larus canus   Faoileán bán

A medium-sized gull, with **adults** showing a slender, pointed yellow-green bill and legs, a dark eye, a white head, tail and underparts, and dark grey upperparts showing a thick, white tertial crescent. White-tipped, black primaries show two large white mirrors. **Winter adults** show a narrow dark band on the bill and a streaked head. **1st year birds** show a pinkish-grey base to a slender, dark-tipped bill, dark spots on head, a dark grey mantle, contrasting pale-edged brown tertials and coverts, and dark brown primaries. In flight, shows a well-defined, dark tail band. **2nd years** as adults, but show dark primary coverts and a broad, dark band on a dull yellowish bill.

Voice and Diet
Common Gulls give shrill, whistling *keee-ya* calls which can develop into longer, trumpeting notes. The calls are shriller and higher-pitched than those of the larger gull species. Feeds on a wide range of insects, molluscs, worms and fish. Will also take offal, dead fish, small birds and mammals and eggs. Can also be found on rubbish tips feeding on scraps and waste.

Ring-billed Gull
Larus delawarensis

A stocky gull similar to, but slightly larger and deeper-chested than, Common Gull. **Adults** show a black ring on a broad, parallel yellow bill. Eye yellow with a dark pupil. Legs yellow. Upperparts paler grey than Common, with smaller mirrors on the primaries and a thinner tertial crescent. Head and underparts white. Head streaked in winter. **1st year birds** show a dark tip to a heavy, orange-pink bill. Head and breast heavily spotted. In flight, shows a pale grey mantle, dark primaries and secondaries, pale grey greater coverts, and a blotchy tail band. **2nd years** as adults, but show dark primary coverts and can show traces of the tail band and secondary bar.

Voice and Diet
Ring-billed Gulls, though rarely heard when found Ireland, give high-pitched, shrill calls similar to those of Common Gull. Feeds on a wide range of molluscs, fish, worms and insects. Like Common Gull, will take offal, dead fish, small birds and mammals and eggs. Can also be found on rubbish tips feeding on scraps and waste.

Mediterranean Gull
Larus melanocephalus

A heavy, stocky gull, similar to Black-headed Gull but showing a broader, more drooped bill. **Summer adults** show a black hood, a black subterminal band, and a yellow tip to a deep red bill. Legs red. Upperparts pale grey which, unlike Black-headed, show pure white primaries. Underparts and tail white. **Winter adults** show a black patch behind eye. **1st winter birds** show a pale base to a dark bill, a pale grey mantle and dark brown primaries. In flight, shows a striking upperwing pattern, resembling Common Gull. Tail shows a thick, dark tail band. **1st summers** show extensive black on the head. **2nd years** as adults, but show variable amounts of black on the primaries.

Voice and Diet
Gives deep, harsh *kee-oh* calls which are deeper in tone and pitch than those of Black-headed Gull. Feeds in association with other gull species, taking a wide assortment of small fish, worms, molluscs and insects. Occasionally found on rubbish tips feeding on waste and scraps.

126

Habitat and Status

A widespread species found along most coastal counties in autumn and winter. Breeds in colonies on small lake or coastal islands, usually nesting on the ground. The main breeding populations are based in western and northern regions. In autumn and winter, numbers increase with the arrival of birds from Europe and Iceland. In winter, found on estuaries, mudflats, coastal fields and on inland lakes and pastures.

Common Gull

2nd winter

Adult (summer)

slender yellow-green bill, dark mantle

1st winter

Habitat and Status

A rare but regular vagrant from North America. First found in Ireland in 1979, Ring-billed Gulls have now become annual visitors. This is probably due to a population expansion in North America. Found with gull flocks on estuaries, mudflats, marshes, inland pastures and rubbish tips. Most records refer to a period from winter to early spring, with some birds occasionally over-summering. May breed in Ireland in the near future.

Ring-billed Gull

Adult (summer)

Adult (winter)

yellow eye, black ring on broad yellowish bill

1st winter

Habitat and Status

Formerly a very rare vagrant from south-east Europe, has now become a widespread annual visitor to coastal counties with a small breeding population established in the south-east. Most reports refer to winter when birds from the Netherlands and Belgium occur. Most sightings are along the east and south coasts, with smaller numbers reported in the south-east, west and north. Found on coastal estuaries and mudflats, with recent reports from inland pastures.

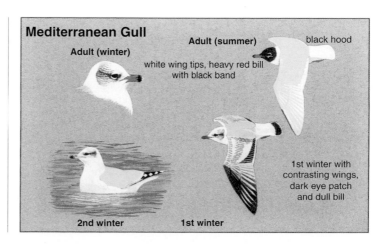

Mediterranean Gull

Adult (winter)

Adult (summer)

black hood

white wing tips, heavy red bill with black band

1st winter with contrasting wings, dark eye patch and dull bill

2nd winter

1st winter

127

Gulls

Black-headed Gull
Larus ridibundus Sléibhín

A small gull, with **summer adults** showing a chocolate-brown hood, white eye crescents, a dark red bill and legs, and white underparts. Upperparts pale grey with black-tipped primaries. In flight, wings show a white leading edge and contrasting dusky underprimaries. Tail white. **Winter adults** show a white head with a dark ear spot and brighter legs and bill. **1st winter birds** similar to adult winter, but wings show a pale brown carpal bar and a black secondary bar. Tail shows a dark band. Like adults, wings show a white leading edge and dusky under-primaries. **1st summers** can show a dark hood. **Juveniles** warm-buff on head, hindneck, sides of breast and upperparts.

Voice and Diet
An extremely noisy gull giving loud, harsh *kuarr* and short, abrupt *kwup* calls. Particularly noisy when nesting. Takes a wide range of food items, including fish, worms, molluscs, insects, seeds, berries and other plant material. Also found on rubbish tips feeding on waste and scraps. Can occasionally be seen disturbing prey by paddling vigorously in wet mud, sand or shallow pools. Will also hawk flying ants and insects in the air.

Bonaparte's Gull (rare)
Larus philadelphia

A dainty gull, smaller than Black-headed Gull. **Summer adults** show a blackish hood, white eye crescents, a black bill, pale red legs, and white underparts. Upperparts pale grey with black-tipped primaries. In flight, shows white leading edges but differs from Black-headed by showing a black edge to white underprimaries. Tail white. **Winter adults** show a white head, a neat, dark ear spot, and a grey wash on sides of breast and hindneck. **1st winter birds** as adult winter, but wings show a blackish-brown covert bar, a black secondary bar, a dark trailing edge to underwing, and white under-primaries. Tail shows a dark band. Dark bill shows a pale base. Legs pale flesh.

Voice and Diet
Rarely heard when found in Ireland, Bonaparte's Gull can occasionally give a harsh, chattering call. Feeds on a wide range of invertebrates, with a tendency to pick from the surface of the water in flight more frequently than Black-headed Gull.

Little Gull
Larus minutus

A tiny gull with rounded wings. **Winter adults** show a white head, black eye crescents and ear spot, a greyish crown and a blackish bill. Underparts white. Upperparts pale grey. In flight, shows pale grey wings, with white-tipped primaries and secondaries forming a white trailing edge, and contrasting blackish underwings. Legs red. **Summer adults** show a black hood and a pink flush on underparts. In flight, **1st winter birds** show a blackish covert bar and leading edge, forming a striking W upperwing pattern similar to 1st year Kittiwake. Underwing whitish. Head as winter adult. Bill blackish. Legs reddish. **2nd winters** as adults, but show black on wing tips and paler underwings.

Voice and Diet
Gives low-pitched, repeated *kek* and harsher, louder *ke-aa* calls. Feeds in a very Black Tern-like manner, flying buoyantly low over the water and dipping to pick food from the surface. Will occasionally hawk flying insects on the wing. Feeds on a variety of small fish, molluscs, worms and insects. Will take plant matter on occasions.

Habitat and Status

A very common widespread resident breeding species found in all counties. Largest breeding populations based in western and north-western regions. Nests in colonies on dunes, coastal islands, moorland pools, bogs and on freshwater lake islands. In winter, numbers increase with birds from Britain and northern Europe. Found in winter on inland pastures and ploughed fields, reservoirs, and on coastal estuaries and mudflats.

Black-headed Gull

Adult (winter)

Juvenile and Adult (summer)

1st winter

Habitat and Status

An extremely rare vagrant from North America which can occur at any time of the year. Some records refer to birds which have remained in one area for prolonged periods, or which have returned to the same area in consecutive years. While Bonaparte's Gull has occurred in all provinces, most records refer to areas from the north-east to the south-east. Usually found associating with gull flocks on mudflats, estuaries, harbours or on coastal lakes.

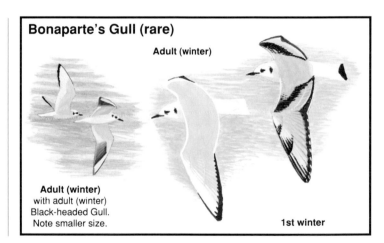

Bonaparte's Gull (rare)

Adult (winter)

Adult (winter) with adult (winter) Black-headed Gull. Note smaller size.

1st winter

Habitat and Status

A scarce but regular winter and passage visitor to coastal counties, with occasional inland sightings. Most records refer to winter months when birds are blown close inshore during bad weather. A regular movement is noted annually off southern and eastern coasts in spring and autumn. Found on coastal stretches, harbours and lagoons. Also frequents coastal lakes and marshes, and, occasionally, inland lakes. Breeds in colonies in central and eastern Europe.

Little Gull

2nd winter

1st winter

Adult (winter)

Adult winter
2nd winter
1st winter

Summer adults

Gulls

Kittiwake
Rissa tridactyla   Saidhbhéar

A slender gull with long, pointed wings. **Summer adults** show a white head, underparts, rump and tail. Upperparts dark grey. In flight, shows clear-cut black wing tips and dark grey coverts fading to a white trailing edge to secondaries and primaries. **Winter adults** show a greyish hindneck and rear crown, and a dark ear spot. Bill greenish-yellow. Legs dark. Eye dark with a red orbital ring. **1st year birds** show a greyish rear crown, a dark ear spot and a black half-collar on the hindneck. In flight, the greyish-white secondaries and inner primaries contrast with the black leading edges and covert bars which form a distinctive W on the wings. Forked tail shows a black terminal band. Bill dark.

Voice and Diet
The distinctive, loud, repeated *kitti-waak* calls are usually only heard at the breeding cliffs. Feeds on a wide range of fish, crustaceans, molluscs, worms and insects. Feeds by picking delicately from the surface in flight or when settled. Occasionally dives.

Sabine's Gull (rare)
Larus sabini

Summer adults show a blackish-grey hood, white underparts, rump and tail, and a yellow-tipped black bill. In flight, shows a black leading edge, dark grey coverts and mantle, and white inner primaries and secondaries forming a striking white triangle. Outer primaries show white tips. **Winter adults** show a dark smudge on the head. Legs dark. **1st years** show a grey-brown mantle extending onto head and sides of breast, grey-brown coverts contrasting with a black leading edge and white 'triangle', and a black terminal band to a forked tail. Bill dark. Immature Kittiwakes can resemble Sabine's Gulls but show a mostly white head, a black W on the wings and a black collar on the neck.

Voice and Diet
Although rarely heard in Ireland, Sabine's Gull can give a harsh, grating, tern-like call. Feeds on a wide range of crustaceans, molluscs, worms, small fish and insects. Feeds by picking off the surface of the water in flight. Will also feed actively on mudflats.

Ross's Gull (rare)
Rhodostethia rosea

A small gull with a wedge-shaped tail. **Winter adults** show a grey-washed crown, dark eye crescents and ear spots, a full or partial dark neck ring, and can show a pink flush on whitish underparts. In flight, slender, pale grey wings show a white trailing edge and a narrow black leading edge. Tail white. Legs reddish. Bill and eye dark. **Summer adults** show a black neck ring and deep pink underparts. **1st winter birds** show a greyish wash on the head, sides of breast and flanks, dark ear spots and eye crescents, and a black W across the wings formed by black leading edges and covert bars which contrast with a white innerwing and grey coverts. Tail shows a dark subterminal band. Flight buoyant.

Voice and Diet
Although rarely heard in Ireland, Ross's Gull can give high-pitched *ar-wo* and *cla* calls. Feeds by delicately picking morsels from the surface of the water in flight. Will also pick food from the water while swimming. Occasionally plunge-dives like Kittiwake. Feeds on small fish and invertebrates.

Habitat and Status

A common, widespread breeding species present in most coastal counties. During the breeding season, found on sheer cliffs, nesting on narrow ledges. Will occasionally build nests on sides of buildings, piers or on light standards. Spring and autumn movements are noted annually from the south-west. In winter, disperses to open oceans and seas, although small numbers are usually present in ports and harbours. Kittiwakes are more pelagic than other gull species and are rarely found inland.

Kittiwake
cliff-nester

1st winter

Adult (summer)

Habitat and Status

A rare but regular autumn passage vagrant from the high Arctic regions of Canada, Greenland and Spitzbergen. Usually seen following strong westerly winds when birds are recorded around the coast. Most records come from western and south-western regions. While most records refer to autumn, there have been several winter and spring reports. Sabine's Gulls are almost wholly pelagic, rarely being found inland. Can follow trawlers at sea.

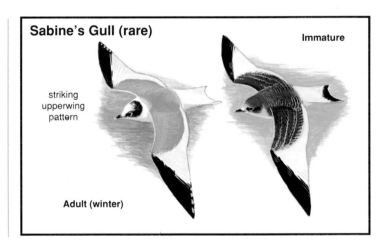

Sabine's Gull (rare)

Immature

striking
upperwing
pattern

Adult (winter)

Habitat and Status

An extremely rare winter vagrant from Arctic regions of Siberia, Canada and Greenland. Most records refer to adult birds. Usually found in coastal fishing ports and harbours, often associating with other gull species. While most records refer to January and February, Ross's Gulls have been recorded in spring.

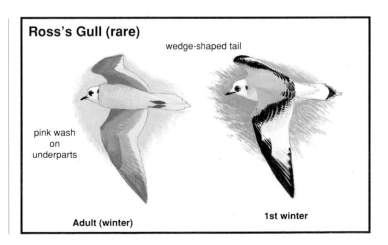

Ross's Gull (rare)

wedge-shaped tail

pink wash
on
underparts

Adult (winter)

1st winter

Terns

Black Tern
Chlidonias niger   Geabhróg dhubh

A small, compact species with short wings and a shallow fork to the tail. **Summer adults** are very distinctive with a black head and underparts, white undertail-coverts, grey upperwings, rump and tail, grey underwings, a black bill and dark legs. **Moulting adults** can show black mottling on underparts. **Immatures** show a diagnostic black shoulder patch, white underparts and a black ear covert and crown patch. Upperwing grey with a strong, conspicuous, black carpal bar. Mantle grey, slightly darker than grey rump and tail. Flight is bouncy with shallow, stiff wing beats. Feeds by picking from the surface while in flight. Does not plunge-dive like other tern species.

Voice and Diet
Not as vocal as other tern species, Black Tern can sometimes give a high-pitched, squeaky *kitt* call. Feeds on a wide variety of insects which are delicately picked from the surface of lakes and marshes.

White-winged Black Tern (rare)
Chlidonias leucopterus

A small, stocky tern with rounded wings, a shallow fork to the tail, and a black bill. **Summer adults** show a black head, mantle and underparts. Contrasting white upperwing shows dark outer primaries and inner secondaries. Underwing shows black coverts and grey flight feathers. Rump, tail and undertail white. **Adults in moult** can show black body and underwing mottling. Legs reddish. **Immatures** show a black ear covert and crown patch, white underparts, and pale wings with a thin carpal bar. A dark mantle contrasts with the wings and the white rump and tail. Lacks shoulder patches of immature Black Tern. Flies with stiff wing beats, picking from the surface of the water in flight.

Voice and Diet
Seldom heard in Ireland, White-winged Black Tern can occasionally give a high-pitched *kitt* call, similar to that of Black Tern. Feeds on a wide variety of insects which, like other marsh terns, are delicately picked from the surface of lakes and marshes.

Whiskered Tern (rare)
Chlidonias hybridus

A bulky tern with a shallow fork to a short tail and short, broad wings. **Summer adults** show a black cap, a white face which contrasts with blackish or dark grey underparts, and white undertail-coverts. Mantle, wings, rump and tail grey. Bill and legs blood-red. Structure, short broad wings and the shallow fork to the tail eliminate any confusion with Arctic Tern which can show very dark underparts. **Adults in moult** can show dark mottling on the underparts. **Immatures** show white underparts, a black ear covert and crown patch, and grey wings which can show brownish feathers on mantle and scapulars. Rump and tail grey. Bill blackish. Wing beats stiff. Feeds by surface-picking in flight.

Voice and Diet
Less vocal than other species of tern, but can give a harsh *ky-it* call on occasions. Like other species of marsh tern, feeds on a wide variety of insects which are skilfully picked from the surface of lakes and marshes.

Habitat and Status

A regular autumn passage migrant from continental Europe. Also recorded irregularly in spring. Successful breeding occurred on one occasion at Lough Erne, Co. Fermanagh, in 1967. Breeding was attempted at the same locality again in 1975 but the nest and eggs were abandoned. Found feeding over freshwater lakes, marshes and reservoirs. Usually found in coastal counties, but has also been reported at inland sites. Black Terns are also occasionally seen during seawatches.

Black Tern

Immature

Adult (winter)
dark overall, grey rump

Adult (summer)

Habitat and Status

A rare spring and autumn vagrant from eastern Europe, with most records referring to August and September. Usually found feeding over freshwater lakes, marshes and reservoirs. Most reports come from coastal counties, although this species has been recorded inland. On passage, can occur at coastal sites.

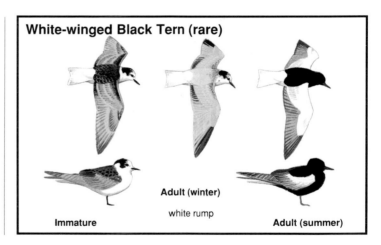

White-winged Black Tern (rare)

Immature

Adult (winter)
white rump

Adult (summer)

Habitat and Status

An extremely rare spring and autumn vagrant from southern and south-eastern Europe. Frequents freshwater lakes, marshes and reservoirs. Although usually found in coastal counties, Whiskered Tern has been recorded inland, with one bird spending time with a tern colony in Co. Tipperary. Seems to prefer deeper water than other marsh terns.

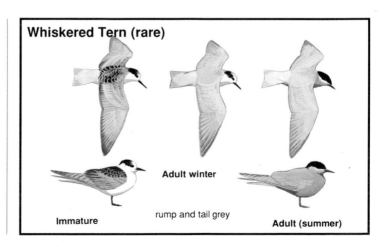

Whiskered Tern (rare)

Immature

Adult winter
rump and tail grey

Adult (summer)

Terns

Common Tern
Sterna hirundo   Geabhróg

An elegant species with a long, black-tipped red bill. **Adults** show a black crown and nape, white cheeks and underparts, and a pale grey mantle and wings. When perched, shows red legs and long wings which are equal to the tail length. Flies lazily on long wings, showing pale grey upperwings with a distinctive dark wedge on the mid-primary and dark outer primaries tips. Underwing silvery-grey with a broad, dark trailing edge on outer primaries. Rump and long tail white. **Juveniles** show a pale base to a dark bill, red legs, a white forehead and lores, and a brownish mantle with pale edges to feathers contrasting with a dark carpal bar. Shows dark grey secondaries and primaries in flight.

Voice and Diet
Gives loud, grating *kee-aaar* and *kiip* calls. Juveniles give hard, repeated *kik* calls. Feeds on a variety of small fish which are skilfully caught by diving from a height following a mid-air hover.

Arctic Tern
Sterna paradisaea   Geabhróg Artach

A dainty species with a shortish, blood-red bill. **Adults** show a rounded black crown and nape, white cheeks, whitish underparts which can show a dark greyish wash, and pale grey upperparts. When perched, shows short red legs and a wing length which is shorter than the long tail streamers. Flies with shallow, quick wing beats and shows a plain grey upperwing with no primary wedges. The underwing is pure white and shows a narrow, black trailing edge to the primaries. Rump and long tail white. **Juveniles** show an all dark bill, pale red legs, a white forehead and lores, a pale grey mantle and wings, and a faint carpal bar. Shows white primaries and secondaries in flight.

Voice and Diet
Gives a *kee-aar* call similar to Common Tern, although shorter and delivered in a less harsh manner. Can also give a whistling *kee-kee* call. Juveniles give harsh *kik-kik* calls. Feeds on a wide range of small fish and invertebrates which are caught by skilful dives following mid-air hovers.

Roseate Tern
Sterna dougallii   Geabhróg rósach

A delicate species with a dull red base to a blackish bill. **Adults** show a black crown and nape, white cheeks, white underparts which show a pink wash in summer, and whitish-grey upperparts. When perched, shows orange-red legs and long tail streamers extending well beyond the wings. Flies lazily and shows a very pale upperwing with grey outer primary wedges in late summer. White underwing lacks a dark trailing edge to the primaries. **Juveniles** show a black cap with a white loral spot, a black bill, and black legs. Mantle shows dark brown scalloping which gives a dark, saddle-like effect in flight. Wings pale with faint greyish primary tips and a faint carpal bar. Underwing whitish.

Voice and Diet
Gives a distinctive, high-pitched *tchu-ick* call, not unlike that of Spotted Redshank. Also gives loud, harsh *raaak* calls. Feeds on a variety of fish which are caught by diving from mid-air hovers.

Habitat and Status

A widespread summer visitor, with breeding populations present in most coastal and some inland counties. Winters off West Africa. Breeding takes place in colonies, usually on small coastal and lake islands. Nest an open scrape on the ground. Found along coastlines, inland rivers and lakes, and off headlands on passage.

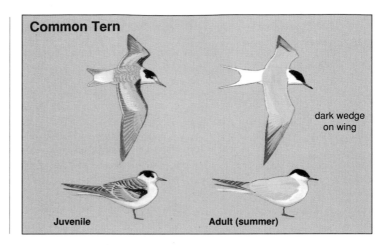

Common Tern

dark wedge on wing

Juvenile   Adult (summer)

Habitat and Status

A widespread summer visitor, with breeding taking place in most coastal counties. Tends to be more maritime in behaviour than Common Tern, although small numbers breed on inland lakes, often in mixed tern colonies. Found along coastal areas and large inland lakes. Nests on small islands and undisturbed shorelines, with the nest an open scrape on the ground. Wintering on the Antarctic pack ice, Arctic Terns are reputed to see more daylight than any other bird species.

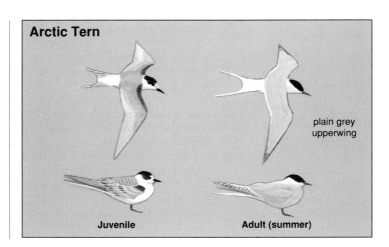

Arctic Tern

plain grey upperwing

Juvenile   Adult (summer)

Habitat and Status

A rare breeding species which, following a serious decline in recent decades, is now beginning to breed successfully in coastal counties in the east, south-east and north. Maritime in habitat, Roseate Terns breed in colonies on small islands or beaches, nesting in hollows or under vegetation. Winters off West Africa.

Roseate Tern

very pale upperwing, very long tail

Juvenile

Adult (summer)

Terns

Forster's Tern (rare)
Sterna forsteri

A slender, long-winged tern. **Summer adults** show a black tip to an orange bill, a black cap, white underparts, and pale grey upperparts. Resembles Common Tern, but in flight the upperwings show whitish inner primaries. Underwing pale grey with a dark leading edge and tips to outer primaries. Rump white. Tail pale grey with white edges. Most Irish records refer to **winter**, when adults show a black ear covert patch, a black bill and pale red legs. **Immatures** similar, but show a greyish wash on the nape, brownish markings on the coverts and tertials, and darker primaries. In winter, does not show a strong carpal bar. Flight is graceful with slow, shallow wing beats.

Voice and Diet
Can give a harsh, low-pitched *krarr* call and a repeated *kik* call which is delivered rapidly. Feeds on a wide range of small fish and invertebrates which are caught by skilful dives following mid-air hovers.

Sandwich Tern
Sterna sandvicensis   Geabhróg scothdhubh

A large, long-winged tern with a slender, yellow-tipped black bill and black legs. **Summer adults** show a black cap with a shaggy crest, white underparts and pale grey upperparts. In flight, shows slender pointed wings with dark wedges to primaries. Rump and short, forked tail white. **Winter adults** show a white forehead, with the black cap and shaggy crest confined to the rear of the crown. Some birds can show a white forehead by the end of the breeding season. **Juveniles** show a slender black bill, a black cap with white speckling on the forehead, and a scalloped mantle and carpal bar. The tertials and tail also show dark markings. Flight is strong and direct, with shallow wing beats.

Voice and Diet
Gives a distinctive, loud, grating *kirr-rik* call. Feeds on a variety of fish which, like other tern species, are caught by skilful dives following mid-air hovers. Will also take worms and molluscs.

Caspian Tern (rare)
Sterna caspia

A very large, heavy tern with a large, thick, orange-red bill showing a dark subterminal band and a pale tip, and longish black legs. **Adults** show a black cap and a short, shaggy crest. Underparts white. Upperparts pale grey, with long wings showing dark tips. In flight, shows a pale grey upperwing with slightly darker tips to the primaries. Underwing very distinctive, showing pale coverts, secondaries and inner primaries which contrast strongly with the blackish outer primaries. Rump white. Short white tail shows a shallow fork. In flight, appears gull-like, the wings being less pointed than in other tern species. Flies with slow, heavy, deliberate wing beats.

Voice and Diet
Rarely heard in Ireland, Caspian Terns can give a deep, loud, harsh *kraah* call. Feeds on a variety of fish which are caught by plunge-diving like other tern species. May also feed on the water in a gull-like manner. Occasionally known to take young birds and eggs.

33-36cm	**Forster's Tern**
38-44cm	**Sandwich Tern**
47-53cm	**Caspian Tern**

Habitat and Status

A very rare vagrant from North America. Most Irish records refer to the winter months in eastern and south-eastern counties. Found feeding on open offshore waters, bays and harbours. Can roost on mudflats or in harbours. Can be faithful to a wintering area, with some birds returning to the same region each year.

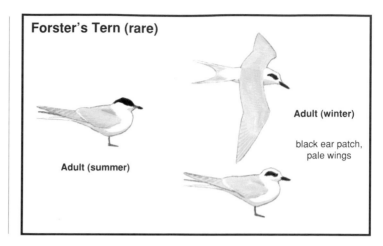

Forster's Tern (rare)

Adult (winter)

black ear patch, pale wings

Adult (summer)

Habitat and Status

A common summer visitor found breeding in noisy colonies on quiet, undisturbed islands or shingle beaches in most coastal regions. Small colonies are also present at some inland sites. Nests in a scrap on open ground or on grass. One of the earliest summer visitors to Ireland, Sandwich Terns can be seen along most coastal regions from early March onwards. Found on open coastal waters, bays and harbours. Most depart by September, wintering off the coast of West Africa.

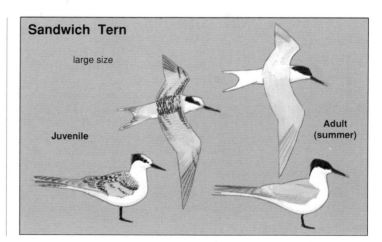

Sandwich Tern

large size

Juvenile

Adult (summer)

Habitat and Status

An extremely rare vagrant from southern and south-eastern Europe. Most records refer to late summer or early autumn. While most reports have been from coastal locations, one record refers to a bird found inland, on Lough Derravaragh, Co. Westmeath, in July 1984. Found on open coastal waters, brackish lagoons and freshwater lakes.

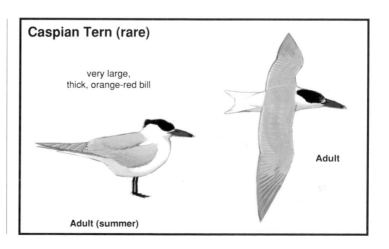

Caspian Tern (rare)

very large, thick, orange-red bill

Adult

Adult (summer)

Terns and Auks

Little Tern
Sterna albifrons   Geabhróg bheag
A tiny, long-winged tern with a black-tipped yellow bill and orange-yellow legs. **Adults** show a white forehead patch which contrasts strongly with a black loral stripe, crown and nape. Upperparts bluish-grey with long wings. Throat, neck and underparts white. In flight, the long wings show a dark leading edge to the primaries. Rump and short, forked tail white. **Immatures** show a dark, brownish bill, yellow-brown legs, a buff to white forehead and lores, a black streaked crown, and a blackish eye patch. Greyish upperparts show brown barring on the mantle and scapulars and, in flight, the wings show a complete dark leading edge. Flight appears bouncy with fast wing beats.

Voice and Diet
Little Terns are generally very noisy around the breeding grounds, giving loud, shrill *krii-ek* calls. Also gives a repeated, sharp *kitt* call and chattering *kirrik-kirrik-kirrik* calls. Feeds on a range of crustaceans and small fish by diving from mid-air hovers.

Guillemot
Uria aalge   Foracha
A slim auk with a dark, pointed bill and dark legs. **Summer adults** show a dark chocolate-brown head, throat, neck and upperparts, with a thin white line formed by white tips to the secondaries. Underparts white with dark flank streaking. The **Bridled forms** show a white eye-ring and a white eye-stripe from behind eye. **Winter adults** shows a white throat, neck and cheeks, with a thin black stripe obvious behind the eye. Crown, nape and hindneck chocolate-brown, forming a collar on sides of breast. In flight, shows white sides to rump, a short, rounded tail, a white trailing edge to secondaries, whitish underwing coverts and dark axillaries. **1st winter birds** show less flank streaking.

Voice and Diet
Extremely noisy at the breeding colonies, with birds making harsh, rolling *oarrr* calls. Away from the breeding grounds, rarely heard to call. Feeds by diving, swimming underwater by flapping the wings. Takes a variety of fish, marine worms, molluscs and crustaceans.

Razorbill
Alca torda   Crosán
A stocky auk with black legs and a dark, stubby bill showing a white band and a thin white line from the eye along the upper mandible. **Summer adults** show a black head, throat, neck and upperparts, with a thin white line formed by white tips to the secondaries. Pointed tail obvious when swimming. White underparts unstreaked. **Winter adults** show a white throat and neck, with white extending behind contrastingly black ear coverts. Crown, nape and hindneck black, forming a short collar on sides of breast. In flight, shows white sides to rump, a longish pointed tail, a white trailing edge to secondaries, and clean whitish underwing coverts. **1st winter birds** similar to winter adults.

Voice and Diet
At the breeding grounds, give low, weak, growling, whistling and grunting calls. Rarely heard away from the breeding colonies. Feeds by diving, swimming underwater by flapping the wings. Feeds on a wide variety of prey items, taking fish, marine worms, molluscs and crustaceans.

Habitat and Status

A summer visitor to most coastal counties except those in northern and north-eastern regions. Rarely found inland. Breeds in small colonies on shingle and sandy beaches, the nest consisting of a scrape in the ground. The eggs and chicks are perfectly camouflaged and difficult to see. Unfortunately, because of this, and their habit of nesting on beaches, Little Terns are prone to human disturbance.

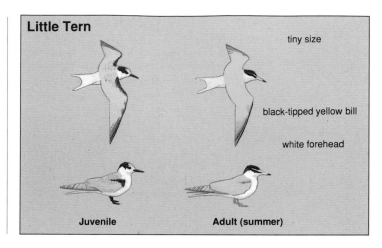

Little Tern

tiny size

black-tipped yellow bill

white forehead

Juvenile   Adult (summer)

Habitat and Status

A common breeding species, with large colonies present in summer on cliffs and islands on southern and western coastal sites. Small colonies also present in eastern and northern regions. Breeds on sheer cliffs, perching precariously on narrow ledges. Juveniles leave the cliffs before they can fly and are fed at sea by the parents. Guillemots winter off the Irish coast and are found in harbours, bays and offshore waters.

Guillemot

Bridled form

Adult (summer)

pointed bill, streaking on flanks

Winter

Habitat and Status

Common breeding species, present in summer among mixed auk colonies on cliffs and islands on southern and western coastal sites. Small colonies are also present in eastern and northern regions. Does not breed on narrow ledges on sheer cliffs, but nests in crevices, under boulders or on sheltered ledges. Juveniles leave the cliffs before they can fly and are fed at sea by the parents. Winters off the Irish coast and are found in harbours, bays and on offshore waters.

Razorbill

Adult (summer)

Winter

thick bill, clean flanks

Auks

Black Guillemot
Cepphus grylle   Foracha dhubh

A striking auk with bright red legs and a dark bill showing a bright red gape. **Summer adults** show an all sooty-black plumage with striking white wing covert patches. In flight, these patches are the most conspicuous feature. **Winter adults** show a very white head with a dark grey area around the eye, a greyish crown and nape, and white underparts with blackish streaking along the flanks. The blackish mantle shows broad white edges to feathers, giving a barred and mottled appearance. The tail and wings remain blackish in winter, the large white wing covert patches being less conspicuous. **Immatures** are similar to winter adults, but show dark barring on wing patches and duller legs.

Voice and Diet
On the breeding areas, can give loud, whistling *spiiiiieh* calls, which can finish in trilling notes. Feeds by diving for marine prey items including fish, worms, molluscs and crustaceans.

Puffin
Fratercula arctica   Puifín

An unmistakable, dumpy, black and white auk with a colourful bill. **Summer adults** show a triangular blue-grey, yellow and reddish-orange bill with a yellow-edged gape. Whitish face shows a greyish wash on the cheeks, and dark shading above eye extending as a thin rear eye-stripe. Crown, nape and neck black. Upperparts and tail black, contrasting with white underparts. Legs bright orange. Eye dark with a red eye-ring. In **winter**, shows a smaller, duller bill, a dusky, greyish face, and yellowish legs. **Immatures** show a stubbier bill, a dark greyish face and dusky rear flanks. Flies with rapid wing beats, showing a black upperwing and rump, and dark underwings. Stands in an upright posture.

Voice and Diet
A normally silent species. However, in the breeding burrows, Puffins can be heard to give low, moaning, growling *arr-ow-arr* calls. Feeds on a wide variety of marine life, taking fish, worms, molluscs and crustaceans. At breeding sites, can often be seen returning from feeding forays with up to ten sand-eels draped cross-wise in the bill.

Little Auk (rare)
Alle alle

A tiny, starling-sized, black and white auk with a stubby bill and a plump, rounded, neckless appearance. **In winter**, shows a black crown and cheeks, a white throat, and white extending up behind the ear coverts. A black, broken collar on the lower throat contrasts with the white underparts. Upperparts black with white tips to secondaries and short, obvious white lines on the scapulars. In **summer**, shows a completely black head and throat with a thin, white crescent above eye. Flies with rapid wing beats, showing a white trailing edge to secondaries and a dark underwing. Could be mistaken for immature Puffin in flight. Legs and eyes dark. Swims buoyantly. Can be very tame.

Voice and Diet
Little Auks are silent when found in Ireland, giving high, chattering calls only on the breeding grounds. Feeds by diving, taking a wide variety of small marine invertebrates and crustaceans.

Habitat and Status

A widespread resident species, present in all Irish coastal counties. Found on rocky cliffs and islands, nesting under boulders, in caves, holes and even using crevices in walls and piers. Breeding occurs in most regions where there is a suitable rocky coastline. In winter, found in sheltered bays and harbours, usually remaining close to shore.

Black Guillemot

striking white wing patches

Winter

Adult (summer)

red legs

Habitat and Status

A summer visitor to some Irish coastal counties, with the highest populations based at colonies in north-western, western and south-western regions. Smaller, more widely scattered colonies are present along north-eastern, eastern and south-eastern coasts. Found on grassy slopes on quiet, undisturbed islands and cliffs, nesting in old rabbit and shearwater burrows. In winter, most birds disperse to the Atlantic and are seldom seen offshore.

Puffin

Adult (summer)

bright bill and legs

Adult (winter)   duller bill and face

Habitat and Status

A rare but regular vagrant which breeds on high Arctic cliffs and winters in the North Atlantic. In autumn, birds can sometimes be seen passing southwards with other auk species. In winter can be seen on seawatches, but can also be found in sheltered harbours. In some years, following gales, wrecks can occur with birds blown along the coastline or occasionally far inland. Also reported in spring when small parties of birds have been seen.

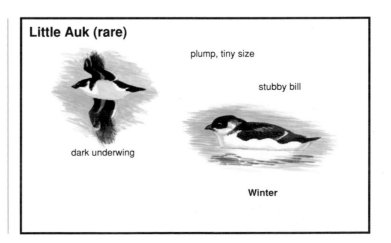

Little Auk (rare)

plump, tiny size

stubby bill

dark underwing

Winter

Doves and Pigeons

Rock Dove
Columba livia   Colm aille

The ancestor of the domestic and feral pigeon, wild Rock Doves are shy and unapproachable. **Adults** show a blue-grey head and neck with a green and purple neck patch. Breast, belly and undertail pale grey. Upperparts pale grey, with two broad black wingbars across tertials and secondaries, and median coverts. Primaries dark grey. Tail blue-grey with a darker terminal band. In flight, shows a small white rump contrasting with grey tail and upperparts, swept-back wings which show striking black bars on the secondaries and median coverts, and silvery-white underwings. Can glide on V-shaped wings. Eye reddish-orange. Bill grey with white cere. Legs pinkish. **Immatures** duller with brownish tones.

Voice and Diet
Gives a soft *coo-roo-coo* song occasionally associated with a strutting, fan-tailed display. Engages in display flights which consist of slow wing beats, wing claps and long glides on V-shaped wings. Feeds on a wide variety of grains, cereals and seeds. Will also take other plant material and occasionally molluscs.

(Feral Pigeon)
Columba livia

Feral Pigeons, the domesticated and tame city ancestor of the Rock Dove, come in an extremely wide variety of colours. Some appear identical to the wild Rock Dove, showing the blue-grey head with purple and green neck patches, two black wingbars on pale grey upperparts, pale grey underparts and white rumps. However, Feral Pigeons tend to show thicker bills. Other common varieties include cinnamon and white, grey and white, and dark blackish-grey. Some show a dark, chequered pattern on the upperparts, while others are almost wholly white. Eye reddish-orange. Legs pinkish-brown. Bill grey with whitish cere. Flies rapidly on swept-back wings. Frequently glides on V-shaped wings.

Voice and Diet
Like the Rock Dove, gives a soft *coo-roo-coo* song occasionally associated with a strutting, fan-tailed display. Also engages in display flights which consist of slow wing beats, wing claps and long glides on V-shaped wings. Feeds on a wide variety of seeds, grains and scraps which can be found in cities and towns.

Stock Dove
Columba oenas   Colm gorm

A stocky, compact species which lacks white in the plumage and shows a dark eye and a pale tip to a bright reddish bill. **Adults** show a blue-grey head with an emerald-green neck patch and a purple-tinged breast. Belly, undertail, mantle and rump blue-grey. Wings show two small blackish bars on the inner coverts and tertials. The secondaries, primaries and primary coverts are dark. Short, blue-grey tail shows a very broad, dark terminal band. In flight, appears compact, short-winged, and shows a distinctive dark border to edge and rear of wings. Underwings greyish. **Immatures** show a browner plumage, a darkish bill and lack the emerald-green neck patches.

Voice and Diet
Gives a deep, sharp *coo-ah* call which can be repeated. Engages in display flights which involve flying straight with slow, deep wing beats with wing claps and glides on shallow, V-shaped wings. Feeds on a wide variety of seeds, cereals and other plant material. Can also take small invertebrates.

Habitat and Status

A resident species, pure wild Rock Doves are now only found along the south-western, north-western and northern coasts. Found in small numbers on rocky sea cliffs, headlands and islands, feeding in coastal fields. Nests in caves and crevices in rocks.

Rock Dove

white cere

double wingbar, pale rump

Habitat and Status

An extremely common, tame, resident species present in all counties. Found in town and city parks and streets. Also found near mills, grain stores and farms. Feral Pigeons have adapted to living close to human habitation. Nests on ledges of buildings or in holes in ruined buildings and out-houses.

(Feral Pigeon)

similar to Rock Dove but in a wide variety of colours

Habitat and Status

A common, widespread resident species found in most counties, with the highest concentrations in eastern and south-eastern regions. Found on farmlands, woodlands, parks and along coastal cliffs and dune systems. Nests in holes in trees, old ruined buildings, cliff crevices and even rabbit burrows.

Stock Dove

emerald-green neck patch

dark rump

two small wingbars

Doves and Pigeons

Woodpigeon
Columba palumbus   Colm coille

A small-headed, plump bird with a longish tail. **Adults** show a grey-blue head, a green and purple gloss on the side of the neck, and conspicuous white neck patches. Breast purplish-brown with rest of underparts creamy greyish-white. Upperparts grey-brown, with a striking white line on bend of wing. Primary coverts and primaries dark. Rump and uppertail blue-grey with a dark terminal band to tail. Flies with swept-back wings, deep chest, head held high, showing white across middle of wing and greyish underwings. Eye yellowish. Bill orange-yellow with white cere. **Immatures** browner, lacking neck patches and showing dark eyes and duller bills. Flushes noisily with wing clatters.

Voice and Diet
Gives a muffled, rhythmic cooing song consisting of *cooo-coo, coo, coo-cu* delivered from a prominent perch. Engages in display flight which involves flying steeply upwards, wing clapping and gliding downwards. This display can be repeated several times. Feeds on a wide variety of seeds, cereals, leaves and other plant material. Can also take some invertebrates.

Collared Dove
Streptopelia decaocto   Fearán baicdhubh

A slim, pale, sandy-brown dove with a longish tail. **Adults** show a pinkish-brown head, with a conspicuous black and white neck collar. Breast pinkish-brown with belly and undertail pale sandy-brown. Upperparts greyish-brown, with a pale greyish bend on the wing and darker primaries. Rump and tail sandy-brown with white outer tips to tail. From below, shows a diagnostic undertail pattern of a very broad white outer band contrasting with dark inner undertail. In flight, shows rounded wings with pale grey middle, dark primaries and pale underwings. Eye dark reddish. Bill slim and dark. Legs pinkish-brown. **Immatures** lack the half-collar, appear duller and show pale edges to upperpart feathers.

Voice and Diet
Gives a deep, cooing song consisting of *coo-cooo-oo*, the emphasis being on the second syllable. In flight or when alarmed, gives a harsh, nasal *cwurr* call. Feeds on a wide variety of grain and seeds, also visiting bird tables to take any available scraps.

Turtle Dove
Streptopelia turtur   Fearán

A small, slender dove with a longish, graduated tail and boldly marked upperparts. **Adults** show a blue-grey head with black and white neck patches. Breast pinkish. Belly and undertail whitish. Mantle and rump grey-brown. Scapulars, lesser and median coverts, inner greater coverts and tertials rufous with black centres. Secondaries, greater and primary coverts pale greyish, contrasting with dark primaries. Tail greyish-brown with a white terminal band and a dark subterminal band. Undertail dark with a narrow white tip. In flight, shows pointed wings with greyish underwings. Eye and legs reddish-brown. Bill dark with reddish cere. **Immatures** duller and lack neck patches.

Voice and Diet
Gives a very distinctive, soft, purring *torr-r-r* song, delivered from a prominent perch. Feeds on a wide variety of seeds and grain.

Habitat and Status

A very common resident species present in all counties. Can be found in many habitats, including towns, cities, parks, gardens, farmlands, woodlands and open country. Will feed in flocks, often in association with other pigeons and doves. Nests in trees, hedges or on the ground.

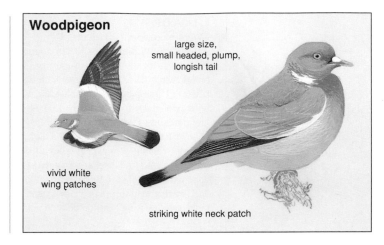

Woodpigeon

large size, small headed, plump, longish tail

vivid white wing patches

striking white neck patch

Habitat and Status

A widespread, common species which was first recorded in Ireland in 1959, breeding in that year in Dublin and Galway. Now found in all counties. Formerly an eastern European species, the range of Collared Dove began to expand westwards in the 1930s. By the 1970s, the species had reached Iceland. Found in towns, parks, gardens and farmlands, often seen in the vicinity of mills. Will also visit bird tables.

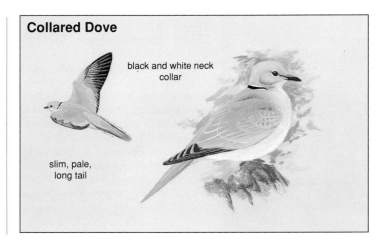

Collared Dove

black and white neck collar

slim, pale, long tail

Habitat and Status

A scarce passage migrant from continental Europe, found in spring and autumn. Some may over-summer and breeding has taken place on occasions. Most frequently found on passage on coastal headlands and islands, but can occur in open country with hedgerows and small woodlands. Nests in bushes and small trees.

Turtle Dove

black and white on tail

small, slender, boldly marked rufous upperparts

Cuckoos and Nightjar

Cuckoo
Cuculus canorus   Cuach

A long-tailed, parasitic species appearing hawk-like in flight. **Adults** show a bluish-grey head, throat and upper breast, while the white underparts show narrow, dark grey barring. Upperparts also bluish-grey, with slightly darker wings which can be held drooped. The long, graduated, dark grey tail shows white spotting. Pointed, dark bill shows a yellowish base. Eyes yellow with a dark pupil. Legs yellow. **Females** can show brownish tones to the upperparts and a buff wash on the breast. **Juveniles** show brownish upperparts with black barring, buffish-white underparts with dark barring, and distinctive white nape patches. Flies with rapid, shallow wing beats on pointed wings.

Voice and Diet
Males give the very distinctive, far-carrying *cuc-coo* call which is usually delivered from a prominent perch or on the wing. Females, though rarely heard, give long, bubbling, chuckling calls and repeated *wah-wah* calls. Feeds on a variety of insects and larvae. The female, when laying an egg in a nest of a foster parent, will usually remove an egg from that nest and eat it.

Nightjar
Caprimulgus europaeus   Tuirne lín

A distinctive, delicately camouflaged, crepuscular bird which flies with easy, buoyant wing beats interspersed with floating glides on raised wings. In flight, shows long wings and tail, a broad, flattened head and a very short wide-gaped bill. **Adult males** show a greyish-brown plumage with a complicated pattern of black, brown, buff and cream barring, mottling, spotting and streaking. In flight, males show white spots to the three outer primaries and white tips to the outer tail feathers. **Adult females** and **immatures** are similar, but lack the white wing spots and tail tips. During daylight hours, Nightjars sit still among ground vegetation or on low, horizontal branches.

Voice and Diet
The song of Nightjar is an unmistakable, rapid, rhythmical churring which rises and falls in pitch. The song can continue for long periods of time. In flight, gives a sharp *quu-ic* call. On the breeding grounds can also engage in loud wing-clapping displays. Feeds on a variety of insects which are caught on the wing.

Yellow-billed Cuckoo (rare)
Coccyzus americanus

A slim, secretive, long-tailed bird which shows a curved bill with a striking yellow lower mandible. **Adults** show a greyish crown and ear coverts, with greyish-brown upperparts contrasting with rufous wing patches. The wing patches are especially obvious in flight or with the wings drooped. The long, graduated, blackish tail shows bold white tips which are very striking from below. Underparts white. Shows a dark eye, a yellow orbital ring and greyish legs. **Immatures** similar, but show a dark grey tail with narrower, more diffuse white tips. Flies with fast, shallow wing beats. Can be easily overlooked, sitting still in deep cover or moving quietly through dense vegetation.

Voice and Diet
Yellow-billed Cuckoos are usually silent outside the breeding season and so are rarely heard in Ireland. Feeds on a variety of insects, but will eat berries and fruit in the autumn. Will feed in cover close to or on the ground.

Habitat and Status

A common summer visitor to all regions, usually arriving by mid-April. Adults depart by July, immatures in August and September. Found on farmlands, moorlands, woodland edges, sand-dunes and coastal islands and headlands. Infamous for laying eggs in other species' nests. The young Cuckoo, on hatching, will systematically remove all other eggs and chicks from the nest, thus receiving the full attention of the unfortunate foster parents.

Cuckoo

hawk-like flight

Adult

long tail, barred underparts

Juvenile

Habitat and Status

Formerly a widespread summer visitor, Nightjar is now a very rare breeding species and passage migrant. Small breeding populations are found most years in some south-western, western and midland counties, with occasional reports from northern and eastern regions. Frequents felled woodland and conifer plantations with open moorland areas. On passage, found on coastal headlands and islands, usually flushed from ground vegetation or trees.

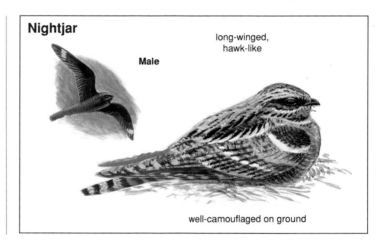

Nightjar

long-winged, hawk-like

Male

well-camouflaged on ground

Habitat and Status

An extremely rare autumn vagrant from North America. Most records refer to late September or October ,with reports from eastern, south-western, western and north-western coastal counties. Some reports also refer to birds either found dead or dying. Frequents areas of scrub or dense bushes, well-vegetated gardens, orchards and woodland edges. Usually keeps in deep cover.

Yellow-billed Cuckoo (rare)

rufous on wings

yellow on bill

long tail

Owls

Barn Owl
Tyto alba Scréachóg reilige

A distinctive species usually encountered as a ghostly white shape flying in the night. Can occasionally hunt at dusk when the delicate plumage can be seen. Shows black eyes set in a white, heart-shaped face. Crown, mantle, wings, rump and tail are orange-buff with varying amounts of grey speckling. Underparts white but can show a buff tinge. **Females** can show more speckling on the upperparts and fine dark spotting on the underparts. **Juveniles** similar to adults but often show tufts of down on the head, mantle and underparts. When perched, appears upright with a large head and longish legs. Flies with grace and ease, moving with slow, deep wing beats. Hovers with dangling legs when hunting.

Voice and Diet
Gives a very eerie, drawn-out screech, often delivered in flight. At the nest, both adults and young give loud snoring and hissing calls. Feeds by flying on rounded, silent wings, hovering and pouncing on prey. Will take small mammals like rats, mice and shrews. Will also feed on small birds and sometimes insects.

Long-eared Owl
Asio otus Ceann cait

A slim, upright, nocturnal species with striking long tufts on the head. A greyish-brown crown contrasts with an orangy face which shows pale eyebrows and striking black vertical lines from the tufts to the bill. Eyes bright orange. Pale buffish-white underparts show dark streaking to belly and onto flanks. Upperparts greyish-brown with fine barring and streaking. In flight, shows an orangy upperwing with mottling on the coverts, barring on the secondaries and primaries, and a distinctive orangy primary patch. Underwing white with fine barring on the tip and a dark carpal patch. Tail shows indistinct barring. In flight shows rounded wings. Flies with deep wing beats interspersed with glides.

Voice and Diet
In spring gives a very distinctive, low, muffled, repeated *oo* call. Can also give a variety of wheezes, barks and screams. One call resembles the *cwurr* call of Collared Dove. Young birds can give a far-carrying, squeaking call. During display flights engages in wing-clapping. Feeds on a wide range of small mammals, including mice, rats and shrews. Will also take birds and insects.

Short-eared Owl
Asio flammeus Ulchabhán réisc

A stocky owl usually seen hunting, roosting on the ground or perched on a post during daylight hours. A pale, sandy-buff crown shows two indistinct tufts, while a pale face shows bright yellow eyes set in black eye-rings. Dark streaking on pale buffish-white underparts usually confined to the breast, with faint flank streaking. Upperparts pale sandy-buff with dark, heavy blotching. In flight, shows a pale buff upperwing with heavy mottling on coverts, strong barring on primaries and secondaries, a white trailing edge, a dark carpal patch, and a striking pale primary patch. Underwing white with a solid dark tip and carpal patch. Tail strongly barred. Flies with slow, deep wing beats. Glides on raised wings.

Voice and Diet
Gives a shrill, barking *kwock* call. Can also give a low-pitched *bo-bo-bo* call near breeding areas. Will engage in flight displays involving wing-claps. Feeds on small mammals, including rats, mice and, where available, voles. Can also take small birds and will occasionally feed on insects.

Habitat and Status

A scarce but widely distributed resident breeding species. While present in most Irish counties, they are absent or in very low numbers in some parts of the west and north-west. Numbers seem to be declining, with birds absent from former breeding areas. Found near old buildings, ruins, farms, church towers, and even in towns and cities. Will also nest in hollows in trees. In winter can be found in woodlands. Hunts over fields and open ground.

Barn Owl

very pale in flight

heart-shaped face with dark eyes

Habitat and Status

A widespread but uncommon resident breeding species. Found in woodlands, favouring areas of pine or spruce. Nests in old crow or Magpie nests, old squirrel dreys and occasionally on the ground. On passage, found on coastal headlands and islands, roosting in small trees or in hedgerows. In the absence of such cover, passage birds may roost on the ground, leading to potential confusion with Short-eared Owl. Many birds seen on passage are probably migrants from the Continent.

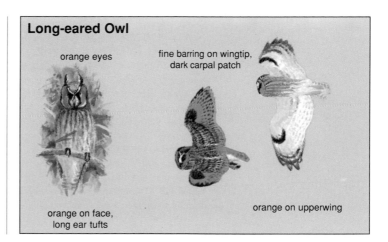

Long-eared Owl

orange eyes

fine barring on wingtip, dark carpal patch

orange on face, long ear tufts

orange on upperwing

Habitat and Status

A scarce, thinly-distributed passage and winter visitor to Ireland from Iceland, northern Europe, Scotland and northern England. Breeding has occurred in the west and south-west, with summering birds being recorded in other regions on occasions. Found on the ground or perched on posts close to rough vegetation, usually in coastal marshes or dunes. Also found in stubble fields, bogs and moorlands. Nests on the ground in heather, grass or gorse.

Short-eared Owl

solid dark wing tips, dark carpal patch

yellow eyes

short, indistinct ear tufts

149

Kingfisher, Bee-eater and Roller

Kingfisher
Alcedo atthis Cruidín

A small, brightly-coloured, short-winged bird with a long, dagger-like bill. **Adults** show a bright blue-green crown and moustachial stripe with pale barring and spotting. Nape dark blue-green. Dark loral stripe contrasts with bright orange-chestnut loral spot and ear coverts. Throat and neck patch white. Underparts bright orange-chestnut. Mantle to rump pale turquoise. Short green-blue wings show pale spotting on the scapulars and coverts. Short tail bright blue. Bill dark with an orange-red base, more extensive on females. **Immatures** greener with paler underparts. Legs orange-red. Eye dark. Flies rapidly with whirring wing beats, the bright turquoise mantle and rump being very conspicuous.

Voice and Diet
Gives a shrill, harsh *chee* or *chrii* call which often attracts attention. The song is seldom heard and consists of a short trill. Feeds on a wide variety of small fish and aquatic insects. Dives into the water from an overhanging branch or open perch, opening wings on impact.

Bee-eater (rare)
Merops apiaster

A brightly-coloured bird with a long, curved bill and long central tail feathers. **Adults** chestnut on crown and nape, with a white and blue forehead and supercilium, black lores and ear coverts, and a yellow throat with a thin black lower border. Underparts bright turquoise. Mantle pale chestnut. Scapulars pale yellow, lesser coverts greenish with chestnut secondaries, median and greater coverts. Primaries blue. Black tips to primaries and secondaries form a trailing edge to wings. Tail greenish-blue with long central feathers. **Immatures** similar, but show greenish upperparts and a shorter tail. Curved bill long and blackish. Eye brown. Flight graceful with rapid wing beats and glides.

Voice and Diet
Gives a very distinctive, bubbling, rolling, liquid *prruip* call which is repeated, loud and far-carrying. Occasionally, when feeding or passing high overhead, can be heard clearly but not seen. Feeds on a wide variety of large flying insects such as bees which are caught on the wing.

Roller (rare)
Coracias garrulus

A large, brightly-coloured bird with a thick, dark, pointed bill. **Summer adults** show a bright turquoise head, a black eye-stripe, a chestnut mantle, dark blue and turquoise wing coverts, and blackish primaries and secondaries. Breast, belly, flanks and undertail bright turquoise. Rump bluish. Tail dark greenish-blue with pale turquoise edges and black tips to outer feathers. **Winter adults** and **immatures** show a dull brownish-green head and breast, and a duller mantle. In flight, shows a dramatic wing pattern, with the dark blue leading edge and turquoise wing coverts contrasting strongly with the blackish primaries and secondaries. The undulating flight appears lazy.

Voice and Diet
Gives a deep, harsh, crow-like *krr-rak* call. Can also be heard to give chattering-type calls. Feeds in a shrike-like manner, swooping down on large insects from a prominent perch on trees, wires or fences.

Habitat and Status

A common resident bird found in all counties. Found along rivers, streams, on lakes, canals and marshes. In winter, can occur on coastal estuaries and bays, occasionally found feeding on channels on tidal marshes. Nests in excavated tunnels on banks of rivers, streams and canals.

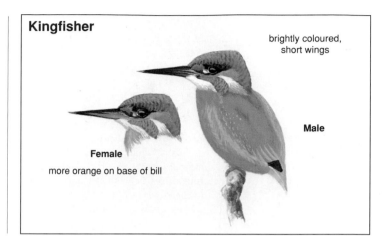

Kingfisher

brightly coloured, short wings

Male

Female
more orange on base of bill

Habitat and Status

An extremely rare spring and autumn vagrant from southern Europe. Found on open country, usually with scattered trees for perching. However, many sightings in Ireland refer to coastal headlands and islands.

Bee-eater (rare)

brightly coloured

Habitat and Status

An extremely rare passage vagrant from southern and central Europe. Found in open country with scattered trees, although when found in Ireland may be close to coastal areas or on islands and headlands.

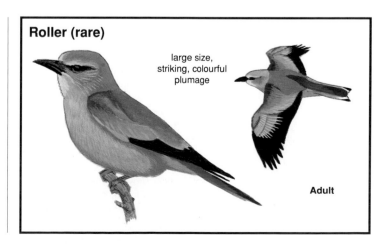

Roller (rare)

large size, striking, colourful plumage

Adult

Swallows and Martins

Swallow
Hirundo rustica   Fáinleog

A familiar summer visitor, easily recognised by the long tail streamers. **Adults** show a glossy bluish head, a dark red forehead and throat patch, and a dark bluish breast band. Lower breast, belly, flanks and undertail-coverts creamy white. Upperparts and rump dark glossy blue. Wings browner. The diagnostic tail shows elongated streamers. White subterminal patches on the central feathers form a distinctive white band on the undertail, and narrow white markings on the uppertail. Tail streamers longest on males. **Immatures** show shorter tail streamers, buffish throat and forehead patches, and a greyish-brown breast band. Flies with effortless swoops and glides. Short legs and bill dark.

Voice and Diet
Gives a high, tinkling *vitt* call, sometimes repeated. Song combines various twittering, warbling and trilling notes. Feeds on a wide variety of insects which are skilfully caught on the wing. Drinks on the wing by swooping low over streams and rivers and dipping the bill into the water.

House Martin
Delichon urbica   Gabhlán binne

A compact bird with a forked tail and a large, conspicuous white rump. **Adults** show a metallic dark blue head and upperparts. Throat, breast, belly, flanks and undertail pure white. Wings appear browner. Large white rump contrasts strongly with the dark upperparts and the dark, metallic blue forked tail which lacks the elongated tail streamers of Swallow. **Immatures** show a brownish wash on the sides of the breast, a dull brownish crown, brownish wings, and white tips to the tertials. In flight, shows a more triangular wing shape than Swallow. Flies with fluttering wing beats, interspersed with frequent glides and swoops. Bill short and dark. Legs and feet feathered white.

Voice and Diet
Gives a clear, hard *tchirrrip* call along with a sharp *tseep* when alarmed. Song consists of weak, chirruping, twittering notes, similar to but less varied than that of Swallow. Feeds on a wide variety of insects which are caught on the wing.

Red-rumped Swallow (rare)
Hirundo daurica

A stocky bird with long, broad tail streamers and a striking pale buff rump. **Adults** show a metallic blue crown, with a chestnut-buff nape and supercilium, and pale buff face. Mantle, scapulars and tertials metallic blue, with remainder of wings brownish. Underparts pale buff with thin streaking. In flight, shows a striking warm-to-pale-buff rump which can appear two-toned, and a long black tail with no white spots or markings. The upper- and undertail-coverts are also black, making the tail appear extremely long and broad-based. **Immatures** show a paler neck collar and rump, and shorter tails. Flies with fluttering wing beats and glides, similar to House Martin. Short bill and eye dark.

Voice and Diet
Gives a short, rasping *tschirrit* call which, on occasions, can resemble the chirruping call made by House Sparrows. Feeds on a wide variety of insects which are skilfully caught on the wing.

Habitat and Status

A very common summer visitor to all counties. Arrives from the wintering grounds in southern Africa by March or April. The nest is made of mud pellets and built under rafters, on ledges and under eaves of old sheds, barns, farm out-houses and porches. Can be very faithful to nest sites, returning year after year to the same location. Found on farmlands, in suburbs, and over lakes and rivers. Will roost in reed-beds.

Swallow

dark, glossy blue upperparts

long tail streamers

dark red throat

Habitat and Status

A very common summer visitor from wintering grounds in Africa. Arrives in March or April, leaves by mid-October, with a few records of birds seen during winter months. Found in towns, villages, farms and around cliffs. Nests in colonies. Builds a nest made of mud which is cupped under eaves of houses, bridges or on cliffs.

House Martin

conspicuous white rump

short, forked tail

Habitat and Status

An extremely rare spring and late autumn visitor from southern Europe. Usually found over open country, sometimes associating with Swallows. Occasionally seen feeding over marshes, lakes and rivers. In the autumn, most records refer to coastal islands and headlands.

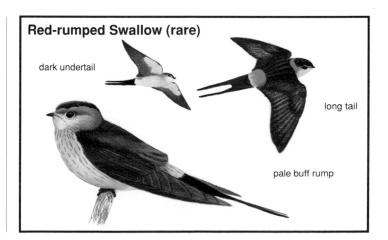

Red-rumped Swallow (rare)

dark undertail

long tail

pale buff rump

153

Martins and Swifts

Sand Martin
Riparia riparia   Gabhlán gainimh

A small brown and white martin with a short tail and a brown breast band. **Adults** show a dull brown crown, nape and ear coverts. Chin and throat are white, contrasting with a broad brown breast band. Lower breast, belly, flanks and undertail-coverts white. Mantle, wings and rump brown. Brown tail is short and shows a very shallow fork. **Immatures** show pale edges to wing and upperpart feathers, creating a scaly appearance. In flight shows brownish underwings. Flies with fluttering wing beats, gliding less frequently than Swallow. Highly gregarious, often seen in large flocks, occasionally associating with Swallows and House Martins. Short bill and eyes dark.

Voice and Diet
Gives a short, sharp, dry *tchrrip* call which can be repeated. Song is a weak, harsh twittering. Feeds on a wide variety of flying insects which are caught on the wing.

Swift
Apus apus   Gabhlán gaoithe

A large, agile, all-dark bird with long, scythe-like wings and a short, forked tail. **Adults** show a small, inconspicuous pale throat patch which can contrast with the sooty-brown head, upperparts and underparts. The sooty-brown tail is short and shows a deep fork which is not always obvious as the tail can be closed to a point. **Immatures** show a slightly larger throat patch and appear browner. Small bill, eye and legs dark. Flies on stiff wings with rapid wing beats and skilful glides. Highly adapted to an aerial life, eating, sleeping and mating on the wing, only perching during the breeding season. Highly gregarious, occasionally forming large, noisy flocks.

Voice and Diet
Gives a long, loud, shrill, piercing screech, often delivered during rapid aerial chases around rooftops. Takes a wide variety of flying insects which are caught on the wing. Feeds by flying with open mouth, swooping on prey items which can then be stored in the throat. This can give the throat a bulging appearance.

Alpine Swift (rare)
Apus melba

A very large, brown and white swift with long, broad-based, scythe-like wings and a short, forked tail which can appear pointed when closed. Head, upperparts, rump and tail brown, similar in tone to Sand Martin. A small white throat patch, which can be difficult to see on occasions, contrasts with a brown breast band. Striking white belly conspicuous against brownish flanks and undertail. Upperwing uniform brown, with underwing showing contrasting, darker lesser and median coverts. Flight appears more lazy than Swift, with longer wings producing slower wing beats. Partial albino Swifts may appear similar but large size, brown upperparts and slower flight of Alpine Swift eliminate confusion.

Voice and Diet
Rarely heard in Ireland, Alpine Swifts can give loud, trilling screeches, similar to but less piercing than the calls of Swift. Feeds on a wide variety of insects which are caught on the wing.

11-13cm	**Sand Martin**
16-18cm	**Swift**
20-23cm	**Alpine Swift**

Habitat and Status

A common summer visitor to all counties from wintering grounds in southern Africa. Sand Martins are subject to fluctuations in numbers, with the species suffering severe population crashes from time to time. Found in areas close to water. Nests in colonies, building tunnels in sand or earth faces. Will roost in reed-beds.

Sand Martin

- brown breast band
- short tail
- white throat

Habitat and Status

A very common passage and summer visitor, arriving in late April, leaving by August or early September. Found over towns, villages, cliffs and open country. Often found feeding over rivers, lakes and marshes. Nests in colonies in holes in eaves, under roof tiles, church towers and cliffs.

Swift

- long scythe-like wings
- dark plumage, paler throat

Habitat and Status

A very rare vagrant from southern Europe, recorded in Ireland between March and September. Usually seen singly, with some records referring to small parties. Highly aerial, birds can be found almost anywhere, with sightings over towns, lakes, marshes, rivers and at coastal headlands and islands.

Alpine Swift (rare)

- large size
- conspicuous white belly and throat

Hoopoe and Woodpeckers

Hoopoe (rare)
Upupa epops   Húpú

An exotic species with a bold plumage and a long, curved bill. Crown shows a long, pinkish-brown, black-tipped crest. This can be fanned, but is usually depressed, giving the head a hammer-like appearance. Apart from a thin, dark eye-stripe, the face, and the nape, throat, mantle and scapulars are pinkish-brown, contrasting with the bold black and white pattern of the wings. Breast pinkish-brown, fading to white on the belly, flanks and undertail. Tail black with a white central band. Flight appears lazy and undulating, the wings closing following each wing beat. In flight, the striking wing pattern and the boldly patterned rump are obvious. Feeds on the ground in a methodical fashion.

Voice and Diet
The distinctive, low *poo-poo-poo* song, from which the species derives its name, is rarely heard in Ireland. On occasions, gives a quiet, chattering alarm call. Feeds in a methodical manner, searching for a wide range of worms, larvae and insects which are either picked off the ground or probed for in soft earth or sand.

Great Spotted Woodpecker (rare)
Dendrocopos major   Mórchnagaire breac

A striking pied woodpecker with a thick, pointed, dark bill, a dark eye and dark legs. **Adult males** show a black crown contrasting with a pale forehead, white cheeks and red and white nape patches. A black moustachial stripe joins a black stripe from the lower nape and continues down side of neck. Lower nape and upperparts black, with large white or buff-fringed oval shoulder patches. Wings blackish with white barring. Throat and underparts white, with a bright red undertail extending up to lower belly. Tail black with white-notched outer feathers. **Females** do not show a red nape patch, while **immatures** show a reddish crown and thinner moustachial stripes. Flight is fast and undulating.

Voice and Diet
Gives a loud, explosive, far-carrying *kiick* call, usually in flight. The drumming, which lasts for approximately one second, is seldom heard in Ireland. Feeds on a wide range of insects and larvae which are picked from tree trunks. Will also feed on seeds and nuts in winter and has been known to visit bird tables for scraps. In spring and summer, will also take eggs and nestlings.

Wryneck (rare)
Jynx torquilla   Cam-mhuin

A shy species with a complex plumage pattern. A brownish central crown stripe extends down nape and onto brownish mantle. Sides of crown greyish, continuing down to form a greyish V on mantle. Brown eye-stripe extends down side of neck. Pale supercilium visible behind eye. Fine barring present on whitish chin and buffish throat. Underparts grey-buff, with dark barring and arrowhead markings. Brownish wings show black, white and grey barring and spots. Rump and long tail greyish, with fine barring and dark bands on tail. Short greyish, pointed bill. Legs brownish. Feet show two toes forward and two behind. Eye brownish with dark pupil. Flies with long glides on closed wings.

Voice and Diet
Wrynecks are silent on passage and so are not heard in Ireland. On the breeding grounds, the calls are shrill and falcon-like. Feeds chiefly on ants which are licked up from the ground, old walls or from tree trunks. When feeding on the ground, hops with raised tail but clings in a woodpecker-like fashion when feeding on tree trunks.

Habitat and Status

A scarce but annual vagrant from southern Europe. Hoopoes have been recorded in every month, but most reports refer to early spring, with a smaller passage noted in autumn. Can be found in a wide range of habitats, including farmland, rough coastal pastures, sand-dunes, parklands and gardens. On passage, occurs on coastal islands and headlands, with most reports originating from the south-east, south and south-west.

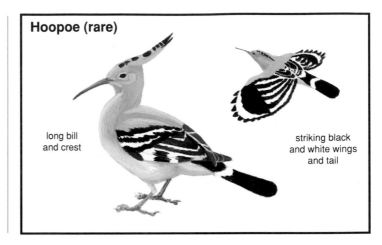

Hoopoe (rare)

long bill and crest

striking black and white wings and tail

Habitat and Status

Great Spotted Woodpecker was once a resident species in Ireland but is now a rare vagrant, usually found in winter. Most records probably refer to birds from northern Europe, where food shortages can result in large influxes into Great Britain and smaller arrivals into Ireland. Found in open woodland, parklands and occasionally gardens where they have been known to visit bird tables.

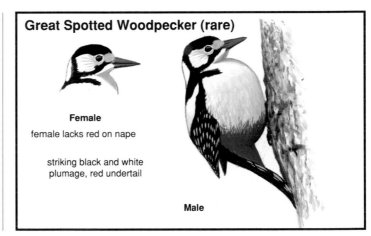

Great Spotted Woodpecker (rare)

Female

female lacks red on nape

striking black and white plumage, red undertail

Male

Habitat and Status

A rare but regular passage vagrant from northern and central Europe, with most records referring to autumn. In spring, small numbers can occur and these may refer to populations from southern Europe. On passage, found on coastal headlands and islands, usually discovered feeding along old walls, on pastures or in gardens and hedgerows with trees.

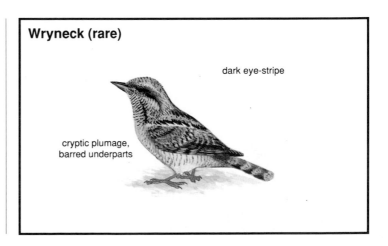

Wryneck (rare)

dark eye-stripe

cryptic plumage, barred underparts

Larks

Skylark
Alauda arvensis   Fuiseog

A large lark, more often heard than seen. **Adults** show a long streaked crest which can be raised or flattened on the head. Face appears plain, with a creamy supercilium, a thin eye-stripe behind the eye and thin streaking on brownish cheeks. Heavy streaking on the buffish breast extends as a malar stripe onto the paler throat. Underparts creamy. Upperparts brown with heavy blackish streaking. Unlike Short-toed Lark, the primaries extend past the tertials. Flight undulating, showing a white trailing edge to the wings and white edges to the long tail. Pale bill thick and pointed. Legs pinkish and show a very long hindclaw. **Immatures** appear scaly and show a very short crest.

Voice and Diet
The familiar song is delivered from high in the air, the bird hovering in a stationary position. Also sings during fluttery display flights. Will occasionally sing from posts or trees. The song consists of a continuous, strong, loud, clear warbling. When flushed or in flight, gives a rippling *chirrup* call. Feeds on a variety of seeds, worms, insects and larvae.

Short-toed Lark (rare)
Calandrella brachydactyla

A dumpy, sparrow-like lark with a thick, pale bill and pale legs. Streaked, sandy-brown crown shows a short crest but usually appears round-headed. Creamy supercilium contrasts with a dark eye-stripe behind the eye. Cheeks show faint streaking. Upperparts pale sandy-brown with thin streaking. The dark-centred median coverts show as a bar across the wing. Unlike Skylark, the primaries are hidden under the long tertials. Underparts whitish, with dark patches on the sides of the breast which may continue as a broken malar stripe. Can show faint streaking across centre of breast. In flight, shows a plain wing with no white trailing edge, and thin white edges to the tail.

Voice and Diet
Gives a short, hard, chirruping *tchi-tchirrp* call which can recall House Martin or House Sparrow. Can also give a clear, drawn-out *tee-oo* call. Feeds on a variety of seeds. Will also take small insects.

Shore Lark (rare)
Eremophila alpestris

A large lark which occurs as a rare winter visitor. Shows a striking pale yellowish face, a black loral stripe which extends onto the cheeks, and a dark eye-stripe behind eye. Rear of cheeks yellowish. Pale yellow supercilium is bordered above by a black stripe which forms short horns on the side of the head. The pale yellowish throat contrasts with a black gorget across the breast. Nape and upperparts pinkish-brown with dark streaking. Underparts whitish and almost unstreaked. In **summer**, the horns are longer, the face and throat yellower, and the cheeks blacker. In flight, shows plain wings and a dark tail with thin, white outer edges. Short bill greyish. Legs dark.

Voice and Diet
Gives a thin, pipit-like *tsee-tsi* call and a whistling-type *tsiu* call. Feeds on the ground, sometimes keeping company with larks and buntings. Feeds on a variety of seeds and insects. May also take small molluscs and crustaceans.

Habitat and Status

A common and formerly widespread, resident breeding species. Has shown a recent population decrease due to habitat loss and changes. Found in a variety of habitats, including moorlands, farmlands, rough pastures, sand-dunes and saltmarshes. Also found on stubble fields in autumn. Nests on the ground in grass or crops. Very inconspicuous on the ground, flushing at the last moment. When returning to the nest, lands some distance away before running, in cover, to the nest site.

Skylark

conspicuous crest — thick, pale bill — a large lark

Habitat and Status

A rare but frequent passage vagrant from southern Europe. Most records refer to autumn, with some birds occurring in spring. Usually found on coastal headlands and islands, frequenting areas of open sandy or stony ground, short grassy areas, stubble fields or dry saltmarshes. Can be quite confiding.

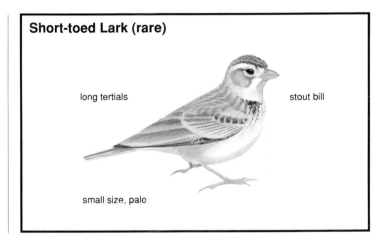

Short-toed Lark (rare)

long tertials — stout bill — small size, pale

Habitat and Status

An extremely rare vagrant from northern Europe. While most records refer to winter, this species has also occurred in spring. Most sightings have involved single birds, although pairs have been recorded, while three were reported present in Co. Kerry during the 1976–77 winter. Found at coastal locations, feeding on stony, shingle or sandy beaches. Also found on stubble fields and waste ground close to the coast. Can associate with larks, buntings and even finches.

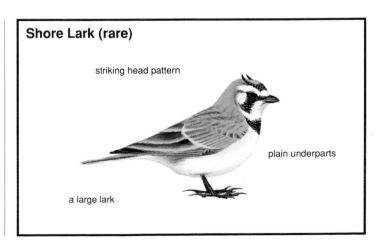

Shore Lark (rare)

striking head pattern — plain underparts — a large lark

Pipits

Meadow Pipit
Anthus pratensis   Riabhóg mhóna

A small, active pipit, similar to Tree Pipit. In **spring**, shows brownish upperparts with dark streaking on the back and crown. A pale supercilium fades behind the eye while a faint eye-stripe behind the eye gives the face a plain appearance. Underparts show a dark malar stripe and heavy streaking which, unlike Tree Pipit, extends as heavy flank streaking. Whitish underparts show a faint buffish wash on the breast. In **autumn**, the upperparts show greenish tones with a strong yellowish-buff wash on the breast and flanks. Rump unstreaked. Tail brownish with white outer feathers. Legs pinkish-orange with a long hindclaw. Bill pale, thin and pointed with a dark tip.

Voice and Diet
Gives a very distinctive, thin *tsip* call which can be repeated and delivered in a strong manner. On the breeding grounds, rises in a display flight, giving a series of accelerated, thin, tinkling, piping notes before descending in a parachuting glide, giving a rapid, musical trill. Feeds on a wide range of small insects, larvae and worms. Will also take seeds in the autumn. Feeds in a busy, active manner.

Tree Pipit (rare)
Anthus trivialis   Riabhóg choille

A small pipit, similar to, but slightly larger and more slender than, Meadow Pipit. In **spring**, shows greenish upperparts with streaking on the back and crown. Supercilium strong behind the eye, contrasting with a prominent eye-stripe which may extend across the lores. Underparts show a dark malar stripe and strong, defined streaking which, unlike Meadow Pipit, becomes thin and faint on the flanks. Underparts show a strong orangy-buff wash on the breast which contrasts with a whiter belly. In **autumn**, the breast can show a creamy wash. Rump unstreaked. Tail shows white outer feathers. Legs pinkish with a short hindclaw. Thick, pale bill shows a dark tip.

Voice and Diet
Gives a very distinctive, buzzing *tzeep* call which can be repeated and delivered in a strong manner. Can also give a very soft *sip* call. The song, while rarely heard in Ireland, is very distinctive, being a very loud, accelerated series of Chaffinch-like notes which are given during a rising display flight, usually launched from a tree or bush. The song finishes with repeated *seea* notes during a descending, parachuting glide. Feeds in a slow, methodical manner, taking a wide range of small insects.

Red-throated Pipit (rare)
Anthus cervinus

A small pipit which resembles a colder-plumaged Meadow Pipit. Usually found in autumn. Cold, brownish upperparts show two pale tramlines which contrast with dark streaking. Unlike Meadow Pipit, the rump is streaked. A pale supercilium contrasts with a streaked crown and a thin, dark eye-stripe. Creamy or whitish underparts show a dark malar stripe which ends as a large dark spot on the sides of the neck as it meets the heavy streaking on the breast. Streaking extends onto flanks as two thick lines. Tail appears shortish in flight and shows white outer feathers. In **summer**, shows a brick-red throat and face. Legs pale pinkish. Bill pale, thin and pointed with a dark tip.

Voice and Diet
Gives a very striking, distinctive call which is often the only way of identifying birds in flight. The call consists of a long, thin *ptseeeee* note which fades and trails off at the end. The call may resemble the flight call given by Redwing. Feeds on a variety of insects, worms and larvae. Will also take seeds on occasions.

Habitat and Status

A very common, widespread breeding species found in all counties. Frequents areas of open country, being present on rough pastures, farmland, sand-dunes, moorlands and bogs. Also found on offshore islands. Nests in a shallow depression on the ground, usually in heavy cover of grass tussocks or heather. In winter, the higher ground is abandoned and many move to more southern counties. In autumn, a good passage movement is noted annually in the south-west.

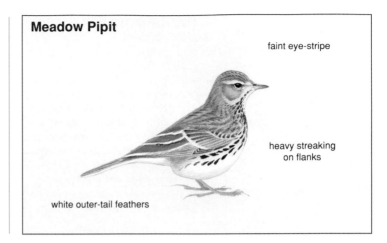

Meadow Pipit

faint eye-stripe

heavy streaking on flanks

white outer-tail feathers

Habitat and Status

A scarce but annual spring and autumn passage migrant from Britain and Europe. Most records refer to the south-east and south-west. Also recorded on several occasions at inland sites. May be a very rare breeding species, with several records of singing birds at suitable locations during summer months. Tends to perch on trees more than Meadow Pipit but, when seen in Ireland, is usually found feeding with other pipits on open, rough pastures and farmland on coastal islands and headlands.

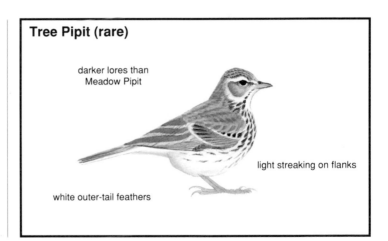

Tree Pipit (rare)

darker lores than Meadow Pipit

light streaking on flanks

white outer-tail feathers

Habitat and Status

A very rare passage vagrant from northern Europe and Scandinavia. Most reports refer to autumn, with very few spring records. Most records are from the south-east and south-west. Found on passage on coastal headlands and islands, feeding on open rough pastures and farmland. Will also perch readily on small trees, bushes and shrubs. Freely associates with other pipits and the distinctive call is often the first and, sometimes only, indication of the bird's presence.

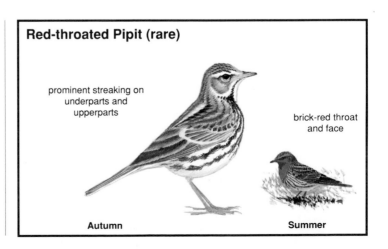

Red-throated Pipit (rare)

prominent streaking on underparts and upperparts

brick-red throat and face

Autumn

Summer

161

Pipits

Olive-backed Pipit (rare)
Anthus hodgsoni

A small pipit similar to Tree Pipit. Upperparts olive-green, appearing plain at a distance, but showing very faint streaking. Crown olive-green with faint streaking. Facial pattern very striking, showing a strong, pale supercilium which contrasts with a dark lateral crown stripe and a thin, dark eye-stripe. The rear of the ear coverts show a whitish teardrop-shaped spot, while the lower rear border is dark. Whitish underparts show a dark malar stripe and heavy streaking which becomes thinner and fainter on the flanks. Rump olive-green and unstreaked. Tail shows white outer feathers. Legs pale pinkish. Pale bill pointed. When perched or feeding, persistently wags the tail.

Voice and Diet
The thin, hoarse *tseep* call is very similar to that of Tree Pipit, but is usually shorter, more hoarse and less buzzing. The call notes can be given twice to form a double-noted call. Feeds on a wide variety of insects.

Rock Pipit
Anthus petrosus   Riabhóg chladaigh

A rather drab pipit, slightly larger and taller than Meadow Pipit. Upperparts dull olive-grey with dark streaking and showing inconspicuous, creamy-buff wingbars. Shows a faint, pale supercilium and a thin, dark eye-stripe which highlights a narrow, pale eye-ring. Ear coverts show a dark lower border. Dull creamy underparts show a dark malar stripe and heavy brown streaking on the breast and flanks. This heavy streaking may even extend onto the paler belly. In flight appears long-winged. Unlike other pipits, the darkish tail shows creamy or buffish outer feathers. Long, dagger-like bill is pale with a dark tip. Legs appear blackish but, when seen well, show a dull pinkish hue.

Voice and Diet
Gives a loud, full, harsh *pseep* call. Song is similar to that of Meadow Pipit but is a louder, more musical series of accelerated notes given during a rising display flight. The song finishes with a loud, strong trill given while descending during a parachuting glide. Feeds on a wide variety of small insects and worms. Also feeds on a variety of prey items found along the coast, including sandhoppers and molluscs. May feed on seeds on occasions.

Water Pipit (rare)
Anthus spinoletta   Riabhóg uisce

A timid pipit, similar to Rock Pipit but showing a more contrasting plumage. In **winter**, shows plain greyish-brown upperparts with faint streaking and contrasting white wingbars and edges to the tertials. Greyish-brown crown shows dark streaking and contrasts with a white supercilium which tapers to a point towards the nape. Underparts whitish, with dark streaking on the breast becoming faint on the flanks. Unlike Rock Pipit, the tail shows white outer feathers. **In summer**, shows a bluish-grey head, a white supercilium and whitish underparts with a pale pink wash on the breast and faint streaking on the flanks. Pale, pointed bill shows a dark tip. Legs dark.

Voice and Diet
Gives a *fist* call which is similar to that of Rock Pipit but sounds thinner and shorter. Feeds on a wide range of insects, larvae and worms. Will occasionally take seeds.

Habitat and Status

An extremely rare vagrant from north-eastern Russia and Asia. Usually found in late autumn, with one winter record. All reports refer to the south-west and south-east. Usually found on rough pastures, farmlands and gardens on coastal headlands and islands. The winter record refers to a bird feeding in an area of waste ground close to a housing estate in Cobh, Co. Cork.

Olive-backed Pipit (rare)

faint streaking on upperparts

distinctive head pattern

heavily streaked underparts

Habitat and Status

A common, resident breeding species found in all coastal counties. Rarely found inland. Frequents areas of rocky coastline and islands, occasionally occurring on mudflats and estuaries in winter. Nests in holes or crevices in rocks or cliffs. While numbers peak at some locations in autumn, this is not due to a strong passage movement but rather reflects a population increase due to recently fledged, immature birds.

Rock Pipit

drab plumage

faint supercilium

dark legs

Habitat and Status

A rare passage and winter visitor from Europe. Most records refer to winter, with several records in spring and early summer. Found on flooded fields, marshes, watercress beds, saltmarshes, or along the fringes of small lakes, usually close to or at coastal locations. Not approachable, flushing at a good distance and flying high before landing again even farther away. Most records refer to eastern and south-eastern counties.

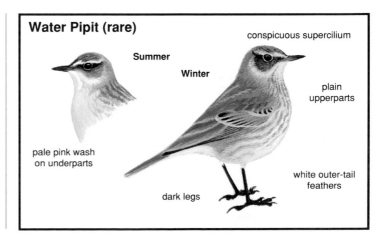

Water Pipit (rare)

Summer

Winter

conspicuous supercilium

plain upperparts

pale pink wash on underparts

dark legs

white outer-tail feathers

Pipits and Wagtails

Richard's Pipit (rare)
Anthus novaeseelandiae

A large, bulky pipit with a thick, thrush-like bill. Upperparts brownish with heavy, dark streaking and dark centres to wing feathers. Nape and crown streaked. Broad, creamy supercilium contrasts with a dark eye-stripe behind the eye. Unlike Tawny Pipit, the lores are pale. Ear coverts appear pale-centred and show a dark moustachial stripe. A thick, dark malar stripe ends with a large dark spot where it meets the diffuse streaking on the breast. Underparts warm-buff, especially on the flanks. Long, dark tail shows white outer feathers and can recall Reed Bunting. Pale, thick bill shows a dark tip. Long orangy legs show a long hindclaw. Has a tendency to hover before perching.

Voice and Diet

Gives a very distinctive, sharp *schreep* call which is delivered in an explosive manner. Feeds on a variety of insects, worms, larvae and seeds.

Tawny Pipit (rare)
Anthus campestris

A large, slender, wagtail-like, pale, sandy pipit. Sandy upperparts, nape and crown lack, or show, faint streaking. Dark centres to median coverts create a striking bar on the plain wing. A very pale supercilium contrasts with a dark eye-stripe. Unlike Richard's Pipit, the lores are dark. Ear coverts sandy with a dark moustachial stripe. A thin, darkish malar stripe fades into faint streaking on the breast. Can lack breast streaking. Underparts creamy. Long tail shows creamy-buff outer feathers. Shows a pale, thin bill. Long, orangy legs show a short hindclaw. Could be confused with immature Yellow Wagtail which shows blackish legs.

Voice and Diet

Gives a soft, drawn-out, wagtail-like *tseeup* call. Can also give a loud, harsh, sparrow-like *chirrup* call. Feeds on a variety of insects, larvae and worms.

Yellow Wagtail
Motacilla flava   Glasóg bhui

A slender, long-tailed species with a thin, pointed, dark bill and dark legs. **Spring males** show bright yellow underparts, throat and supercilium which contrast with a yellow-green crown, ear coverts and upperparts. Dark wings show two narrow white bars and thin white edges to the tertials. Rump greenish. Tail dark with white outer feathers. **Females** show brownish-green upperparts with a pale, yellow-washed supercilium, throat and breast. **Immatures** similar to females with a pale supercilium and chin, and can show a dark malar stripe and breast band. **Blue-headed**, **Ashy-headed** and **Grey-headed** races occasionally occur and show distinctive head patterns.

Voice and Diet

Gives a very distinctive, thin, musical *tsweep* call which is given both on the ground when feeding or in flight. Can also give a short, warbling song which consists of simple, thin *tsip-tsip* notes. The song can be given in flight or from a perch. Feeds on a wide range of small insects and larvae. Can often be found associating with cattle, flitting suddenly into the air to catch insects disturbed by the feeding animals.

Habitat and Status

A rare but regular vagrant from Siberia. Most records refer to late autumn, with occasional winter records. Usually found on rough pastures, short turf and farmland on coastal headlands and islands. Also has a tendency to feed in very long grass and could be easily overlooked. Most Irish records refer to southern counties.

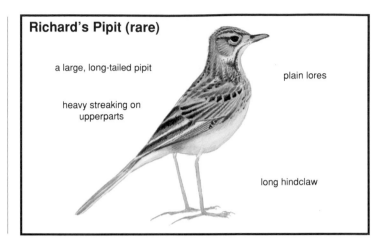

Richard's Pipit (rare)

a large, long-tailed pipit

plain lores

heavy streaking on upperparts

long hindclaw

Habitat and Status

A rare spring and autumn passage vagrant from southern Europe. Most records refer to southern counties. Found feeding on short grass, rough pastures and farmlands, usually on coastal headlands and islands. Has also been recorded on open, sandy areas and short turf close to coastal locations.

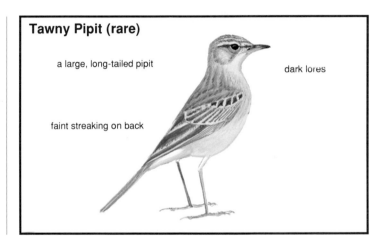

Tawny Pipit (rare)

a large, long-tailed pipit

dark lores

faint streaking on back

Habitat and Status

A scarce but regular spring and autumn passage migrant occurring annually. Also a rare breeding species with proved, or suspected, breeding taking place in several counties in recent years. On passage, found at coastal locations, feeding in rough pastures, marshes and short turf. In summer, frequents lowland rough pastures, farmlands, marshes and wet meadows. Nests on the ground in cover of grass tussocks or crops. Other races are scarce to rare vagrants.

Yellow Wagtail

Blue-headed

Ashy-headed

Grey-headed

Female

Male

dark legs

Wagtails

Grey Wagtail
Motacilla cinerea   Glasóg liath

A bright bird with a long, constantly wagging tail. **Summer males** show a grey head and mantle, a white supercilium, a black throat and white sub-moustachial stripes. Wings darker, with white-edged tertials. Tail black with white edges. Rump bright yellowish-green. Breast, undertail and centre of belly bright yellow. Flanks white. **Females** differ by showing a white throat, buffish supercilium, greenish ear coverts and paler breast. **Winter males** similar to females, but show a buff-yellow breast. **Immatures** similar to winter adults, but upperparts greyish-brown. Legs pinkish. Bill thin and dark. Appears slim and long-tailed in flight, with a white wingbar and a dark underwing covert bar.

Voice and Diet
Gives a sharp, abrupt, loud *stzit* or *stzitzi* call. Song consists of a twittering, trilling warble. Feeds on a wide variety of insects which are caught among stones. Will also take molluscs and sandhoppers.

Pied Wagtail
Motacilla alba yarrellii   Glasóg shráide

A black and white bird with a long, constantly wagging tail. **Summer males** show a white face and forehead, with a black crown and nape meeting a black bib. Back, wings and rump black. Wings show white bars and white-edged tertials. Tail black with white outer edges. Underparts white with dark grey flanks. **Summer females** show a blackish-grey back. **Winter adults** show a white throat, a black, crescent-shaped breast band and a blackish-grey back. **Juveniles** show a brownish-grey crown and back, a black rump, a buff-tinged face and throat, a messy breast band and greyish flanks. **1st winter** birds similar to winter adults, but show greyish upperparts. Legs and thin, pointed bill black.

Voice and Diet
Gives a loud, shrill *tchissick* call with an abrupt *tchik* call given in alarm. Song consists of twitters and warbles. Feeds in an active, fast manner, taking a wide variety of insects and seeds.

(White Wagtail)
Motacilla alba alba   Glasóg bhán

A black, grey and white bird with a long, constantly wagging tail. **Summer males** show a white face and forehead, with a black crown and nape which do not meet the black bib. Back ash-grey, contrasting with crown and blackish wings which show white bars and white-edged tertials. Greyish rump contrasts with black, white-edged tail. Underparts white with clean flanks. On **summer females**, grey of back extends onto nape. **Winter adults** differ by showing a white throat and a black, crescent-shaped breast band. **Immatures** show a grey crown, back and rump, paler wings with fainter bars, a thin, messy breast band and clean flanks. Can show pale yellow tones to face and throat. Legs and bill black.

Voice and Diet
White Wagtails give the same calls as those of Pied Wagtail, with a loud, shrill *tchissick* call given in flight and an abrupt *tchik* call given in alarm. Rarely heard in song in Ireland. Feeds in the same active, fast manner as Pied Wagtail, taking a wide variety of insects and seeds.

Habitat and Status

A common, widespread, resident species, with small passage movements noted in the autumn. Found in all counties, usually along fast-moving rivers and streams. Can also occur in cities, feeding along dockland areas and around park ponds. Nests in holes or on ledges under bridges, walls or old buildings close to or over water.

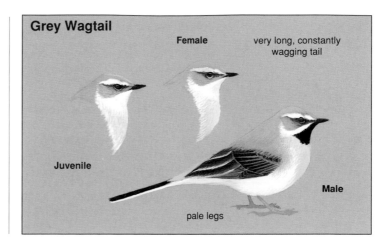

Habitat and Status

A very common, widespread, resident species found in all counties. In autumn, birds from Scotland and northern England may occur on passage. Found in a wide range of habitats, including towns, gardens, farms and shorelines. In winter, can occasionally be found roosting in large colonies in city centres. Nests in holes in walls, banks, out-houses, rocks or under stones or plants.

Habitat and Status

This race of Pied Wagtail is an uncommon spring and autumn passage migrant from Iceland and continental Europe. Found in open country at coastal headlands, islands, shorelines, lagoons and coastal wetlands and lakes. Occasionally associates with Pied Wagtail flocks. In spring, most records refer to northern and north-western coasts, with the south and south-east recording the highest numbers in autumn. Along the east coast is considered scarce at all times.

Dunnock, Robin and Bluethroat

Dunnock
Prunella modularis   Donnóg

A small, rather drab, grey and brown bird with a dark, slender, pointed bill. **Adults** show a grey head with brownish crown and ear coverts. Mantle rufous-brown with blackish streaks. The rufous-brown wings show dark centres to the feathers, adding to the streaked appearance of the upperparts. Rump and tail greyish-brown. The breast, belly, flanks and undertail are grey, with brown streaking present on the flanks. Eye deep reddish-brown. **Immatures** show a browner head with a white throat, dark streaking on buffish breast and flanks, and less rufous upperparts. Usually seen singly, feeding near cover. Moves with a shuffling gait, twitching the wings on occasions.

Voice and Diet
Gives a high, piping *tseep* call. The song is a hurried, high, pleasant, broken jingle. Sings from a prominent perch. Feeds on a variety of small insects and seeds. Will visit bird tables, but usually prefers to feed on the ground below them, taking scraps that might have fallen.

Robin
Erithacus rubecula   Spideog

A familiar, cheeky, rotund bird with a bright orange-red breast. **Adults** unmistakable, with an olive-brown crown, nape and upperparts. The lores, ear coverts and breast are bright orange-red, with a grey border from behind eye to the sides of the breast. Belly and undertail white. **Juvenile** birds show a brownish head and wings, with the mantle, face and breast strongly barred. **Immatures** are similar to adults, but have pale tips to greater coverts showing as a narrow wingbar. Eye appears large and rounded. Bill dark, thin and pointed. Legs thin and blackish. Hops along the ground, frequently pausing in an upright stance with flicks of the tail and wings. A highly territorial species, usually solitary.

Voice and Diet
Gives a sharp, harsh *tic* or *tic-tic* call which can be repeated. Also gives softer *tsiip* and *tsee* calls. Song is a variety of short, high, liquid warbling phrases. Feeds on a wide selection of small insects, worms and also seeds. Will frequently visit bird tables.

Bluethroat (rare)
Luscinia svecica

Males and females of this skulking, Robin-like bird show a brownish crown, nape and ear coverts, a whitish supercilium, a dark coronal stripe, and brownish upperparts and tail with rufous patches on the base of the tail. Underparts whitish. **Adult males**, however, show a bright blue throat and breast with a red or white central patch (depending on the race), and a black, white and rufous lower border. **Females** show whitish sub-moustachial stripes, a buff-white throat and breast which can show blue and chestnut tones, and a black malar stripe meeting a broken black breast band. **Immatures** resemble females. Pointed bill dark. Eye dark. Has a Robin-like stance, with drooped wings and cocked tail.

Voice and Diet
Gives a sharp *tac* call and can also be heard to give a softer *wheet* call. Feeds in a chat-like fashion, taking a wide variety of small insects, berries and seeds.

Habitat and Status

A very common, widespread, resident species. Found in areas with good cover and undergrowth. Present in towns and cities, being found in parks and gardens. In country areas, found along hedgerows and woodland fringes. Nests in dense cover in bushes and small trees.

Dunnock

dull grey and brown plumage

brown streaking on flanks

Habitat and Status

A very common and widespread resident species found in all counties. In spring and autumn, some vagrants from continental Europe may occur in Ireland. Found in gardens, parks, hedgerows and woodlands. Nests in holes in walls, trees, in ivy or on ledges. Occasionally found nesting in most unusual places such as tin cans or watering cans.

Robin

unstreaked upperparts

conspicuous orange-red face and breast

Habitat and Status

A very rare spring and autumn passage vagrant from northern and central Europe. Both races have been recorded, the Red-spotted being from northern Europe and the White-spotted from central Europe. Very skulking on passage, seeking deep cover and undergrowth. Usually found on coastal islands and headlands in Ireland.

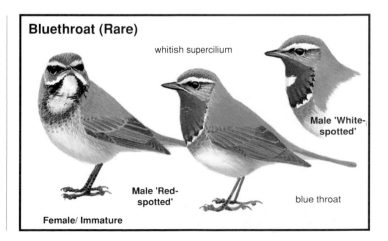

Bluethroat (Rare)

whitish supercilium

Male 'White-spotted'

Male 'Red-spotted'

blue throat

Female/ Immature

Redstarts and Nightingale

Black Redstart

Phoenicurus ochruros Earrdheargan dubh

A dark bird which shows a conspicuous, bright orange-red tail and rump in flight. **Winter adult males** have a blackish-grey crown, nape and mantle, with blackish wings showing white patches. Cheeks and throat blackish, extending onto breast. Belly and undertail pale greyish. In **summer**, the upperparts, the throat and the breast are black. **Females** are greyish-brown on upperparts and on underparts from the chin to the belly. Undertail paler. **Immatures** similar to adult females. In all plumages, the rump and tail are orange-red with dark central tail feathers. The tail can sometimes be flicked. Bill thin, dark and pointed. Legs blackish. Dark eye shows a very thin eye-ring.

Voice and Diet
The scratchy, hissing song of Black Redstart is rarely heard in Ireland. Usually silent on passage, wintering birds can occasionally give a short, soft *tsit* call. Feeds on a wide range of insects. Will also take berries.

Redstart

Phoenicurus phoenicurus Earrdheargán

A slim bird which shows a striking orange-red tail and rump in flight. **Summer males** show a black throat and ear coverts, a white forehead and supercilium, orange-red underparts and a blue-grey crown, nape and mantle. Undertail pale. Wings brownish. **Autumn** and **1st winter males** show pale mottling on underparts and throat, with immatures being browner above with an obscure supercilium. **Adult females** are warm brown above and creamy-buff below, usually with a white chin. Can show a peach wash on breast and flanks. **Immature females** similar. All plumages show an orange-red rump and tail with dark central tail feathers. Eye dark with a pale eye-ring. Thin, pointed bill dark. Legs dark.

Voice and Diet
Gives a Willow Warbler-like *hooweet* call, occasionally preceded by *tchuc* calls. The song consists of hurried warbling notes and twitters, and ends weakly. The song can recall a mixture between Chaffinch and Robin. Feeds on a wide variety of insects. Will also take berries.

Nightingale (rare)

Luscinia megarhynchos Filiméala

A sturdy, rather plain, skulking species with a deep chestnut-red, rounded tail. **Adults** show a warm brown crown, nape and upperparts, with slightly paler ear coverts. The longish wings can occasionally be drooped, emphasising the chestnut-red tail which can be held cocked. Underparts buff-brown with a whitish throat and belly. Can occasionally show a greyish wash along the flanks. **Immatures** show pale tips to greater coverts and tertials. The dark eye is conspicuous in the plain face and shows a white eye-ring. The pointed bill is horn-coloured. Legs brownish. An extremely skulking species, moving and feeding in deep cover. Resembles Robin in flight and when on the ground.

Voice and Diet
As Nightingale is only a passage vagrant, the beautiful, rich song for which this species is renowned has only been heard once in Ireland, in Co. Kildare in May 1955. On passage can give loud *tac* calls. Can also be heard to give *weet* calls on occasions. Feeds on a wide variety of insects, worms and larvae. Will also take berries.

Habitat and Status

An uncommon but regular spring and autumn passage migrant from central Europe. Each year, small numbers over-winter. Unlike Redstart, prefers open areas. Found on fields, rocky beaches, around power stations and old ruined buildings. Wintering birds are usually found at coastal locations. Tends to perch prominently on open rocks, walls or even on the top of buildings.

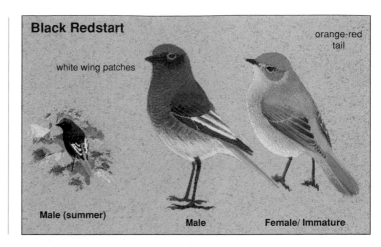

Black Redstart

white wing patches

orange-red tail

Male (summer)

Male

Female/ Immature

Habitat and Status

A very rare breeding species, and an uncommon but regular spring and autumn migrant. In summer, occurs in mature deciduous woodland, with most breeding records referring to eastern counties. Breeding has also been recorded in the north, north-west and south-west. Nests in holes in trees or old walls. On migration, can be found in gardens and areas with good cover on coastal headlands and islands.

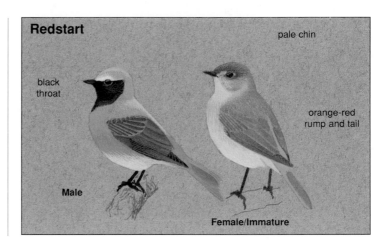

Redstart

pale chin

black throat

orange-red rump and tail

Male

Female/Immature

Habitat and Status

An extremely rare spring and autumn passage vagrant from Europe. With the exception of one bird found in song in Co. Kildare in 1955, most records refer to coastal islands in the south-east and south-west. A skulking species, Nightingales are found in areas of dense cover in gardens, in bramble patches or along hedgerows.

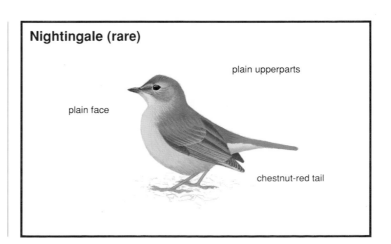

Nightingale (rare)

plain upperparts

plain face

chestnut-red tail

Chats

Whinchat
Saxicola rubetra   Caislín aitinn

A striking species, with **summer males** showing a blackish crown and ear coverts, a white supercilium and dark-streaked brownish upperparts and rump. Wings dark with white inner wing coverts and primary coverts. Underparts buff, with a white border to cheeks and a whitish belly and undertail. **Females** show a brown crown and cheeks, a creamy supercilium, and paler buff breast and flanks which can show spotting. Upperparts fawn, with white tips to dark-centred feathers. Wings show a small white covert patch and a pale tertial panel. **Autumn males** and **immatures** similar to females. In all plumages, the short tail shows white or buffish-white patches on the base. Pointed bill, eye and legs dark.

Voice and Diet
Gives short, sharp *stic-stic* or *tu-stic-stic* calls, which can be repeated. Can also give a low churring-type call. The song is a brief, twittering, variable warble. Feeds on a wide variety of insects, larvae, worms and spiders which are taken both on the ground and from plants.

Stonechat
Saxicola torquata   Caislín cloch

A smart species, with **summer males** showing a black head and throat, a reddish-orange breast and striking white neck patches. Belly and undertail whitish. Mantle blackish with brown streaking. Wings dark with white inner covert patches. Rump whitish with dark streaking. Tail dark. In **winter**, shows buffish tips to upperpart feathers, mottling on throat and a duller breast. **Adult females** show a brown head and throat, a faint supercilium, pale sides to neck, and streaked, brown upperparts with white wing patches. Breast reddish-buff. **Immatures** similar. Eye, bill and legs dark. **Siberian races** show an unstreaked white or pale rump, females and immatures showing a pale plumage and a white throat.

Voice and Diet
Gives sharp, repeated *tsack-tsack* or *weet-tsack-tsack* calls which sound like stones clicked together. Song consists of a variety of repeated, high-pitched phrases which are delivered from a prominent perch or during a song flight. Song may recall that of Dunnock. Feeds on a wide variety of insects, larvae and worms. Also takes seeds on occasions.

Wheatear
Oenanthe oenanthe   Clochrán

An upright species with a white rump and a black inverted T on a short white tail. **Summer males** show a greyish crown and mantle, a white supercilium, and a black eye mask with white lower cheeks. Wings blackish. Breast buffish. Belly and undertail white. **Autumn males** show brownish-grey upperparts and buff-edged wing feathers. **Adult females** show a brownish mask, a creamy supercilium, brownish-grey upperparts, brownish wings and a buffish breast. **Autumn females** show browner upperparts and buff-edged wing feathers. **Immatures** have brownish upperparts, a creamy or whitish supercilium, buff-edged wing feathers and sandy-buff underparts. Eye, pointed bill and legs dark.

Voice and Diet
Gives harsh *chack* or *weet-chack* calls. Song consists of harsh chack-type phrases combined with whistles, warbles and wheezing notes. Song can be delivered from a perch or during a display flight. Feeds on a wide range of insects.

Habitat and Status

A regular spring and autumn passage migrant along eastern and southern coastal counties. Also a summer visitor, breeding in many counties, usually at sites away from the coast. Frequents areas of rough pasture, mountain valleys, young conifer plantations and bogland edges. On passage, found on rough pastures and open areas along the coast. Nests in grass tussocks or bracken, occasionally at the base of a bush or small tree.

Whinchat

striking white supercilium

Male

Female

Autumn

Habitat and Status

A common resident species found in most counties. Frequents rough pasture, young forestry plantations and mountain valleys, usually in areas with gorse, heather or bracken. In winter, moves to low-lying areas and coastal locations. A small number also migrate to Europe in autumn. Nests in gorse or in thick cover. The rare Siberian Stonechat is an extremely rare autumn vagrant, found on coastal headlands and islands.

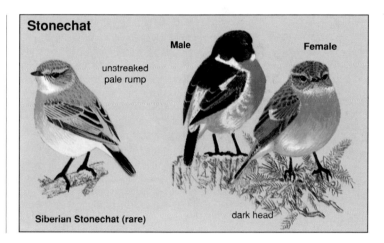

Stonechat

Male

Female

unstreaked pale rump

Siberian Stonechat (rare)

dark head

Habitat and Status

A common summer visitor and passage migrant. Wheatears are often the first migrants to return to Ireland in spring, some birds arriving in early March. Found on mountains, moorlands and at coastal locations. Frequents areas of low grass, rough pastures and dunes, where they feed on open ground or perch prominently on rocks or fences. Nests in holes in walls, scree, rocks or even old rabbit burrows. On passage, found along coastal shingle banks, beaches, islands and headlands.

Wheatear

striking tail pattern

Male

Female

Thrushes

Blackbird

Turdus merula   Céirseach

The striking **male** shows an all black plumage which contrasts with a bright orange-yellow bill and yellow eye-ring. The **female** is dull brown with a pale throat and slightly paler underparts which can often show indistinct spotting. The bill of the female is dark with a dull yellowish base. **Immature females** are slightly paler than adults. **Immature males** are dark blackish-brown with paler underparts, and differ from adult males by lacking an orange bill and yellow eye-ring. The wings are short and do not show pale edges, this being a very useful feature to identify semi-albinistic birds which can appear very similar to Ring Ouzel. Runs along ground, frequently pausing with tail and head in the air.

Voice and Diet
Blackbirds are highly excitable birds and give loud, strong *chuck, chuck* alarm calls which usually end in an excited screech. In flight, can give a *tsee* call, thinner than that of Redwing. Song is loud and fluty, with a variety of melodic notes, usually delivered from a prominent perch. Feeds on worms, slugs, snails, insects, as well as berries and fallen fruit such as apples.

Ring Ouzel

Turdus torquatus   Lon creige

A shy, long-winged and more streamlined bird than the Blackbird with a conspicuous white crescent-shaped patch on the breast. **Males** are black, with silvery edges to the wing feathers, long primaries and a pure white breast patch. The shorter, thicker bill is lemon-yellow in colour. Males also lack the yellow eye-ring of male Blackbird. **Females** are dark blackish-brown and show a duller breast patch and bill. **Immatures** are dark brown and lack the white breast patch, although this can appear as a pale brownish patch on some young males. Best separated from immature Blackbirds by silvery-white edges to the wing feathers, clearly visible even in flight, and by the long primaries.

Voice and Diet
Can give a loud, harsh, hollow, chattering *chak-chak* call. The song is a series of lonely piping notes, often finished with a chatter. Usually sings from a prominent perch. Feeds on worms, slugs, insects, seeds and berries.

Fieldfare

Turdus pilaris   Sacán

A large, striking thrush with contrasting upperparts and heavily spotted underparts. Head and nape grey with a thin pale supercilium. Shows a blackish eye-stripe, a dark border to the ear coverts, and blackish centres to the crown feathers. Mantle chestnut-brown, with brown wings showing dark centres to the tertials and primaries. Rump grey, contrasting strongly with the black tail. Throat white with dark malar stripe and spotting. Breast yellow-buff with very heavy inverted arrowhead spotting, fading onto whitish flanks and belly. Bill pale yellow with a dark tip. Eye and legs blackish. In flight shows a whitish underwing. Usually seen in large, mixed thrush flocks.

Voice and Diet
In flight gives a soft *tsee*, similar to but not as drawn-out as Redwing. Also gives a harsh, chattering *chik-chak-chak* call. Feeds on insects, worms, slugs and berries as well as windfall fruit.

Habitat and Status

A very familiar, common bird of gardens, towns, farmlands and woodlands. Usually solitary or in pairs, Blackbirds are highly territorial and will engage in noisy disputes with neighbours. Nests in bushes and hedgerows as well as in trees, old walls and out-houses.

Blackbird

black plumage, orange-yellow bill and eye-ring

brown with pale throat

Male   **Female**

Habitat and Status

An uncommon bird of mountainous regions, often found on areas of scree and replacing Blackbird at higher altitudes. Nests in grass on steep, rocky outcrops. A summer visitor from southern Europe and North Africa, usually arriving in early spring and departing throughout the autumn, with some birds seen as late as November. On migration, occurs in fields and along hedgerows on coastal islands and headlands. In general, a shy, retiring bird.

Ring Ouzel

lemon-yellow bill

Male

white breast crescent

long wings

Female

Habitat and Status

A common winter visitor from Scandinavia and northern Europe, arriving in late autumn/early winter and departing in early spring. Found on open fields and open woodlands, moving in large flocks which often include Redwings. During hard weather will visit town gardens to feed on berry bushes. On migration, found along hedgerows and in fields on coastal islands and headlands.

Fieldfare

grey rump and head, black tail, brown back

heavily marked underparts

Thrushes

Song Thrush
Turdus philomelos   Smólach

A small, shy thrush with warm brown upperparts and heavily spotted underparts. The black eye is not conspicuous in the warm yellow-buff face. Ear coverts spotted and bordered by spots. The spotting on the throat forms a malar stripe. Breast and flanks yellow-buff with arrowhead spotting, heaviest on the breast. Crown, nape and mantle warm brown, with wings and tail the same tone. Therefore, the upperparts appear uniform and lack the contrasts of Mistle Thrush. **Young birds** similar to adults, but show pale spotting on the mantle. In flight shows an orange-red underwing. Bill brownish, with the base of the lower mandible yellow-brown. Legs pale. Rarely seen in flocks.

Voice and Diet
Can give a soft *tsip* call, often heard in flight. When alarmed, gives a sharp *chi-chip-chip* call. The song is loud and wandering, consisting of sharp, melodic notes. The diagnostic feature of the song is that each phrase is repeated twice. Feeds on worms, slugs, insects and berries. Also feeds on snails by smashing the shells on a favourite stone. Broken snail shells close to such an anvil stone are often a good indication of the presence of a Song Thrush.

Mistle Thrush
Turdus viscivorus   Liatráisc

A large, pot-bellied thrush with heavy spotting on the underparts, and long wings and tail. Large black eye conspicuous in a rather pale face. Shows a dark ear covert border and dark spots on a pale throat. Breast and flanks pale buff with heavy, broad, wedge-shaped spotting. Crown, nape and mantle greyish-brown with contrasting wings due to white tips on median and greater coverts and dark centres to the tertials and primaries. Long tail greyish-brown but with diagnostic white tips to the outer-tail feathers. In flight, shows a whitish underwing. **Juveniles** similar, but show pale edges to upperpart feathers. Legs pale. Bill horn-coloured.

Voice and Diet
When alarmed gives a diagnostic rattling *prrr-rr-rr-rr* call which is repeated continuously. This sounds very like the rattles that were once carried by football supporters. The song is quite Blackbird-like, but with the melodic phrases uttered in a faster and sharper tone. Usually sings from a prominent perch. Feeds on insects, worms, fruit and berries. Is also known to take nestlings occasionally.

Redwing
Turdus iliacus   Deargán sneachta

A striking, dark brown thrush with a white supercilium, heavy underpart streaking, and a bright red flash on the flanks. Crown and nape dark brown with broad white supercilium and sub-moustachial stripe. Ear coverts brown. Mantle, tail and wings uniform dark brown, with **immatures** showing pale tips to greater coverts and tertials. Underparts creamy white, with heavy breast streaking extending onto throat as a malar stripe, and fading onto flanks. The most striking feature is the bright red patch on the flanks. In flight shows a reddish under-wing. Eye dark. Legs pale. Bill dark with a yellow base. Usually seen in large, mixed thrush flocks.

Voice and Diet
The call is a soft, long *tseep*, often repeated and which can be heard at night as flocks pass overhead on migration. Can also give a sharp *chich-up* call. Feeds on berries, insects, worms and slugs.

Habitat and Status

A common bird found in gardens, parks and woodlands. In recent years, breeding numbers appear to have decreased slightly. In winter, the population increases with the arrival of birds from Scotland and northern England. A shy thrush, preferring areas of dense cover. Nests in trees or hedges and occasionally in old out-houses.

Song Thrush

warm brown upperparts

yellow-buff face

heavily spotted underparts

Habitat and Status

A common resident bird of parks, woodlands, graveyards, towns and mountains. Less shy than Song Thrush, being found on more open ground away from cover. Nests in trees. In late summer and winter, they are highly gregarious, often forming quite large flocks. In hard weather can visit gardens.

Mistle Thrush

a large thrush

pale face

wings contrast with upperparts

heavily spotted underparts

white tips to outer tail

Habitat and Status

A common winter visitor to all counties, arriving in late autumn and departing by early spring. Found in large flocks on open fields or open woodlands. Perches frequently in large flocks along hedgerows and trees. In autumn, lone birds can often be found on coastal islands and headlands. Can also be found alone or in small parties in town gardens feeding on berries. Breeds in northern Europe and Iceland.

Redwing

striking white supercilium

bright red flank patch

heavily streaked underparts

Dipper, Wren and Waxwing

Dipper

Cinclus cinclus   Gabha dubh

A plump, short-tailed species with a striking plumage. Seen along fast-flowing rivers, perching on rocks and bobbing continuously before plunging into the water. **Adults** show a dark brown head, a blackish mantle, wings, rump and tail, and a striking white throat and breast. This white gorget is bordered below by a dull chestnut band which fades into the blackish belly and flanks. Short bill dark. Legs greyish. When perched, flashes a white eyelid when blinking. **Juveniles** show a dark greyish head and upperparts, and a dirty, off-white gorget. Flight fast and direct, usually low over the water. Irish Dippers belong to a specific race (see Introduction).

Voice and Diet

Gives a loud, sharp *zit-zit* call, usually in flight. Can also give a hard *klink* note. The song is a sweet mixture of rippling, warbling and grating notes. Feeds by walking along the bottom of a stream or swimming on or below the surface of the water, searching for a variety of aquatic insects. Also takes molluscs, crustaceans, small fish, worms and tadpoles.

Wren

Troglodytes troglodytes   Dreoilín

A tiny, busy species which shows very short, rounded wings and a stubby cocked tail. **Adults** show a rufous-brown head and a striking pale buff supercilium. Upperparts and short wings rufous-brown with dark barring. Short, cocked, rufous-brown tail also shows thin, dark bars. Underparts pale buff with dark brown barring on the flanks and white spots on the undertail. Thin, pointed dark bill is slightly curved. **Juveniles** similar, but show mottling on the crown and throat, a fainter supercilium, and lack spots on the undertail. A very active bird, constantly on the move, usually in deep cover. Flight is fast and straight, flying with rapid, whirring wing beats.

Voice and Diet

Gives harsh, loud, repeated *tic* calls when alarmed or disturbed. Can also give grating, churring calls. The song consists of harsh, rattling, shrill, warbling notes, followed by a rapid trill. The song is remarkably loud and far-carrying for such a small bird. Feeds on a wide variety of small insects and spiders. Will also take some seeds and can be attracted to bird tables.

Waxwing

Bombycilla garrulus   Síodeiteach

A tame, plump, colourful species. **Adults** show a pinkish-brown head with a long crest, a black eye mask, a black bib, sharply defined on males, and a white line from the bill. The cheeks are pinkish-brown but show warm chestnut tones. Upperparts greyish-brown. Wings show white and yellow V-tips to the black primaries, white and bright red waxy tips to the secondaries and white-tipped primary coverts. Rump grey. Tail shows a black subterminal band and a bright yellow tip. Underparts pinkish-brown with deep rufous-brown undertail-coverts. Short, dark bill slightly hooked. **Immatures** show paler, duller wings. In flight, appears very Starling-like, showing a short tail and triangular wings.

Voice and Diet

Gives a very distinctive, weak, trilling *sirrrrr* call, which may recall the distant ringing of a modern telephone. Feeds acrobatically and voraciously on a variety of berries and buds in winter. Will often sit for long periods during feeding. Will also eat fruit. In spring can sometimes be seen fly-catching, chasing insects on the wing and returning to a prominent perch.

Habitat and Status

A scarce but widely distributed resident breeding species present in all counties. Found along fast-flowing streams and rivers, usually in upland regions. Dippers also occur on suitable stretches of water in low-lying areas. Builds a domed nest on walls, ledges, under bridges or among tree roots, always nesting above or close to water. In winter, many birds leave upland regions. Birds of the Continental race have occurred in Ireland in late autumn and winter.

Dipper

plump, short-tailed bird

striking white throat and breast

Habitat and Status

An extremely common, widespread, resident breeding species present in large numbers in every county. Found in a wide range of habitats, including gardens, parks, hedgerows, farmland, woodlands, reeds, upland scrub and moorlands. Builds a domed nest in ivy, hedgerows, old buildings and broken walls. Small movements are noted at some coastal islands each year and it is believed that these are local birds dispersing in search of food.

Wren

thin pointed bill

barring on rufous upperparts and flanks

small size, short tail

Habitat and Status

An uncommon to rare winter visitor from Scandinavia, found in very small numbers annually. In some years, Waxwings irrupt in search of food, and can occur throughout the country. Found anywhere with a plentiful supply of berries. Usually reported in town and city gardens where their exotic plumage and tameness often attract attention. Most records refer to northern and eastern coastal counties. Have been recorded in midland, western and south-western regions.

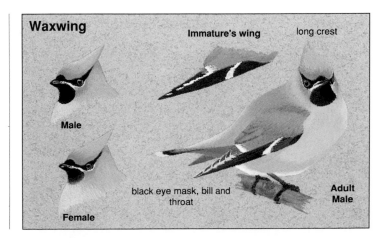

Waxwing

Immature's wing

long crest

Male

black eye mask, bill and throat

Female

Adult Male

Warblers

Blackcap
Sylvia atricapilla   Caipín dubh

A very striking warbler with a distinctive black or chestnut crown, a longish tail and a thin, long bill. **Adult males** show a glossy black cap extending down to eye level, greyish cheeks, nape and mantle, and brownish-grey wings. Rump and tail greyish. Throat, neck and breast pale grey, with flanks and belly showing a greyish wash. Undertail whitish. **Adult females** are more greyish-brown on the upper and underparts and show a bright chestnut cap. **Immature males** show brownish tones on cap, while **immature females** appear more yellow-brown on crown. Black eye shows a thin, whitish orbital ring. Bill black. Moves in a slow, deliberate manner. Can be skulking on occasions.

Voice and Diet
When alarmed, gives a hard, often repeated *tacc* call and also harsh, churring calls. Song is shorter than the similar Garden Warbler, containing a rich variety of melodic, soft, clear, warbling notes. Song occasionally starts with squeaky or scratchy notes. Sings from deep in cover. Feeds on a wide range of insects in summer, taking berries in autumn and winter. Will also visit gardens to feed on windfall apples.

Whitethroat
Sylvia communis   Gilphíb

A large, slim, long-tailed warbler with pinkish legs. **Adult males** show a grey crown, ear coverts and nape, a brownish mantle and brownish wings with bright, conspicuous, rufous edges to secondaries and tertials. Rump brown. Long tail grey-brown with narrow, striking, white outer-tail feathers. White throat contrasts with greyish-white underparts which can show a pinkish-buff wash on breast and flanks. **Adult females** and **immatures** similar, but show brownish heads, with immatures also showing buff-white edges to tail. Eyes pale and show a broken, narrow, white orbital ring. Bill greyish. Can perch prominently but can also be very skulking.

Voice and Diet
Gives a loud, harsh *tcak* call when disturbed or alarmed. Can also a give hoarse *tchar* call and quiet *whet, whet, whit-whit-whit* calls. Song consists of short, rapid, scratchy, warbling notes given from a prominent perch or during a dancing, aerial display flight. Feeds on a wide variety of insects. Will also feed on berries in autumn.

Lesser Whitethroat
Sylvia curruca   Gilphíb bheag

A smart, compact, short-tailed warbler with steel-grey legs. **Adults** show a grey forehead, crown and nape, and darker lores and ear coverts which can appear as a dark mask. Upperparts dark greyish-brown, the wing feathers lacking rufous edges. Rump grey. Short tail greyish-brown with white outer-tail feathers. Throat white, with underparts greyish-white, occasionally showing a pinkish-buff wash on breast and flanks. In autumn, adults can appear paler grey on the upperparts. Dark eye shows no orbital ring. **Immatures** show greyish-brown heads, creamy white throats and buffish tones on breast and flanks. Tail also shows off-white outer-tail feathers. Short, dark greyish bill.

Voice and Diet
Gives a loud, abrupt, harsh *tcack* call when disturbed or alarmed. Can also give a *charr* call. Rarely heard singing in Ireland. Song consists of soft warbling notes followed by a fast, far-carrying, single-note rattle. Feeds on a wide variety of insects, taking berries in autumn.

Habitat and Status

An uncommon local breeding species found in most counties. A regular passage migrant seen on coastal headlands and islands in spring and autumn. Small numbers also winter in Ireland and these are believed to be late autumn arrivals from northern and eastern Europe. Frequents mixed woodland with good undergrowth. Also found along hedgerows and gardens. Nests in hedges and brambles.

Blackcap — black cap (Male), chestnut cap (Female)

Habitat and Status

A widespread summer visitor and passage migrant. Whitethroat numbers took a drastic decline in the late 1960s. Since then, populations have increased but have not reached their former numbers. Found in open areas with hedges and scrub. Often found on woodland edges but never in woods or forests. On migration, found along hedgerows and in gardens on coastal headlands and islands. Nests low in dense cover.

Whitethroat — striking white throat (Male), rufous on wings (Female)

Habitat and Status

An extremely rare breeding species, but a regular spring and autumn passage migrant from Europe. Breeding has taken place on several occasions in the south-east. Frequents areas of dense vegetation with brambles, bushes and small trees. On passage, found along hedgerows and in gardens on coastal headlands and islands. Nests in dense hedges and bushes.

Lesser Whitethroat — Male (summer), Female, white throat, dark cheeks, greyish-brown upperparts

Warblers

Garden Warbler
Sylvia borin   Ceolaire garraí

A stocky, rounded, featureless warbler with a thick, greyish bill and grey legs. **Adults** show an olive-brown head with a faint, pale supercilium, a thin eye-ring, and a greyish area on the side of neck. A large, round eye is very conspicuous in a plain face, giving a gentle expression. Mantle, rump and wings plain olive-brown, with slightly darker centres to tertials. Short, olive-brown tail is unmarked. Throat creamy-white, with breast and flanks showing a buffish-grey wash. Belly and undertail whitish. **Immatures** show warmer olive-brown upperparts and buffish flanks. Can be skulking. Moves in a slow, deliberate manner, occasionally with drooped wings.

Voice and Diet
Gives a short, hard *tchack* call and a quick, repeated *churr* call when disturbed or alarmed. Song is a prolonged, soft, even, melodic warbling similar to but quieter and faster than that of Blackcap. Usually sings from deep cover. Feeds on a wide variety of insects. Also takes berries in autumn.

Barred Warbler (rare)
Sylvia nisoria

A large, stocky warbler resembling a huge Garden Warbler. **Immatures** show a pale grey head, a plain face with a thin, dark eye-stripe, and a narrow, pale eye-ring. Upperparts pale sandy-grey. Wings show whitish tips to median coverts, pale grey edges to greater coverts, and pale tips and edges to primaries and tertials. Long greyish tail shows narrow white outer-tail feathers. Underparts white with a buffish wash along the flanks. Flanks and undertail can also show faint buffish barring. Eye brown. Hefty dark bill shows a pale grey base on lower mandible. Legs grey. Moves in a slow, heavy manner. **Summer adults** show strong barring on the underparts and a pale eye.

Voice and Diet
Gives a loud, harsh, solid *tchack* call delivered in an almost chat-like manner. Can also give low churring and grating calls. Takes a wide variety of insects. Will also feed on berries.

Subalpine Warbler (rare)
Sylvia cantillans

A small, dainty warbler with a red eye, a reddish eye-ring and orange-orche legs. **Adult males** show a blue-grey head, thin white moustachial stripes, and bright pinkish or orange-brown throat, breast and flanks. Upperparts blue-grey with browner wings. Tail greyish with white outer feathers. Belly and undertail whitish. **Females** similar, but show washed-out pinkish-buff underparts and fainter moustachial stripes. **Immature males** similar to drab adult males. **Immature females** show pale sandy-grey upperparts, creamy underparts with buff flanks, white undertail, and a pale eye-ring. **Immatures** show buffish-white edges to tail. Bill greyish with a dark tip on adults, horn-coloured on immatures.

Voice and Diet
Gives a sharp, quiet *tec* call. Can also give fast, chattering calls when alarmed. Feeds in an active fashion, taking a wide range of insects and small spiders.

Habitat and Status

An uncommon breeding species, with the main populations based in midland and some northern counties. Also breeds in very small numbers in eastern, south-eastern, south-western and north-western regions. A regular passage migrant, more numerous in autumn than spring. Found in woodland with dense undergrowth. Nests in low brambles and bushes. On passage, found along hedgerows and in gardens on coastal headlands and islands.

Garden Warbler

grey on side of neck

plain face

Habitat and Status

A rare but regular autumn vagrant from central and eastern Europe. Most birds found in Ireland are immatures. As Barred Warbler is an extremely skulking species, preferring to move in deep cover, they can be easily missed. Found along hedgerows, bushes, brambles and areas of dense vegetation on coastal headlands and islands.

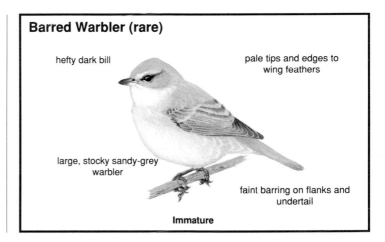

Barred Warbler (rare)

hefty dark bill

pale tips and edges to wing feathers

large, stocky sandy-grey warbler

faint barring on flanks and undertail

Immature

Habitat and Status

A rare but regular passage vagrant from southern Europe, occurring in autumn and especially in spring. Found on coastal headlands and islands, with most records referring to the south-east and south-west. Can be very skulking, seeking deep cover in hedgerows, bushes and brambles.

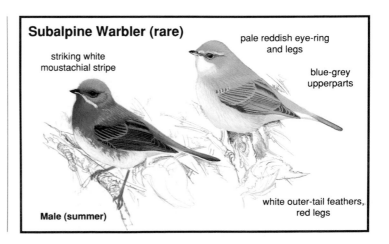

Subalpine Warbler (rare)

striking white moustachial stripe

pale reddish eye-ring and legs

blue-grey upperparts

white outer-tail feathers, red legs

Male (summer)

Warblers

Dartford Warbler (rare)
Sylvia undata   Ceolaire fraoigh

A distinctive, small, dark, skulking warbler with short, drooped wings and a long tail which is often held cocked. **Males** show brownish upperparts and wings, a dark grey head, and a plum-coloured throat and breast with small white spots on the throat. Belly whitish. Long tail greyish-brown with a narrow white border. **Females** show paler brown upperparts with a brownish-grey head. Underparts pale plum or pinkish-buff with white spots on throat and a whitish belly. Eye and orbital ring reddish-orange. Legs bright yellow-orange. Bill long, pointed and dark with a yellow-orange base. **Immatures** similar to female, but show dark eyes with a duller orbital ring and duller legs.

Voice and Diet
Gives sharp, metallic *tchirr* and short, hard *tic* calls. Can occasionally give a combination of both calls, resulting in an excited *tchirr-tic-tic* call. Feeds in a jerky, active manner, taking a wide range of insects and spiders.

Sedge Warbler
Acrocephalus schoenobaenus   Ceolaire cíbe

A pale brown warbler with streaked upperparts and a creamy-white supercilium. Adults show pale brown upperparts with dark streaking, heaviest on the crown. A broad, creamy-white supercilium is bordered by a dark lateral crown-stripe and a dark eye-stripe. Cheeks brownish. Clean underparts creamy, with a yellow-buff wash on sides of breast and flanks. Wings long with pale edges to dark-centred feathers. Unstreaked rump warm buff, contrasting with upperparts in flight. Tail feathers pale brown and rounded. **Immatures** similar, but show buffier plumage, a pale buff central crown-stripe and spotting on breast. Pointed bill dark with a paler base. Gape bright orange-red. Legs brownish.

Voice and Diet
Gives short, loud *tuc* and *chirr* calls. Song is a loud, fast sequence of harsh, grating, chattering notes mixed with musical and trilling notes. Sedge Warblers can also mimic other species and may include such notes within the song. Can sing from dense cover or perched prominently on top of reeds or sedges. Will also engage in short, singing, display flights. Feeds on a variety of insects, worms and spiders. Will also take berries.

Aquatic Warbler (rare)
Acrocephalus paludicola

A streaked, yellow-buff warbler resembling Sedge Warbler. **Adults** and **immatures** show a dark crown with a well-defined yellow-buff crown-stripe unlike the thin, messy crown-stripe of immature Sedge Warbler. Broad supercilium yellowish-buff. **Immatures** show pale lores with a broad dark eye-stripe confined to rear of eye. Some adults may show dark lores. Cheeks pale brown. Heavily streaked upperparts yellow-buff with two conspicuous lines on mantle. Rump yellow-buff and streaked. Pointed tail feathers give a spiky appearance in flight. Underparts pale cream and can show faint breast and flank streaking. Bill appears thicker and paler than Sedge Warbler. Legs pink.

Voice and Diet
Gives short, loud *tuc* and *churr* calls, almost identical to those of Sedge Warbler but delivered in a deeper tone. Feeds on a wide variety of insects and spiders.

Habitat and Status

An extremely rare autumn vagrant from Europe. Most records refer to birds found on coastal islands in the south-east and south-west. Frequents areas of dense gorse, heather and brambles, moving and feeding in thick cover. Could be easily overlooked due to its skulking nature. In calm and good weather, however, Dartford Warblers can occasionally perch on the tops of gorse or bushes, allowing excellent views.

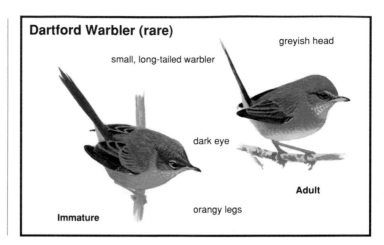

Dartford Warbler (rare)

small, long-tailed warbler

greyish head

dark eye

Adult

Immature

orangy legs

Habitat and Status

A common summer visitor present in suitable areas in all counties. Also breeds on some coastal islands with good, dense cover. Sedge Warblers are found in a wide range of habitats, including reed-beds, marshes, hedgerows and bushes close to ditches or wetlands, and dense vegetation near water. Nests in reeds, sedges or bushes above shallow water. On passage, can be found along hedgerows or in gardens on coastal headlands and islands.

Sedge Warbler

striking white supercilium

dark lores

thin, pale central crown-stripe

Adult

Immature

Habitat and Status

A very rare passage vagrant from central Europe. Most records refer to autumn, with just one record from early summer. Usually found in open reed-beds, sedges and areas of damp, tangled vegetation. A skulking species which moves low in dense vegetation. Could be easily overlooked. Migration routes and the wintering areas are virtually unknown.

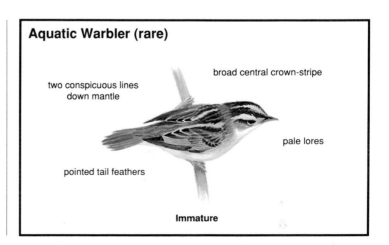

Aquatic Warbler (rare)

broad central crown-stripe

two conspicuous lines down mantle

pale lores

pointed tail feathers

Immature

Warblers

Reed Warbler
Acrocephalus scirpaceus   Ceolaire giolcaí

A plain, warm brown warbler with short wings and a rounded tail. **Adults** show a warm brown head, a faint supercilium and brownish cheeks. Upperparts and wings warm brown, with short, plain primaries appearing bunched. Rump shows rufous tones. Rounded tail warm brown. Throat and underparts white with warm buff on sides of breast and flanks. This can make the throat appear conspicuously white. Undertail clean white. **Immatures** almost identical, but show a stronger rufous tone on the rump. Long, slender bill pinkish-yellow with a darker upper edge. Legs brownish-grey with yellowish feet. Eye dark and obvious in a plain face. Moves up reeds in a jerky manner. Flight low and undulating.

Voice and Diet
Gives a short, harsh, low *tchurr*. Song is distinctive, resembling that of Sedge Warbler but delivered in a lower pitch, a slower manner and containing the repeated phrases of *jac-jac-jac, cerr-cerr-cerr*, interspersed with more liquid notes. Feeds on a variety of aquatic insects, spiders, slugs, worms and molluscs. Will also feed on berries in the autumn.

Savi's Warbler (rare)
Locustella luscinioides

A large, dull brown species which resembles Reed Warbler. **Adults** and **immatures** similar, showing a dull brown, rounded head with a distinct, thin supercilium and a pale, narrow eye-ring. Upperparts dull brown with short wings showing curved primaries. Lacks the warmer tones and straight primaries of Reed Warbler. Rump dull brown. The rich brown tail can be held cocked and appears rounded in flight. Underparts dull buff with a white throat. Undertail-coverts warm buff with paler buff tips. Long, pointed bill shows black upper and yellowish lower mandibles. Legs brownish or pinkish. Unlike Reed Warbler, walks up and down a perch in a skulking manner.

Voice and Diet
Song is similar to the reeling song of Grasshopper Warbler, but is lower-pitched and more buzzing. The call is occasionally preceded by *tic* calls which quicken as they emerge into the song. Tends to sing in shorter bursts than Grasshopper Warbler. Can give a quiet *tsck*, similar to the call of Robin. Feeds on a variety of insects and spiders.

Grasshopper Warbler
Locustella naevia   Ceolaire casarnaí

A shy, heavily streaked, olive-brown warbler. **Adults** and **immatures** similar, showing olive-brown upperparts with heavy streaking on the crown, mantle and rump, a faint supercilium and brownish cheeks. Wings show dark centres to feathers and short, curved primaries. Rounded tail can be held cocked. Underparts buffish-white with a whitish throat and yellow-buff sides to breast and flanks. Breast and flanks can show thin streaking. Undertail-coverts can also show dark streaking. Legs pale pink or orange. Pointed bill shows a dark upper and a pinkish lower mandible. Heavy streaking eliminates confusion with Savi's Warbler. A skulking species that moves carefully through dense vegetation.

Voice and Diet
The distinctive song is a far-carrying, single, reeling note which may recall the winding of an angler's reel. The song can also have a ventriloquial effect when the bird turns its head. The song can be given for lengthy periods, either day or night. Also gives a short, sharp *twhick* call. Feeds on a variety of insects and spiders.

Habitat and Status

Formerly a rare autumn vagrant to Ireland, in recent years Reed Warblers have become an established breeding species, with the main populations based in eastern and southern counties. In some areas, good numbers are present each summer and it seems likely that this colonisation will continue. Found in reed-beds, sedges and vegetation close to water. Nests in reeds and occasionally in hedges or bushes. On passage, can be found along hedgerows or in gardens on coastal headlands and islands.

Reed Warbler

plain, warm-brown warbler

long, pointed bill

Habitat and Status

A very rare vagrant from Europe, with summer records from western, south-western, south-eastern and eastern counties. While breeding has not been proven, potential pairs have been seen in Cork and Dublin. Found in extensive reed-beds with or without scattered bushes and trees. Although a very skulking species, the distinctive song usually attracts attention.

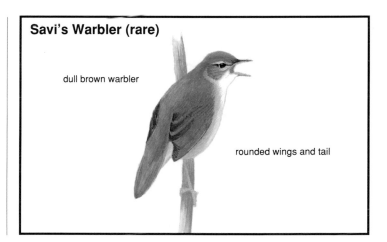

Savi's Warbler (rare)

dull brown warbler

rounded wings and tail

Habitat and Status

A common breeding species found in suitable habitats in all counties. Frequents areas of marshland with scattered trees and bushes, moorlands with bushes and gorse, neglected hedgerows, and in rough pastureland with long grass. Also found in young conifer plantations. A skulking species, difficult to see. Nests on or just above the ground in grass tussocks or undergrowth. On passage, found on coastal headlands and islands.

Grasshopper Warbler

heavily streaked upperparts and crown

very skulking

rounded tail

Willow Warbler

Phylloscopus trochilus   Ceolaire sailí

A small, busy warbler, very similar to Chiffchaff but showing pale legs and a pale orange base to a thin, dark, pointed bill. Long wings give Willow Warbler an attenuated, slim appearance. **Spring adults** show pale green upperparts, a well-defined, yellowish supercilium, a strong eye-stripe and blotchy ear coverts. Pale panel obvious on the closed wing. Green tail shows a shallow fork. Underparts show a bright yellow wash on the throat and breast and a clean whitish belly and undertail. In **autumn** shows green upperparts and a lemon-yellow supercilium and underparts. Unlike Chiffchaff, does not flick the tail when feeding. In flight, appears long-winged and flycatcher-like.

Voice and Diet

The song is distinctive, consisting of thin, pleasant, liquid notes which are delivered softly at first, but which grow louder before the notes descend and fade away. The song is usually finished by a fast *tswee* note. Also gives a loud *hoo-eet* call. Feeds on a wide range of small insects and spiders which are quickly picked off foliage. Will also engage in fly-catching, hovering and chasing insects in flight. Occasionally eats berries in the autumn.

Chiffchaff

Phylloscopus collybita   Tiuf-teaf

A small, active warbler, very similar to Willow Warbler but showing dark legs and a thin, dark, pointed bill with very little orange on the base. Short wings give Chiffchaff a rotund appearance. When feeding, constantly flicks the tail. **Spring adults** show dull, olive-green upperparts, a short, yellowish supercilium, and a dark eye-stripe with pale crescents obvious above and below the eye. Plain wings show blackish alula. Underparts olive-yellow and can show buffish tones. In **autumn** shows olive-green upperparts and buffish underparts. Chiffchaffs of the **Siberian race**, *tristis*, show beige upperparts, whitish underparts, a pale supercilium and can show a short, pale wingbar.

Voice and Diet

The song is diagnostic, consisting of repeated *chiff-chaff* notes. The song can sometimes vary and the same phrase can be repeated. The song usually commences with wheezing-type noises. Also gives a sharp, short *hweet* call, similar to the call of Willow Warbler. Feeds on small insects and spiders which are picked quickly from foliage.

Wood Warbler

Phylloscopus sibilatrix   Ceolaire coille

A very striking, brightly-coloured warbler, larger and more slender and attenuated in appearance than Willow Warbler. Upperparts very bright green, with very long wings showing conspicuous green edges to dark-centred feathers. Green crown and dark eye-stripe both contrast with the striking bright yellow supercilium, ear coverts and throat. Rump and tail bright green. Underparts are frosty, silky white and contrast strongly with the bright yellow throat. The yellow of the throat fades into the white of the upper breast but can appear very clear-cut. Legs pale. Bill shows a pale, orangy base. When feeding, does not flick the tail but can droop the long wings.

Voice and Diet

The song is distinctive, consisting of repeated *tseep-tseep* notes which are then followed by a fast, shivering trill. On occasions the song only comprises of the trill. The song can be given during gliding display flights. Also gives a plaintive *tseu* call. Feeds on a wide variety of small insects and spiders. Will occasionally eat berries in the autumn.

Habitat and Status

An extremely common passage and summer visitor found in all counties. Arrives in early spring, with most birds departing by September. Unlike Chiffchaff, never found in winter. Frequents a wide range of habitats, including woodlands, hedgerows, copses and any areas with bushes and scrub. Builds a domed nest in good cover on or near the ground. On passage, found in gardens and hedgerows on islands, headlands and coastal stretches.

Willow Warbler

long wings

pale legs

Habitat and Status

A very common passage and summer visitor, present in all counties. Small numbers occur each winter. Found in open woodland with undergrowth and a mixture of trees and mature hedgerows, brambles and scrub. Nests in deep cover above the ground. On passage, found along hedgerows, gardens and reeds at coastal locations. The Siberian race, *tristis*, is a rare late autumn vagrant, usually found on coastal headlands and islands.

Chiffchaff

short wings

pale wingbar

dark legs

Tristis **Chiffchaff (rare)**

Habitat and Status

A rare breeding species found in very small numbers in eastern, northern, western and south-western counties. Has also been reported summering in midland counties. Most summer records refer to birds in song with breeding not always proved. Found in areas of oak woodland and mature deciduous forests, building a domed nest in cover on the ground. Occasionally found on passage, feeding in gardens and trees on coastal headlands and islands.

Wood Warbler

yellow throat and face

long wings

pale legs

bright edges to wing feathers

Warblers

Greenish Warbler (rare)
Phylloscopus trochiloides

A busy, active warbler similar to the Siberian *tristis* race of Chiffchaff. Flicks the wings when feeding. Most sightings refer to **1st winter birds** which show a greyish-green crown with a long white or yellowish supercilium which broadens behind the eye and contrasts with a dark eye-stripe. Upperparts greyish-green with bright edges to wing feathers and a clear-cut white or yellowish greater covert bar. Can also show a fainter median covert bar. Tail greenish with bright edges. Underparts whitish. Bill yellowish or pinkish-yellow with a dark culmen and tip. Legs brownish. *Tristis* Chiffchaffs differ by showing a duller plumage, a diffuse, less clear-cut wingbar and a dark bill.

Voice and Diet
Gives a soft, distinctive *soo-wee* call which can be delivered in a louder, more excited manner when agitated. The call can occasionally resemble a softer version of that given by Pied Wagtail. Feeds in a very busy, active manner, moving quickly through foliage in search of small insects and spiders.

Arctic Warbler (rare)
Phylloscopus borealis

A chunky warbler similar to, but larger than, Greenish Warbler. Most sightings refer to **1st winter birds** which show a greenish crown with a very long, whitish supercilium which kinks upwards as it extends beyond the ear coverts. A dark eye-stripe contrasts with pale mottling on the ear coverts, which also show a dark border. Greenish upperparts show a whitish greater covert bar and can frequently show a median covert bar. Underparts whitish. Legs orange-yellow. Yellowish bill longer and heavier than Greenish Warbler with a dark culmen and tip. Greenish Warbler differs by showing a shorter supercilium, usually only one wingbar, a slimmer, shorter bill, and darker legs.

Voice and Diet
Gives a distinctive, short, hard, metallic *zik* call, quite unlike that of Greenish Warbler. The calls can become louder and sharper if agitated. Feeds in an active manner and may recall Wood Warbler in behaviour. Takes a wide variety of insects, larvae and spiders.

Radde's Warbler (rare)
Phylloscopus schwarzi

A chunky, brownish warbler, heavier in appearance than Chiffchaff and showing a heavy, pale, pinkish-orange bill and thick, pale, yellowish legs. Most sightings refer to **1st winter birds** which show a brownish crown with a dark upper border to a prominent supercilium which is broader and buffish before the eye, becoming creamy behind the eye. Thick dark eye-stripe contrasts with pale mottling on the ear coverts. Upperparts brownish, with olive tones on wings, rump and tail. Underparts creamy-yellow with a buff wash on sides of breast and along flanks. Undertail-coverts usually warm rusty-buff. Can be skulking, moving heavily through low cover or feeding on the ground.

Voice and Diet
Gives a distinctive, soft, but sharp *tchwet* call, usually delivered from deep cover. This can occasionally be repeated to give a staggered *tchwet-tet-tet* call. Feeds on the ground or in low cover and takes a wide variety of insects, larvae and spiders.

Habitat and Status

A very rare autumn vagrant from north-eastern and eastern Europe. All Irish records refer to a period between late August and early October, with the majority of sightings being in September. It should be noted that most *tristis* Chiffchaffs do not occur in Ireland until late autumn, usually from mid-October onwards. On passage, found in well-vegetated gardens, hedgerows and trees on coastal headlands and islands. All reports refer to south-eastern and south-western counties.

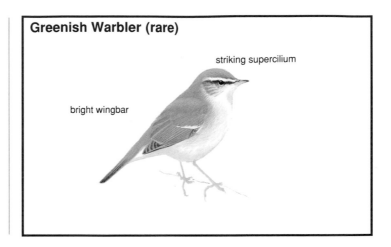

Greenish Warbler (rare)

striking supercilium

bright wingbar

Habitat and Status

An extremely rare autumn vagrant from northern Europe. All Irish records refer to September and October, with records from north-western, western and south-western counties. On passage, found in well-vegetated gardens, along hedgerows and in trees on coastal headlands and islands.

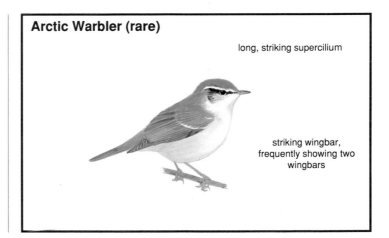

Arctic Warbler (rare)

long, striking supercilium

striking wingbar, frequently showing two wingbars

Habitat and Status

An extremely rare autumn vagrant from Siberia. Most records refer to late autumn, usually from mid to late October. Birds have been recorded in south-eastern, southern and south-western regions. Frequents areas of dense scrub, thick hedgerows and gardens on coastal headlands and islands. Due to their skulking nature and ground-feeding behaviour, Radde's Warblers may be easily overlooked.

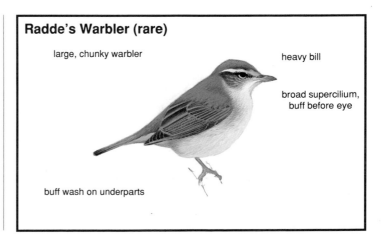

Radde's Warbler (rare)

large, chunky warbler

heavy bill

broad supercilium, buff before eye

buff wash on underparts

Warblers

Bonelli's Warbler (rare)
Phylloscopus bonelli
A drab warbler, slightly larger than Chiffchaff and showing a large black eye on a plain face. Pale greenish-grey head lacks a prominent eye-stripe and supercilium. Underparts white with a pale buff wash. Pale greenish-grey upperparts contrast with green edges to the wing feathers which form a deep green panel on the closed wing. Tertials also striking, showing darker centres. In flight, the pale yellow rump can be seen, while the tail shows bright green edges. Pointed bill shows a dark upper mandible and an orange cutting edge and lower mandible. Legs greyish-brown. Lack of a prominent eye-stripe and supercilium eliminates possible confusion with any unusually pale *Phylloscopus* warblers.

Voice and Diet
Gives a very loud, far-carrying *hoo-eet* call which, although similar to that of Willow Warbler, rises sharply on the second phrase. An extremely busy, active feeder, picking insects from foliage and occasionally fly-catching.

Icterine Warbler (rare)
Hippolais icterina   Ceolaire ictireach
A sturdy, slim, long-winged warbler similar to Melodious Warbler. Shows a long, sloping forehead and a plain-faced appearance. Lacks any dark stripe between the eye and bill. Shows a very faint supercilium. In **autumn** shows a pale, greyish-green head and upperparts. Unlike Melodious, pale edges to the tertials create a panel on the closed wing, while the primary projection is about equal to the length of the tertials. Tail square-ended. Underparts creamy, with a pale yellow wash on the chin and throat. Long, wide, orange bill shows a dark culmen. Legs bluish-grey. **Spring adults** show brighter upperparts and yellowish underparts. Feeds in an active, lively manner.

Voice and Diet
Although usually silent on migration, Icterine Warblers can occasionally give a brief, hard *teck* call, not unlike that of a *Sylvia* warbler. Feeds on a wide variety of insects and larvae. Will also feed on ripe fruit and berries.

Melodious Warbler (rare)
Hippolais polyglotta
A rounded, short-winged warbler similar to Icterine Warbler. Like Icterine, appears plain-faced, lacking any dark stripe between the eye and bill, and showing a faint supercilium. However, head shape appears more rounded. In **autumn**, head and upperparts olive-green. Wings appear plain, lacking the pale wing panel of Icterine. Primary projection short, being about half the length of the tertials with the primaries appearing bunched. Tail square-ended. Underparts yellowish, brightest on the throat and upper breast. Long, wide, orange bill shows a dark culmen. Legs brownish. **Spring adults** show brighter upperparts and yellower underparts. Feeds in a slow, methodical manner.

Voice and Diet
Like Icterine, Melodious Warblers are usually silent on migration, but can occasionally give a brief, House Sparrow-like chattering call. Feeds on a wide variety of insects and larvae. Like Icterine, can occasionally feed on ripe fruit and berries.

11-12cm **Bonelli's Warbler**
13-14cm **Icterine Warbler**
12-13cm **Melodious Warbler**

Habitat and Status
An extremely rare autumn vagrant from southern and central Europe. All records refer to south-eastern and south-western islands and headlands. Usually found in well-vegetated gardens with trees and bushes. Can be very active and difficult to follow.

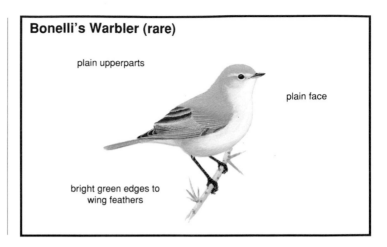

Bonelli's Warbler (rare)

plain upperparts

plain face

bright green edges to wing feathers

Habitat and Status
A rare passage migrant from northern and eastern Europe. Recorded on an almost annual basis, with most records referring to autumn. Smaller numbers have been recorded in spring, while one bird was present in Co. Dublin in November 1982. Most reports originate in southern counties where birds are seen in gardens and hedgerows on coastal headlands and islands.

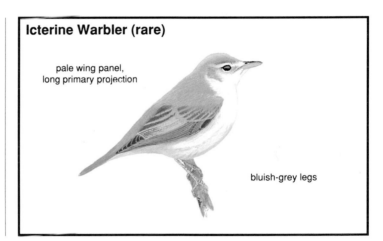

Icterine Warbler (rare)

pale wing panel, long primary projection

bluish-grey legs

Habitat and Status
A rare passage migrant from southern and south-western Europe. Recorded almost annually, Melodious Warblers tend to be more scarce than Icterine Warblers. Most records refer to autumn, with smaller numbers in spring. Also tends to occur earlier in autumn than Icterine. Most reports originate in southern counties where birds are seen in gardens and hedgerows on coastal headlands and islands. Tends to be more skulking than Icterine. Could be overlooked in dense cover.

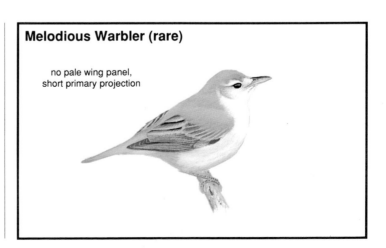

Melodious Warbler (rare)

no pale wing panel, short primary projection

193

Warblers

Yellow-browed Warbler
Phylloscopus inornatus

A small, bright, busy warbler, similar to Pallas's Warbler. Most records refer to **1st year birds** which show a bright olive-green crown, nape and upperparts, and greyish-white underparts which can show a faint yellowish wash along the flanks. Pale greenish ear coverts show faint blotches. A bright creamy-yellow supercilium appears upcurved behind the eye and contrasts with a dark eye-stripe. Darker wings show two creamy-yellow wingbars on the greater and median coverts, and pale yellowish edges to dark tertials. Unlike Pallas's, Yellow-browed shows an olive-green rump. Short tail olive-green. Legs pale. Thin, pale bill shows a dark tip.

Voice and Diet
Yellow-browed Warblers tend to call frequently, giving a strong, sharp, loud *chue-eep* call, with the second phrase higher pitched. Feeds in a busy, active manner, taking a wide variety of small insects and spiders. Can also catch insects on the wing.

Pallas's Warbler (rare)
Phylloscopus proregulus

A tiny, active, brightly-coloured warbler, similar to Yellow-browed Warbler but showing a bright yellow rump. Shows an olive-green crown with a contrasting creamy-yellow central crown-stripe, a broad creamy-yellow supercilium and a dark eye-stripe. Upperparts bright olive-green, with darker wings showing two bright yellow wingbars formed by tips to the greater and median coverts. Dark tertials show broad white edges. Frosty-white underparts often show a yellow wash on the sides of the breast and flanks. Frequently hovers when feeding, revealing the bright yellow rump. Thin, pointed bill dark. Legs pale. Moves in a Goldcrest-like manner but can be extremely skulking.

Voice and Diet
A usually silent species, Pallas's can give a faint, quiet *chu-ee* call. Feeds actively in cover, taking a wide range of small insects and spiders. Also fly-catches on the wing. During feeding hovers, can delicately pick insects from the surface of leaves.

Yellow-rumped Warbler (rare)
Dendroica coronata

A rather drab warbler showing dull upperparts but yellowish patches on the sides of the breast. All records refer to **1st year birds** which show a dull brownish head with a faint, pale supercilium and, occasionally, a yellowish crown patch. A clean white throat contrasts with creamy underparts which show bright yellow patches on the sides of the breast, and streaking from sides of breast onto flanks. Brownish upperparts show strong, dark streaking. Rump bright yellow. Blue-grey wings show two thin whitish wingbars and white edges to dark tertials. Greyish tail shows white spots on the outermost two or three feathers, conspicuous from below. Thin, pointed bill dark. Legs dark.

Voice and Diet
Can occasionally give a sharp *tikk* call. Feeds in an easy, methodical manner, taking a wide variety of insects. Also feeds on berries and seeds in the autumn.

10–11cm **Yellow-browed Warbler**
9–10cm **Pallas's Warbler**
13–14cm **Yellow-rumped Warbler**

Habitat and Status

A rare but regular late autumn vagrant from northern Siberia. Usually found along hedgerows or in well-vegetated gardens on coastal headlands and islands. Most records refer to south-western regions, although recorded along all coastal regions.

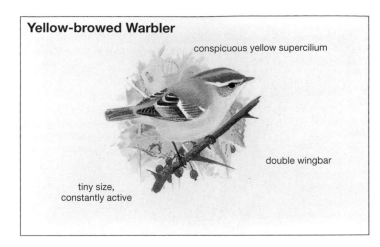

Yellow-browed Warbler

conspicuous yellow supercilium

double wingbar

tiny size, constantly active

Habitat and Status

An extremely rare, late autumn vagrant from southern Siberia. Like Yellow-browed Warbler, usually seen along hedgerows and in well-vegetated gardens on coastal headlands and islands. Most records refer to southern coastal counties. Despite their Goldcrest-like manner, Pallas's Warbler can prove to be frustratingly skulking and therefore difficult to see.

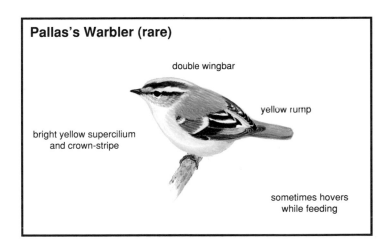

Pallas's Warbler (rare)

double wingbar

yellow rump

bright yellow supercilium and crown-stripe

sometimes hovers while feeding

Habitat and Status

An extremely rare autumn vagrant from North America. Found along hedgerows and in well-vegetated gardens on coastal islands and headlands. Can also feed on the ground and can occasionally be very approachable. Most records refer to Cape Clear Island off the coast of Co. Cork, but this species has also been recorded on Loop Head, Co. Clare.

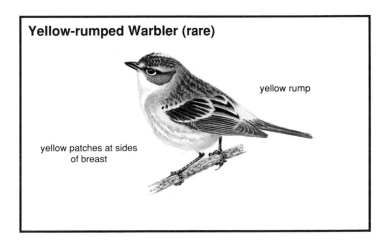

Yellow-rumped Warbler (rare)

yellow rump

yellow patches at sides of breast

Crests and Vireo

Goldcrest
Regulus regulus   Cíorbhuí

This tiny, active bird is Ireland's smallest species. **Males** show a black-edged, orange-yellow crown, and a dull greenish nape and upperparts. Wings show two white bars, white edges to the tertials and a dark wing panel. A large pale area around the dark eye gives the face a plain, open expression. The rump and short, forked tail are dull greenish. Underparts dull whitish, occasionally showing a greenish wash across the breast or along flanks. **Females** similar, but show a pure yellow, black-edged crown. **Juveniles** appear brownish on the head, lacking the yellow crown, and showing darkish crown edges. Small, thin, pointed bill dark. Legs dark.

Voice and Diet
Gives soft, high-pitched, repeated *zii* calls. The song is also very soft and high-pitched, consisting of repeated *ziida-ziida* notes, and ending in a short twitter. Feeds in a busy, active manner, taking a wide variety of spiders and small insects.

Firecrest
Regulus ignicapillus   Lasairchíor

A tiny, busy species, similar to Goldcrest but showing a striking head pattern and a very bright plumage. Like Goldcrest, **males** show a black-edged, orange-yellow crown but differ by showing a broad white supercilium and a dark eye-stripe. The ear coverts are greenish and highlight a small, pale crescent below the dark eye. The upperparts appear bright green with distinctive bronzy patches on the shoulders. The wings show two narrow white wingbars. Rump and short forked tail greenish. Underparts whitish, appearing cleaner than on Goldcrest. **Females** similar, but show a yellowish crown. Small, thin, pointed bill dark. Legs dark.

Voice and Diet
Gives a repeated *zit* call, which, although similar to Goldcrest, is lower-pitched and delivered in a quieter, less persistent manner. Feeds actively, taking a wide range of small insects and spiders.

Red-eyed Vireo (rare)
Vireo olivaceus

A heavy, North American, warbler-like species, best identified by the very distinctive head pattern. **Adults** and **immatures** show a blue-grey crown bordered by a black lateral crown-stripe, and a whitish supercilium contrasting strongly with a dark eye-stripe. Ear coverts pale olive-green. Upperparts olive-green. Wings and tail slightly darker. Underparts silky white but can show a yellowish wash on the flanks and undertail. The strong, darkish bill shows a hooked tip. Legs bluish-grey. Most sightings in Ireland refer to immature birds which show a brownish iris, while adults show a conspicuous, bright red iris. Moves in a slow, deliberate manner and can be confiding.

Voice and Diet
Rarely heard in Ireland, Red-eyed Vireo can give a short, sharp, scolding *chew* call. Feeds in a deliberate manner, taking a wide range of insects. Will also feed actively on a variety of berries.

Habitat and Status

A common breeding species found in all counties. In autumn and spring, occurs as a passage migrant on coastal headlands and islands. In winter, numbers may increase with the arrival of birds from Britain and northern Europe. Found in a variety of habitats, including deciduous and coniferous woodland, and in gardens with good vegetation. Nests under thick cover in conifers, or occasionally in ivy.

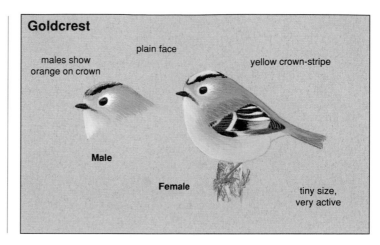

Habitat and Status

A scarce but regular passage migrant, occurring almost annually. Most records refer to birds seen in autumn, with small numbers occurring in spring. There are also several winter records. On passage, found in gardens and trees on coastal headlands and islands, with most records referring to regions along the southern coastline.

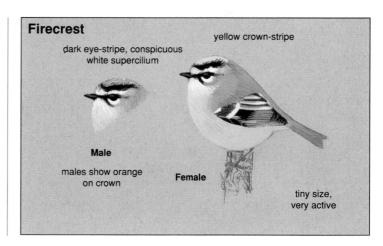

Habitat and Status

A very rare autumn vagrant from North America, with most sightings in October. Most reports refer to coastal islands and headlands in the south-west, with other records from the south and south-east. Found in mature gardens with a mixture of trees and good undergrowth for cover.

Flycatchers

Spotted Flycatcher
Muscicapa striata   Cuilire liath

An upright, rather drab bird, usually seen chasing insects in mid-air, hovering and twisting before returning to an open perch. Plain grey-brown upperparts show dark streaking confined to the steep forehead. Wings show pale edges to the tertials, greater coverts and long primaries. A habit of drooping and repeatedly flicking the wings exposes the grey-brown tail. The tail, which can be wagged slowly, does not show white edges or basal patches. Greyish-white underparts show brown streaking on the breast and diffuse streaking on the pale throat. Sexes alike. Long, pointed, thick black bill can sometimes be heard to snap when fly-catching. Legs dark.

Voice and Diet
Call is a soft, scratchy *tsee* or *tsee-tuc*. The song is short, containing thin scratchy *tsip-tsic* notes repeated at intervals. Song is delivered from a perch. As the name suggests, feeds on all forms of insects, usually caught on the wing.

Pied Flycatcher
Ficedula hypoleuca   Cuilire alabhreac

Behaves in a manner very similar to Spotted Flycatcher, but appears smaller and more rotund. **Summer plumage males** show a black head with a small white forehead patch, bold white patches on black wings, and white edges to a black tail. Underparts white. **Females** show grey-brown upperparts, white wing patches, blackish tails with white edges and whitish underparts. **Autumn males** similar to females, but retain the white forehead patch. **Immatures** similar to females, but show a thin pale wingbar on the median coverts, and usually lack a whitish primary base patch. Holds the wings drooped and flicks the wings and tail often. Shows a thin, pointed black bill and dark legs.

Voice and Diet
Call is a sharp *whiit* or, on occasions, a shorter *tik*. These calls can often be combined to give a *whiit-tik*. The song can often be confused with Redstart and consists of strong, repeated *zee-iit* notes, often mingled with more scratchy, liquid notes. Feeds on insects, usually caught on the wing.

Red-breasted Flycatcher (rare)
Ficedula parva

A small, charming, rotund bird. **Autumn adults** show a grey-brown head and upperparts and creamy, buff-washed underparts. Plain wings are usually held drooped, allowing white patches on the base of the black tail to be seen easily. Tail often held cocked, showing a pure white undertail. A large black eye and a broad white orbital ring give an innocent facial expression. **Immatures** similar, but show pale edges to wing coverts. **Summer males** show an orange-red throat patch, although this plumage is rarely seen in Ireland. Legs dark and bill blackish. Although feeds like other flycatchers, Red-breasted can be quite skulking and warbler-like in behaviour.

Voice and Diet
Call is a short wren-like *trr-trr*, delivered as a soft, low trill. Can also give a sharp *chic* call. Feeds on insects which are caught on the wing or picked off foliage in a warbler-like manner.

Habitat and Status

A bird of open wooded areas including parks and gardens. Prefers areas with open ground where fly-catching flights can be made easily. A widespread summer visitor, Spotted Flycatcher is usually one of the last migrants to arrive. Nests in holes of trees, in walls, buildings or creeping plants such as ivy.

Spotted Flycatcher

streaked crown and underparts

upright stance

Habitat and Status

An extremely rare Irish breeding bird of deciduous woodlands. Nests are built in holes of trees and walls. Will also use nest boxes. A regular passage migrant with most records referring to autumn. On passage, found in gardens and along hedgerows on coastal headlands and islands.

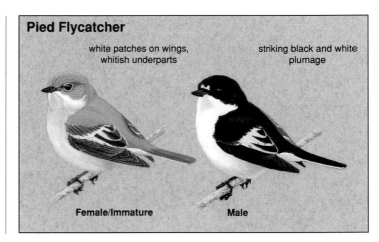

Pied Flycatcher

white patches on wings, whitish underparts

striking black and white plumage

Female/Immature   **Male**

Habitat and Status

Rare but regular vagrant to Ireland from eastern Europe, usually occurring in late autumn. Normally found frequenting gardens or well-vegetated areas on coastal headlands and islands. Their skulking behaviour can make them easy to overlook.

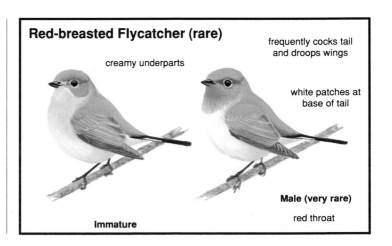

Red-breasted Flycatcher (rare)

frequently cocks tail and droops wings

creamy underparts

white patches at base of tail

Male (very rare)

red throat

Immature

Tits

Coal Tit
Parus ater   Meantán dubh

A small, active bird, appearing quite large-headed and short-tailed. **Adults** show a black head and chin contrasting with striking yellowish-white cheeks and nape patch. Underparts yellowish-white with buff tones on flanks. Upperparts greyish olive-buff with slightly darker wings showing two whitish wingbars. Rump olive-buff. Forked tail dark buff-grey. Small, stubby bill blackish. Legs dark. **Juveniles** show browner upperparts, sooty-black head and chin, and yellower cheeks, nape patch and underparts. Ireland has a specific race of Coal Tit (see Introduction). Those of the **British race** show whiter cheeks and underparts, and more olive-grey upperparts.

Voice and Diet
Gives a variety of calls, including a high-pitched, piping *tsuu* and a thin *tzee-tzee-tzee* call which is not unlike that of Goldcrest. The song is a repeated *teecho-teecho-teecho* which is similar to but sweeter and more piping than that of Great Tit. Feeds on insects, spiders and seeds. In winter, a common visitor to suburban gardens, feeding on seed and nut-feeders. Will also eat fat and, on occasions, meat.

Blue Tit
Parus caeruleus   Meantán gorm

An active, cheeky, colourful bird with a short, stubby, black bill and dark legs. **Adults** show a pale blue crown, with a white lower border and cheeks contrasting with a black bib and eye-stripe. Dark blue collar and nape highlight a white nape spot. Underparts bright yellow, with a dark mark down the centre of the belly. Upperparts green, with one white wingbar on bright blue wings. Rump green. Short, forked tail blue. **Juveniles** show a greenish-brown crown and hindneck, yellowish cheeks, crown border and nape patch, a diffuse black bib, more olive-green upperparts, and greenish-blue wings and tail. An extremely acrobatic species when feeding.

Voice and Diet
Gives a wide range of calls, including a rapid *tzee-tzee-tzee-tzit* and harsh churring notes. The song begins with two or three *tzee* notes which are followed by a fast, liquid trill. Feeds on a wide variety of insects, spiders, fruit, seeds, berries and grain. A common visitor to garden feeding stations, taking nuts and seeds. Has also developed an annoying habit of tearing open milk bottle tops to drink the creamy head.

Great Tit
Parus major   Meantán mór

A large, striking, handsome tit with a dark, pointed bill and dark greyish legs. **Adult males** show a shining blackish-blue head and throat with white cheeks and a pale yellowish nape spot. Bright yellow underparts show a black central band from the throat onto the whitish undertail-coverts. Band thickest on centre of belly. Upperparts olive-green, with bluish-grey wings showing a white wingbar and obvious white edges to the tertials. Forked, bluish-grey tail shows distinctive white outer edges. **Adult females** similar, but show a narrower band on the underparts. **Juveniles** appear duller overall, with yellowish cheeks and brownish tones to upperparts.

Voice and Diet
Gives a very large range of calls which have a metallic quality, usually louder than those of other tits. Calls include a Chaffinch-like *tzink*, a fast, repeated, short *tui*, thin, high-pitched *tzee-tzee-tzee* and harsh churring notes. Song repeated, loud *teecho-teecho-teecho* notes, similar to Coal Tit. Feeds on a variety of insects, spiders, worms, fruit, seeds and berries. A common winter visitor to nut and seed feeders. Occasionally kills young birds.

Habitat and Status

An extremely common and widespread resident breeding species found in all counties. Frequents coniferous and deciduous woodlands, parks and gardens. Nests in holes close to the ground, using old tree stumps, walls and rocks. Will also nest in banks or in actual holes in the ground. In winter, a common visitor to garden feeding stations. The British race occurs widely and can be found associating with native birds. Continental race very rare.

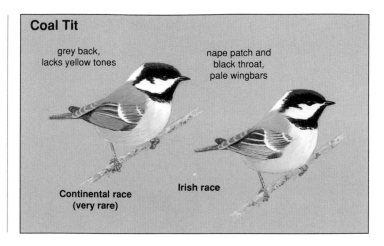

Coal Tit

grey back, lacks yellow tones

nape patch and black throat, pale wingbars

Continental race (very rare)

Irish race

Habitat and Status

An extremely common and widespread resident breeding species found in all counties. Frequents deciduous woodlands, parks, gardens, hedgerows and ditches. Nests in holes in trees or walls and will frequently use nest boxes if available. In winter, extremely common in suburban gardens. Also found in areas of reeds in winter. Occasionally associates with other tit species to form large roving parties.

Blue Tit

striking facial pattern and blue crown

bright yellow underparts

Habitat and Status

An extremely common and widespread resident breeding species found in all counties. Frequents orchards, deciduous woodlands, parks, gardens and hedgerows. Nests in holes in trees and, less frequently, in walls. Like Blue Tits, will frequently use nest boxes. In winter, extremely common in suburban gardens, feeding and aggressively defending nut and seed feeders. Occasionally associates with other tit species to form large roving parties.

Great Tit

males show broad black band down centre of yellow underparts, narrower on females

white cheeks

females duller

Female

Male

Tits and Treecreeper

Long-tailed Tit

Aegithalos caudatus   Meantán earrfhada

A tiny, active bird with a small black bill, a rounded, fluffed-up body, and an extremely long tail. **Adults** show a white head with a black stripe from above eye onto side of neck and meeting black mantle. Throat and breast whitish, with belly, flanks and undertail showing a pinkish wash. Pinkish scapulars contrast with mantle. Wings dark, showing striking white edges. Rump dark. The long, graduated tail is black with white outer edges. **Immatures** show dark cheeks, a shorter tail, browner upperparts with whitish scapulars, and whitish underparts showing very little pink. Flight appears weak and undulating, with long tail conspicuous. A busy, gregarious, active bird, constantly on the move.

Voice and Diet

Gives a variety of calls including a distinctive, low *tsupp,* a trilling *tsrrup* and a repeated *tsee-tsee-tsee* call. Song is seldom heard and consists of a mixture of call notes. Feeds in an acrobatic manner, taking small insects and spiders.

Bearded Tit (rare)

Panurus biarmicus   Meantán croiméalach

A distinctive, tit-like bird with a long tail. **Adult males** show a pale grey head with black lores and moustaches, a short, orange bill and an orange-yellow eye. Underparts pinkish-grey with black undertail-coverts. Mantle and rump tawny-brown. Short wings show black centres to feathers with broad white and buff edges. Long, graduated, tawny-brown tail shows narrow white edges. **Females** differ by showing a tawny head lacking black moustaches, with greyer breast and a duller bill and eye. Legs blackish. **Immatures** similar to females but show black down centre of back and on sides of tail. **Immature males** also show black lores. Flight low and weak, usually on whirring wings.

Voice and Diet

Gives a distinctive, pinging, *tching* call which often reveals the bird's presence. This call can sometimes be followed by a trilling *tirr* call. Also gives a range of *tick* notes and squeaky calls. Feeds in an acrobatic manner, taking insects and reed seeds.

Treecreeper

Certhia familiaris   Snag

A small, brown and white bird which moves up trees in a mouse-like, spiralling fashion. **Adults** show a thin, down-curved bill, a whitish supercilium, and streaked brownish crown and cheeks. Throat, breast, belly and undertail white with pale buff flanks. Mantle and wings show a complicated pattern of brown with pale buff and dark streaking and pale wingbars. Rump rufous-brown. Tail brown with stiff, pointed feathers which are pressed against the tree trunk for support. **Immatures** show brown flecks on breast and flanks, duller white underparts and colder brown upperparts. Climbs up trees in a jerky manner before dropping down to the base of another to begin again. Usually solitary.

Voice and Diet

Gives a thin, high-pitched *tzeu* call and a softer *tset*. Song almost Goldcrest-like, consisting of *tzee-tzee-tzee-tsizzi-tzee*, starting slowly but accelerating towards the finish. Feeds on a wide variety of insects which are caught with the thin bill.

13–15cm **Long-tailed Tit**
16–17cm **Bearded Tit**
12–14cm **Treecreeper**

Habitat and Status

A common resident species present in all counties. Found in woodlands and woodland edges, hedgerows, parklands and gardens. In winter, can often associate with other tit species, forming large, roving flocks on occasions. Prolonged hard winter weather can sometimes reduce populations. Nests in thorny bushes or high in trees, building an oval, mossy nest.

Long-tailed Tit

black head stripe and mantle

long tail

pinkish on back and underparts

Habitat and Status

A rare species which has bred in Ireland. Most sightings refer to the eastern, south-eastern and south-western regions where small numbers become established and resident from time to time. Severe winters, however, tend to reduce the populations drastically. Bearded Tits have also been recorded on coastal islands in autumn. Found in large, extensive reed-beds.

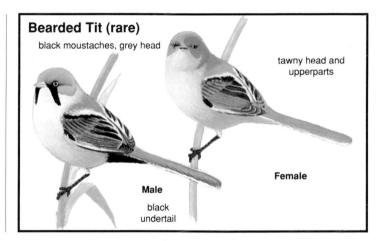

Bearded Tit (rare)

black moustaches, grey head

tawny head and upperparts

Male

black undertail

Female

Habitat and Status

A common resident species found in all counties, although not common in some parts of south-western, western and north-western counties. Found in deciduous and coniferous woodlands, parks and gardens. Tends to feed on trees with gnarled bark. Nests behind bark, in ivy or in crevices in trees.

Treecreeper

curved bill

streaked brown plumage

creeps mouse-like up tree trunks

Shrikes

Red-backed Shrike (rare)
Lanius collurio   Scréachán droimrua

Males show a grey head, a black mask through eye onto ear coverts, a white supercilium, and a rust-red mantle and wing coverts, with the remaining wing feathers darker brown. Rump grey. A black tail shows broad white patches at the base. White underparts can show a peach wash on the breast. **Females** rufous-red on upperparts and head, with a dark brown eye mask and a white supercilium. Tail colour as mantle, with white edges. Rump grey-brown. Underparts white with faint barring. **Immatures** similar to females, with crescent-shaped barring on sides of breast and flanks, and barring on the upperparts. Rump and tail brown. Bill dark, females showing a paler base. Legs dark.

Voice and Diet
Although rarely heard in Ireland, the call is a sharp, falcon-like *che-ek*. Feeds on small birds and insects, catching them by swooping down from a prominent perch. Like other shrikes, can sometimes be observed impaling prey items on thorns.

Woodchat Shrike (rare)
Lanius senator

A striking shrike with a deep chestnut crown and nape which extend as far as the black mantle. A broad black mask runs from the forehead through the eye and onto the ear coverts. Wings black, with white scapulars forming large white wing patches. White base to primaries obvious in flight. Black tail shows broad white edges and contrasts with the white rump. Underparts white. **Females** show duller colours and faint crescents on breast and flanks. **Immatures** greyish-brown on head and upperparts, with barring on upper and underparts. White centres to scapulars, white tips to median coverts and a whitish rump separate them from immature Red-backed. Bill dark. Legs dark. Large, rounded eye is blackish.

Voice and Diet
Although rarely heard in Ireland, the call comprises of harsh chattering notes. Feeds on insects or small birds which are caught by swooping down from a perch. Like all shrikes, Woodchats can occasionally impale prey on thorns.

Great Grey Shrike (rare)
Lanius excubitor

Large, long-tailed, grey, black and white shrike with a thick, dark bill. Usually seen on prominent perches from where they can swoop down on prey items. Forehead, crown and nape pale grey, extending onto mantle. Black mask from base of bill through eye onto ear coverts. A thin white supercilium meets over the bill. Short wings black with small area of white on the base of the primaries forming thin white bar on open wing. Scapulars tipped white. Rump grey. Long black tail shows white outer-tail feathers with white tips to outermost feathers. Underparts white. **Females** and **immatures** similar, but can show faint barring on the underparts. Legs and bill dark.

Voice and Diet
Gives a harsh, angry, falcon-like *shikk-shikk* call. Feeds on small mammals, birds and insects. Catches prey by swooping down from a prominent perch. Can also create a store of prey items by impaling them on thorns to be consumed at leisure. This practice lends shrikes their other name, 'Butcher-birds'.

Habitat and Status

A rare European visitor to Ireland, mainly occurring in autumn when immatures are found on coastal headlands and islands. Sits on prominent perches like telegraph wires or bushes where prey can easily be spotted. Usually found in areas of open ground with convenient perches.

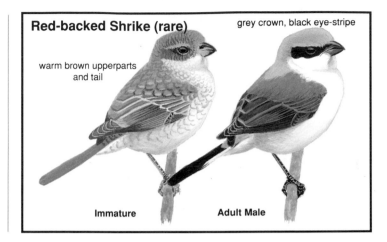

Red-backed Shrike (rare)

grey crown, black eye-stripe

warm brown upperparts and tail

Immature

Adult Male

Habitat and Status

A rare bird from central and southern Europe, more likely to be seen in spring when the birds are in full summer plumage. Immatures can occur in early autumn. Usually found on coastal headlands and islands where they perch on bushes or small trees. Woodchats can easily be overlooked, as they do not always sit on prominent perches like other shrikes.

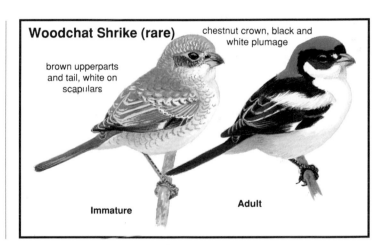

Woodchat Shrike (rare)

chestnut crown, black and white plumage

brown upperparts and tail, white on scapulars

Immature

Adult

Habitat and Status

A very rare late autumn and winter visitor from northern Europe. Normally found in open areas like farmland, with scattered trees and telegraph poles and wires. Easily seen because of its habit of sitting on prominent perches.

Great Grey Shrike (rare)

black eye-stripe

long tail

largish size

Crows

Rook

Corvus frugilegus   Rúcach

A common, scraggy-looking crow with a long, pointed grey bill and a whitish face patch. Forehead steep and, despite the rounded crown, often appears flat-headed. Complete plumage glossy black with a purple sheen. Along with the grey bill and whitish face patch which extends from base of bill to chin and throat, one of the most diagnostic features is the shaggy feathers which cover the upper legs. This creates a baggy-trousers effect and is particularly useful when separating **immature** birds, which lack the pale bill and face patch, from Carrion Crows. In flight has narrow wings, primary fingers and a long, slightly rounded tail. Moves in large flocks, often with Jackdaws.

Voice and Diet

A very noisy species, especially when roosting at dusk. Gives a sharp, grumpy *kaarg* call which is repeated continuously, often with a whole flock calling at once. Feeds on many items, including root crops, berries, insects, worms and slugs.

Hooded Crow

Corvus corone   Feannóg

An unmistakable grey and black crow with a dark, thick-set, blunt bill. Black head, breast, wings and tail contrast strongly with the grey mantle and underparts. Lacks the baggy-trousers effect of Rook. In flight, shows black rounded wings with primary fingers and a short, black, square tail. **Immatures** are duller grey, often with mantle markings, and with brownish wings and tails. Usually solitary, but can occur in small parties, often with Rooks and Jackdaws. **Carrion Crows**, the all-black race, occur on occasions from Britian and Europe and can be separated from immature Rooks by the blunt, thicker bill and tidier leg feathers.

Voice and Diet

Gives a loud, harsh *kaaw*, flatter in tone than Rook. Will also give a honking nasal-type *kraa* call. Takes a wide variety of food, including carrion, small birds and mammals, eggs, insects and grain. Along the coast can occasionally be seen to drop molluscs onto hard surfaces in an attempt to crack open the shells.

Raven

Corvus corax   Fiach dubh

The largest member of the crow family, Ravens are strong, powerful birds with a deep, heavy, dark bill and shaggy throat feathers. The complete plumage is glossy black with a purple or green sheen. In flight, the long wings have obvious primary fingers. The thick bill, along with the shaggy throat, give a large-headed profile in flight, while the diagnostic long, wedge-shaped tail is easy to see. Overall, the flight is strong and powerful, with the birds often performing acrobatic tumbles in the air. When soaring, can look like large raptors. Usually seen alone, in pairs or in small family parties. Rarely associates with other crow species.

Voice and Diet

Gives a very distinctive deep, loud, honking *prruc-pruc* call which can carry great distances. Also gives a variety of softer, quieter, croaking calls. Feeds on carrion of all kinds, but will kill weak or injured small mammals and birds. Also feeds on eggs, slugs, worms, insects and occasionally on grain.

Habitat and Status

An extremely common resident bird found on farmland, parks, towns and cities. Feeds in large, often mixed flocks on open land. In recent years, Rooks have tended to feed on road sides and have learned some road sense, often casually hopping out of the way of traffic. However, many are killed on the roads, although these may be young, inexperienced birds. Nests in the very tops of trees in large colonies called rookeries.

Rook

pale grey bill, whitish face patch, all black plumage

Adult

shaggy leg feathers

Immature

darker bill, no face patch

Habitat and Status

A common resident bird found in a wide variety of habitats, including woodland, farmland, towns, parks, coastal areas and mountains. Nests in trees, on cliffs or in old buildings. The Carrion Crow can occur at any time of the year, although most records refer to autumn and winter. When found in Ireland, Carrion Crows are usually seen in coastal locations.

Hooded Crow

grey and black plumage

Carrion Crow
all black plumage, lacks shaggy leg feathers

Hooded Crow

Habitat and Status

A common resident bird of mountain glens and coastal cliffs. Nests are built on cliff outcrops or in trees, with some pairs nesting as early as January or February. A carrion eater, Ravens often suffer as a result of taking poisoned bait.

Raven

long, wedge-shaped tail

thick bill, shaggy throat

enormous size

Crows

Jackdaw
Corvus monedula   Cág

A cheeky, small, compact crow with a glossy black plumage. Nape pale ash-grey, which creates a black-capped appearance. Upper and underparts glossy black. Bill dark and pointed, considerably shorter than in other crow species. Legs dark. Eye is a whitish-grey with a dark pupil, this being a diagnostic feature. **Immatures** lack the pale grey nape and show darker eyes. In flight, has pointed wings and a short tail. Flight appears easy and buoyant, with fast wing beats interspersed with glides. On the ground, hops cheekily and is highly inquisitive. A gregarious species, Jackdaws are usually found in large flocks, often associating with Rooks.

Voice and Diet
A commonly heard bird which gives a characteristic *jak-jak* call, often repeated. Will also frequently give a *kee-yaw*, which is flatter and shorter than the similar calls of Chough. Feeds on a wide variety of food, including slugs, insects and their larvae, as well as berries and fruit. Also known to steal eggs and nestlings.

Chough
Pyrrhocorax pyrrhocorax   Cág cosdearg

An absolute acrobat of the air, this Jackdaw-sized glossy black crow is easily identified by the long, thin, curved red bill, red legs and the distinctive *chauuh* call. **Immatures** show a pale orange bill and paler legs. The long, pointed bill is used for probing and can sometimes appear stained as a result. A shy bird, usually seen in small parties. In flight, the wings appear rounded with long primary fingers. The tail is slightly rounded. Choughs seem to enjoy themselves in flight, with easy, buoyant wing beats interspersed with swoops on closed wings. On the ground, walks or hops in a sideways manner. Sometimes associates with other crows, particularly Jackdaws.

Voice and Diet
Gives a distinctive, loud, high-pitched *chauuh* call which, although similar to that of Jackdaw, is delivered in a more explosive manner. Feeds by probing in fields or sand-dunes for worms, slugs, insects and larvae. Will also take grain.

Magpie
Pica pica   Snag breac

A boldly-patterned, cheeky bird with a long, wedge-shaped tail. Initially appears black and white but, when seen well, reveals an elaborate variety of colours. Head, mantle and breast black with a bluish-purple gloss. The wings are black with blue and green sheens, but show white scapulars and white, black-edged primaries. Undertail and rump black. Long tail appears black, but shows green, purple and bronze sheens. Flies with long trailing tail and white scapulars and primaries contrasting strongly with otherwise black upperparts. Belly and flanks white. **Immatures** show a duller plumage and shorter tail. Stout, pointed dark bill. Legs and eyes dark.

Voice and Diet
A very vocal bird giving a loud, chattering *chacka-chacka-chack* call which is repeated harshly both in flight and when alarmed. Feeds on insects, slugs and seeds, but also steals eggs and nestlings, making this species unpopular with many people.

Habitat and Status

An abundant resident bird found in woodlands, parks, towns, cities, farmland and quarries. Nests in holes in trees, cliffs or occasionally on chimney pots. Often seen on open land in large flocks.

Jackdaw

pale grey nape

neat, triangular bill, pale eye

blackish plumage

Habitat and Status

An uncommon bird of rugged headlands and islands. Found along southern, western and northern coastal areas. Choughs are very rare in most eastern regions. Feeds in sand-dune areas or on short-cropped grass known as machair. Nests in coastal cliff holes or caves.

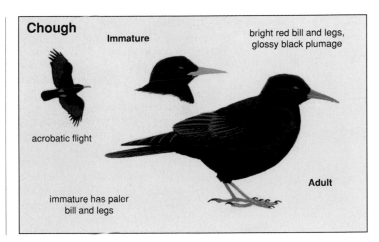

Chough

Immature

bright red bill and legs, glossy black plumage

acrobatic flight

Adult

immature has paler bill and legs

Habitat and Status

A very common resident species found in towns, cities, parks and open farmland. Often seen alone or in pairs, although sometimes forms small parties. Walks in a deliberate manner while searching for food. Builds a large, domed nest in trees or bushes. Can often remain faithful to the same nesting site.

Magpie

striking plumage

long tail

Crows and Starlings

Jay
Garrulus glandarius   Scréachóg

A stocky, skulking species with a stout, dark bill, and showing a white rump and a black tail. **Adults** show a black-streaked, whitish crown, a broad black moustachial stripe, a white throat and purplish-brown cheeks, nape and mantle. Black wings show a bright blue and black barred wing patch, a conspicuous white panel formed by white bases to the secondaries, and deep chestnut inner edges to the tertials. Underparts pinkish-brown, fading to white on the centre of the belly. Undertail-coverts white. Flight appears laboured, with the white rump contrasting strongly with the black tail. Jays in Ireland belong to a specific race (see Introduction).

Voice and Diet
The very distinctive call can be the first indication of the presence of a Jay. Gives very harsh, loud *skkaaaa* and loud, barking *kaa* calls. Can also give a subdued mewing-type note. Feeds on fruit, berries, nuts and acorns. Known to bury food in the autumn, utilising hidden stores during hard winter periods. Also feeds on insects, worms, slugs, eggs, nestlings and small mammals.

Starling
Sturnus vulgaris   Druid

A busy species showing a long, pointed bill, a short tail and triangular wings in flight. **Summer males** show a purple and green gloss to a blackish head and underparts, buff edges to mantle and wing feathers, and a grey base to a yellow bill. **Females** similar, but show some pale underpart spots, a pink base to the bill and a thin white eye circle. **Winter males** show buff spotting on the upperparts, white spotting on the head and underparts, and a brown bill. **Winter females** show larger underpart spotting. Legs pinkish. **Juveniles** greyish-brown with a white throat, dark lores, a dark bill and dark legs. **Immatures in moult** show a mixture of juvenile and adult winter plumages.

Voice and Diet
A noisy species with a variety of calls. Very talented mimics. Usual calls comprise harsh, grating *tzheerr* and thin, whistling *tzoo-ee* notes. Song a rambling selection of warbling, whistling and clicking. Some mimicry may be included. Feeds on the ground in noisy flocks, probing with open bills in search of insects, worms and slugs. Also feeds on grain, fruit, berries, scraps and insects.

Rose-coloured Starling (rare)
Sturnus roseus

A stocky species with a shorter and stubbier bill than Starling. **Adults** show a black head, breast, wings and tail contrasting with a pink mantle, rump and belly. Crown shows elongated rear feathers. Bill and legs pink. In winter, pink is obscured by buff fringes. **Juveniles** appear similar to juvenile Starling, but show pale lores, a sandy-grey head and upperparts, darker wings with buff edges to the feathers, pale buff underparts and rump, and a white throat. Unlike juvenile Starling, the stubbier bill is pale yellow with a reddish tip, and the legs are pale pink. Juveniles usually occur when immature Starlings are in an adult-like 1st winter plumage.

Voice and Diet
Rose-coloured Starlings give grating *tzheerr* and whistling *tzoo-ee* calls, similar to Starling but delivered in a higher-pitched, harsher tone. Freely associates with Starlings, feeding on the ground, probing with open bills for insects, worms and slugs. Also feeds on grain, fruit and berries. Occasionally hawks insects.

Habitat and Status

A widely distributed resident breeding species. While present in all counties, Jays are relatively uncommon in some northern, north-western, western and south-western counties. Frequents deciduous and coniferous woodlands, open mature parklands and, occasionally in winter, orchards and suburban gardens. Nests in trees or large, mature bushes. British Jays appear paler.

Jay

streaked crown,
black moustaches,
bright blue wing patches

white rump

Habitat and Status

A common, widespread breeding species present in all counties in a wide range of habitats — cities, farmland, woodland, islands, shorelines. Nests in holes in trees or buildings, usually in loose colonies. In early autumn, immature birds may disperse in large flocks to headlands and islands. In late autumn, birds arrive from the Continent and in hard winters, from northern and central Europe. Can form huge winter roosting flocks, usually in reed-beds, woodlands, on buildings or cliffs.

Starling

adult all dark in summer

dark brown upperparts, dark lores and bill

Adult (winter)   **Immature**

Habitat and Status

A very rare vagrant from south-eastern Europe. Most records refer to a period from June to November, with birds found in a variety of habitats. Occurs in autumn on coastal islands and headlands, associating with Starlings on open and rough pastures. In summer and late autumn, can be found at any location, usually with flocks of Starlings. Has occurred in all regions, with most reports referring to coastal counties.

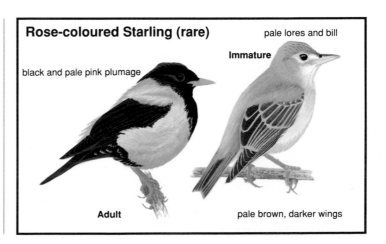

Rose-coloured Starling (rare)

pale lores and bill

Immature

black and pale pink plumage

Adult   pale brown, darker wings

Oriole, Grosbeak and Finches

Golden Oriole (rare)
Oriolus oriolus   Óiréal órga

A shy, slender, Starling-sized bird with a striking plumage and a pinkish-red bill. **Males** show a bright sulphur-yellow head, mantle and underparts contrasting with a black loral patch and black wings. In flight, shows conspicuous yellow primary coverts and bright yellow outer tips to a black tail. **Females** appear duller, with a yellow-green head and upperparts, browner wings, and paler underparts which usually show brown streaking. Tail blackish, with rump and outer-tail tips pale yellow. Some old females can appear as bright as males, but show greyish lores and greenish tones to the upperparts. **Immatures** similar to females. Flight strong and undulating.

Voice and Diet
Both sexes can occasionally give harsh, scratching, Jay-like calls. The distinctive, loud, clear, fluty song is rarely heard in Ireland. Golden Orioles feed on insects in spring and summer but will eat a variety of fruits and berries at all times.

Rose-breasted Grosbeak (rare)
Pheucticus ludovicianus

A large, stocky bird showing a huge, pale bill. Usually seen in immature plumage when found in Ireland. **Immature males** show a dark brown crown with a pale central stripe, a white supercilium and dark ear coverts. Brown upperparts show dark streaking. Wings show whitish tips to median and greater coverts, whitish primary bases and pale-tipped tertials. Underwing coverts pinkish. Pale underparts heavily streaked on yellowish-buff breast and flanks. Can show pink on breast and throat. **Immature females** and **adult females** similar, but lack pink on underparts and show yellow underwing coverts. **Adult males** are strikingly black and white and show a bright red breast patch.

Voice and Diet
Rose-breasted Grosbeak can give a sharp, metallic *keck* call. Feeds on a wide variety of insects but in autumn usually found feeding on seeds and berries. Berries occasionally stain the bill, giving it a darker appearance.

Hawfinch (rare)
Coccothraustes coccothraustes   Glasán gobmhór

A bull-necked, stout finch with a very large, bluish-grey bill. **Adult males** show a warm brown crown and ear coverts, a black bib and lores, and a grey hindneck. Mantle and scapulars rich dark brown. Glossy blackish wings show a white covert patch. Rump and white-tipped tail warm brown. Underparts pinkish-brown with white undertail. In flight, shows a striking white wing patch and a whitish, transparent band on the primaries. Bill paler in winter. Eye brown with a black pupil. **Adult females** similar, but appear duller, with greyish tones on the head, rump and upperparts. A secretive species, but tends to perch openly in the upper branches of tall trees.

Voice and Diet
Hawfinches can be difficult to see, but can draw attention to their presence by giving a distinctive, explosive *tzik* call. Can also give a thin *tzriip* call. Feeds on a variety of seeds, kernels and berries. Will also feed on beechmast. The enormous bill can exert great pressure, opening the toughest seeds and kernels with apparent ease. Also feeds on insects in summer.

Habitat and Status

A rare but regular spring passage migrant from Europe. Extremely rare in autumn. Most records refer to a period from mid-April to mid-June, with numbers peaking in early May. Most are found in mature or well-vegetated gardens on coastal headlands and islands. A skulking and often elusive species, with a tendency to sit tight in deep cover. Usually first seen in flight. Most reports refer to south-eastern and south-western coastal counties. Occasionally found inland.

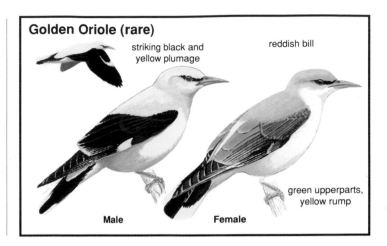

Golden Oriole (rare)

striking black and yellow plumage

reddish bill

green upperparts, yellow rump

Male

Female

Habitat and Status

An extremely rare autumn vagrant from North America. Found along hedgerows, in gardens and dense scrub on coastal headlands and islands. Most records refer to the south-west, with one report from the south-east. Most Irish records have been seen in October. Can occasionally be very confiding and tame.

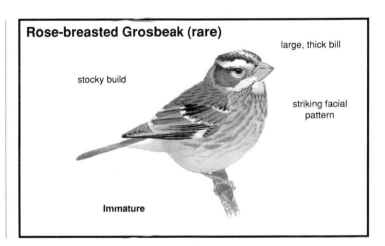

Rose-breasted Grosbeak (rare)

large, thick bill

stocky build

striking facial pattern

Immature

Habitat and Status

Formerly a regular winter visitor to the east, midlands and south-west, Hawfinches are now rare vagrants from Europe. Recorded in all seasons, but most recent reports refer to autumn. Seen in open woodlands, mature parks and orchards in winter, spring and summer. In autumn, found on coastal headlands and islands. Feeds in trees and on the ground. In the autumn of 1988, a major influx occurred, with large numbers seen at migration points along the south-west.

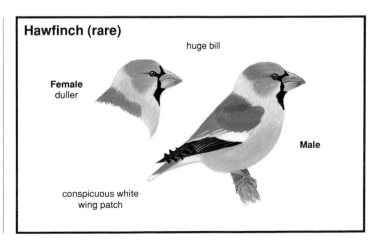

Hawfinch (rare)

huge bill

Female duller

Male

conspicuous white wing patch

Finches

Chaffinch
Fringilla coelebs   Rí rua

Summer males show a blue-grey crown and nape, a reddish-pink breast and cheeks, and a chestnut-coloured mantle. Dark wings show a broad white shoulder patch, white-tipped greater coverts and white bases to the primaries. Primaries and tertials also show olive-green edges. Forked tail shows white outer feathers. Rump olive-green. In winter the plumage is paler. **Females** show similar wing markings, but the upperparts and head are greyish-brown. The centre of the crown and the nape are paler, creating dark lines from side of neck onto sides of crown. Underparts pale greyish-brown. **Immatures** similar to females. Thick bill blue-grey. Can form large flocks in winter.

Voice and Diet
Calls frequently, giving a loud *pinnk* call or, in flight, a *chhip* call. In spring and summer, males can be heard to give a *whiit* call. Song consists of scratchy chipping-type notes finished rapidly with a *ptsse-eeo* note. Feeds on seeds, berries, fruit and occasionally insects.

Brambling
Fringilla montifringilla   Breacán

A colourful finch with a black and orange plumage and a white rump. **Winter males** show a mottled brown head and mantle, and grey from behind eye onto nape and sides of neck. A bright orange shoulder patch and two buff wingbars are obvious on blackish wings. Upper breast orange, fading to a white lower breast, belly and undertail. Shows diffuse spotting on flanks. Deeply notched blackish tail contrasts with the white rump. **Females** similar, but show a paler head and shoulder patch, and an orange wash on the breast. **Summer males** show a black head and mantle, and orange on the throat, breast and scapulars. Thick bill black on summer males, paler on females. Legs pale.

Voice and Diet
Calls include a Chaffinch-like *chick* in flight and a *tsueek* when on the ground. Feeds on seeds and berries but also favours beechmast.

Goldfinch
Carduelis carduelis   Lasair choille

A charming finch with colourful head and wing markings, and a white rump. Sexes alike. **Adults** show a bright red forehead and chin, black before eye, and white cheeks and throat. Crown and sides of neck black. Mantle buff-brown, extending onto lower throat, sides of breast and along flanks. Underparts white. Wings black with a bright yellow patch, yellow bases to primaries and white tips to primaries, secondaries and tertials. Rump white. The black, notched tail shows white tips. **Immatures** show a greyish-brown head and mantle, and duller wing markings. Thick bill whitish-grey and pointed. Legs pale. Rarely associates with other finch flocks. Flight undulating.

Voice and Diet
The twittering, chattering *ptswit-wit-wit* flight call is unmistakable. Can also give a loud *ee-uu* call. The song is a trill consisting of a variety of twittering notes. Feeds on a variety of seeds and is often found feeding on the tops of thistles or teazels. Also takes small insects.

Habitat and Status

An abundant finch, found in every county. Frequents gardens, parklands, hedgerows and woodland. In winter, found in farmyards and on open fields when resident birds are joined by birds from northern Europe. Nests in bushes and low trees.

Chaffinch

white wingbars, dull grey and brown head pattern

blue-grey crown and nape, pinkish underparts

Female

Male

Habitat and Status

An uncommon winter visitor from northern Europe. Found in mixed finch flocks on farmlands, open fields and beech woodland. In late autumn, occurs on coastal headlands and islands. Numbers can fluctuate from winter to winter, with flocks of several hundred birds occasionally recorded.

Brambling

pale wingbars and rump

brown upperparts, pale orange underparts

striking black and orange plumage

Male

Female

Habitat and Status

A common finch found on open ground such as parks, gardens and woodland edges. Can be seen on waste ground where thistles are likely to grow. A resident species, Goldfinches nest in bushes and trees.

Goldfinch

yellow wing patches

conspicuous red, black and white head pattern

white rump

Finches and Buntings

Greenfinch
Carduelis chloris   Glasán darach

A chunky finch with bright yellow wing and tail flashes, a thick, pale bill and pale legs. **Summer males** show an olive-green head and upperparts, and bright yellow-green underparts. Greyish wings show a bright yellow flash on the primaries. Rump yellow-green. Dark, forked tail shows yellow flashes at base. **Winter males** show brown tones to upperparts and head. **Adult females** show a faintly streaked, greyish-brown head and upperparts with yellow-tinged, whitish underparts and dull yellow wing and tail flashes. **Immatures**, while showing streaked brownish heads and upperparts, pale, streaked underparts and a brownish rump, do show yellow wing and tail flashes.

Voice and Diet
In flight gives a distinctive, soft, deep, trilling *chit* which is usually repeated. In spring, males can give a long, drawn-out, nasal *tsueee* note. The twittering song consists of a variety of call notes and is delivered from a prominent perch or during a slow, wing-flapping, bat-like flight display. Feeds on a variety of berries, seeds, fruit and occasionally insects. A regular winter visitor to nut feeders in gardens.

Siskin
Carduelis spinus   Siscín

An agile finch which shows two thick yellow wingbars, a pointed, pale bill and dark legs. **Adult males** show a black crown and chin, olive-green ear coverts, and a yellowish supercilium, throat and breast. Upperparts olive-green with faint streaking. Yellow-edged, black wings show two broad yellow wingbars. Yellow-green rump unstreaked. Short, dark, forked tail shows yellow base. Underparts white with dark streaking along flanks. **Adult females** show heavily streaked greyish-green upperparts and head. Wings similar to males. Underparts whitish with heavy streaking. **Immatures** similar to females, but appear browner on the upperparts and show a greyish rump.

Voice and Diet
Gives distinctive, loud, shrill *tseu* or more extended *tseu-eet* calls. Song consists of a combination of call notes and more warbling, twittering notes. The song can be delivered either from a prominent perch or during a Greenfinch-like, slow, flapping display flight. Feeds on a wide range of tree seeds and will readily visit nut and seed feeders in gardens during winter.

Yellowhammer
Emberiza citrinella   Buíóg

A striking bunting, **summer males** showing a bright yellow head and underparts with olive-brown head streaking, a chestnut ear covert border and moustachial stripe, a diffuse chestnut breast band, and dark streaking on chestnut-washed flanks. Chestnut upperparts show dark streaking. Chestnut rump unstreaked. Tail shows white outer edges. **Winter males** show heavier head and underpart streaking, and darker head markings. **Females** show a pale yellow head with olive-brown ear covert border, moustachial and malar stripes. Underparts yellowish with brown breast and flank streaking. Upperparts as male. **Immatures** duller than females with finer streaking. Bill greyish. Legs pinkish.

Voice and Diet
Gives a sharp, loud, metallic *tzwik* call. The song is a distinctive combination of repeated, high-pitched, tinkling notes finishing in a drawn-out, wheezy *chueee* note. This song is traditionally transcribed as *little-bit-of-bread-and-no-cheese*, the emphasis being on the *cheese*. Feeds on a wide range of seeds, corn, grain, berries and fruit. In summer, feeds on insects, spiders and worms.

Habitat and Status

An extremely common, widespread, resident species found in all counties. In winter, birds from Britain and the Continent can occur. Found in a wide range of habitats, nesting in hedgerows, bushes and trees in gardens, parks, woodland edges and farmland. In winter, can be found in quite large flocks on farmlands and yards, arable fields and coastal saltmarshes. Also a common winter visitor to city and town gardens, feeding on nut and seed feeders.

Greenfinch

bright yellow tail and wing flashes

thick, pale bill

Female

Male

Habitat and Status

A common, widespread, resident species found in all counties. In summer, frequents conifer plantations and occasionally areas of mixed woodlands. Nests high in conifers. In winter is found in areas with alder, birch and larch trees. Has become a regular visitor to gardens in towns and cities, feeding on nut and seed feeders. Highly gregarious, often found in quite large flocks. Will readily associate with other species, including Redpolls.

Siskin

two yellow wingbars and unstreaked yellow-green rump

black crown and chin

Male

Female

streaked head and upperparts

Habitat and Status

An uncommon but widespread, resident species formerly found in all counties. Population decreases, noted in the 1990s, have continued and the species is now absent from many former strongholds. Still found in some northern, eastern and south-eastern counties, with small populations still resident in western regions. Frequents hedgerows on arable farmland, woodland edges, overgrown scrub and gorse slopes and young conifer plantations. Nests on or near the ground in overgrown bases of hedges and brambles.

Yellowhammer

Male

striking head pattern

unstreaked chestnut rump

white outer-tail feathers

Female

217

Finches

Linnet
Carduelis cannabina   Gleoiseach

A small brownish finch with a heavy, greyish bill and white flashes on the wings and tail. **Summer males** show a bright red forehead and breast, a grey head, a pale throat and whitish underparts. Warm brown upperparts show faint streaks and an inconspicuous wingbar. Dark primaries show extensive white flashes on outer feathers. Short, forked tail shows striking white sides. **Winter males** show a streaked grey head, with pale areas above and below eye and on cheeks. Whitish underparts show faint streaking on buff breast and flanks. **Females** similar to winter males, but show a browner head with heavy streaking on upper- and underparts. **Immatures** show a pale-buff face and less streaking.

Voice and Diet
In flight gives a twittering, musical *tret-tret-terret* call and a drawn-out *tsweet*. Song consists of a variety of twittering, trilling, fluty notes which are delivered from a prominent perch. Feeds on a wide range of plant seeds and some insects.

Twite
Carduelis flavirostris   Gleoiseach sléibhe

A heavily-streaked finch, similar to Linnet but with a pale yellow bill in winter and less extensive white wing and tail flashes. **Summer males** show a warm buff face, throat and breast, and streaked, brownish ear coverts, nape and crown. Underparts whitish with streaking from breast onto flanks. Heavily-streaked brownish upperparts show a conspicuous pale wingbar and white flashes on outer primaries. Rump pinkish. Forked tail shows white sides. Bill dark. **Winter males** show a pale yellow bill, a buffish-pink rump and streaked, buff flanks. **Females** similar to males, but show a streaked buffish rump. Best told from Linnet by buff face and throat, small, paler bill and heavier streaking.

Voice and Diet
In flight gives a harsh, nasal, metallic *tchweek* call which can often be the first indication of the presence of a Twite among a large, mixed finch flock. Can also give twittering calls which are similar to but harder than Linnets, and a softer *tseee* call. Song consists of a range of twittering, trilling, musical notes delivered from a prominent perch. Feeds on a variety of plant seeds and some insects.

Lesser Redpoll
Carduelis carbaret   Deargéadan coiteann

A heavily-streaked brownish finch with a black-tipped yellow bill and which is smaller and more arboreal in behaviour than Linnet. **Males** show a bright red forehead, a black chin and pinkish-red tones on head, breast and upper flanks. Underparts whitish with dark flank streaking. Crown and upperparts tawny-brown with heavy streaking. Wings show two obvious whitish-buff wingbars but lack white primary flashes of Linnet. Rump pinkish. Forked, brownish tail does not show white sides. Duller in winter. **Females** show heavier underpart streaking and lack strong pinkish-red tones. **Immatures** similar to females, showing a red forehead but no pinkish-red tones to head and breast.

Voice and Diet
In flight, gives a twittering, rhythmic, repeated *chei-chei-chei* call. Can also occasionally give a drawn-out *tsweeck*. Song consists of a variety of trilling notes interspersed with call notes. Song can be delivered from a prominent perch but can also be given during a circling, slow, flapping flight display. Feeds on a wide range of tree seeds, particularly those of birch and alder. Will also take some insects.

Habitat and Status

A widespread and common breeding species present in all counties. Frequents a variety of habitats, including farmlands, rough pastures, waste ground, sand-dunes, saltmarshes, scrubland and young plantations. Nests in dense cover on the ground or in brambles and bushes. Many Irish birds winter in southern continental Europe. In winter, the largest populations can be found in eastern and southern regions, usually at coastal locations.

Linnet

Male (summer)

Male (winter)

Female

white flashes on wings

Habitat and Status

An uncommon resident species, with breeding populations based in northern, north-western, western and south-western counties. Nests on the ground in heather, old stone walls or gorse, frequenting areas of open, upland moorlands and pastures. In winter, more commonly found along coastal stubble and crop fields, salt-marshes and estuaries, occurring regularly along more eastern regions. Feeds on the ground and can be quite approachable.

Twite

streaked buffish rump

pale yellow bill, pinkish rump

Female

Male

Habitat and Status

A widespread breeding species, present in all counties. During the breeding season, found in a variety of woodlands which usually include some birch or alder. Also found in upland conifer plantations. Nests in high bushes, young conifers and woodland edges. In autumn and winter, tends to leave more mountainous and western areas. Can associate with Siskins and occasionally visits bird tables in town gardens. Largest winter populations are in north-eastern and midland counties.

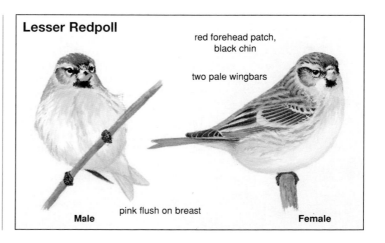

Lesser Redpoll

red forehead patch, black chin

two pale wingbars

pink flush on breast

Male

Female

Finches

Crossbill
Loxia curvirostra   Crosghob
Stocky, large-headed finch with long wings and a short, deeply-forked tail. The large bill is crossed at the tip, an adaptation for taking seeds from the cones of coniferous trees. When feeding, pulls the cones from the trees, holding them in the feet while extracting the seeds. **Males** have an orange-red head, upperparts and underparts, the rump being slightly brighter. **Females** are dull greyish-green with a bright yellow-green rump. The wings of both sexes are brownish. **Immatures** are pale greyish-green and heavily streaked. Eye and legs blackish. Highly gregarious, often moving in large, noisy flocks. Flight strong and undulating. Often seen perched on the very tops of trees.

Voice and Diet
A noisy species, continuously calling to each other both in flight and when feeding. Call consists of a short, sharp *chip*. In song, gives a series of trills along with high pitched *tir-ee* notes. Feeds mainly on conifer seeds, although will take berries and occasionally insects.

Bullfinch
Pyrrhula pyrrhula   Corcrán coille
Plump, thick-necked finch with a short, dark, thickset bill. **Males** show a black crown and upper nape, continuing down below the eye and onto the chin. The cheeks, throat, breast and upper belly are bright pink-red, with the lower belly and undertail white. The mantle is blue-grey and extends up the nape. The black wings show a broad white wingbar. Black tail appears square-ended. Most obvious feature in flight is the broad white rump. Duller **females** show pinkish-buff cheeks, breast and upper belly, with a greyish-brown mantle. Black crown duller. **Immatures** do not show a black cap. Black eye blends into black cap. Thick, short bill blackish-grey. Legs blackish.

Voice and Diet
Gives a soft *dieu* call. The song is a quiet variety of creaking notes. Feeds on seeds, berries and occasionally insects. Also has a liking for fresh buds of apple trees and is considered a pest in orchards.

Scarlet Rosefinch (rare)
Carpodacus erythrinus
Stout, thick-billed finch, usually found in Ireland in the drab female or immature plumage. **Summer males** show a bright pink-red head and breast, often extending down onto the whitish belly and flanks. Upperparts streaked greyish-brown. Rump pinkish-red. Notched tail greyish-brown. **Immatures** and **females** are extremely plain and nondescript, with greyish-brown upperparts and head. The paler underparts show faint streaking and an inconspicuous malar stripe. Brownish wings show two diagnostic pale wingbars on the median and greater coverts. Large black beady eye stands out in a plain face. The thick, short bill is dark horn-coloured. Legs brownish.

Voice and Diet
Occasionally heard to call in Ireland, giving a quiet *teu-ic* call. Has also been heard to sing when seen in spring. The song consists of loud, far-carrying *teu-teu* notes. Feeds primarily on seeds.

Habitat and Status

Usually found in coniferous forests, frequently visiting pools to drink. An uncommon breeding bird in Ireland, nesting high in conifer trees as early as February. Populations can fluctuate drastically, with large influxes occurring in certain years. In autumn, can be found on coastal headlands and islands.

Crossbill

grey-green plumage

crossed mandibles

orange-red plumage

Female

Male

Habitat and Status

A common resident species found in open parkland, woods, orchards and well-developed gardens. Builds nests in bushes or brambles. Unlike other finches, Bullfinches are more often seen in pairs than in flocks.

Bullfinch

heavy dark bill

white rump

broad white wingbar

Female

Male

Habitat and Status

A rare but regular vagrant to Ireland from eastern Europe. Although small numbers have been recorded in spring, they are usually found in autumn on coastal islands and headlands. Feeds in fields, but perches openly on hedgerows, bushes or in gardens. Often associates with other feeding finch flocks.

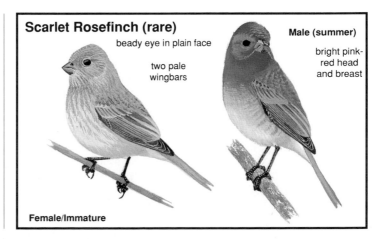

Scarlet Rosefinch (rare)

beady eye in plain face

two pale wingbars

Male (summer)

bright pink-red head and breast

Female/Immature

Sparrows and Buntings

House Sparrow
Passer domesticus   Gealbhan binne

House Sparrows are one of the most common, successful species found in Ireland. **Males** show a grey forehead and crown, a brownish-grey nape, a black throat and chin patch, and pale cheeks. Underparts greyish-white. Chestnut upper-parts show broad dark streaks and contrast with a grey rump and uppertail-coverts. **Females** appear duller, with streaked, paler upperparts, and show a brownish crown and a pale supercilium. Underparts greyish-white. Shows a thick, short bill. A highly gregarious species, feeding and roosting in large, noisy flocks. Easily attracted to gardens to feed on any available scraps. Can occasionally be seen taking communal dust baths.

Voice and Diet
Gives a loud, repeated *chirrp* or *chirp* call. When alarmed, gives the same note delivered with more urgency. Flight call is a short *zwit*. Although primarily a seed-eater, almost any available food is taken. Recently, House Sparrows have learned to feed from nut feeders left out for tits and finches.

Tree Sparrow
Passer montanus   Gealbhan crainn

Tree Sparrows are slightly smaller and more colourful than the very similar House Sparrow. **Males** and **females** are identical. Shows a striking head pattern with a deep chestnut crown and a distinctive black spot on white cheeks. The black throat and chin patch are neater than House Sparrow. Shows a white neck collar and streaked chestnut upper-parts. Tail and rump warm brown. Underparts greyish-white. Thick bill short and dark. **Immatures** show a brownish-grey tinge to the centre of the crown, buffish-grey underparts and a yellowish base to the bill. Occasionally joins House Sparrow flocks in the winter.

Voice and Diet
Gives a distinctive, sharp, repeated *tek* call. When perched, can also give a loud *tritt* call which can be difficult to hear if within a mixed flock of sparrows. Feeds on a wide variety of seeds and cereals. Although primarily a seed-eater, Tree Sparrows will occasionally eat insects.

Corn Bunting (rare)
Emberiza calandra   Gealóg bhuachair

A large, heavily-streaked, brownish bunting with a large, thick bill. **Summer adults** show a streaked brownish crown, a pale supercilium and a broad dark border to heavily-streaked ear coverts. Underparts whitish with a thick malar stripe meeting heavy streaking on the sides of the breast, and continuing onto the flanks. Upperparts greyish-brown with heavy dark streaking on the mantle, and dark centres to the wing feathers. Long brownish tail does not show white outer feathers. **Winter adults** and **immatures** appear duller, with whitish-buff underparts. Shows a very thick, pinkish bill. Legs and largish feet pinkish-orange. Usually seen perched prominently on telegraph wires and fences.

Voice and Diet
Gives a low, sharp *tikk* call. The far-carrying song is a fast, complicated jingle of rattles and chirps. The distinctive song has often been described as sounding like rattling keys. Feeds on a wide variety of seeds and cereals but will take some insects on occasion.

Habitat and Status

A very common resident town and city species, usually found close to human habitation. In Ireland they are present in all counties. Nests in holes and cavities, often under roof tiles. On occasions, nests in trees and bushes, constructing a dome-shaped nest with a side entrance.

House Sparrow

grey forehead and crown

Male

streaked, pale upperparts and pale supercilium

extensive black bib

Female

Habitat and Status

A widespread but scarce resident species, found in all regions. Found on open farmland and less frequently in towns and villages. Tree Sparrows breed in widely scattered colonies. Nests in holes in trees and old buildings.

Tree Sparrow

deep chestnut crown

striking black spot on white cheeks

small, neat black bib

Habitat and Status

Formerly found in most counties at the beginning of the twentieth century, the range of the Corn Bunting had diminished steadily until the species no longer bred in Ireland from the 1990s. Now a rare winter and passage visitor from Europe, although small pockets of birds may still exist in remote western regions. Found on coastal farmland and open country. Nests on the ground in long grass or thistles.

Corn Bunting (rare)

large, heavily-streaked bunting

thick, pale bill

lacks white on tail

Buntings

Reed Bunting
Emberiza schoeniclus   Gealóg ghiolcaí

A striking bunting with a long, white-edged tail. **Summer males** show a black head and throat contrasting with a white moustachial stripe and neck collar. Upperparts rufous with black streaking and centres to wing feathers. Underparts whitish with flank streaking. In **winter**, black on head and throat obscured by buffish tips. **Adult females** and **immatures** show a brownish crown with a thin, dark, lateral crown-stripe and buff supercilium. Ear coverts and lores brownish, with a dark eye-stripe from behind eye forming a dark ear covert border and a moustachial stripe meeting the bill. Creamy throat shows a malar stripe. Breast and flanks streaked. Bill greyish. Legs brownish.

Voice and Diet
Song consists of repeated, hurried *tzik-tzik-tzik-tzizzizik* notes. The song is usually delivered from the tops of reed-stems or from bushes. Most frequently-heard calls include a loud, shrill *tswee* and a harsh *chink*. Feeds on a wide range of insects and larvae in summer, taking mostly seeds in winter.

Little Bunting (rare)
Emberiza pusilla

A small bunting with a striking head pattern. **Adult males, females** and **immatures** similar, showing a warm brown crown, a black lateral crown-stripe, a buff supercilium behind eye, chestnut lores and ear coverts, and a pale spot on rear ear coverts. Eye shows a pale orbital ring. Eye-stripe behind eye forms a dark border to rear of ear coverts but, unlike Reed Bunting, there is no moustachial stripe. Thin malar stripe does not meet bill. White underparts show breast and flank streaking. Upperparts buff with black streaking. Whitish median covert tips form a wingbar. Greater coverts can show pale tips. Outer-tails white. Short bill greyish with a straight culmen. Legs pinkish.

Voice and Diet
When found on passage, Little Bunting can give very distinctive, Robin-like *tick* or thrush-like *tsip* calls which are unlike the calls given by Reed Bunting. Feeds on the ground in a low, crouched manner, taking a variety of seeds and occasionally insects.

Rustic Bunting (rare)
Emberiza rustica

Autumn adults and **immatures** show white underparts, with chestnut breast streaking extending and broadening onto flanks. Pale nape patch contrasts with a streaked brown crown which can appear crested. Supercilium buff before eye, creamy-buff and prominent behind eye. Lores and ear coverts brownish with a pale buff rear spot. Dark stripe behind eye forms ear covert border and thin moustachial stripe. Pale throat shows malar stripe. Dark-streaked chestnut upperparts show wingbars formed by pale median and greater covert tips. Outer-tail feathers white. **Summer males** show a black crown and cheeks, and a white supercilium and nape patch. Bill pinkish with a grey tip. Legs pinkish-brown.

Voice and Diet
On passage, Rustic Buntings can give a hard, sharp, Robin-like *tsip* call which can be repeated. Care should be taken, as the call of Little Bunting is very similar. Feeds on the ground, taking a variety of seeds and plant material and occasionally insects.

14-16cm **Reed Bunting**
13-14cm **Little Bunting**
14-15cm **Rustic Bunting**

Habitat and Status

A common, resident, widely-distributed species present in all counties. Found in a wide range of habitats, including reed-beds, marshes, hedgerows, sand-dunes and young conifer plantations. Nests on or near the ground in tussocks, rank vegetation or bushes. In winter are altitudinal migrants, leaving more mountainous regions in favour of low-lying or coastal habitat. Can also be found on farmlands in winter.

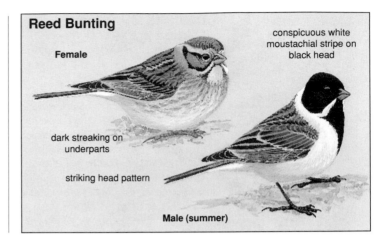

Reed Bunting

Female

conspicuous white moustachial stripe on black head

dark streaking on underparts

striking head pattern

Male (summer)

Habitat and Status

A very rare vagrant from northern Scandinavia and Siberia. Most records refer to autumn, although reported both in spring and winter. While most recent records refer to south-western regions, birds have been seen in north-western, western, eastern and south-eastern counties. Found on coastal headlands and islands in rough pastures, crop fields and short grass. Often perches on top of low bushes. Associates with other species, including buntings and finches.

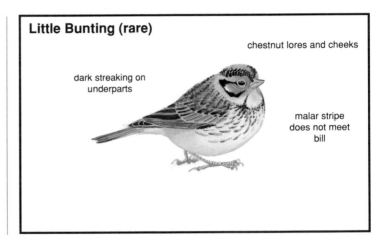

Little Bunting (rare)

chestnut lores and cheeks

dark streaking on underparts

malar stripe does not meet bill

Habitat and Status

A very rare vagrant from northern Scandinavia and Siberia. Most records refer to autumn, although Rustic Bunting has been recorded in spring. Most records refer to south-western regions. Found on coastal headlands and islands in rough pastures, crop fields and short grass. Often perches in the open on top of low bushes, wires or fence posts. Can sometimes associate with other species.

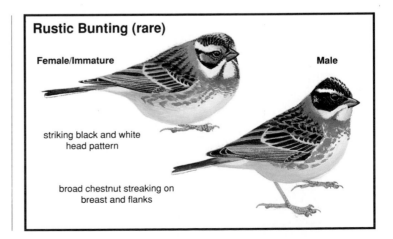

Rustic Bunting (rare)

Female/Immature

Male

striking black and white head pattern

broad chestnut streaking on breast and flanks

225

Buntings

Lapland Bunting
Calcarius lapponicus

A long-winged bunting with a short, yellowish bill. **Winter males** and **females** show a buff crown, a black lateral crown-stripe, and buff lores, ear coverts and supercilium. Black eye-stripe forms a thick border to ear coverts and continues as a moustachial stripe. Nape chestnut or warm buff. White tips to median and greater coverts, and chestnut greater coverts, contrasted with streaked, buff upperparts. Creamy underparts show a malar stripe and streaking on breast and flanks. **Winter males** tend to be brighter with dark blotching on the breast. **1st winters** show a dull head and nape. **Summer males** show a black head and throat with white from eye to sides of breast. Legs dark.

Voice and Diet
In flight or when flushed, gives a very distinctive, dry, rippling, rattling *trickitick* call which can often be followed by a softer, descending *teuu*. This latter call can resemble that of Snow Bunting but is softer. Moves on the ground in a low, crouched manner, feeding on a wide range of seeds. Will occasionally take insects.

Snow Bunting
Plectrophenax nivalis   Gealóg shneachta

A striking, tame bunting with a yellowish bill and dark legs. **Winter male**s show a warm buff crown, cheeks and breast sides and a pale buff nape. Underparts white. Dark-streaked, pale buff upperparts contrast with white inner wings and black primaries. In flight, shows white sides to black tail. **Females** show dull buff upperparts, crown, cheeks and sides of breast with streaking on nape and upperparts. Wings show brown primaries and less white, with dark bases to coverts and markings on secondaries. Underparts creamy with buff flanks. **Immatures** are very dull, showing a very small area of white on the wings. **Summer males** show a black and white plumage and a black bill.

Voice and Diet
In flight or when flushed, gives a rippling, musical *tirrirrirrip* call. Also gives a plaintive *teu* call which is louder and more whistling than the similar call of Lapland Bunting. Feeds on the ground, taking a variety of seeds and other plant material. Will occasionally take insects.

Ortolan Bunting (rare)
Emberiza hortulana

A long-winged bunting always showing a pale orbital ring, and pale reddish-pink bill and legs. **Adult males** show a greyish-olive head, nape and upper breast, and a pale yellow throat and moustachial stripe. Underparts orange-buff. Warm brown upperparts show dark streaking and pale wingbars formed by tips to median and greater coverts. Tail dark with white outer edges. **Adult females** similar, but show brownish tones to head and breast, thin breast streaking and paler underparts. **Immatures** similar to females, but show a brownish head, a pale throat and moustachial stripe, a streaked grey-buff breast, thin streaking on pale buff underparts and streaked, brownish upperparts.

Voice and Diet
Gives a variety of calls, including a soft, liquid *tsip*, a harder *twick*, and a louder, sharper *tseu*. Feeds on the ground, taking a wide assortment of seeds and other plant material. Will also take insects on occasion.

Habitat and Status

A scarce but regular autumn and winter visitor. On passage, found on northern, western and south-western coastal islands and headlands, frequenting crop and stubble fields, pastures and moorland. In winter, found along coastal counties, including eastern and south-eastern areas. In winter is normally found on coastal stubble and crop fields and saltmarshes. Can be very tame and hard to flush and as a result may be easily overlooked.

Lapland Bunting

1st winter

Summer Male (rare)

Male (winter)

long wings, yellow bill

Habitat and Status

An uncommon but regular autumn passage migrant and winter visitor. On passage, found on coastal headlands and islands, frequenting pastures and moorlands. Winters in small numbers along most coastal counties, the largest populations in northern regions. Less numerous on southern coasts. Frequents coastal shingle banks, dunes, stubble and crop fields, piers and harbours. Can also winter inland, usually on mountain tops. Occasionally occurs in spring.

Snow Bunting

Female (winter)

yellow bill, black legs

white underparts and wing patches

Male (winter)

Habitat and Status

A rare autumn passage migrant from continental Europe. Also occurs as a rare vagrant in spring. Most records refer to south-western and south-eastern coastal locations, with reports also from northern, western and eastern regions. On passage, found on coastal islands and headlands, frequenting stubble and crop fields, pastures and areas of scrub. Feeds on the ground, but does perch openly. A shy species which could be overlooked. Tends to flush easily.

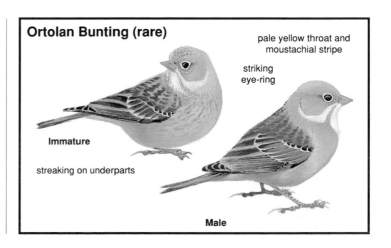

Ortolan Bunting (rare)

pale yellow throat and moustachial stripe

striking eye-ring

Immature

streaking on underparts

Male

Rare Species

Rare Species Accounts

The following species are considered to be extremely rare vagrants to Ireland and require great caution in their identification. All species that appear in this section require full documented evidence to be submitted to the respective rarities committees which are listed at the back.

Pied-billed Grebe
Podilymbus podiceps

A stocky grebe, slightly larger than Little Grebe and showing a thick, short, stubby bill. In summer shows a whitish bill with a thick black band, a dark crown and nape, a greyish head and neck, and a black throat patch. Shows dark brown upperparts and dingy-buff flanks. Belly and undertail white. In winter, the bill is yellowish-grey, the throat is whitish and the head and neck are warm brownish-buff.
Range: North America

Soft-plumaged Petrel
Pterodroma mollis

An agile petrel, similar in size to Manx Shearwater. Shows a dark, blackish head and cheeks, a whitish forehead, a dark grey nape and back, dark upperwings and a long pale tail. White underparts contrast strongly with blackish underwings. Can show a diffuse greyish patch on the sides of the breast near the base of the wings.
Range: Cape Verde Islands and small islands off Madeira

Bulwer's Petrel
Bulweria bulweria

A large species, intermediate in size between petrels and shearwaters. Shows an all-dark plumage, with long wings showing pale upperwing bars. The long, tapering tail appears wedge-shaped when spread. Flies with swooping wing beats interspersed with glides over the water.
Range: Azores and Madeira

Swinhoe's Petrel
Oceanodroma monorhis

All all-dark petrel, very similar in size and shape to Leach's Petrel. Shows long, angled wings with a contrasting pale panel on the upperwing, pale shafts to the primary feathers which are almost impossible to see in the field, and dark underwings. Unlike Leach's Petrel, shows an all-dark rump. Tail shows a shallow fork.
Range: Eastern Asia

Madeiran Petrel
Oceanodroma castro

A white-romped petrel very similar to both Leach's and Wilson's Petrels. Shows a shallow fork to the tail, a dark body, long, broad, angled wings and a pale upperwing bar. Unlike Wilson's, the toes do not project past the tail. Differs from Leach's by showing a less conspicuous wingbar, and more extensive white on the rump which extends onto the sides of the rear flanks and undertail-coverts. Flies with quick, shallow wing beats.
Range: Azores, Madeira and Portugal

Magnificent Frigatebird
Fregata magnificens

An enormous seabird with long, angled wings and a long, forked tail. Adult males show an all-dark plumage with a red throat patch. Adult females differ by showing a whitish breast patch and a pale upperwing bar. Immatures similar to females, but show a whitish head and more extensive white on the underparts. Very skilled in the air, flying with slow wing beats and long glides. Often soars to great heights. Rarely lands on the water, picking food from the surface in flight. Will also steal food from other seabirds.
Range: Tropical Atlantic and east Pacific

Double-crested Cormorant
Phalacrocorax auritus

Similar but smaller than Cormorant with bright orange lores, chin and bill. Adults show a glossy black plumage with pale-edged wing feathers and wispy crests in summer plumage. Immatures appear dark brown above with a pale brown foreneck and breast, and a dark belly and undertail. This plumage is the opposite to that shown in immature Cormorant where the neck and upper breast is dark and the belly white. Immature Double-crested also show the striking orange lores, chin and bill.
Range: North America

American Bittern
Botaurus lentiginosus

Very similar to but smaller than Bittern. Differs by showing a brown crown and forehead, a dark eye-stripe, a black stripe from the base of the bill along the side of the neck, broad brown stripes on the foreneck and no barring on the sides of the neck. The long, greenish-yellow bill tends to show a

dark culmen. Unlike Bittern, the primary coverts and flight feathers do not show any barring and appear uniformly dark in flight.
Range: North America

Squacco Heron
Ardeola ralloides

A small, thickset heron with a short neck and elongated crown feathers forming a long, striped, cream and black mane. Appears yellow-buff on head, breast and upperparts, the mantle showing a peach wash. In flight shows strikingly white wings, rump and tail. In summer, the thick pointed bill shows a blue-grey base and a dark tip, while the legs are pinkish. In winter shows browner upperparts, a streaked breast, a dark tip to a yellow-green bill, and greenish legs.
Range: Southern Europe

Cattle Egret
Bubulcus ibis

A stocky, short-necked egret, smaller than Little Egret. In summer, shows a white plumage with long pinkish-buff crown, breast and mantle feathers. Bill and legs reddish. In winter, shows a white plumage with pale buff tones on the breast, crown and mantle, a yellow bill and dark green legs. In flight shows rounded wings. Usually found in grasslands and dry habitats, often associating with livestock.
Range: Southern Europe

Great White Egret
Egretta alba

A very large, slim, elegant egret similar in size to Grey Heron. Shows a long slender neck, an all-white plumage with long, wispy scapular aigrettes and loose breast feathering. In summer, shows a yellow base to a dark bill,

black lower legs and yellowish upper legs. In winter, loses the scapular aigrettes and shows a dark tip to a yellow bill.
Range: South-eastern Europe and North America

Black Stork
Ciconia nigra

A large, striking species, similar in size to White Stork. Adults show a glossy black head, upper breast and upperparts, and white underparts. Long, dagger-like bill and legs scarlet-red. In flight, shows dark underwings which contrast with white axillaries and underparts. Soars on long, broad wings and with neck extended. Immatures show a greyish-brown head and upper breast, brownish-black upperparts, and greyish-green legs and bill.
Range: South-western and eastern Europe

Lesser White-fronted Goose
Anser erythropus

Appears very similar to White-fronted Goose, but is smaller and daintier, with a shorter neck and a rounded head. Shows a diagnostic yellow eye-ring at all ages. Plumage as White-fronted, but

shows more extensive white on the face extending as a point onto the forehead. Tends to show less black barring on the belly. Pinkish bill appears short and triangular. Legs orange-yellow. Immatures lack the white face patch and black barring on the belly. Told by the yellow eye-ring, structure and the short, pinkish bill.
Range: Northern Europe

Ruddy Shelduck
Tadorna ferruginea

A large, goose-like duck with a short, black bill and dark legs. Males show an orange-brown body, dark wing tips and tail, a pale yellow-buff head, a creamy face and a black neck collar. Females similar, but show a whiter face and lack the black neck collar. In flight, shows a striking white forewing, a dark green speculum and dark wing tips. Behaviour as Shelduck.
Range: Southern and south-eastern Europe, North Africa

Mandarin Duck
Aix galericulata

A medium-sized but very striking and colourful Asian species with a large-headed, crested appearance. Males show a bright red bill with a white stripe from above the eye to the rear of the nape. Forehead appears green, contrasting with the orange cheeks and

lores. Breast dark with two white stripes. Upperparts dark with striking orange sails on back. Undertail white. Females similar in shape but show a paler bill, have a greyish head and a white throat, dark brown upperparts and greyish underparts with pale buff spotting. A small feral population is now established in Co. Down.
Range: Feral population established in Great Britain

Green-winged Teal
Anas carolinensis

Similar in size and structure to Teal. Males differ by showing a bold white vertical bar on the side of the breast and by lacking a horizontal white stripe on the upperparts. Head dark rufous with a dark green face mask showing a thin, dull yellow border. Breast orange-buff with dark spotting, upperparts dark brownish-grey, flanks grey with fine vermiculations and yellow, black-bordered undertail patches. On Teal, the head appears brighter with obvious yellow lines around face mask and onto base of bill while the flanks appear more coarsely vermiculated. Female Green-winged Teal very difficult to separate from female Teal tending to show a darker line on the cheek and a whiter wingbar in flight.
Range: North America

Lesser Scaup
Aythya affinis
Very similar to Scaup, but appearing smaller, with a peaked rear crown, and showing a blue-grey bill with a narrow black nail. Males show a purple gloss to a black head, unlike the green of

Scaup, and a black breast. The scapulars appear more vermiculated than Scaup while the flanks show greyish tones. Tail, rump and undertail black. In flight, shows a dark upperwing with a white wingbar on secondaries fading to grey on the primaries. Scaup show a white wingbar across the secondaries to the outer primaries. Females resemble female Scaup and are best told by the narrow black nail on the blue-grey bill, the wingbar pattern and structural differences.
Range: North America

Bufflehead
Bucephala albeola

A small, Teal-sized duck. Males very distinctive showing a glossy black head with a large white patch on the rear of the head, white underparts and black and white upperparts. Females and immatures show a brownish-grey head with a striking white oval patch on the rear of the cheek, dark brownish upperparts and greyish underparts. Bill, short, pale grey in males, darker in females.
Range: North America

Hooded Merganser
Mergus cucullatus
A striking species, smaller than Red-breasted Merganser and showing a long, narrow bill. Males show an erectile fan crest on a black head and a long white stripe behind the eye which, when the crest is raised, appears as a striking white patch. The white breast shows two black stripes, while the

blackish upperparts with diagnostic white shafts to the tertials contrast with the orange-brown flanks. Narrow bill black. Iris yellow. Females show a brownish head with a fuller crest than female Red-breasted Merganser. The breast and flanks are brownish, with darker upperparts showing white shafts to the tertials. Dark bill shows a yellowish base. Iris brownish.
Range: North America

Honey Buzzard
Pernis apivorus

Similar in size to Buzzard, showing longer, slender wings and a small protruding head. Upperparts greyish-brown with a greyish head and nape and three unevenly spaced bands on the brownish uppertail. Underparts and underwing coverts show heavy barring, with conspicuous dark bands on the flight feathers and tail. Unlike Buzzard, tends to soar and glide on flat wings while the wing beats appear deeper and more elastic.
Range: Great Britain and Europe

Griffon Vulture
Gyps fulvus
An enormous raptor with a featherless, greyish head, very broad, long wings and a short tail. In flight shows sandy-brown upperparts and upperwing-coverts contrasting with dark flight feathers and tail. Underparts streaked

brown with pale brown underwing coverts. In flight shows very long wings held in an acute V when soaring.
Range: Southern Europe

Bald Eagle
Haliaeetus leucocephalus
A large, Golden Eagle-sized raptor. Adults very distinctive showing a large, yellow bill, brown wings, and brown upper and underparts contrasting strongly with a striking white head, tail and undertail. Juveniles appear dark, brown overall with a dark bill, white axillaries and whitish centres to the tail feathers. Immature birds show white patches on the head, tail and on the breast and wing feathers with a distinctive white triangle on the back. The bill gradually turns yellow as the bird matures which can take up to four years.
Range: North America

Spotted Eagle
Aquila clanga
A large raptor, smaller than Golden Eagle, and showing a uniformly dark brown plumage, no barring on the flight feathers and tail, and a pale U on the uppertail-coverts. Immatures similar, but show white spotting on the scapulars and upperwing coverts, and a larger, more conspicuous U on the uppertail-coverts. In flight, wings appear broad and are held slightly bowed when soaring.
Range: Eastern and north-eastern Europe

Lesser Kestrel
Falco naumanni
A smaller, slimmer falcon than Kestrel with narrower wings and a wedge-tipped tail. Adult males show a blue-grey head without moustachials,

chestnut upperparts which show no spotting or barring, and a blue-grey tail with white tips and a black subterminal band. Underparts buffish with light spotting. In flight, shows chestnut and blue-grey upperwing coverts, while the underwings are whitish with faint spotting on the coverts and dark trailing edges and tips. Females appear similar to female Kestrel, but show thinner barring on the upperparts, a diffuse moustachial and paler, lightly spotted underparts. Lesser Kestrels show whitish claws, unlike the black claws of Kestrel. Hawks for insects on the wing, tending to hover less frequently.
Range: Southern Europe

Capercaillie
Tetrao urogallus
A very large gamebird extinct in Ireland since the eighteenth century. Males show a blackish-grey head, breast and tail, a brown mantle and wings, white shoulder patches, and white on the belly, undertail and tail. Males also show a striking red wattle above the eye and a whitish bill. Females are heavily barred and show an orange-buff head, breast and tail, brownish upperparts and wings, and whitish underparts.
Range: Scotland; central and northern Europe

Sora
Porzana carolina
A very distinctive rail, with adults showing a black face-mask and throat, a black-centred, unstreaked chestnut crown, bluish-grey cheeks, neck and breast, broad barring on the flanks, and buff-white undertail-coverts. The warm brown upperparts show dark centres to the mantle feathers, scapulars and tertials. Bill yellow. Legs greenish. Immatures similar, but show

a creamy supercilium and throat, warm-buff cheeks and breast, and a duller yellowish-green bill. Resembles Spotted Crake, but shows no red base to the bill or white spots on the neck and breast.
Range: North America

Little Crake
Porzana parva
A very small, shy crake. Males show a blue-grey face and underparts with faint, whitish barring on lower flanks, bolder barring on the undertail, and an olive-brown crown. Upperparts olive-brown with diffuse whitish streaking. Bill greenish with a red base. Legs green. Females similar, but show a pale grey face, a whitish throat and pale buff underparts with diffuse white barring on greyish flanks. Immatures resemble females, but can show grey and buff barring extending from the flanks onto the sides of the breast, whitish spotting on the scapulars and wing coverts, and a dull greenish bill.
Range: Eastern and central Europe

Baillon's Crake
Porzana pusilla
A very shy crake, similar to but smaller than Little Crake. Adults show a dark blue-grey face and underparts, with very heavy black and white barring on the flanks extending onto the undertail. Crown and upperparts rufous-brown, with white and black spotting and streaking on the mantle and wings. Bill olive-green. Legs pale brownish or greyish-green. Immatures show pale brown underparts, with brown barring on the sides of the breast becoming black and white on the flanks and undertail. Bill brownish.
Range: Southern and south-eastern Europe

Rare Species

American Coot
Fulica americana
Very similar to Coot, but shows a dark band on the white bill, a reddish-brown top to the white shield, and white sides to the undertail-coverts. Head and neck appear black, and contrast slightly with the greyish body.
Range: North America

Sandhill Crane
Grus canadensis
A tall species, similar to but smaller than European Crane. Adults show a bright red forehead patch, a pale grey plumage which can show brown staining, and a long, pointed dark bill. Legs greyish. Immatures lack the red forehead patch of adults and show a rufous-brown head and neck, and rufous tips to the wing feathers. Bill dark brownish.
Range: North America

Little Bustard
Tetrax tetrax
A duck-sized, stocky, thick-necked species showing a short bill. Males show a sandy-brown crown, a blue-grey face and throat, a striking black and white neck patch, fine dark barring on sandy-brown upperparts, and whitish underparts. Females show fine dark barring on a sandy-brown head, neck and upperparts, and whitish underparts. In flight, black primary coverts and wing tips contrast strongly with the extensive white on the wings. Glides on bowed wings in a grouse-like manner.
Range: Southern and south-eastern Europe

Great Bustard
Otis tarda
A very heavy, stocky, thick-necked species similar in size to a large goose.

Males show a greyish head with long white whiskers on the sides of the white throat, a rufous breast band and white underparts. Upperparts rufous-brown with black barring and a prominent white secondary panel. Tail rufous-brown with black barring. Bill short and thick. Females similar, but appear smaller and lack the rufous breast band. In flight, shows a broad white panel across the upper primaries and secondaries contrasting with a black trailing edge.
Range: Southern, central and south-eastern Europe

Stone Curlew
Burhinus oedicnemus
A striking, stocky species with staring, bright yellow eyes and a shortish, thick, yellow-based black bill. Shows whitish stripes above and below the eye, a heavily streaked brownish crown, breast and upperparts, a white belly and a cinnamon-washed undertail. Tail considerably longer than wings. In flight, dark wings contrast with two black-edged wingbars. Sturdy, long legs yellowish.
Range: Europe

Cream-coloured Courser
Cursorius cursor
A sandy-coloured, plover-like species with a short, dark, decurved bill and long creamy legs. A striking white supercilium extends onto nape and is bordered below by a broad black eye-stripe from behind eye. Rear of sandy crown shows a bluish-grey tinge. Underwings black. White-tipped tail shows a black subterminal band. Immatures show less defined head markings.
Range: North Africa and Middle East

Collared Pratincole
Glareola pratincola
A long-winged, tern-like wader which shows a greyish-buff head, upperparts and sides of breast, a white belly and a creamy, black-bordered throat. Short dark bill shows a red base. In flight, shows a dark, white-edged, forked tail, and a white rump and uppertail-coverts. Upperwing shows darker outer primaries, a paler inner wing and a white trailing edge to the secondaries. Underwing shows reddish-brown axillaries and coverts, but can appear black at a distance.
Range: Southern Europe

Black-winged Pratincole
Glareola nordmanni
Very similar to Collared Pratincole, showing a black-bordered, creamy throat, a white belly, a white-edged, dark forked tail, and a white rump and uppertail coverts. However, head, upperparts and sides of breast appear darker and the short dark bill shows a smaller red base. In flight, does not show any contrast between outer and inner wings, and lacks a white trailing edge to secondaries. Underwing-coverts and axillaries black.
Range: Eastern Europe

Pacific Golden Plover
Pluvialis fulva
Very similar to American Golden Plover but shows a slightly longer, heavier bill, a shorter primary projection, and a tertial length which is equal to or only slightly shorter than the tail. Like American Golden Plover, shows a dusky, grey underwing. Summer plumaged birds appear more as Golden Plover, showing a black face and underparts with a white supercilium extending down as a white

flank stripe. Vent also whitish. White flank stripe can show dark markings and therefore does not appear as clean as on Golden Plover. Shows yellow-buff spotting on the mantle and whitish spotting on wing coverts. Immatures appear more yellow-buff than immature American Golden Plover, with larger, yellow-buff spotting on the upperparts, and brownish streaking on crown, nape, breast and flanks. Head pattern less striking than on American Golden Plover, but shows a distinctive streak before the eye and a dark patch on the rear of ear coverts.
Range: Siberia

Sociable Plover
Chettusia gregaria

An upright plover, similar in size to Lapwing. In winter plumage, shows a striking white supercilium contrasting with a dark crown and eye-stripe, greyish brown upperparts and breast, and a pale belly and undersail. In summer plumage shows a black crown, yellow-buff cheeks, and a black and deep chestnut belly patch. In flight, the broad rounded wings show black primaries, white secondaries and greater coverts, and greyish-brown coverts and scapulars. This striking upperwing pattern shows a strong resemblance to that of Sabine's Gull. White tail shows a broad black subterminal band. Can associate with Lapwing flocks.
Range: South-eastern Russia

Great Knot
Calidris tenuirostris

Very similar to Knot but appearing slightly larger with a longer, more decurved bill, a smaller headed appearance and longer wings. In summer shows extensive head streaking and dark, broad spotting and 'arrowhead' markings on breast and flanks. Upperparts show pale-edged, dark feathering contrasting with warm, reddish-brown scapulars. Immatures and winter adults similar to Knot but show more extensive spotting on the breast. Legs greenish in colour.
Range: North-east Siberia

Western Sandpiper
Calidris mauri

Very similar to Semipalmated Sandpiper, but the longer legs and the longer, slightly decurved bill give a more Dunlin-like profile. Juveniles show a streaked, greyish crown and upperparts with contrasting rufous edges to upper scapulars and centre of mantle. Underparts clean white with streaking on sides of breast. Face appears plainer than on juvenile Semipalmated, lacking the strong eye-stripe and supercilium. Summer adults show heavy arrowhead streaking on breast and onto flanks, heavy streaking on the warm buff crown, striking rufous ear coverts, warm buff, black and white scapulars, and streaked upperparts. Also shows small webbing between toes. Legs black.
Range: North America

Red-necked Stint
Calidris ruficollis

Similar in size and structure to Little Stint, but tends to appear longer-winged and also shows a shorter bill. Summer adults show a reddish-orange upper breast, throat and cheeks, extending onto supercilium and crown which shows black streaking. Underparts white with black breast streaking extending onto sides of breast as distinctive arrowhead markings. Upperparts greyish with some rufous, black-tipped scapulars. May also be confused with summer plumaged Sanderling which appear bigger overall, show a longer bill, more

extensive reddish-orange colouring on the breast sides and upperparts, and also lack a hind claw. Juvenile Red-necked Stint appear similar to juvenile Little Stint but show greyish wing-coverts, indistinct white 'braces' on the mantle and a brown wash across the breast.
Range: North-east Siberia

Long-toed Stint
Calidris subminuta

A very small wader which tends to stand upright and tall thus recalling a miniature Wood Sandpiper in structure and stance. Summer adults show a warm brown, dark-streaked crown, a white supercilium which does not reach the base of the bill and warm brown cheeks. Shows rufous fringes to the mantle feathers, scapulars and tertials. Underparts white with dark streaking on sides of breast. Bill long, dark and pointed with a pale base to the lower mandible. Legs yellowish-green with long toes that extend beyond the tail in flight. Juveniles similar but show white mantle 'braces' and rufous scapulars and tertials which contrast with greyish wing coverts. In all plumages resembles Least Sandpiper with key differences being: the supercilium reaches the bill base; shows shorter legs; toes do not extend beyond tail in flight; shows warm rufous fringes to both scapulars and coverts in juvenile plumage and overall shape and stance.
Range: Siberia

Sharp-tailed Sandpiper
Calidris acuminata

Similar is size and shape to Pectoral Sandpiper but lacks the sharply defined breast band of Pectoral in all plumages. Summer adults very distinctive showing a striking rufous, dark streaked crown, a bold white supercilium, prominent behind the eye, and a white stripe below dark

streaked ear-coverts. Underparts show a warm brown washed breast with heavy streaking from the throat onto breast and extending as dark, arrowhead markings onto sides of breast, flanks and to undertail. Upperparts show black centres and whitish edges to feathers with thin white mantle stripes. Bill dark with a paler base and appears slightly shorter than that of Pectoral Sandpiper. Legs greenish-yellow. Immatures resemble immature Pectorals but differ by showing more extensive white around the eye, a whiter supercilium, particularly behind the eye and by showing an unstreaked, orange-buff breast with streaking confined to the breast sides. Gives a soft 'weeep' call, unlike the harsh 'krrit' call of Pectoral Sandpiper.
Range: Eastern Siberia

Stilt Sandpiper
Micropalama himantopus
A tall, upright sandpiper with long, greenish legs and a long, dark bill showing a slight droop towards the tip. Summer adults show heavy streaking on a warm buff crown, a whitish supercilium and chestnut ear coverts. Neck heavily streaked, fading onto heavy dark barring on the breast, belly and undertail. Dark upperparts show warm buff edges to upper scapulars. In winter, shows plain grey upperparts and whitish underparts. Immatures show dark streaking on a greyish-buff crown, a pale supercilium, a dark eye-stripe, dark streaking on the nape, neck, breast and flanks, and greyish upperparts with warm buff edges on upper scapulars and mantle. In flight, shows uniformly dark upperwings and a pale, whitish rump, more obvious in winter plumage. Legs project beyond tail in flight.
Range: North America

Great Snipe
Gallinago media
A stocky species, slightly larger than Snipe with a shorter bill. Rarely calls when flushed and does not zig-zag in flight. Rounded wings and body give a Woodcock-like profile. Differs from Snipe by showing a more heavily-barred belly, two distinctive white borders to darker greater coverts, and white outer-tail feathers.
Range: Northern and north-eastern Europe, and Siberia

Short-billed Dowitcher
Limnodromus griseus
Very similar to Long-billed Dowitcher, but shows a slightly shorter bill, although there is considerable overlap between these species. Juvenile birds show warmer tones than juvenile Long-billed, and show distinctive warm orange edges and notches to tertials, greater coverts and scapulars. Summer adults show pale orange underparts with a whitish belly and dark spotting on the sides of the breast. In flight shows a white wedge on back. Call is a rattling *chu-tu-tut*, very unlike the clear *keek* call of Long-billed.
Range: North America

Eskimo Curlew
Numenius borealis
Smaller than Whimbrel and showing a smaller, shorter bill. Shows a dark-streaked crown with a paler central stripe, a pale supercilium and a dark eye-stripe. Pale cinnamon-buff neck and underparts show heavy streaking. Belly cleaner. Upperpart feathers show pale buff notches. In flight, shows a brown rump and cinnamon-washed underwing coverts. Primaries

uniformly dark, lacking any barring. Could be confused with Hudsonian Whimbrel which also shows a dark brown rump.
Range: North America

Upland Sandpiper
Bartramia longicauda
A distinctive species with a long, slender neck, a small head and a long, wedge-shaped tail. Thin, straight, yellow bill shows a black tip. Legs yellow. Crown shows dark streaking and highlights an inconspicuous, pale supercilium. Brown-buff neck and breast shows heavy streaking fading to barring on whiter belly and flanks. Dark upperpart feathers show paler edges. In flight, shows uniformly dark wings and a contrastingly dark back, rump and uppertail coverts.
Range: North Amenca

Marsh Sandpiper
Tringa stagnatilis
A slender, elegant wader recalling a small Greenshank but showing a long, very fine, dark bill and long, slim, greenish legs. Summer adults show a pale supercilium and thin, dark streaking on a brownish-grey crown, cheeks and breast. Grey-brown upperparts show heavy, dark mottling. Underparts white. Winter adults show pale grey upperparts, a white supercilium and clean white underparts. Juveniles show dark grey upperparts with thin white feather fringes, faint dark grey streaking on crown and sides of breast, a white supercilium, and dark ear coverts. In flight, shows a white rump and wedge up back, and plain, uniformly dark upperwings. Long legs extend beyond tail in flight.
Range: Eastern Europe

Solitary Sandpiper
Tringa solitaria

Very similar to Green Sandpiper. Shows pale spots on olive-brown upperparts, a prominent white orbital ring, and a short, pale supercilium. Crown, neck and sides of breast streaked. Underparts white. Dark, straight bill shows a slightly paler base. Legs greenish. In flight, differs from Green Sandpiper by showing a dark rump, uppertail-coverts and centre to tail. Outer-tail conspicuously white with black barring. Underwings dark.
Range: North America

Terek Sandpiper
Xenus cinereus

A very distinctive wader, larger than a Common Sandpiper and showing a very long, dark, upcurved bill with a yellowish base. Legs appear short and are a striking yellow-orange colour. Summer adults show greyish upperparts with a contrasting black stripe on the carpal area, a greyish crown and a white supercilium. White underparts show a greyish wash and light streaking on the sides of the breast. Juveniles similar but show dark centres to the scapulars and coverts, and duller legs. In flight can appear very Redshank-like showing a white trailing edge to the wing but shows a greyish tail and rump.
Range: North-eastern Europe and Siberia

Gull-billed Tern
Gelochelidon nilotica

A stocky, broad-winged tern, resembling Sandwich Tern but showing a shorter, stubby, all-black bill. Summer adults show a black cap, grey upperparts and white underparts. Rump and short, forked tail grey. Immatures show a dark eye-stripe, dark streaking on the crown, and buff mottling on the wings and back. Winter adults show a white head with a thin black eye-stripe.
Range: Southern and eastern Europe

Royal Tern
Sterna maxima

A large, heavy tern with a thick orange-yellow bill. Adults show dark legs, a black cap with a short, shaggy rear crest, pale grey upperparts and white underparts. Rump and forked tail whitish. Winter adults show a white forehead and crown. Immatures show a white forehead and lores, brown markings on upperparts, dark tips to tail feathers, and pale legs. Could be confused with Caspian Tern, but shows white tips to the under-primaries.
Range: North America and north-west Africa

Lesser Crested Tern
Sterna bengalensis

A large, Sandwich Tern-sized bird showing dark grey upperparts and white underparts. Like Sandwich Tern, shows a shaggy crest to the black crown but differs by having a long, bright orange-yellow bill which is quite broad at the base. In flight shows a greyish rump and tail centre. Tail is also short and distinctly forked. Legs black. In winter shows a white forehead. Immatures show a winter adult-like head, a more yellowish bill and dark centres to the coverts, tertials and scapulars.
Range: North and North-west Africa

Elegant Tern
Sterna elegans

A slender, Sandwich Tern-sized species showing a long, drooping, yellow-orange bill. Adults show dark legs, a black cap with a long, shaggy rear crest, pale grey upperparts and white underparts. Rump and forked tail whitish. Winter adults show a white forehead and crown. Immatures show a white forehead and lores, dark markings on upperparts, dark tips to tail feathers, and pale legs.
Range: Pacific Coast of North America

Bridled Tern
Sterna anaethetus

A distinctive tern showing a thick, black bill and legs. Adults show greyish-brown upperparts, rump and forked tail. A black cap contrasts with a striking white forehead which extends as a white supercilium above and behind eye. Also shows a narrow white neck band. Immatures show a less distinctive head pattern and pale fringes to upperpart feathers.
Range: North-west Africa and the Red Sea

Franklin's Gull
Larus pipixcan

A dark-backed, 'hooded' gull, slightly smaller than Black-headed Gull. Summer adults show a black hood with

striking white eye crescents, white underparts and dark, slate-grey upperparts with large white tips to the primaries. In flight shows a white trailing edge to the wings, extensive white on the wing tips and a pale grey-centred tail. Bill short and red with a dark tip. Legs bright red. Winter adults show a reduced hood, confined to the rear of the crown and behind the eye, a dark bill and dull-coloured legs. First-year birds appear similar to adult winter but show greyish-brown wing coverts, black wing tips and a neat black tail band. Second-year birds also similar to adult winters but differ by showing more black on wing tips. In all plumages can be confused with Laughing Gull, but differs in being smaller, with a shorter bill (long and drooped in Laughing), shorter legs and, in adult plumage, showing extensive white areas on the wing tips.
Range: North America

Caspian Gull
Larus cachinnans
Similar to both Yellow-legged and Herring Gulls but appearing longer-billed, longer-winged with a more slender, tall, long-necked look and a flatter crown. Adults show a white head and underparts, dark grey upperparts with an obvious white tertial crescent and black wing tips with obvious white spots. Also shows white inner primary webs which appear as white 'tongues' intruding onto the black of the wing tip. Long, slender bill appears pale, washed out yellow in colour, with a small red gonys spot. Eye usually appears dark and small in the head. Legs appear long and are usually a pinkish yellow in colour. First-year birds appear very white headed with greyish upperparts and brownish bands on the wing coverts as well as having dark streaking on the base of the hind-neck. Bill dark. Legs pale. As birds mature, the upperparts become grey with the

white on the primary tips only reached at full adulthood. Bill slowly forms adult pattern, with second and third-year birds showing a dark ring towards the tip.
Range: Eastern Europe, Black Sea and Caspian Sea

Brünnich's Guillemot
Uria lomvia
Very similar to Guillemot, but shows a thicker, stubbier bill with a distinctive white stripe on the base of the upper mandible. Brünnich's Guillemot also lacks flank streaking and shows a steep forehead. In winter, black of the crown extends down to cover the ear coverts. Therefore, does not show the black eye-stripe of winter-plumaged Guillemot. Short tail may be held cocked.
Range: Arctic islands and cliffs

Pallas's Sandgrouse
Syrrhaptes paradoxus
A dove-like species with a short, stubby bill and along, pointed tail. Males show a grey and rufous head, a grey breast, pale buff underparts and a black belly patch. Brownish upperparts show heavy barring. Wings show grey outer primaries, black inner primaries and secondaries, and pale buff coverts. Females appear duller and show more extensive barring on the wing coverts and head.
Range: Central Asia

Great Spotted Cuckoo
Clamator glandarius
A striking species, larger than than Cuckoo and showing a long, white-edged, graduated tail. Adults show a crested grey cap, greyish-brown upperparts with bold white spots on the wing feathers, creamy underparts and a yellowish throat. Immatures show a

black crown, smaller wing spots and warm rufous on the primaries. In flight may resemble Magpie.
Range: Southern Europe

Black-billed Cuckoo
Coccyzus erythrophthalmus
Very similar to Yellow-billed Cuckoo, but shows little or no rufous on the wings, paler undertail feathers with smaller white tips, and a dark bill. Adults show a completely black bill and a red orbital ring. Immatures show a grey base to a dark bill and a pale yellow-buff orbital ring.
Range: North America

Scops Owl
Otus scops

A very slim, upright owl smaller than Little Owl. Shows a rufous to greyish-brown plumage with delicate black streaking and pale spotting. Also shows ear tufts which, when raised, gives Scops Owl a very flat-faced appearance. Eyes yellow. Song a repetitive low whistle.
Range: Southern Europe

Snowy Owl
Nyctea scandiaca
An enormous, diurnal owl with yellow eyes and long, broad, rounded wings.

Males are pure white with scattered dark spots. The larger females show extensive brown barring and spotting on the head, upperparts and underparts. Usually only the face, throat and legs are pure white.
Range: Alaska, Canada, Greenland, Iceland and Scandinavia

Little Owl
Athene noctua

A small, squat owl with a large, rounded head and bright yellow eyes. Head and upperparts brownish with extensive white streaking and spotting. Underparts whitish with broad dark streaking. Diurnal and crepuscular in behaviour.
Range: Continental Europe

Common Nighthawk
Chordeiles minor

Very similar to, but slightly smaller than Nightjar showing a cryptic combination of finely barred, greyish upperparts and barred underparts. Dark, greyish crown finely barred with pale cheeks showing dark streaking. In flight shows long, pointed wings with all dark primaries and strongly contrasting white primary patches. Flies with slow wing beats and frequent glides. Rump grey with dark barring, tail dark with slight fork. Adults show a white throat patch which is duller, or lacking, on immatures.
Range: North America

Needle-tailed Swift
Hirundapus caudacutus

A large swift with swept-back wings. Shows a dark plumage with a white forehead, throat and upper breast, and a diagnostic white U-shaped patch on the undertail. Dark upperparts show a pale greyish patch on the back. Short tail is square-ended. Could be confused with semi-albinistic Swifts.
Range: Asia

Pallid Swift
Apus pallidus

Very similar in size and shape to Swift but shows a browner plumage and slightly broader wings. In flight shows a pale brown head with a thin dark eye mask, a large, whitish throat patch, and pale-fringed brownish underparts. Underwings show a strong contrast between darker wing-coverts and pale secondaries and inner primaries. Outer primaries dark. Upperwing shows similar pattern. From above shows a dark 'saddle' on the mantle contrasting with paler rump and head. Tail brownish with a shallow fork.
Range: Southern and Eastern Europe

Little Swift
Apus affinis

A small, all-dark swift with a conspicuous square white rump patch, and a whitish forehead and throat patch. Tail almost square-ended. Wings short and broad. Flight is slower than Swift, and appears almost bat-like.
Range: Africa and Asia

Chimney Swift
Chaetura pelagica

A small, compact, all-dark swift showing broad wings and a short, squared tail which, on very close view, shows thin spines. Shows an all-dark, brown plumage with paler throat and breast. Flight fast, with fluttering wingbeats and frequent glides,

recalling House Martin. Can also look bat-like on occasions.
Range: North America

Belted Kingfisher
Ceryle alcyon

A very large kingfisher with a long, dagger-like, dark bill. Males show a blue-grey head with a shaggy crest on the rear crown, a white loral spot, neck collar and throat, and blue-grey upperparts with small whitish spots on the wing feathers. White underparts show a broad, blue-grey breast band and flank markings. Long blue-grey tail shows white barring. Females similar, but show a second, lower, bright rufous breast band, and some rufous along the flanks.
Range: North America

Rare Species

Green Woodpecker
Picus viridis

A large, brightly coloured woodpecker with a strong, pointed dark bill and a bright yellowish rump. Males have a bright red crown, a black face mask and black moustachials which show a red central stripe. Upperparts dull green with dark, barred, flight feathers. Underparts pale greyish-green with barring on the ventral region. Short, graduated dark tail shows faint barring. Females similar, but lack the red central stripe to the black moustachials.
Range: Continental Europe

Yellow-bellied Sapsucker
Sphyrapicus varius

A brightly-marked woodpecker with a red crown, a bold black and white face pattern, and black upperparts showing white barring and a large white wing patch. Males show a black-bordered red throat patch. Whitish underparts show a lemon-yellow wash and black barring on the flanks and vent. Rump white. Females similar, but show a diffuse red crown patch, and a black-bordered white throat patch. On immatures, dark brown mottling replaces the black of the head pattern and flanks. Upperparts blackish with pale, yellow-washed barring on the back, and a bright white wing patch. Underparts also show a lemon-yellow wash. Immature males show a diffuse reddish throat patch. Immature females show a whitish throat.
Range: North America

Northern Flicker
Colaptes auratus

A medium-sized Woodpecker showing a plain greyish head with a small red nape patch and buff-brown face and throat. Males show a distinctive black malar stripe — lacking on females. Upperparts pale buff with black barring and spotting. Pale underparts show a black breast patch, and extensive black spotting. Tail dark and contrasts strongly with a white rump, especially obvious in flight. Underwings show a bright yellow wash. Bill long, dark and pointed.
Range: North America

Woodlark
Lullula arborea

Very similar to Skylark, but shows a shorter tail, an ill-defined crest, and a striking whitish supercilium which almost meets on the nape. Warm, rufous-brown ear coverts are unstreaked. Crown and upperparts brownish, with heavy, dark streaking. Whitish underparts show a buff-washed breast with clear, dark spotting. In flight, the rounded wings show two black and white patches on the leading edge, but lack the white trailing edge as shown by Skylark. Short tail shows brown sides and conspicuous white tips.
Range: Continental Europe

Cliff Swallow
Petrochelidon pyrrhonota

A House Martin-like species showing a pale orange rump and a dark, square

tail which lacks streamers. Crown bluish black contrasting with a whitish forehead and reddish cheeks and sides of neck. Nape pale reddish grey, forming a distinctive collar. Chin, throat and upper breast black. Underparts whitish. Upperparts bluish black with some white streaking. Wings dark and broad. Can appear similar to Red-rumped Swallow but lacks the tail streamers and dark ventral area of that species. Immatures appear duller overall.
Range: North America

Buff-bellied Pipit
Anthus rubescens

Initially similar to Water Pipit in both summer and winter plumages. However, Buff-bellied Pipit shows plain, unmarked lores, a more defined malar stripe, and stronger breast and flank streaking. In summer, shows streaked greyish upperparts, and orange-buff underparts with dark streaking. In winter, the greyish-brown upperparts show very faint streaking. The warm buff underparts show dark streaking on the breast, fading and becoming more diffuse on the flanks. Tail shows white outer feathers. Legs dark. The Asian subspecies shows heavier upperpart streaking and

whitish-buff underparts in winter, and pale legs. The flight call is very similar to Meadow Pipit.
Range: North America and Asia

Citrine Wagtail
Motacilla citreola

A striking wagtail with a heavy black pointed bill and a long black, white-edged tail. Males show a bright yellow head and underparts with white undertail-coverts. A black half collar contrasts with pale grey upperparts. Blackish wings show two broad white wingbars and white edges to tertials. Females show a greyish-brown crown and ear coverts, a grey nape, a yellow supercilium and throat, and diffuse yellow underparts. Immatures show a greyish crown and nape, with a whitish supercilium continuing around pale grey ear coverts and onto sides of breast. The whitish breast can show diffuse spots forming an indistinct gorget. Upperparts and rump grey with wings showing two broad white wingbars and white tertial edges as on adults. Underparts whitish. Undertail-coverts white. Legs dark.
Range: Eastern Europe and Asia

Gray Catbird
Dumetella carolinensis
A very distinctive thrush-like species with a longish tail. Adults show an all bluish-grey plumage with a neat black cap and striking rufous undertail-coverts. Adults also show a brownish-red iris. Immatures similar, but show brownish tones to the wing feathers and a duller iris.
Range: North America

Rufous Bush Robin
Cercotrichas galactotes
A slim chat-like species with a long, graduated, rufous tail showing striking black and white tips. Shows a clear, whitish supercilium, a dark eye-stripe, plain whitish ear coverts, a rufous-brown crown and upperparts, and whitish underparts. When perched, often cocks or fans the bright tail.
Range: Southern Europe and North Africa

Thrush Nightingale
Luscinia luscinia
Very similar to Nightingale, but tends to appear slightly darker on the upperparts and shows a darker, less rufous tail. The whitish underparts also show faint mottling on the grey-washed breast which can continue to form a diffuse malar stripe.
Range: Eastern Europe

Pied Wheatear
Oenanthe pleschanka
Smaller and slimmer than Wheatear, showing a larger white rump and more white on the tail due to a narrower black tail-band. Summer males shows a white crown and nape contrasting with black face mask, back and wings. Underparts whitish-buff, with white undertail coverts. Females quite dark, showing a greyish throat and upper breast, a dark, greyish-brown head with an inconspicuous supercilium, uniformly dark, greyish-brown

upperparts, and whitish underparts. 1st year females similar, but show buff fringes to wing feathers and buffish underparts. 1st year males show pale fringes to a blackish face mask, a dark greyish-brown crown and upperparts, buff fringes to the wing feathers and a buffish wash on the breast.
Range: South-eastern Europe

Isabelline Wheatear
Oenanthe isabellina
A slim, pale, upright species very similar to female Wheatear. On Isabelline Wheatear, the wings never appear darker than the upperparts and show pale centres to the wing coverts which contrast with the darker alula. Also shows a broad, creamy supercilium and a shorter tail with a broader black tail-hand. Underwing coverts and axillaries are also white.
Range: South-eastern Europe and Middle East

Black-eared Wheatear
Oenanthe hispanica
A smaller, slimmer species than Wheatear, showing a very narrow black tail-band. Some inner tail feathers are almost pure white, but show small black spots on the tips. Adult males show a pale buff crown and mantle, a black eye mask, and either a black or whitish throat. Wings black. Rump white. Underparts show buffish tones on the breast fading to white on the belly and undertail. Females show either dark brownish upperparts with a greyish-brown throat and a dark eye mask, or paler buffish upperparts with a pale throat. Underparts creamy with a warm buff wash on the breast.
Range: Southern Europe

Rare Species

Desert Wheatear
Oenanthe deserti

A small wheatear showing an almost wholly black tail and a narrow, buff-tinged white rump. Adult males show a creamy-buff crown and upperparts, with a striking black throat and ear coverts which meet the black wings. Wings can show a white stripe on the scapulars. Underparts pale creamy-buff. 1st year males similar, but show pale fringes to blackish throat feathers, buff edges to wing feathers and appear duller above and below. Females show a pale buff crown and upperparts, darker ear coverts, pale buff fringes to wing feathers and creamy-buff underparts.
Range: North Africa and Middle East

Rock Thrush
Monticola saxatilis

A striking species showing a dark-centred, chestnut tail. Males show a bluish head and breast, deep chestnut underparts, and dark bluish upperparts with a white patch on lower back. The dark brown wings show chestnut underwing coverts and axillaries. Females show strong barring on the brownish upperparts and warm brown underparts.
Range: Southern Europe

White's Thrush
Zoothera dauma

A large striking species, slightly bigger than Mistle Thrush. The brownish head, upperparts and rump, and the whitish underparts, show extensive, large, dark crescentic barring. In flight, shows bold black and white bands on the underwing. Tail shows striking white outer tips and paler central feathers.
Range: Siberia

Siberian Thrush
Zoothera sibirica

A Song Thrush-sized species which shows distinctive black and white bands on the underwing. Adult males show a dark bill, a dark bluish-grey plumage with a bold white supercilium, a whitish rear belly, and black spotting on a whitish undertail. Immature males similar, but show a creamy supercilium and throat, and pale grey mottling on dark underparts. Females show a creamy supercilium, a brown crown, ear coverts and upperparts, a dark malar stripe on a pale throat, and brown barring and spotting on pale underparts.
Range: Siberia

Swainson's Thrush
Catharus ustulatus

A small, shy species, very similar to Grey-cheeked Thrush. Shows a warm, olive-brown crown, nape and upperparts. Warm brown ear coverts highlight a large, pale buff eye-ring and a pale buff supercilium before the eye. The warm buff throat shows a malar stripe extending as spotting onto a warm buff upperbreast. This spotting becomes more diffuse and fades into the whitish-grey underparts. Bill dark with a pale yellowish base.
Range: North America

Grey-cheeked Thrush
Catharus minimus

An elusive, small thrush very similar to Swainson's Thrush. Shows a cold greyish-brown crown, nape and upperparts, greyish ear coverts, and a diffuse, pale eye-ring. Spotting on the throat fades into the greyish-white underparts. Breast shows a faint buff wash. Dark bill shows a pinkish-yellow base.
Range: North America

Hermit Thrush
Catharus guttatus

A small, shy species, similar in size to both Grey-cheeked and Swainson's Thrushes. Shows a warm brown head and cheeks, a striking white eye-ring,

warm brown upperparts and a reddish-brown tail, which is very distinctive in flight. Underparts whitish with bold black spotting on the breast and a buff wash on the breast sides, flanks and undertail. Bill pinkish with a dark tip. Legs pink. Immatures show pale buff tips to greater coverts creating a pale wingbar.

Range: North America

American Robin
Turdus migratorius

A very distinctive, bright, Blackbird-sized thrush. Males show a blackish head contrasting with a broken white eye-ring, a black-streaked, whitish throat, and bluish-grey upperparts. Underparts are brick-red with white on the rear belly. White undertail shows black spotting. Bluish-grey tail shows white tips to outer feathers. Females similar, but shows paler upperparts and a browner head. Thick, pointed, yellow bill shows a dark tip.

Range: North America

Cetti's Warbler
Cettia cetti

A sturdy, skulky warbler showing a dull chestnut-brown crown, upperparts and wings, a whitish supercilium, and pale greyish-white underparts. Shows a broad, rounded chestnut-brown tail, very striking in flight. Tends to be very elusive and difficult to see.

Range: Continental Europe

Fan-tailed Warbler
Cisticola juncidis

A small, short-winged warbler with a short tail often held cocked to reveal the conspicuous black and white tips. Crown and upperparts pale buff with heavy, dark streaking. Shows a pale buff supercilium and a beady dark eye set in a plain face. Throat whitish,

fading onto a warm buff breast and flanks. Fast, active species, difficult to observe. Flight weak and undulating. Flight call is a hard, repeated *chit*.

Range: Southern Europe and North Africa

Pallas's Grasshopper Warbler
Locustella certhiola

A very shy, skulking species which resembles Grasshopper Warbler. Shows a heavily-streaked, greyish-brown crown, a prominent whitish supercilium, and streaked, rufous-brown upperparts. Tertials show small whitish tips or spots on inner webs. Underparts creamy-buff, occasionally showing a rufous wash on the breast, flanks and undertail. Breast shows diffuse spotting. Unlike Grasshopper Warbler, the undertail coverts lack dark streaks. Pallas's Grasshopper Warbler also shows a distinctive undertail pattern with brown fading to black towards the tip, and showing pale, whitish tips on all but the central feathers. Uppertail appears more rufous-brown.

Range: Asia

Paddyfield Warbler
Acrocephalus agricola

A stocky, short-winged warbler similar to Reed Warbler and showing a brown crown and upperparts, greyish-brown sides to the neck, a warm rufous-brown rump, and long rounded tail. Pale whitish underparts show a warm buff wash on the flanks. Unlike Reed Warbler, shows a conspicuous whitish supercilium, broadening behind the eye, bordered below by a dark eye-stripe and above by a darkish coronal stripe. The short, dark bill shows a yellowish base to the lower mandible.

Range: Eastern Europe

Blyth's Reed Warbler
Acrocephalus dumetorum

Very similar to both Reed and Marsh Warbler, but shows a more greyish-brown head and upperparts with a slightly warmer rump and tail. The short wings lack any contrasting dark centres or pale edges to the feathers. Shows a sloped forehead and a whitish supercilium, prominent before the eye. Also shows a whitish eye-ring, although this is not as conspicuous as on Marsh Warbler. The greyish-white underparts show a yellowish tinge to the breast and flanks. Shows a long, heavy bill, with the paler lower mandible sometimes showing a dark mark towards the tip. Legs usually darker than on Reed or Marsh Warblers.

Range: North-eastern Europe and Asia

Marsh Warbler
Acrocephalus palustris

Extremely similar to Reed Warbler, but shows a more rounded crown and paler brown upperparts which lack strong rufous tones, even on the rump. Shows a short, pale supercilium and a conspicuous pale eye-ring. Underparts creamy-white with a faint buff wash. Wings appear more contrasting than on Reed and Blyth's Reed Warbler, showing narrow pale edges to darker tertials and secondaries. The longer primaries do not appear as bunched as those on Reed Warbler, and show striking pale crescentic tips. The alula, when visible, are darker than the wing coverts. The legs usually appear paler than on Reed Warbler and show yellowish feet. Also shows pale claws, which are dark on Reed Warbler.

Range: South-eastern and Central Europe

Rare Species

Great Reed Warbler
Acrocephalus arundinaceus
An enormous, long-tailed bird resembling a huge Reed Warbler. Shows a warm brown crown, upperparts, rump and tail. The long wings show contrasting dark centres and pale edges to the feathers, while the primaries show pale tips. Shows a prominent white supercilium and greyish-brown ear coverts. Underparts greyish-white with a warm buff wash on the flanks. Shows a large, heavy bill with a pale base to the lower mandible, and thick, dark legs.
Range: Continental Europe

Olivaceous Warbler
Hippolais pallida
A plain warbler which initially resembles Booted Warbler. Shows a more sloped forehead, a longer, slender bill with a bright yellow lower mandible, and olive tones to a greyish-buff crown and upperparts. Also shows a faint supercilium and eye-ring on a plain face. Lores pale. Underparts whitish. Appears longer winged than Booted Warbler. Legs bluish-grey.
Range: Southern Europe and North Africa

Sardinian Warbler
Sylvia melanocephala
A Whitethroat-sized warbler with males showing a very striking plumage of a black head with a white throat, a bright

red orbital and eye-ring, grey upperparts with dark-centred tertials and whitish underparts showing a grey wash across the breast and flanks. Long, dark tail shows white edges and white tips to all but central feathers forming a very distinctive tail pattern. Legs pinkish. Females show a greyish head with a white throat and a pale brownish eye-ring and a thin, reddish orbital ring. Underparts whitish, with a brownish wash on breast and flanks. Upperparts pale brown with brown-edged, black tertials. Both sexes show a thin, dark, pointed bill with a distinctive grey base to the lower mandible.
Range: Southern and Eastern Europe.

Dusky Warbler
Phylloscopus fuscatus

A Chiffchaff-like warbler showing dark brown upperparts and crown, and greyish-white underparts with a buff wash along the flanks. Shows a conspicuous rust-tinged, whitish supercilium, dark brown ear coverts, pale, flesh-coloured legs and a pale bill. Also resembles Radde's Warbler which shows a thicker, heavier bill, yellowish legs, more yellowish-buff tones to the underparts, a broader, buff and cream supercilium, and mottled ear coverts. Tends to be extremely skulking and feeds close to the ground. Gives a very loud *thek* call from deep in cover.
Range: Siberia

Marsh Tit
Parus palustris
Initially similar to Coal Tit in size and structure. Shows an all-black, glossy crown, a small black bib, white cheeks and brownish upperparts. The wings appear plain, lacking wingbars. The underparts are greyish-white with buffish flanks. Short, stubby bill and legs dark. Tail shows inconspicuous white edges.
Range: Continental Europe

Isabelline Shrike
Lanius isabellinus
Similar in size and shape to Red-backed Shrike with a striking, orange-red uppertail. Adults show sandy, greyish-brown upperparts, white underparts with a buff wash on the flanks, a small white patch on the primaries and a narrow, black eye-mask. Sexes similar. Immatures resemble young Red-backed Shrike but appear paler overall, show a bright orange-red tail, a paler eye mask and lack barring on the upperparts. Underparts show faint barring on the flanks. Thick, hooked bill shows a dark tip and a pinkish base.
Range: Central Asia and Southern Siberia

Brown Shrike
Lanius cristatus
A Red-backed Shrike-sized bird, showing short, dark wings and a long, rounded, brown tail. Brown upperparts contrast with a black eye mask, a white supercilium and a brownish-grey crown. Shows a white throat and chin and pale underparts, with a strong yellow-buff wash on the breast and flanks. Immatures show a fainter eye mask and some barring on the sides of the breast and flanks. Bill long, pointed and dark tipped.
Range: Siberia and East Asia

Lesser Grey Shrike
Lanius minor

Resembles a small, long-winged, short-tailed Great Grey Shrike. Adults unmistakable, showing a broad black face patch from over the forehead to behind the eye. The whitish underparts show a delicate, salmon-pink wash on the breast and upper belly. 1st year birds can be more easily confused with Great Grey Shrike, as the black face mask does not extend over the forehead. However, Lesser Grey lacks a white supercilium, shows longer wings with obvious pale tips and edges to the primaries, has an inconspicuous white scapular stripe but a larger white primary patch. Lesser Grey also shows a smaller, stubbier bill.
Range: Southern, Central and Eastern Europe

Philadelphia Vireo
Vireo philadelphicus

Initially similar to Red-eyed Vireo, but is smaller and has a more rounded crown. Shows a bluish-grey crown and nape, a dark eye-stripe and a whitish supercilium. Can also show a whitish crescent below the eye. Upperparts olive-green and contrast with bright, yellowish underparts. Short, stout dark

bill shows a slightly hooked tip. Legs bluish-grey.
Range: North America

Mealy Redpoll
Carduelis flammea

Similar to Lesser Redpoll but appearing slightly larger. In all plumages usually shows a brighter plumage with white underparts showing streaking on the sides of the breast and flanks, and a paler head with more extensive red on the forehead. Lesser Redpoll tends to appear more buff on the breast and flanks. Mealy Redpoll also differs from Lesser Redpoll by showing crisp white wingbars, white-edged wing feathers, a streaked white rump and white 'tramlines' on the mantle (Lesser Redpoll shows buffish wingbars and feather edges as well as a streaked brown rump). Undertail white with a broad, dark centre to the longest undertail covert, forming a very noticeable undertail streak. Spring males show extensive red on the throat and breast. Shows a small, conical, yellow bill contrasting with black on the chin and lores. Legs black.
Range: Scandinavia, Greenland and Iceland

Arctic Redpoll
Carduelis hornemanni

Similar to Mealy Redpoll but usually shows a brighter, crisper plumage with white underparts showing streaking on the sides of the breast and becoming thin, or absent on the flanks. Head appears quite pale with dark crown

streaking and paler red on the forehead. Arctic Redpoll also differs from Mealy Redpoll by showing an unstreaked white rump, sometimes very bright and obvious on males, broader white 'tramlines' on the mantle and a pure white undertail with a very narrow dark centre to the longest undertail covert, forming a very thin undertail streak which can be absent in some birds. Some males appear so white and bright that they have been referred to as resembling a 'ball of cottonwool'. Spring males show a pale pink wash on the throat and breast. Shows a small, conical, yellow bill contrasting with black on the chin and lores. Legs black.
Range: Scandinavia

Serin
Serinus serinus

A small, dumpy finch with a short, stubby bill and showing a bright yellow rump, especially in flight. Males show a bright yellow forehead, supercilium, throat and breast. Crown and ear coverts dull greenish with light streaking. Ear coverts also show a bright yellow lower patch and crescent below the eye. Underparts white with heavy dark streaking. Upperparts appear dull green with dark streaking. Lacks conspicuous wingbars. Females appear duller, showing a faint yellow wash on the face and breast, heavily streaked whitish underparts and streaked dull greenish upperparts.
Range: Continental Europe

Two-barred Crossbill
Loxia leucoptera

Very similar to Crossbill, but shows two broad white wingbars and prominent white tips to the tertials. Many Crossbills may also have similar markings, but never show such broad wingbars widening on the inner coverts, or well-defined white tertial tips. Two-barred

Crossbill is smaller than Crossbill, and usually shows a slimmer bill. Males also show a pinker, paler plumage than Crossbill and can have pale edges to brownish scapulars. Females of both species show similar colourations.
Range: Northern Europe

Black-and-white Warbler
Mniotilta varia

An unmistakable, striking species. Males show a black crown with a white central stripe, a white supercilium, and black ear coverts and throat. Upperparts black with white streaks. Underparts white, with black streaking extending from throat onto breast, flanks and undertail. Females show a whitish throat, a buffish tinge to the supercilium before the eye, and buff-washed rear flanks. 1st year birds similar to females but lack buffish tones. Legs dark. Pointed bill shows a pale base. Feeds by moving along tree trunks and branches in a Treecreeper-like manner.
Range: North America

Northern Parula
Parula americana

Colourful species showing a very bright plumage. 1st year males show a bluish face, a greenish crown, and a bright yellow throat and breast broken by a bluish band. The breast also shows bright rufous patches. Belly and undertail white. Upperparts and wings bluish with a yellowish-green mantle, two prominent white wingbars, and greenish edges to wing feathers. Rump and short tail bluish. Summer males show a brighter blue head and upperparts, and a black, spotted breast band. 1st year and summer females similar to males, but lack the black band and the rufous patches on the breast. Upperparts also appear more greenish-blue. Moves in a tit-like fashion.
Range: North America

Blue-winged Warbler
Vermivora pinus

An extremely striking species showing bright yellow underparts and crown. Adults show a dark bill, a contrasting black eyestripe, olive-green nape and back, and two broad white wingbars on bluish-grey wings. Rump olive, tail bluish with white outer feathers, and undertail contrastingly white. Immature birds similar but show a more olive crown with a yellow forehead, a dark eyestripe, narrower, duller wingbars and a pale bill. Very active and tit-like when feeding, constantly flicking tail.
Range: North America

Yellow Warbler
Dendroica petechia
A very distinctive, bright warbler, slightly larger than a Wood Warbler.

Adult males show a dark eye and bill, a bright yellow face and underparts with reddish streaking on the breast and flanks. Upperparts bright yellow-green with unique yellow tail spots visible when tail is spread. Legs pale reddish. Females appear slightly duller and lack the breast and flank streaking. Immatures appear even duller than females with a dull greenish-brown upperparts, yellow-washed, pale underparts, a yellowish undertail and a pale eye ring and loral area. Can be very shy and skulking.
Range: North America

Blackpoll Warbler
Dendroica striata

1st year birds show a dull olive-green crown, ear coverts and upperparts, a pale yellow-buff supercilium, diffuse dark streaking on the mantle, two white wing bars, and white edges to the tertials. Pale yellow-buff to whitish underparts show faint streaking from the breast onto flanks. Undertail white. In all plumages shows distinctive white spots towards the tips of the outermost tail feathers. Summer males show a striking black crown and moustachial stripe, white cheeks, black streaked underparts, and dark streaking on olive-grey upperparts. Legs pale yellow-brown with paler feet.
Range: North America

American Redstart
Setophaga ruticilla

A very colourful species, easily recognised. 1st year males and females show a bluish-grey head with a thin, pale, inconspicuous supercilium before the eye, and narrow white eye crescents. Whitish underparts show a yellow or orange-yellow patch on the sides of the breast. Upperparts brownish-green with a bright yellow wing patch. The long, brownish-green tail, which is often held cocked, reveals bright yellow patches at the base. Summer males show a black head, breast, upperparts and tail, white underparts, and striking orange breast, wing and tail patches.
Range: North America

Ovenbird
Seiurus aurocapillus

A very skulking species which moves along the ground, usually in cover. Shows a bright olive-green head and upperparts with a striking, black-bordered, orange central crown-stripe. The large black eye shows conspicuous white eye-rings. White underparts show heavy black streaking, fading on the buff-washed flanks. White throat also shows a strong black malar stripe. Legs pale pinkish. Dark bill shows a pinkish base.
Range: North America

Northern Waterthrush
Seiurus noveboracensis

A skulky, terrestrial species, usually found close to water. Shows a dull olive-brown crown and ear coverts, a dark eye stripe, and a very long, striking, yellowish-buff supercilium. Upperparts and tail plain dull olive-brown. Whitish underparts show heavy black streaking from the throat to the flanks and belly. Flanks can show a yellowish-buff wash.

Legs pinkish. Dark bill shows a pinkish base. Has a habit of constantly bobbing the head and tail in a Common Sandpiper-like manner.
Range: North America

Scarlet Tanager
Piranga olivacea

A large, finch-like species with a thick, pale bill. Summer males show a bright red plumage with a contrasting black tail and wings. Females show greenish upperparts with brownish wings and yellowish-green underparts. Females also tend to show a darker bill. 1st year males very similar to females, but show black on the scapulars and on some wing feathers. Underwing-coverts whitish.
Range: North America

Fox Sparrow
Zonotrichia iliaca

A large bunting with a thick, pale bill. Shows a grey and blotched rufous crown, a grey supercilium and sides of neck, and bright chestnut ear coverts. White throat and underparts show a thick chestnut malar stripe and streaking, extending onto the flanks. The streaking may form a chestnut patch on the sides of the breast. Mantle olive-brown with a rufous wash and dark streaking. The wings are chestnut and show two thin, pale wingbars and darker centres to the feathers. Rump and long tail bright chestnut, very conspicuous in flight.
Range: North America

White-throated Sparrow
Zonotrichia albicollis

A large species showing a thick, horn-coloured bill. Adults show a white central crown-stripe, a black lateral crown-stripe and eye-stripe, and a

conspicuous supercilium, bright yellow before the eye, and white above and behind the eye. A white throat shows a very faint, thin malar stripe. Cheeks and underparts greyish, fading to buff on the flanks which also show diffuse buff streaking. Undertail white. Upperparts brown with dark streaking. Brown wings show dark centres to the feathers and two white bars. Immatures show a buffish central crown-stripe and supercilium, and a thicker, darker malar stripe on a dirty, whitish throat. Underparts show stronger streaking on the breast. Legs pale brown.
Range: North America.

Dark-eyed Junco
Junco hyemalis

A distinctive bunting with a thick, pale, pinkish-white bill. Males show a slate-grey head, breast, flanks and upperparts contrasting with a bold white belly and undertail. Long slate-grey tail shows broad, conspicuous white outer edges. Females appear more greyish-brown on the head and upperparts. Immatures similar to adults, but show stronger brownish fringes to mantle and flanks, and browner wing feathers. The bill on immatures can also appear slightly darker.
Range: North America

Rare Species

Pine Bunting
Emberiza leucocephalos

A Yellowhammer-sized bunting with summer males showing a striking head pattern including a black-bordered white crown and ear-coverts, and an orange-brown supercilium and throat. Underparts white with a streaked, rufous washed, breast and flanks. Nape greyish brown with warmer brown upperparts showing black streaking. Wings show dark centres to feathers with warm brown edges and thin white tips to coverts, and white-edged primaries. Rump warm red-brown similar to Yellowhammer. Winter males appear greyish brown on the head but still show black-bordered, white ear-coverts. Females show a paler brown supercilium, dark-bordered whitish ear-coverts, a white throat and a dark malar stripe meeting dark breast streaking. Immatures appear very similar to immature Yellowhammer but differ by showing streaked, white underparts with no yellowish wash, and white edges to the primaries (yellowish on Yellowhammer). Bill conical in shape with a pale grey lower mandible and a dark upper mandible. Legs pinkish.
Range: Siberia

Yellow-breasted Bunting
Emberiza aureola

Summer males are unmistakable, showing a deep brown head and upperparts, a black face and throat, bright yellow underparts showing a deep brown breast band, and dark streaking along the flanks. Also shows a conspicuous white carpal patch and a narrow white wingbar. Females show a brown-streaked crown with a pale yellow-buff central crown and supercilium. A dark eye-stripe forms a border to the brownish ear coverts which also shows a pale rear patch.

Underparts pale yellow with faint streaking on the sides of the breast and flanks. Pale yellow throat shows a very faint malar stripe, if any. Upperparts pale buff with dark streaking. Wings show two pale bars. Warm brown rump appears heavily streaked. 1st year birds similar to females, but show paler yellowish underparts and heavier streaking on the breast and flanks.
Range: Northern Europe

Black-headed Bunting
Emberiza melanocephala

Summer males show a black crown and cheeks, bright yellow sides of neck and underparts, and a bright chestnut nape, sides of breast and upperparts. Darker wings show two whitish bars. Females show a greyish-brown crown, cheeks, nape and upperparts, with a faint chestnut tinge on the mantle and sides of the breast. Underparts very pale, washed-out lemon-yellow. 1st year birds show a pale brown, streaked head and upperparts, pale wingbars and pale buff underparts. Also shows a very faint malar stripe and dark streaking on the breast which fades and becomes diffuse on the flanks. Most striking feature of immature birds is the bright yellow undertail. In all plumages, does not show white on the tail. Bill greyish.
Range: South-eastern Europe

Indigo Bunting
Passerina cyanea

A small bunting with large pale bill. Summer males show a bright blue plumage with blackish centres to the wing feathers. In winter, the blue is partially obscured by brownish fringes to the feathers. Females appear very

drab, showing a brown head and upperparts, and pale buff underparts with faint streaking on the breast and flanks. Females show faint bluish tones to the tail and wings. 1st year birds appear similar to females, but can show paler tips to the greater coverts which form an indistinct wing bar. 1st year males can also show some bluish feathers on the mantle and underparts.
Range: North America

Bobolink
Dolichonyx oryzivorus

A large bunting-like species with diagnostic pointed tail feathers. 1st year birds show a striking head pattern of a yellow-buff crown, a blackish lateral crown-stripe, and a broad yellow-buff supercilium. Cheeks and lores pale buff, with a dark eye-stripe prominent behind the eye and forming a border to the rear of the ear coverts. Upperparts pale brown with dark streaking and pale yellow-buff braces. Wings show indistinct bars but have conspicuous white edges to dark tertials. Brownish tail shows very pointed feathers. Underparts yellow-buff with faint streaking on the sides of the breast and flanks. Females similar

to 1st years, but show buff edges to the tertials. Summer males show a black head, underparts and tail, a pale yellow nape, pale yellow-buff fringes to mantle feathers, and a white scapular patch and rump. Blackish wings show pale buff fringes to some feathers. Winter males resemble females, but show extensive black feathering on the underparts.
Range: North America

Footnotes to Rare Species Accounts

The following species have been recorded in Ireland, but are considered to have escaped or to have been released from captivity, or were not specifically identified.

Greater Flamingo *Phoenicopterus ruber*
Baikal Teal *Anas formosa*

Booted Eagle *Hieraaetus pennatus*
Red-legged Partridge *Alectoris rufa*
Black Wheatear/White-crowned Black Wheatear *Oenanthe leucura/ Oenanthe leucopyga*
Red-headed Bunting *Emberiza bruniceps*

The following species has been recorded in Ireland but is now extinct.

Great Auk *Pinguinus impennis*

List of Rare Birds requiring documentation

As of 1 January 2001 the following species require full documentation to verify sightings:

Black-throated Diver *see footnote 1 below*
White-billed Diver
Pied-billed Grebe
Black-necked Grebe
Black-browed Albatross
Madeiran Soft-plumaged Petrel
Swinhoe's Petrel
Fea's Soft-plumaged Petrel
Bulwer's Petrel
Cory's Shearwater *see footnote 2 below*
Little Shearwater
Wilson's Petrel
Madeira Petrel
Double-crested Cormorant
Bittern
American Bittern
Little Bittern
Night Heron
Squacco Heron
Cattle Egret
Great White Egret
Purple Heron
Black Stork
White Stork
Glossy Ibis
Spoonbill
Bewick's Swan (of the subspecies *C. c. columbianus*)
Bean Goose
White-fronted Goose (of the subspecies *A. a. albifrons*)
Lesser White-fronted Goose
Snow Goose
Canada Goose (excluding feral birds)
Brent Goose (of the subspecies *B. b. nigricans*)
Ruddy Shelduck
American Wigeon
American Black Duck
Blue-winged Teal
Red-crested Pochard
Ring-necked Duck
Ferruginous Duck
Lesser Scaup
King Eider

Surf Scoter
Bufflehead
Hooded Merganser
Honey Buzzard
Black Kite
Red Kite
White-tailed Eagle
Bald Eagle
Griffon Vulture
Montagu's Harrier
Goshawk
Rough-legged Buzzard
Spotted Eagle
Golden Eagle
Booted Eagle
Lesser Kestrel
Red-footed Falcon
Hobby
Gyrfalcon
Spotted Crake
Sora
Little Crake
Baillon's Crake
American Coot
Crane
Sandhill Crane
Little Bustard
Great Bustard
Black-winged Stilt
Avocet
Stone Curlew
Cream-coloured Courser
Collared Pratincole
Black-winged Pratincole
Little Ringed Plover
Killdeer
Kentish Plover
Dotterel
American Golden Plover
Pacific Golden Plover
Sociable Plover
Great Knot
Semipalmated Sandpiper
Western Sandpiper
Red-necked Stint
Temminck's Stint
Long-toed Stint

Least Sandpiper
White-rumped Sandpiper
Baird's Sandpiper
Sharp-tailed Sandpiper
Broad-billed Sandpiper
Stilt Sandpiper
Buff-breasted Sandpiper
Snipe (of the subspecies *G. g. delicata*)
Great Snipe
Short-billed Dowitcher
Long-billed Dowitcher
Eskimo Curlew
Hudsonian Whimbrel
Upland Sandpiper
Marsh Sandpiper
Greater Yellowlegs
Lesser Yellowlegs
Solitary Sandpiper
Terek Sandpiper
Spotted Sandpiper
Wilson's Phalarope
Red-necked Phalarope
Long-tailed Skua
Laughing Gull
Franklin's Gull
Bonaparte's Gull
Lesser Black-backed Gull (other than *L. f. graellsii*)
Herring Gull (of the subspecies *L. a. smithsonianus*)
Caspian Gull
Iceland Gull (of the subspecies *L. g. kumlieni*)
Ross's Gull
Ivory Gull
Gull-billed Tern
Caspian Tern
Lesser Crested Tern
Elegant Tern
Forster's Tern
Whiskered Tern
White-winged Black Tern
Brünnich's Guillemot
Little Auk
Pallas's Sandgrouse
Great Spotted Cuckoo

List of Rare Birds requiring documentation

Black-billed Cuckoo
Yellow-billed Cuckoo
Barn Owl (of the subspecies
    T. a. guttata)
Scops Owl
Snowy Owl
Little Owl
Common Nighthawk
White-throated Needletail
Chimney Swift
Pallid Swift
Alpine Swift
Little Swift
Belted Kingfisher
Bee-eater
Roller
Wryneck
Green Woodpecker
Yellow-bellied Sapsucker
Great Spotted Woodpecker
Short-toed Lark
Woodlark
Shore Lark
Red-rumped Swallow
Cliff Swallow
Richard's Pipit
Tawny Pipit
Olive-backed Pipit
Pechora Pipit
Red-throated Pipit
Rock Pipit (of the subspecies
    A. p. littoralis)
Water Pipit
Buff-bellied Pipit
Yellow Wagtail (other than
    M. f. flavissima)
Citrine Wagtail
Grey Catbird
Dipper (of the subspecies
    C. c. cinclus)
Rufous Bush Robin

Thrush Nightingale
Nightingale
Bluethroat
Stonechat (of the subspecies
    S. t. maura or *S. t. stejnegeri*)
Isabelline Wheatear
Pied Wheatear
Black-eared Wheatear
Desert Wheatear
Rock Thrush
White's Thrush
Siberian Thrush
Swainson's Thrush
Grey-cheeked Thrush
Hermit Thrush
American Robin
Cetti's Warbler
Fan-tailed Warbler
Pallas's Grasshopper Warbler
Savi's Warbler
Aquatic Warbler
Paddyfield Warbler
Blyth's Reed Warbler
Marsh Warbler
Great Reed Warbler
Olivaceous Warbler
Icterine Warbler
Melodious Warbler
Dartford Warbler
Subalpine Warbler
Sardinian Warbler
Barred Warbler
Lesser Whitethroat (of the subspecies
    S. c. blythi)
Greenish Warbler
Arctic Warbler
Pallas's Warbler
Radde's Warbler
Dusky Warbler
Bonelli's Warbler
Red-breasted Flycatcher

Bearded Tit
Marsh Tit
Coal Tit (of the subspecies *P. a. ater*)
Golden Oriole
Red-backed Shrike
Isabelline Shrike
Brown Shrike
Lesser Grey Shrike
Great Grey Shrike
Woodchat Shrike
Rose-coloured Starling
Philadelphia Vireo
Red-eyed Vireo
Serin
Mealy Redpoll
Arctic Redpoll
Two-barred Crossbill
Common Rosefinch
Hawfinch
Black-and-white Warbler
Northern Parula
Blue-winged Warbler
Yellow Warbler
Yellow-rumped Warbler
Blackpoll Warbler
American Redstart
Ovenbird
Northern Waterthrush
Scarlet Tanager
Fox Sparrow
White-throated Sparrow
Dark-eyed Junco
Pine Bunting
Ortolan Bunting
Rustic Bunting
Little Bunting
Yellow-breasted Bunting
Black-headed Bunting
Rose-breasted Grosbeak
Indigo Bunting
Bobolink

Footnote 1. Except in the Ballyvaughan area of Co. Clare, in Donegal Bay and off the south Wexford coast.
Footnote 2. Except off the south-west coast between Old Head of Kinsale, Co. Cork and Bridges of Ross, Co. Clare
(but not including Cape Clear Island where descriptions are still required in accordance with the policy of the
Cape Clear Bird Observatory Recorder). Descriptions are also required from all areas for any claims of the subspecies
diomedea or *edwardsii*.

Useful Addresses, Websites and Phone Numbers

Websites of the author and artist

BirdsIreland – www.birdsireland.com
Offering information, news and suggested trips for a birdwatching visit to Ireland. Author Eric Dempsey can be hired as Tour Leader through this website.

oclery.com – www.oclery.com
A gallery of bird and wildlife paintings by artist Michael O'Clery. Many recent works are shown, including original plates from this book, and can be purchased online.

BirdWatch Ireland

We would encourage everyone with an interest in Irish birds to join BirdWatch Ireland. Visit their website
www.birdwatchireland.ie
or contact them at:
BirdWatch Ireland
Ruttledge House, 8 Longford Place,
Monkstown, Co. Dublin
Email: bird@indigo.ie
Phone: +353-1-2804322

Useful websites

BirdWatch Ireland
www.birdwatchireland.ie
Ireland's largest bird conservation group.

Their website has news, education features, local branch information, schools projects, etc. You can join by subscribing through their online shop.

Irish Rare Birds Committee
www.birdwatchireland.ie/irbc.html
Addresses, recent species reviews and various lists.

Irish Bird Network
Electronic bulletin board for Irish birdwatchers. Topical discussion, news and views. To subscribe (for free) send an email to listserv@listserv.hea.ie . Leave the subject area blank, and type Subscribe IBN your name where 'your name' is your own name. You will receive a response seeking confirmation. Follow the instructions.

Wild Ireland
www.wildireland.ie

RSPB
www.rspb.org.uk/

One of the largest bird conservation groups in the world, with information for Northern Ireland.

Dutch Birding
www.dutchbirding.nl

Useful identification articles for the serious birder

British Birds
www.britishbirds.co.uk

British Ornithologists Union
www.bou.org.uk

IrishBirding.com
www.irishbirding.com

Rare bird news phone numbers

For all the latest rare bird news in Ireland, call:
From the Republic of Ireland:
1550 111 700
Calls cost 74 cent per minute.

From Northern Ireland, call:
0901 063 0600
Calls cost 60p per minute.

For a weekly summary of rare bird news, call:
Republic of Ireland: 1550 111 701
Calls cost 74 cent per minute.

To phone in sightings of rare bird news call (01) 8307364, leaving full details and a contact number.

Bibliography

Bird, D., 'Pallas's Grasshopper Warbler and Swainson's Thrush on Cape Clear Island, Co. Cork', *Irish Birding News,* Vol. 1, 1990.

Bird, D., 'Isabelline Wheatear on Mizen Head, Co. Cork', *Irish Birding News,* Vol. 3, 1993.

Brazier, H., Dowdall, J.F., Fitzharris, J.E. and Grace, K., 'Thirty-third Irish Bird Report, 1985', *Irish Birds,* Vol. 3, 287–336.

Brazier, H. and Merne, O.J., 'Breeding Seabirds on the Blasket Islands, Co. Kerry', *Irish Birds,* Vol. 4, No. 1.

Caschera, V., Dowdall, J. and Fitzharris, J., 'Olive-backed Pipits in Co. Cork, October 1990', *Irish Birding News,* Vol. 1, 1990.

Chandler, R.T., *North American Shorebirds,* 1989.

Cooney, T., Haslam, B., Madden, B., O'Donnell, M., O'Flanagan, C. and O'Keefe, P., *Irish East Coast Bird Report,* annual since 1980, Irish Wildbird Conservancy.

Cramp, S., Bourne, W.P. and Saunders, D., *The Seabirds of Britain and Ireland,* Taplinger, 1974.

D'Arcy, G., *The Guide to the Birds of Ireland,* Irish Wildlife Publications, 1981.

Delin, H. and Svensson, L., *Photographic Guide to the Birds of Britain and Europe,* Hamlyn.

Dempsey, E., 'The Waxwing Irruption of 1990–91', *Irish Birding News*, Vol. 1, 1991.

Dempsey, E., 'Northern Gulls in Ireland in Winter 1990–91', *Irish Birding News*, Vol. 1, 1991.

Dempsey, E., 'Monthly Rare Bird Reports, June 2000–June 2001, *www.birdsireland.com*

Dempsey, E. and McGeehan, A., 'Long-tailed Skuas in Ireland in Autumn 1991', *Irish Birding News*, Vol. 2, 1992.

Dowdall, J., 'Identification of Nearctic Thrushes', *Irish Birding News*, Vol. 2, 1992.

Farrand, J. Jr., *The Audobon Society Master Guide to Birding,* Vols. 1, 2 and 3, Alfred A. Knopf, 1983.

Farrell, S., 'Red-footed Falcon on Cape Clear', *Irish Birding News,* Vol. 1, 1991.

Ferguson-Lees. J., Willis, I. and Sharrock, J.T.R., *The Shell Guide to the Birds on Britain and Ireland,* Michael Joseph, 1983.

Fitzharris, J., 'American Waders in Ireland', *Irish Birding News,* Vol. 1, 1990.

Foster, S., 'Red-footed Falcon in Co. Galway', *Irish Birding News,* Vol. 1, 1991.

Garner, M., 'Identification of Yellow-legged Gulls in Britain', *British Birds,* 1997.

Garner, M., Quinn, D. and Glover, B., 'Identification of Yellow-legged Gulls in Britain — Part 2', *British Birds,* 1997.

Grace, K. and Lancaster, A.A.K., 'The Garinish Yellow Wagtail', *Irish Birding News*, Vol. 1, 1990.

Grace, K. and Lancaster, A.A.K., 'Ovenbird on Dursey Island, Co. Cork', *Irish Birding News*, Vol. 1, 1990.

Grace, K., 'Analysis of Irish Rustic and Little Bunting Records', *Irish Birding News*, Vol. 1, 1991.

Grace, K., 'Quizbird No. 4 Solution (Red-necked Phalarope)', *Irish Birding News*, Vol. 3, 1992.

Grant, P.J., *Gulls: A Guide to Identification,* Second Edition, T. and A.D. Poyser, 1982.

Grant, P.J. and Jonsson, L., 'The Identification of Stints and Peeps', *British Birds,* Vol. 77, 1984.

Hammond, N. and Everett, M., *Birds of Britain and Europe,* Pan Books, 1980.

Harris, A., Tucker, L. and Vinicombe, K., *The Macmillan Field Guide to Bird Identification*, 1989.

Harrison, P., *Seabirds: An Identification Guide,* 1983.

Harrison, P., *A Field Guide to Seabirds of the World*, The Stephen Greene Press, 1987.

Hayman. P., Marchant, J. and Prater, T., *Shorebirds: An Identification Guide to the Waders of the World,* Helm, 1986.

Hollom, P.A.D., *The Popular Handbook of British Birds,* 1980.

Hollom, P.A.D., *The Popular Handbook of Rarer British Birds,* 1980.

Hoogendoorn, W. and Steinhaus, H., 'Nearctic Gulls in the Western Palearctic', *Dutch Birding,* September 1990.

Hutchinson, C.D., *Where to Watch Birds in Ireland*, Country House, 1986.

Hutchinson, C.D., *Birds in Ireland*, T. and A.D. Poyser, 1989.

Irish Rare Birds Committee, Checklist of the Birds of Ireland, BirdWatch Ireland, 1998.

Johnson, J. and Smiddy, P., 'Black Stork in Co. Dublin — a species new to Ireland', *Irish Birds,* Vol. 4, No. 1.

Jonsson, L., *Birds of Europe with North Africa and the Middle East,* Helm, 1992.

Kaufman. K., *A Field Guide to Advanced Birding*, Houghton Mifflin, 1990.

Kavanagh, B., 'Bird on the Brink', *Wings* 20, 16–17, BirdWatch Ireland, 2001.

Kelly, A., 'Grey-cheeked Thrush on Cape Clear Island, Co. Cork', *Irish Birding News,* Vol. 1, 1990.

Lack, P., *The Atlas of Wintering Birds in Britain and Ireland*, T. and A.D. Poyser, 1986.

Lewington, I., Alström, P. and Colston, P., *A Field Guide to the Rare Birds of Britain and Europe*, Domino Books, 1991.

Lovatt, J.K., *Birds of Hook Head 1883–1983,* Irish Wildbird Conservancy, no date.

Madge, S. and Burn, H., *Wildfowl: An Identification Guide to the Ducks, Geese and Swans of the World,* Helm.

Mayes, F. and Stowe, R., 'The Status and Distribution of Corncrake in Ireland, 1988', *Irish Birds,* Vol. 4, No. 1.

McGeehan, A., 'Olivaceous Warbler on Cape Clear, Co. Cork', *Irish Birding News,* Vol. 1, 1990.

McGeehan, A., 'Brünnich's Guillemot: Rare or Overlooked?' *Irish Birding News,* Vol. 1, 1991.

McGeehan, A., 'Soft-plumaged Petrel in Co. Down', *Irish Birding News,* Vol. 2, 1991.

McGeehan, A., 'Quizbird No. 2 Solution (Semipalmated Sandpiper)', *Irish Birding News,* Vol. 2, 1991.

McGrath, D. and Walsh, P., *Where to Watch Birds in Waterford,* Irish Wildbird Conservancy.

Bibliography

Mitchell, F., et. al., *The Book of the Irish Countryside*, The Blackstaff Press, 1987.

Mullarney, K., 'Short-billed Dowitcher in Co. Wexford — An Addition to the Irish List', *Irish Birds,* Vol. 3, No. 4, 1988.

Mullarney, K., 'Brünnich's Guillemot in Co. Wexford — An Addition to the Irish List', *Irish Birds,* Vol. 3, No. 4, 1988.

Mullarney, K., 'Loral Pattern of Juvenile Semipalmated and Ringed Plovers', *Irish Birding News*, Vol. 1, 1991.

Mullarney, K., Svensson, L., Zetterstrom, D. and Grant, P.J., *Collins Bird Guide*, HarperCollins*Publishers*, 1999.

Murphy, C., 'First Recorded Breeding Record of Whooper Swans in Ireland', *Irish Birding News,* Vol. 3, 1992.

National Geographic Society, *Field Guide to the Birds of North America,* National Geographic Society, 1983.

Newton, S. et al, 'Birds of Conservation Concern in Ireland', *Irish Birds*, Vol. 6, 333–42, 1999.

Ogilvie, M.A., *Ducks of Britain and Europe,* 1975.

Olsen, K.M. and Larsson, H., *Terns of Europe and North America*, Christopher Helm, 1995.

O'Sullivan, O., Smiddy, P., Milne, P., McAdams, D. and Dempsey, E., 'Irish Bird Report', annual, 1986–99, in *Irish Birds*.

Perry, K.W., *The Irish Dipper,* 1986.

Porter, R.F., Willis, I., Christensen, S. and Nielson, B.P., *Flight Identification of European Raptors,* T. and A.D. Poyser, 1976.

Prater, A.J., *Estuary Birds of Britain and Ireland,* T. and A.D. Poyser, 1981.

Ruttledge, R.F., *A List of the Birds of Ireland,* 1974.

Ruttledge, R.F., 'Exceptional Influx of Little Gulls on the North Wicklow Coast', *Irish Birding News,* Vol. 1, 1990.

Sharrock, J.T.R., *The Atlas of Breeding Birds in Britain and Ireland,* T. and A.D. Poyser, 1976.

Sharrock, J.T.R. and E.M., *Rare Birds in Britain and Ireland,* 1976.

Sibley, D., *The North American Bird Guide*, Pica Press, 2000.

Smiddy, P., 'Marsh Warbler in Co. Cork — A Species New to Ireland', *Irish Birding News,* Vol. 3, 1992.

ten Cate, M., *List of North-west European Birds in Eight Languages,* Corrib Conservation Centre, 1985.

Species Index

Species Index

LATIN

Accipiter gentilis, 74–5
  nisus, 74–5
Acrocephalus agricola, 241
  arundinaceus, 242
  dumetorum, 241
  paludicola, 184–5
  palustris, 241
  schoenobaenus, 184–5
  scirpaceus, 186–7
Actitis hypoleucos, 112–13
  macularia, 112–13
Aegithalos caudatus, 202–3
Aix galericulata, 229–30
Alauda arvensis, 158–9
Alca torda, 138–9
Alcedo atthis, 150–51
Alectoris rufa, 247
Alle alle, 140–41
Anas acuta, 60–61
  americana, 60–61
  carolinensis, 230
  clypeata, 50–51
  crecca, 56–7
  discors, 56–7
  formosa, 247
  penelope, 60–61
  platyrhynchos, 58–9
  querquedula, 56–7
  rubripes, 58–9
  strepera, 58–9
Anser albifrons, 46–7
  anser, 48–9
  brachyrhynchus, 46–7
  caerulescens, 48–9
  erythropus, 229
  fabalis, 46–7
Anthus campestris, 164–5
  cervinus, 160–61
  hodgsoni, 162–3
  novaeseelandiae, 164–5
  petrosus, 162–3
  pratensis, 160–61
  rubescens, 238–9
  spinoletta, 162–3

  trivialis, 160–61
Apus affinis, 237
  apus, 154–5
  melba, 154–5
  pallidus, 237
Aquila chrysaetos, 70–71
  clanga, 231
Ardea cinerea, 40–41
  purpurea, 40–41
Ardeola ralloides, 229
Arenaria interpres, 104–5
Asio flammeus, 148–9
  otus, 148–9
Athene noctua, 237
Aythya affinis, 230
  collaris, 52–3
  ferina, 54–5
  fuligula, 52–3
  marila, 52–3
  nyroca, 54–5

Bartramia longicauda, 234
Bombycilla garrulus, 178–9
Botaurus lentiginosus, 228–9
  stellaris, 36–7
Branta bernicla, 44–5
  canadensis, 44–5
  leucopsis, 44–5
Bubulcus ibis, 229
Bucephala albeola, 230
  clangula, 50–51
Bulweria bulweria, 228
Burhinus oedicnemus, 232
Buteo buteo, 72–3
  lagopus, 72–3

Calandrella brachydactyla, 158–9
Calcarius lapponicus, 226–7
Calidris acuminata, 233–4
  alba, 96–7
  alpina, 98–9
  bairdii, 100–101
  canutus, 100–101
  ferruginea, 98–9
  fuscicollis, 100–101
  maritima, 102–3

  mauri, 233
  melanotos, 94–5
  minuta, 96–7
  minutilla, 102–3
  pusilla, 96–7
  ruficollis, 233
  subminuta, 233
  temminckii, 102–3
  tenuirostris, 233
Calonectris diomedea, 28–9
Caprimulgus europaeus, 146–7
Carduelis cannabina, 218–19
  carbaret, 218–19
  carduelis, 214–15
  chloris, 216–17
  flammea, 243
  flavirostris, 218–19
  hornemanni, 243
  spinus, 216–17
Carpodacus erythrinus, 220–21
Catharus guttatus, 240–41
  minimus, 240
  ustulatus, 240
Cepphus grylle, 140–41
Cercotrichas galactotes, 239
Certhia familiaris, 202–3
Ceryle alcyon, 237
Cettia cetti, 241
Chaetura pelagica, 237
Charadrius alexandrinus, 88–9
  dubius, 88–9
  hiaticula, 88–9
  morinellus, 90–91
  vociferus, 90–91
Chettusia gregaria, 233
Chlidonias hybridus, 132–3
  leucopterus, 132–3
  niger, 132–3
Chordeiles minor, 237
Ciconia ciconia, 38–9
  nigra, 229
Cinclus cinclus, 5, 178–9
Circus aeruginosus, 68–9
  cyaneus, 68–9
  pygargus, 68–9
Cisticola juncidis, 241

Species Index

Species Index

Species Index

IRISH

Species Index